"In Ted Peters's *God in Cosmic History: Where Science and History Meet Religion*, one of America's top contemporary theologians insightfully connects our new scientific story of the universe to the long human quest for God. Such a delicate task is one that few writers are qualified to carry out in a manner that is both fully respectful of the natural sciences and also deeply rooted in religious wisdom. Ted Peters is the embodiment of such skill. His book should have wide appeal to readers of many backgrounds. Strongly recommended."

—John F. Haught
Georgetown University

Author Acknowledgments

Thinking about Cosmic History is like sitting on a pile of ping pong balls. The more I sit on it, the more balls (each ball representing a good idea) zip away in unpredictable directions. When I reach out to pull one back into the pile, another zips out in a different direction. It might never be the case that I will get all those ping pong balls to sit quietly in a single unified pile.

Others in my professional life have helped me chase those unruly balls and bring them back into order. My colleagues at Dominican University who are engaged in the Big History program—Harlan Stelmach, Scott Sinclair, Lindsey Dean, Michael Morrissey, and Cynthia Taylor—prompted me to both appreciate Big History and explore the deficit in the point of view big historians bring to their craft. It was while team-teaching a course with Lindsey Dean on the Axial Age that the vision of this book appeared before my inner eyes. I thank Robert John Russell at the Center for Theology and the Natural Sciences, for his critical review of my fundamental ideas. I'm grateful to other colleagues for their critical review of selected sections: Judith Berling, Daren Erisman, and Rita Sherma.

Robert Bellah and Eric Voegelin have now passed away, but my engagement with their writings and in person has persuaded me to take the Axial Period in Cosmic History very seriously.

I wish finally to thank Rick Warner, President of the World History Association, for writing the foreword and, of course, for affirming the value of melding Big History with World History in light of Cosmic History.

Publisher Acknowledgments

Thank you to the following individuals who reviewed this work in progress.

Paul Seungoh Chung, *Toronto Presbyterian Church, Toronto, Ontario* and *University of St. Michael's College, Toronto, Ontario*

Kirk Wegter-McNelly, *Union College, Schenectady, New York*

Gayle E. Woloschak, *Northwestern University, Evanston, Illinois*

GOD IN
COSMIC HISTORY

Where Science & History Meet Religion

TED PETERS

Forward by Rick Warner

ANSELM
ACADEMIC

Created by the publishing team of Anselm Academic.

The scriptural quotations contained herein are from the New Revised Standard Version of the Bible. Copyright © 1993 and 1989 by the Division of Christian Education of the National Council of the Churches of Christ in the United States of America. All rights reserved.

Cover image in public domain

Copyright © 2017 by Ted Peters. All rights reserved. No part of this book may be reproduced by any means without the written permission of the publisher, Anselm Academic, Christian Brothers Publications, 702 Terrace Heights, Winona, Minnesota 55987-1320, www.anselmacademic.org.

Printed in the United States of America

7077

ISBN 978-1-59982-813-8

Dedication

I dedicate this volume to today's grandchildren,
who will become the next generation of Cosmic History's
beloved children: Kayla, Jessica, Jacqueline, David, Maddie
Lulu, Nina, Lydia, Jack, Will, Reynold, and Alice Rose.

Contents

Foreword

In recent decades, an increase in connections between distant parts of the world has hastened the process of globalization. Thanks in part to rapidly improving communication and transportation systems, our planet has grown smaller. Parallel to the increasing economic, cultural, and environmental interactions, our interest in distinct peoples and their histories has grown significantly. In the academic world, courses and research in what is now called "the new World History" have grown at a rapid pace.

A growing group of world historians has turned to *Big History*, a movement developed by historian David Christian and others over the past twenty-five years. Big History describes the past in its largest spatial and temporal limits, from the big bang some 13.8 billion years ago to the future. Human history is understood not only within a global context, as in World History, but within a galactic—or cosmic—context. The big story reveals a pattern of increasing complexity in the universe. Given its broad context, Big History is by nature interdisciplinary, with strong involvement from the natural sciences.

Big historians describe their story as a modern cosmology, from the cosmogony of the big bang down to the present environmental context. Like many other origin stories, Big History does not offer a completely comprehensible answer to the questions, "What is on the outside of the universe?" or, "What happened before the big bang?" Science also has its limitations.

Science has played an important role in shaping the modern mind, and yet some people doubt a number of science's claims, sometimes raising objections on the basis of religious beliefs; witness, for example, religious-based objections to the theory of evolution and the idea that climate change is anthropogenic or caused by humans. Such debates set up an apparent dichotomy of religion versus science. It appears that science and religion are at war. This book, *God in Cosmic History*, will dig beneath the apparent dichotomy to uncover what is underneath.

Science does not actually preclude the "question of God." Through Cosmic History this question can be asked and made more complex, interesting, and fruitful. With this book, theology has joined physics, geology, chemistry, biology, and other disciplines in the quiver of the big historian to open up intellectual spaces for fresh interpretations of history.

Rick Warner
Wabash College
President, World History Association, 2016–2018

PART ONE

Cosmic History and the Origin of All Things

A set of questions orient this book: Is God the author of cosmic history? Does history author itself? Might there be a co-authorship? Before tackling these questions, a more basic question must be addressed: does a strictly scientific account of natural history and human history require that we raise the question of God? Cosmic historians answer this question affirmatively for two reasons. First, throughout most of human history our ancestors believed in divine reality, and this belief significantly influenced the course of events that the historian chronicles. Second, cosmic historians are convinced that a strictly scientific interpretation of either nature or humanity cannot on its own render a full account of reality. The method of scientific research is deliberately narrow; it stipulates that no supernatural or non-natural explanations can be considered. It is necessary, then, to go beyond what science presupposes to ask about a more comprehensive and inclusive reality, to ask about ultimate reality.

The chapters that follow will tell the story of cosmic history as big historians tell it. Subsequent chapters will turn to the conceptual set or worldview out of which the big historian tells this story. This book will look at both the story and the story-teller. Critical consciousness will permit the cosmic historian to find the question of God hidden beneath the story as the big historian tells it.

Why Is History Getting Bigger?

S ome things make me feel small. I feel small when I stand next to a professional basketball center, who may rise to more than seven feet tall. I feel small when the media showers attention on celebrities, on rock stars whose success makes me envious. I feel small when a television news show reports on congressional gridlock in Washington, because national officials seem to possess so much economic and political power compared to my marginal and fragile status. I feel small when astronomers tell me that the Milky Way's uncountable stars may number from two hundred to four hundred billion, and that beyond the Milky Way are another one hundred seventy billion galaxies. I feel small because I am small, and the world is very big.

Through the efforts of big historians, history has gotten bigger too. Big historians are no longer satisfied with World History, with merely tracing five or six thousand years of recorded human history. Rather, historians now want to place human history within a larger context, namely, nature's history. Nature's history is big. It goes back perhaps 13.82 billion years, according to a recent scientific calculation.[1] Compared to nature's cosmic history, recorded human history is about the size of a minnow compared to the ocean, or a penny compared to the national debt.

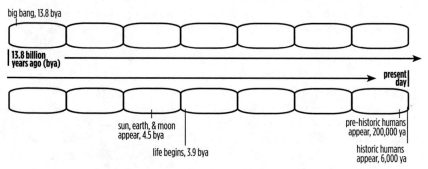

Cosmic History begins with the Big Bang 13.8 billion years ago. Earth has existed for 4.5 billion years. Note what a small fraction of cosmic time is human time.

---

1. On March 21, 2013 the Planck space telescope team released the highest precision map yet of the cosmic microwave background, revealing that the universe is a little older than previous estimates: 13.82 billion years. Mark Peplow, "Planck Snaps Infant Universe," *Nature* 495, no. 7442 (March 28, 2013): 417–18, at 417.

The human soul hungers to be valued. People thirst for meaning. No matter how big the cosmic story becomes, each of us wants to be a valued character in that story. Can big historians or world historians assist in the human quest for a meaningful role in the cosmic story?

History Is Contingent

No matter how big or how small, what makes history historical is contingency. Events are contingent. This means that, prior to an event, what will happen is unpredictable. Looking backward after the event, one realizes that it could have happened differently. Suppose a person plans to purchase a new computer. The buyer weighs the merits and costs of both a PC and an Apple. In advance, no one can predict which will get purchased. Following the purchase of the PC, one may look backward and say, "It could've been the Apple."

Some events in nature are predictable. One can safely predict that the planet Earth will complete an orbit of the sun over the next 365.256 days. Other events in nature are contingent. One cannot accurately predict the weather one month from now; too many of the factors that contribute to meteorological events are contingent. Similarly, future events in human history are contingent, because no one can predict which decisions will be made by human beings with free will. Both natural history and human history include contingent events.

The very existence of the cosmos is contingent. The cosmos is an event, a very large and important event, to be sure. Yet, looking backward, it is possible to see that the cosmos in which we happily live might never have come into existence. There could be nothing instead of something. That we live today in this cosmos is itself contingent. Events that occur within the history of this cosmos are also contingent, both natural and human events. Therefore, one significant definition of *history* is the chronicle and interpretation of past contingent events.

What Is History?

The term *history* in this book will have four slightly different yet overlapping meanings. First, history is what happened. The term *history* can refer to events that took place in the past, regardless of whether anyone was there to record them. Known past events become data for the historian to chronicle and interpret. To say that something is "history" usually means that it belongs to the past. To know what happened in the past is to gain historical knowledge.

Second, history is also an academic discipline that chronicles and interprets past contingent events. "History is at one and the same time happening and consciousness of this happening, history and knowledge of history," writes philosopher Karl Jaspers (1883–1969).[2]

Historians tell about the past in the form of a narrative, a story. In the German language, the same word is used for both history and story (*Geschichte*). In English the two terms are connected by spelling: *story* and hi*story*. Because of the role of interpretation, no historian will tell a story exactly like another historian. A Yankee historian in the northern United States, for example, will tell the story of the "Civil War." A southern historian will tell the story of the "War between the States." There was only one war, but two different histories. Aware of the important role that interpretation plays, big historian Fred Spier remarks, "All historical accounts are reconstructions of some sort."[3] According to this second meaning, history is what historians do. Historians chronicle and interpret events.

Third, to be historical is to be finite. In this third use, *history*—sometimes called *historicity*—is the recognition that human beings are finite rather than infinite, temporal rather than eternal, mortal rather than immortal. To admit that one is a historical being is to say, in effect, that one expects to die. This understanding of one's own historicity stands out in sharp relief against the discovery of eternal reality during the axial breakthrough. The axial breakthrough will be discussed later.

The fourth meaning of *history*—or, more specifically, *effective history*—refers to the influence of the past on one's consciousness today. In this case, effective history is what happens now within one's psyche. The past influences each of us in our consciousness. We are not continually aware of this influence, however, because the past is present in one's self-understanding at the level of pre-understanding. A pre-understanding is a structure already present in our mind that enables us to filter, shape, grasp, admit, and integrate a new experience into our understanding. The pre-understanding makes interpretation possible. And every new experience involves interpretation. Effective history lurks in our pre-understanding just waiting to give shape to any new experience.

The primary means by which the past influences the human psyche today is through language. Each person inherits one or more languages. The English language is about eight centuries old, and it passes on the influence of Greek, Latin, and German going back more than a thousand years prior to that. When an English speaker formulates a sentence, a long list of meanings and connotations accompany each word in that sentence. Every time people speak, they say far more than they had consciously intended to say. This is due to the influence of effective history inside our consciousness. When we understand what someone has just said, we draw upon more than two thousand years of co-meaning.

2. Karl Jaspers, *The Origin and Goal of History*, trans. Michael Bullock (London: Routledge, 1953, 2010), 234.

3. Fred Spier, *Big History and the Future of Humanity* (Oxford: Wiley Blackwell, 2015), 2.

To say, "God bless you!" following someone's sneeze, for example, carries twenty centuries of meaning. In biblical times, it was thought that evil entities—called elemental spirits or *archontes* in the Greek language—floated aimlessly in the air just waiting to get inside a person. Once inside, these elemental spirits would do damage, precipitate disease, or cause insanity. By quickly saying, "God bless you," one prays aloud that the divine spirit will protect the sneezing person from the elemental spirits. Even though most people today don't know or don't think about the original reason for "God bless you," all these ancient meanings are co-present whenever they utter this phrase.

In grasping effective history, one must recognize that *the said* is always dependent on *the unsaid*. In French, *parole* is dependent on *langue*. In German, *das Gesagte* is dependent on *das Ungesagte*. Each sentence a person utters is what gets said. The said draws simultaneously on a gigantic library of co-meanings shelved in the unsaid. No one can control or even manage the unsaid. Virtually every time people speak they say more than they intend to say. In this way, effective history lives on today within the mind of an individual and within his or her culture at the preconscious level.[4]

One can sharply contrast the first and fourth meanings of *history*. According to the first meaning, *history* refers to past events that are now completed, objective, dead, and factual. According to the fourth meaning, *history* is ongoing, subjective, alive, and creative. Whether we realize it or not, our consciousness is drenched in history.

This explains the near-magic of studying history. When one studies history, one grows in self-understanding. With definitions two and three in mind, to chronicle and interpret past events is to grow in understanding one's own historicity. To study the past is to study one's self. This is not actually magic, but almost.

World History within Big History

Working from within the first meaning of *history*, note that nature has its own history apart from human history. Nature's history was not predetermined. Natural events were and are contingent. Just like human beings making decisions as expressions of free will, nature had its own history of contingent events and unpredictable developments before humanity arrived on the scene.

Human beings are fully embedded in nature. In addition to being fully natural, we have inherited from nature the indisputable thrust toward

---

4. The fourth meaning of *history* is a hermeneutical concept developed by philosophers Hans-Georg Gadamer and Paul Ricoeur. Gadamer refers to it as *Wirkungsgeschichte*, usually translated as *effective history*. Hans-Georg Gadamer, *Wahrheit und Methode: Grundzüge einer philosophischen Hermeneutik*, 2nd ed. (Tübingen: J. C. B. Mohr, 1965) and Paul Ricoeur, *The Conflict of Interpretations: Essays in Hermeneutics*, ed. Don Ihde (Evanston, IL: Northwestern University Press, 1974).

unpredictability, creativity, and newness. Even without the appearance of *Homo sapiens*, nature would be historical and creative. With *Homo sapiens* on the scene, the speed of creativity in the cosmos only increases. Cosmic and terrestrial history can be understood only backward, only by chronicling *past* contingent happenings. This signifies that the eyes of human beings should also be open toward the future, a future that will differ from the past. This also signifies that the moment has come to place human history within Cosmic History.

Imagine a set of Russian nesting dolls, sometimes called *matryoshka dolls*. Each doll of increasing size fits within a still larger doll, so that, when assembled, the entire set looks like a single doll. Now imagine that your life story—which is itself a history—is the smallest doll. Your life story fits within a larger history, namely, the history of your family or families. This family history, in turn, fits within a larger history of your nation, your ethnicity, or your religious tradition. This larger history fits within a more inclusive world history, the history all people on planet Earth.

The Russian doll analogy suggests that World History should fit within a still larger history. What is *World History*? "Put simply, World History is macrohistory. It is transregional, transnational, and transcultural," says the World History Association.[5] World History is big, to be sure. But can we find a nest for World History that is yet bigger?

Yes, say the big historians. They propose to fit World History into a still larger Russian doll, namely, Big History. Harvard sociobiologist E. O. Wilson formulates the challenge: "History makes no sense without prehistory, and prehistory makes no sense without biology."[6] Big historians have taken up the challenge and are placing human history within biological history and placing all of this within the physical history of the cosmos.

What Is Big History?

"Big History seeks to understand the integrated history of the Cosmos, Earth, Life, and Humanity, using the best available empirical evidence and scholarly methods."[7] Ken Gilbert of the International Big History Association builds the biggest nest conceivable. "The cosmos itself, beginning with the Big Bang, has now come to be seen, not as an inert or static backdrop for the planet, but an ever-changing manifestation in which everything is essentially historical

---

5. World History Association, "What Is World History?," *http://www.thewha.org/about-wha/what-is-world-history/*.

6. Edward O. Wilson, *The Social Conquest of Earth* (New York: Norton, 2012), 287.

7. International Big History Association, "What Is Big History?," *http://www.ibhanet.org/*. This definition derives in part from the work of Walter Alvarez, who has been teaching Big History at the University of California at Berkeley since 2006. See *http://eps.berkeley.edu/people/walter-alvarez/*.

and developmental."[8] What in this book is termed *Cosmic History* corresponds roughly, though not exhaustively, to this understanding of Big History.

Cosmic History—the subject matter of this book—shares with Big History two important ideas: first, that human interaction with the natural world counts as history; and, second, that the scope of history goes all the way back to the origin of the cosmos, to the big bang. There are, however, three items that this book's version of Cosmic History adds that we don't find in either World History or Big History: first, raising the question of human meaning through remembering the past and expecting the future; second, tracing the differentiation of human consciousness; and third, raising the question of God while analyzing how the historian tries to reconstruct the historical story.

Cosmic History will borrow the skills of the theologian to interrogate history. *Theology* is reflection on faith in God. Theology is to religion what botany is to a four-leaf clover. One can find theologians circulating among Jews, Christians, Muslims, and Hindus. Here we will ask, might a theologian's analysis of history illuminate dimensions of reality missed by other historians?

The History of the Future

Can we connect the future to Cosmic History? Yes, by applying two concepts, *futurum*, and *adventus*. Both are Latin terms for the future. The first, *futurum*, projects a future as an extension of the past. In the case of Cosmic History, some scientists forecast a future in which the entire universe will wind down like a clock and simply drop off into permanent sleep. Called *heat-death*, this permanent sleep consists of an unending state of equilibrium in which nothing happens. This forecast relies on physical *futurum*, the future of nature's history as natural scientists forecast it.

When we turn to human history, however, what we observe is a spirit of defiance, rejection of fatalism, resistance to *futurum*. Voices rise up above the din of events that cry out for more than what historicity alone can deliver. These voices cry out for judgment against the existing social order, while anticipating a future social order that is cured of its evils, healed of its wounds, perfected in its delivery of fulfillment. Why did Zoroaster in ancient Persia dream of paradise? Why did Chinese Buddhists look forward to the Pure Land? Why did disciples of Plato appeal to an eternal standard of justice and an ideal republic? Why did the prophet Isaiah (Isa. 11) envision a "peaceable kingdom" where a lion will lie down with a lamb and a human baby can walk among wild animals without fear? Why does the New Testament promise an everlasting kingdom of God? The

---

8. Ken Gilbert, "The Universal Breakthroughs of Big History: Developing a Unified Theory," in *Teaching and Researching Big History: Exploring a New Scholarly Field*, ed. Leonid Grinin, David Baker, Esther Quaedackers, and Audrey Korotayev (Volgograd, Russia: Uchitel, 2014), 122–46, at 128–29.

future presupposed in all these visions is *adventus*, the advent of a new reality that transforms the present reality. *Adventus* goes beyond what *futurum* can deliver; it promises redemption, healing, renewal. Anticipations of both *futurum* and *adventus* can be found in our chronicles of the human gaze at history. Anticipations of *adventus* precipitate human self-understanding according to the third meaning of *history* mentioned above: human beings are temporal but they look forward to what is eternal. The context of remembering the past and anticipating a future conditioned by eternity gives our historical life meaning, ultimate meaning.

Premodern, Modern, and Postmodern Consciousness

Recall the first two meanings of *history* mentioned above: history is what happened plus history is the chronicle and interpretation of what happened. History is both what happened and the story of what happened. Among the contingent events to be chronicled are jumps in human consciousness. Human consciousness has not always been what we today presume it to be. What goes on within the human mind has changed over time. This change cannot be described as a gradual evolution. Rather, the history of human consciousness is punctuated with leaps in cognition, leaps in knowingness, and leaps in self-awareness.

In order to map the temporal terrain, we will divide the history of human consciousness into three eras: premodern, modern, and postmodern. The first era, the premodern, is subdivided into three periods: spoken language, written language, and the Axial Period. Today's concept of history, which depends on writing, was born in the premodern era, just prior to the Axial Age. The modern era, which is characterized principally by critical consciousness, is divided into two periods: the rational and the relativistic. The rational period watched the triumph of science and technology, whereas the relativistic period redefined history as the collection of multiple culturally specific perspectives. The emerging postmodern era has not yet arrived; it would be premature to subdivide it into periods. There are, however, three distinguishable side-by-side themes in the postmodern mind: quantum contingency, holism, and deconstruction.

You the reader may feel that a bucket of jig saw puzzle pieces has just been dumped on you. Shortly these puzzle pieces will get picked up and put in place. In the meantime, here is the take-away point: each period within each era represents a threshold crossing for consciousness, a leap from more compact thinking to more differentiated thinking. The type of consciousness of one period is seldom if ever lost; rather, each new period adds something without deleting what had come before.

One leap that will draw special attention in this book, *God in Cosmic History*, is the axial leap, which took place in some city-states during the first millennium before the common era. Some scholars refer to this as the *axial breakthrough.* The breakthrough insight is that ephemeral physical history (intra-cosmic history) is distinguishable from a transcendent eternal (supra-cosmic) reality. What people experience in the physical world is material, temporal, changeable, and subject to death. The reality that transcends earthly experience is spiritual, eternal, unchangeable, and life-giving. The former is called *history* according to its third meaning, whereas the latter is thought by axial experiencers to be the ultimate reality, which transcends history. Our axial ancestors drilled deep into the interior of the human psyche and asked, can we find ultimate reality within the human soul? Can we find a window open to the infinite while housed within finite human thinking? Can we envision an end or goal to history that will judge and renew the tragedy and injustice that has befallen the creatures within history? Does eternal life promise more than temporal death?

This leap in human self-understanding may be termed a *differentiation in human consciousness.* This differentiation in human consciousness took place during the premodern Axial Period in three regions: China, India, and the Mesopotamian-Mediterranean region. The breakthrough erupted into the grand religious traditions we now know as Hinduism, Buddhism, Daoism, Confucianism, Judaism, Christianity, and Islam.

Prior to crossing the axial threshold, human consciousness combined three dimensions of reality into a compact conceptual arrangement: self, society, and cosmos. The subsequent axial mind was shocked by its insight into a transcendent reality that reordered self, society, and cosmos. In fact, this axial shock made intra-cosmic history appear alienated or estranged from ultimate reality. The ordering of self and society, according to axial experiencers, is grounded in a supra-cosmic order that transcends the mundane. This supra-cosmic order becomes the ideal for which humans strive and by which humans judge themselves when missing the mark.

In this axial perspective three salient features appear. First, ultimate reality is mysterious, divine, and supra-cosmic. Second, a transcendent model of a just and peaceful social order judges the historical social order as deficient, estranged, and self-destructive. Third, a deepened sense of the individual self produces an inner soul with immediate access to the transcendent mystery and to the vision of a just society. The value of the self is discovered in its immediate relationship to the ultimate. Axial consciousness is much more differentiated than the pre-axial consciousness that preceded it in history.

Philosopher Charles Taylor astutely describes the axial leap in thinking as "disembedding." The compact human consciousness we inherited from our pre-axial forbearers is thoroughly embedded in the ordinary world. For hunter-gatherers and early farmers, the goal of human striving was species survival at minimum and human flourishing at maximum. The axial breakthrough to transcendence during the premodern city-state period designates, first, "going beyond the human world or the cosmos." But, second, "it can mean the discovery or invention of a new standpoint form from which the existing order in the cosmos or society can be criticized or denounced."[9] Post-axial thinkers live simultaneously in two realms, so to speak, the mundane and the transcendent.

The axial insight inherited by modern Europe and North America comes in two forms, the rational form from Greece and the prophetic form from Israel. As rational, the breakthrough insight is that all of physical nature and human nature is grounded in a divine structure of reason. As prophetic, the breakthrough is the realization that God's order of justice is not the historical order of this world. To grasp the divine mind is to think rationally, and to grasp the divine will is to render judgment against the status quo. God's future will drastically alter what has been the case in history. God promises transformation, redemption, and salvation, according to adherents to the various biblical traditions. Axial reasoning regarding nature and axial prophecy regarding future change contributed decisively to the rise of modern science. In the paragraphs that follow, we will trace the crossing of this threshold.

Premodern, Modern, and Postmodern Consciousness

ERAS	PERIODS	TYPES OF CONSCIOUSNESS
Premodern 200,000 years ago	1. spoken language 2. written language	compact
	3. axial	differentiated
Modern 1650 CE to present	1. rational (1650–present) 2. relativistic (1800–present)	critical
Post-Modern 1900 CE to present	1. quest for meaning of quantum contingency (1920–present) 2. quest for holism (1920–present) 3. quest for deconstructionist relativity (1970–present)	post-critical

Another leap, the leap to the modern Western world, is also given special attention in the pages to follow. Key to this leap is critical consciousness. This leap feels like a liberation of the present era from the precedents of the past. Modern thinking takes many forms: objectifying what had been subjective,

---

9. Charles Taylor, "What Was the Axial Revolution?," in *The Axial Age and Its Consequences*, ed. Robert N. Bellah and Hans Joas (Cambridge, MA: Harvard University Press, 2012), 30–46, at 30.

scientizing what had been personal, secularizing what had been sacred, naturalizing what had been enchanted, democratizing what had been authoritarian. At the heart of this critical consciousness is the ability to hold two contradictory thoughts together while bracketing out preference or commitment. This is important: critical consciousness includes the capacity to hold together two opposing thoughts and consider their relative merits before making a judgment. Modern people are particularly good at this. This entire book is an exercise in critical thinking.

Within the modern era, two periods appear. The first period extends the rational insight of the axial breakthrough in Greece, namely, the insight that reality both seen and unseen obeys the laws of reason. This commitment to reason is responsible for the rocket-like launch of modern science. The launch of science was followed quickly by the concept of historical or cultural relativity, however. The key doctrine of relativity is that people in different historical or cultural contexts interpret things differently. All people interpret contextually. The meaning of the *said* is dependent on the *unsaid* specific to the speaker's cultural context. The shift from reason to relativity did not mark a departure from rational science, only an augment. Both reason and relativity in the modern era share critical consciousness.

These four punctuations in the history of human consciousness are marked by significant leaps: the leap to spoken language, to written language, to the axial insight, and to the cultural acceptance of critical consciousness. These leaps are now part of human history. These past leaps live on in the effective history all modern people share in their library of the *unsaid*.

What about the future? Modern Western and even global culture is witnessing restlessness with modern critical consciousness. Spiritual prophets are pining for the emergence of a post-modern and post-critical holism, in some cases even a retrieval of mystical awareness. The modern human psyche seeks an integration of the self with the other, an integration of science with the arts, an integration of technology with meaning, an integration of society with morality. Could postmodern consciousness deliver this integration?

Modern people who are hungry for postmodernity miss the loss of premodern embedded consciousness and frequently bypass language for non-linguistic yoga or meditation in order to retrieve immediate consciousness. The modern removal from embeddedness in the world by critical consciousness leaves a cold feeling, a yearning to become reintegrated. The pursuit of immediate consciousness becomes identified with a quest for holism. What we see here among our postmodern peers is an already differentiated critical consciousness yearning to de-differentiate. The new holism is not here yet, even though it appears on the Christmas list of today's disgruntled moderns.

Holistic reintegration is only one item on the postmodernist's wish list. There are three postmodern quests: (1) seeking for re-integrated wholeness, (2) discerning the import of the rediscovery of contingency in quantum physics, and (3) deconstructing the modern mind by expanding the role of contextual relativity. Of these three postmodern quests, only quantum contingency is discussed in this text.

The interpretation of history in this book, *God in Cosmic History*, is influenced principally by the work of three scholars: sociologist Robert Bellah (1927–2013), philosopher Eric Voegelin (1901–1985), and theologian Paul Tillich (1886–1965). According to Bellah, human history is grounded in natural history. "History goes all the way back and any distinction between history and prehistory is arbitrary. That means that biological history—that is, evolution—is part of the human story all the way through."[10] The effective history of the concept of evolution will be given extensive attention in the chapters to come.

According to Voegelin, human consciousness has differentiated over the millennia, and this differentiation is essential to history itself. Prior to the axial breakthrough, our ancestors did not enjoy a rich and complex interior life. A new depth of soul appeared during the Axial Period; and this new insight made civilization ready for the appearance of the modern world. "Consciousness differentiates in a process called history; and in the process of history [humanity] discovers reality to be engaged in a movement toward the Beyond of its present structure. A cosmos that moves from its divine Beginning toward a divine Beyond of itself is mysterious indeed."[11] Key to the differentiation of consciousness is awareness of a powerful transcendent reality that promises a future different from the past. Historical consciousness requires more than merely the chronicle of past contingent events; it also requires reliance upon a transcendent ground combined with anticipation of newness in the future.

Systematic theologian Paul Tillich, more poignantly than Bellah or Voegelin, interrogates history to locate the question of God. He locates God in the human search for ultimate reality. "God is the answer to the question implied in [human] finitude; [*God*] is the name for that which concerns [humanity] ultimately."[12] Like a prospector, wherever the dimension of ultimacy sparkles, people will dig for the divine gold.

Asking the God Question

Is Cosmic History a story that tells itself? Is God the author of the cosmic story? These are the questions that orient this book.

---

10. Robert N. Bellah, *Religion in Human Evolution from the Paleolithic to the Axial Age* (Cambridge, MA: Harvard University Press, 2011), xi.

11. Eric Voegelin, *Order and History*, 5 vols. (Baton Rouge: Louisiana State University Press, 1956–1987), 4:19.

12. Paul Tillich, *Systematic Theology*, 3 vols. (Chicago: University of Chicago Press, 1951–1963), 1:211, italics added.

Within history the question of God arises in two modes. First, history as the chronicle of events includes some events wherein answers to the question of God were proposed. Pre-axial religious worldviews included gods and goddesses within the cosmos as foragers, farmers, and early citizens perceived them, and formulated their worldview in mythical and narrative symbolism. Post-axial religious traditions—Daoism, Confucianism, Hinduism, Buddhism, Judaism, Christianity, Islam, and others—also belong within any account of world history. Because our ancestors asked the question of God, this question becomes a topic for historical study. "The human idea of God has a history," observes religious scholar Karen Armstrong, "since it has always meant something slightly different to each group of people who have used it at various points of time."[13]

The historian of religion may wish to report and examine traditional claims regarding divine reality, to rethink these claims, so to speak. This study will rethink the question of God as it arose during the Axial Period approximately 2500 years ago. We will give special attention to the purported axial breakthrough, because the ultimate reality reported by axial seers and sages is transcendent, beyond the cosmos and beyond the history of the cosmos. It is also more real than the cosmos.

In the first mode, the cosmic historian will chronicle human answers to the God question. "Human experience of transcendence has been a fact of life," says Armstrong; therefore, it should be included among the topics historians chronicle.[14] As Rick Warner mentioned in this book's foreword, many world historians do chronicle past answers to the God question. Big historians to date, however, have sidelined this component of human history.

In the second mode, the cosmic historian will pursue the God question by interrogating history. The cosmic historian will give history a cross-examination, so to speak. Such a cross-examination could only come from contemporary critical consciousness, from our willingness to question assumptions and draw out implications.

As we have just hinted, one of the reasons for selecting the Axial Period for special attention is that sages and seers in diverse parts of the world at that time claimed to have experienced transcendent reality, an ultimate reality that many of them termed *God*. Nothing short of ultimate reality counts as divine in the axial and post-axial spiritual quest. "Only if God is ultimate reality," writes Tillich, "only then can [God] be the object of surrender, obedience, and assent. Faith in anything which has only preliminary reality is idolatrous."[15] Treating something less than ultimate as if it were ultimate is idolatry, says Tillich. The

---

13. Karen Armstrong, *A History of God: The 4000 Year Quest of Judaism, Christianity, and Islam* (New York: Alfred A. Knopf, 1994), xx.

14. Ibid., xxi.

15. Paul Tillich, *Biblical Religion and the Search for Ultimate Reality* (Chicago: University of Chicago Press, 1955), 59.

cosmic historian must interrogate history to identify the dimension of ultimacy and the practice of idolatry.

Neither the big historian nor the world historian routinely asks the question of ultimacy, even though world historians are more likely to chronicle those who did ask the question of ultimacy in the past. The self-appointed missions of world historians and big historians differ in another orientation. World History is a product of the second period within modernity, relativism. What concerns the world historian is understanding different cultures in different contexts.

Big History, in contrast, returns to the earlier period within the Enlightenment, the rationalist period. Big History considers itself scientific. Because big historians think of themselves as scientific, the history they construct usually focuses on energy flows, natural processes, and the way nature has influenced human political or social organization. Like other scientists, the scholarly method of big historians is tacitly materialistic and naturalistic. *Materialism* is the assumption that our reality is made up of matter and energy—that is, the only reality to be investigated is material reality. *Naturalism* is the assumption that all reality is natural, only natural. No supernatural or supranatural[16] dimension to reality exists or, if it does exist, it does not count in scientific measurements. The compass big historians follow points toward secularism, naturalism, materialism, and scientism. Like other scientists, big historians look at what is physical, not what is metaphysical.

In order to ask the question of God, therefore, one must supplement what big historians and world historians presuppose. This book will pose supra-cosmic questions that most big historians and world historians refrain from asking. Posing supra-cosmic questions makes the cosmos itself look different, even more magnificent and more awe-inspiring.

Review Questions

1. What is World History? Big History? Cosmic History?
2. Compare and contrast the four meanings of *history*.
3. Why should we ask the God question within the context of Cosmic History?
4. Compare and contrast premodern, modern, and postmodern consciousness.

Discussion Questions

1. Can you provide examples of effective history from your own experience?
2. Do you use the word *contingency* very often? What does it refer to?

---

16. To be supranatural is to be above nature. This is a more accurate term than "supernatural," which could mean natural plus.

3. If the course of all events would be determined in advance and nothing would be contingent, would we still have history?

4. The Cosmic Historian should ask the question of God for two reasons. Which of these two reasons do you believe is the most important?

Additional Resources

Print Sources

Christian, David, Cynthia Stokes Brown, and Craig Benjamin. *Big History: Between Nothing and Everything*. New York: McGraw Hill, 2014.

> This is the single most important text to date in the field of Big History. In the opening pages we learn what the big historians think about Big History. Notice how the concept of Big History begins with the big bang story of origin and then compares it with mythical stories of origin told by our ancestors. The central point of the concept of Big History is to nest human history within nature's history. Big bang cosmology is the biggest nest scientists can think of.

Dunn, Ross E., and Laura J. Mitchell. *Panorama: A World History*. New York: McGraw Hill, 2015.

> Familiarize yourself with the field of World History by looking at this volume, a leading textbook. Do you think it should stand alone or should it find a nest within the larger Big History project?

Web Sources

History.com, *http://www.history.com/shows/big-history*.

> This site provides information about sixteen videos on Big History topics available from iTunes and provides a free study guide for each.

International Big History Association, *http://www.ibhanet.org/*.

> This site provides information about the field of Big History by big historians.

World History Association, *http://www.thewha.org/*.

> This association, founded in 1982, promotes historical studies that focus on human community as a whole.

Big Bang Cosmology

Cosmology is a voyage of the human spirit.

—Owen Gingerich[1]

The story of the cosmos cannot begin with "once upon a time." This is because the cosmos starts when time itself starts. The story starts at a time before there was any time; when all things were only one thing. Everything in today's world was one and only one thing. Some scientists call that one thing a *singularity*. The singularity was small, really small. Perhaps the size of a golf ball. Perhaps the size of a ball bearing or even a BB. Perhaps the size of a single atom. By all accounts, it was small.

It was also very compact. Everything in physical reality was packed into that tiny singularity. It was unusually heavy. This singularity was dumb; it did not speak. It did not move. It was undifferentiated. As of yet, the forces of nature had not distinguished themselves: matter and energy were interchangeable, and time and space did not yet exist.

Then the singularity exploded. This explosion is called the *big bang*. As the big bang banged, it expanded and disintegrated and sent material flying out in every direction. Like the explosion of a hand grenade, it sent shrapnel outward. Time had now begun and space had been established.

Today planet Earth is a piece of that shrapnel flying outward and away from the original big bang. The shrapnel from that original explosion has been flying away from its point of origin for 13.8 billion years now and will keep on flying away from the origin for perhaps another 65 to 100 billion years. The big bang has not ceased banging. The universe is continuing to expand at a rate of 74.3 kilometers per second per megaparsec. This means that for "every megaparsec (about 3 million light years) you go out, the Universe is expanding 74.2 km/sec faster."[2]

---

1. Owen Gingerich, "Mankind's Place in the Universe," *Nature* 457, no. 7225 (January 1, 2009): 28–29, at 29.

2. Phil Plait, "The Universe Is Expanding at 74.2 km/sec/Mpc," *Bad Astronomy*, May 7, 2009, *http:// blogs.discovermagazine.com/badastronomy/2009/05/07/the-universe-is-expanding-at-742-kmsecmpc/#. V7IYiigrKUk.*

Why are we talking about the big bang origin of the physical universe? Because it belongs to Big History. According to big historian Fred Spier, Big History is "the approach to history that places human history within the context of cosmic history, from the beginning of the universe up until life on Earth today."[3] With this in mind, it is time to go back to the beginning of all beginnings, the singularity.

The Early Universe

Just what happened as the singularity became a multiplicity? What is the history of how the one became many, how simplicity became complexity?

First, attend to an important scientific principle, the law of entropy. According to this law, hot things cool off. Unless heat is added, a hot thing will continue to cool until it freezes. The universe as a whole began very hot. After the big bang, the universe had only one direction to go: from hot to cold. Everything that has happened over the last 13.8 billion years involves cooling, if not freezing. If the universe lasts another 65 to 100 billion years, it will freeze into an equilibrium state and cease to have any activity. The universe will die a heat-death. A variant on this scenario is the "Big RIP" (Rest In Peace), a hypothesis that forecasts that all the matter of the universe—from galaxies to atoms and even space-time itself—will be progressively torn apart by the heartless expansion of the universe. Whether via heat-death or the Big RIP, our cosmos will go to sleep and never wake up. There is more to the law of entropy than this, but this will suffice for the moment.

No one knows exactly what happened in the very earliest moments of the big bang, but within a tiny fraction of a second, as this new universe started to cool, gravitational forces started to act.

Today there are four fundamental forces operative in the universe: (1) gravity, (2) electromagnetism, (3) the strong subatomic (nuclear) force, and (4) the weak subatomic (nuclear) force. But when the universe was a singularity, all four of these forces were one. As the universe cooled, these forces started to differentiate or separate. The first cooling or freezing separated out the strong subatomic nuclear force from gravity and what would become the other two. Later, the weak subatomic nuclear force and the electromagnetic forces became distinguishable. This left gravity to itself.[4]

This sequence suggests an important philosophical observation: the laws of nature are not eternal; rather the laws of nature are temporal. There was a time

---

3. Fred Spier, *Big History and the Future of Humanity* (Oxford: Wiley Blackwell, 2015), 1.

4. Albert Einstein had hoped that during his career he could find a grand unified field theory that would account for all four of these forces in a single concept, a theory of everything. He failed to realize this dream. Today's cosmologists still believe that each of the four forces differentiated from a prior unity in big bang history.

before which the laws of nature we know today did not exist. Only as the history of the cosmos proceeds do the laws of nature emerge.

Next, still well within the first second after t=0 (time=0), a rapid inflation in size took place. Imagine throwing a pebble into a calm lake, then watching the ripples expand and expand. The universe expanded like ripples in a lake surface, on a single plane, not like a balloon that increases in size everywhere. The cosmos is shaped more like a bicycle wheel than a balloon. This expansion was speedy. In the early universe, the singularity inflated faster than the speed of light to the size of a galaxy. Following the inflation period, the universe continued to expand, to be sure, but at a decreased rate. The material in the inflation was not distributed evenly in all directions. This resulted in regions of dense matter that were separated by vast spatial voids. Some physicists believe that inflation explains why the universe is roughly flat rather than significantly curved.

Immediately following inflation, the universe was still too hot and too dense for the formation of nuclei (the center of an atom, made up of subatomic particles such as protons and neutrons), let alone the formation of entire atoms. Any nuclei that might try to form would be destroyed by collisions with speeding smaller particles. When the temperature dropped to a mere ten million degrees, the strong subatomic (nuclear) force became effective, leading eventually to the formation of nuclei. The era of the atom was coming to birth.

But first comes the era of quarks. A quark is an elementary particle, smaller than an atom, which becomes an indispensable component of matter. In the era of quarks, three of the four forces are in play: gravity, the strong subatomic force, and a combination of the weak subatomic force with electromagnetism, which is called the *electroweak force*.

Then the combined electroweak force split into electromagnetism and the weak subatomic force. The four forces—gravity, electromagnetism, the strong subatomic force, and the weak subatomic force—have taken their present form. Also, fundamental particles have gained mass.

The universe had existed now for three entire seconds after t=0. Temporal history has begun.

Then began the dance of plasma. Plasma is like a cloud of cotton candy made up of unbounded positively and negatively charged subatomic particles getting ready to take physical form. The dance of the plasma lasted for about 380,000 years (400,000 years, rounded off), cooling in the process. The plasma dance began to wind down when the universe cooled to a temperature comparable to that of the sun. At this stage, hydrogen and helium *atoms* began to form.

The dancing plasma was not all at the same density. It was lumpy, or asymmetrical. The asymmetrical lumps formed as galaxies, and the cosmos we now know began to take its present shape.

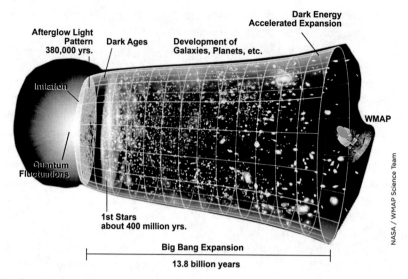

This timeline represents the development of the universe over 13.8 billion years, beginning with the big bang. The far left depicts the earliest moment science can probe, when a period of "inflation" produced a burst of growth in the universe.

Galaxies, Stars, and Planets

Even after the first 380,000 years, the cosmos remained relatively simple. The first atoms to form were the simple ones: hydrogen and helium. These two gasses still compose 75 percent of the visible universe.[5] Vast clouds of hydrogen and helium simply drifted in the cosmos.

Gravity pulls more strongly from regions where the mass is greater. A gravity tug-of-war broke out, so to speak, leading to clustering, clumping, and consolidating. Centers of gravity formed in discrete regions separated from other regions. A process of centering, differentiation, and emergence was taking place.

This centering process drew more and more mass into smaller locations, increasing density. By packing more atoms into smaller places, the temperature increased. The universe as a whole was cooling down (and still is today), but in selected regions it was heating up. With increased temperature, protons in atomic nuclei could fuse, leading to more complex nuclei and more complex elements.

When protons fuse, they emit energy. A portion of their matter is converted to energy. Actually, they explode. It is the fusion of protons that explodes in today's H-bomb (hydrogen bomb). So, in the ancient universe, when hydrogen atoms fused to produce helium atoms, energy and heat and activity produced

---

5. Astrophysicists are acutely aware of dark matter, but the precise quantity has yet to be calculated.

continuous explosions—that is, they produced furnaces. Such a furnace has been creative. Gaseous clouds would collapse only to be heated in the central furnace and then fly back out in more complex form. These furnaces became manufacturing plants, so to speak—manufacturing hot spots that would become our galaxies.

When galaxies emerge, a new level of complexity emerges. A galaxy is a collection of stars, interstellar gas, dust, and dark matter all bound together by a center of gravity. The center of gravity is like the axel on a bicycle wheel; everything else circles around it. That center of gravity takes the form of a black hole.

Our particular galaxy is called the Milky Way. Beyond the Milky Way are more galaxies. Some scientists estimate that there are 170 billion galaxies in the observable universe, each with its own collection of stars. Just as stars are clustered in galaxies, so also galaxies are clustered in groups of galaxies, known as superclusters. Galaxies are separated by voids, or at least what looks like empty space. The entire universe is expanding at an increased rate due to dark energy while, at the same time, galaxy superclusters exhibit internal attraction due to the gravitational force. Voids vaster than those separating galaxies separate the superclusters.

Included within these galaxies are stars. A star is basically a hydrogen bomb in a state of continued detonation. At its core the thermonuclear fusion of hydrogen and helium releases energy that travels through the star's interior, then radiates into the space surrounding it. Each star will continue to emit light and heat as long as enough hydrogen remains to fuel the process.

As the supply of hydrogen within a star diminishes over time and nears exhaustion, elements heavier than helium begin to appear. Our sun's mass is about three quarters hydrogen, with helium making up most of the remainder. But the sun also includes small quantities of oxygen, carbon, neon, and iron. These elements are requisite for life on planet Earth, where atoms bind together to form molecules. Molecules form cells, and cells form humans.

The star at the center of our solar system, the sun, was born less than five billion years ago. It's now middle-aged. It has five more billion years before it dies. It will not die quietly. Approximately four billion years into the future, the sun's hydrogen supply will be greatly diminished. Fusion in the core will cease; but fusion in the outer layers will continue and outer temperatures will rise. This will cause the sun to expand into a red giant, which will destroy Mercury, Venus, and perhaps Earth. All life in our solar system will come to an end. In the contingent cosmos, nothing is permanent.

Entropy and Emergence

Why does the cosmos have this story? Why not some other story? Why any story at all? Why didn't the original singularity just sit there in a state of equilibrium and do nothing for all of eternity? Why did the simplicity of the singularity over time lead to complexity and the emergence of new things? These questions can be answered by looking at the law of entropy and its curious byproduct, creativity in open systems.

First, note that energy in the universe is always *conserved*. This means that energy can be *transformed*, but it cannot be *created* or *destroyed*. This is called by physicists the *first law of thermodynamics* or, sometimes, the *conservation of energy*.

Second, heat always goes to cold. Heat cannot spontaneously flow from a colder location to a hotter location. To say it another way, in a closed system over time any differences in temperature (or pressure) tend to even out. Hot goes to cold. Order goes to disorder. High pressure goes to low pressure. No party balloon will expand all by itself; one has to force air or helium into it. After a pin prick, all the gas within the balloon immediately departs and merges with the surrounding atmosphere. All active states go toward equilibrium. This is called the *second law of thermodynamics*, also known as the *law of entropy*.

Third, the state of being cold is called *equilibrium*. The *third law of thermodynamics* tells us that, as a system approaches absolute zero, the entropy of the system approaches a final value, or a state of equilibrium. This has enormous implications for our cosmic future. As the cosmos winds down, it will eventually reach a final state of equilibrium. Some call this *heat death*. Cosmic history will end in heat death.[6] Just like a human person, the cosmos has its own birth, history, and death. The cosmos has historicity.

Currently the cosmos is in a state that is far from equilibrium. Everywhere hot things are turning cold. High pressure is turning to low pressure. The logs in the fireplace burn down. Cars run out of gas.

One might object that not everything is running down. Some things are heating up. A homeowner puts new logs in the fireplace. A teenager refills the gas tank. A driver increases the pressure in the car's tires. So why are new things emerging in the cosmos? Because the law of entropy applies only to a *closed* system.

An environmental system is "closed" when no outside energy is being introduced. Take a Starbucks or Peets coffee cup as an example. The coffee barista pours lip-burning, hot coffee into a cup. Then the customer takes a seat and opens a book to read. In time, the coffee cools just a tad, so the customer gingerly takes the first sip. As the coffee cools, progressively her sips grow in size. Eventually, she is drinking a full mouthful. At some point, she may even rush to finish the cup before the coffee drops to room temperature.

Nothing is more orderly than a routine cup of coffee in the morning accompanied by a relaxing chair and favorite reading matter or game on the iPad. The coffee cup is a closed system. No outside energy is being introduced. Therefore, the temperature in the cup has only one direction to go: from hot to cold (or to

---

6. Because of the second law of thermodynamics, observes Fred Spier, "the history of the universe must also be the history of increasing disorder. Any local rise in complexity must, therefore, inevitably have been accompanied by a larger rise in disorder elsewhere." Spier, *Big History*, 53.

room temperature). If the drinker placed this coffee cup in the microwave and zapped it for fifty seconds, however, it would heat up again. In the microwave the coffee cup is an open system; it is receiving energy from an outside source. With energy input, the temperature can go from cold to hot. In sum, the law of entropy applies only to closed systems.

The Earth is an open system, continuously receiving energy from the sun. The sun has served as Earth's microwave for nearly five billion years now. In local closed systems such as a coffee cup, the law of entropy applies. To the Earth as a whole, however, just the opposite is the case. The Earth is constantly on the receiving end of energy input. Earth is an open system. The Earth is anti-entropic. What could this mean?

Uncontrolled energy input leads to chaos. If the coffee drinker accidently microwaves that coffee for ten minutes rather than one minute, the coffee will boil over, splatter, and make a big mess. Whenever excessive energy is poured into a system, chaos of this sort results. The chaos destroys whatever was previously in order.

But here is something surprising, something uncanny: emergence. Over time, this chaos leads to creativity, and this creativity leads to a new and unpredicted higher order. Yes, chaos destroys, but nature does not stop there. In time the chaos leads to a new and higher level of order, a more complex form of order than had existed prior to the energy input. A variety of brownie ingredients placed in a heated oven leads to something creative, something that could be created only in an open system with energy input, namely, fresh brownies. The new traits exhibited by the good-tasting brownies are called *emergent properties*.

Earth is one of these open systems, and life on Earth is an emergent phenomenon. New properties are emerging. Every minute for billions of years our planet has received energy from the sun, progressing through temporary chaos toward new and ever more complex levels of unpredicted order. Each person is also an open system, receiving daily energy input through food, and then generating free decisions, which lead, in many cases, to innovation.

The law of entropy cannot tell us why the cosmos has this particular story, yet it could predict that the cosmos would have some sort of story. Because of the asymmetry built into the initial conditions, the singularity was not destined to simply sit in equilibrium waiting. The big bang banged, and the emergent human race on planet Earth is ready and willing to think about it.

The God Question

As the infant universe grew, it matured into a stunningly beautiful and brilliant creature. Among its creative accomplishments, the magnificent cosmos has given birth to us. We *Homo sapiens* are the product of the sun's energy producing chaos on Earth that has led to a higher form of order. Human beings represent that higher order. Our existence as *Homo sapiens* is contingent, historical, and, most importantly, a gift we could not have asked for. We are children of the big bang.

The story just told is a *cosmogony*. *Cosmogony* refers to an account of the origin of the cosmos. The field we know as *cosmology* refers to the study of the universe, which includes big bang cosmogony. In archaic societies, our ancestors told myths about the origin of the cosmos—cosmogonic myths—as they understood their world. According to these myths, gods and goddesses were responsible for creation. Is appeal to divine action necessary in today's big bang cosmogony?

On the one hand, it appears that the progress of scientific knowledge reduces or eliminates the need for divine action to explain the origin of our cosmos. It appears that the importance of our planet and the importance of human life may be diminished when we realize what a small role we play in this huge and expansive universe. On the other hand, there is good reason to believe that the entire cosmos is the product of divine creation and that the human mind is a gift given us so that we can appreciate it. "*The unity, beauty, and comprehensibility of the universe point to a creator*," writes astronomer Bernard Carr at Queen Mary College in London.[7] Big bang cosmology prompts within the human soul the question, is God the author of the cosmic story?

Conclusion

What about the question of meaning? What does the big bang story mean? As a scientific story, it has no meaning. Scientific stories are always meaningless, because the methods of science exclude meaningfulness at the outset. Even so, the story of the big bang cannot help but inspire in us a sense of wonder, awe, and appreciation.

Columbia University physicist Brian Greene wonders out loud whether we might get a clue from this cosmology about the meaning of our human existence. "Cosmology has the ability to grab hold of us at a deep, visceral level because an understanding of how things began feels—at least to some—like the closest we may ever come to understanding *why* they began." Then he offers a discouraging afterthought: "[But] no such scientific connection [between *how* and *why*] is ever found."[8] Even if cosmology prompts within us questions about meaning, and perhaps even about God's creative role, scientific cosmology cannot provide answers.

---

7. Bernard Carr, "Cosmology and Religion," in *The Oxford Handbook of Religion and Science*, ed. Philip Clayton and Zachary Simpson (Oxford: Oxford University Press, 2006), 139–55, at 150. Italics in original.

8. Brian Greene, *The Elegant Universe* (New York: Norton, 1999), 364.

We today will not learn the meaning of existence from big bang theory for two reasons. First, science is unable to provide the meaning of anything. Second, because open systems lead to creativity, innovation, and newness, the meaning of existence is more likely to be found in the future rather than the past. As exciting as the story of the cosmos is, it will remain meaningless as long as it is restricted to a scientific account of past events. Just as a shark swims in the ocean and never flies like an eagle to a mountain top, so also the scientist swims only in facts and theories without ever flying to the heavenly realms of meaning and divinity. Because big historians have elected to swim only in the scientific ocean, we cannot expect them to provide meaning or ask the God question.

History as a discipline is the chronicle and interpretation of past contingent events. This chapter has chronicled the events surrounding the big bang origin of the cosmos. How might a cosmic historian interpret this chronicle so as to perceive its meaning? Without meaning, how could the cosmic historian ask the question of God?

Review Questions

1. Is a greenhouse an open or closed system? Is a space station an open or closed system?
2. What are the three laws of thermodynamics? What do these three forecast for the future of our cosmos?
3. According to far-from-equilibrium dynamics, what accounts for the creativity on planet Earth?
4. How should one use the terms *cosmology* and *cosmogony*?

Discussion Questions

1. Have you thought of nature as history? Does it make sense for you to think that the natural world would have a history even if no human beings were present to chronicle this history?
2. Because no person was present at the big bang to measure the singularity or watch inflation or record the course of natural events, how do scientists know what happened? What data would you rely on if you were a scientist? How much imagination goes into telling the story of the big bang?
3. In light of the big bang story of origin, what do you think is the relationship between time and space?
4. Why must this chronicle of big bang history be devoid of meaning? If someone would want to pose the question of God, how should it be asked?

Additional Resources

Print Sources

Carr, Bernard. "Cosmology and Religion." In *The Oxford Handbook of Religion and Science*, edited by Philip Clayton and Zachary Simpson, 139–55. Oxford: Oxford University Press, 2006.

This brief but amazingly comprehensive chapter provides a summary-exposition of both cosmological and atomic physics. It then draws out religious implications. On the one hand, the expanding scope of cosmology—from geocentrism to heliocentrism to cosmocentrism—tends to make human beings feel increasingly insignificant. On the other hand, the anthropic principle (discussed in the book) returns human consciousness to a place of cosmic significance. Similarly, on the one hand, the advance of science seems to reduce the role that a creator deity can play. On the other hand, the unity, beauty, and comprehensibility of the cosmos point to God as the creator. The best short read.

Christian, David, Cynthia Stokes Brown, and Craig Benjamin. *Big History: Between Nothing and Everything*. New York: McGraw Hill, 2014.

Chapter 1 of this book deals with the first three thresholds. Again, notice how the concept of Big History begins with the big bang story of origin and then compares it with mythical stories of origin told by our ancestors. The central point of the concept of Big History is to nest human history within nature's history. Big bang cosmology is the biggest nest scientists can think of.

Moritz, Joshua M. *Science and Religion: Beyond Warfare and Toward Understanding*. Winona, MN: Anselm Academic, 2015.

Chapter 5, on the creation of the cosmos, poses the philosophical and theological question, why is there something and not nothing?

Russell, Robert John. *Cosmology from Alpha to Omega*. Minneapolis: Fortress, 2008.

This book, written by a hybrid physicist-theologian, is for the advanced student. It demonstrates how the question of God arises out of big bang cosmology.

Web Sources

"Cosmos: A Space-Time Odyssey 2014." *http://geektv.me/watch-online/cosmos-a-space-time-odyssey*.

Narrated by physicist and educator Neil deGrasse Tyson, this made-for-television reiteration of Carl Sagan's series on the cosmos provides an informative visual treat. The big bang bangs on the screen, and the viewer relives cosmic history in this imaginative yet scientifically sound story.

"God and the Universe." Season 6, episode 7 of *The Universe*. The History Channel. *http://www.history.com/shows/the-universe.*

"Monty Python Universe Song," *https://www.youtube.com/watch?v=yq4uCWtQE24.* A humorous description of the universe.

3

Sun, Earth, and Moon

Whenever I am prone to doubt and wonder,
I check myself, and say, the mighty One
Who made the solar system cannot blunder,
And for the best all things are being done.

—S. A. Nagel, "God and Man"

The term Cosmic *History* refers to the history of everything, history in its largest scope. The previous chapter opened with the big bang story, the origin of the universe. What comes now is local history, natural history specific to planet Earth. Relative to the size of the cosmos, Earth is tiny. Photos of Earth taken from the other side of Saturn depict our entire planet as a barely discernible white pinhead.

No matter how tiny, this is *our* Earth. That is, we human beings belong to Earth's history. We were born here and, yes, we will pass away here. All of our ancestors were born, lived, died, and passed their genes down to us here on Earth. Every human word spoken, every song sung, every philosophical idea thought, every picture painted, every love enjoyed, every heart broken, every goal frustrated, and every achievement celebrated has taken place in this one location, Earth.

Life on Earth has been dramatic, to be sure, but does it have meaning? No meaning of Earth's history can be seen when looking through scientific glasses. Might we discern meaning if we looked through other glasses? In what follows, we will read this chapter in the cosmic story through scientific lenses.

Laniakea

Your biography constitutes a history, a mini-history placed within the larger World History. Human world history finds its context in Earth's planetary history. This planet belongs to the larger history of the sun and the solar system which, in turn, sits on the Orion Spur on the outer edge of our galaxy, the Milky

Way. But the Milky Way is by no means a loner. The Milky Way's story belongs within a still larger ongoing story, namely, that of a local supercluster of galaxies separated by voids yet still within a gargantuan supercluster of superclusters named Laniakea. A Hawaiian word for "immesurable heavens," Laniakea includes 100,000 large galaxies stretching across 400 million light years.

The cosmos as a whole is expanding at an accelerated rate due to an as yet unidentified force, dark energy. Galactic superclusters such as Laniakea can be identified because each exhibits internal dynamics due to the force of gravity. "Galaxies flow in currents, swirl in eddies and collect in pools to indirectly reveal the structure, dynamics, origins, and futures of the largest accumulations of matter in the universe," write astronomers Noam Libeskind and Brent Tully.[1] Superclusters are separated by voids larger than the voids that separate one galaxy from another.

Every history enjoys a context within a still larger history, but the largest context is cosmic history. Cosmic history purportedly began with the big bang and will end in heat death. Earth's history is a chapter within the larger cosmic story.

The Solar System

Earth's history is nested within its immediate context, our sun's history. What happened?

Imagine an immensely large molecular cloud, a billowing haze of primitive atoms that will eventually become the things we know. Because of the asymmetry of the particles in the cloud and because of the second law of thermodynamics, which says that active states go toward equilibrium, there is movement, a whirling movement. In this movement, gravity exerts its attractive force. A centering process draws more and more mass into a smaller location, increasing the mass's density. Packing more atoms into a smaller place increases the temperature. As mass collects, its gravitational pull increases. With this increase in gravitational pull, more mass is drawn toward the hot center, as the rest of the cloud swirls around the mass in the shape of a disk; this is called the *solar nebula*. The system feeds on itself, becoming increasingly dense until our sun forms.

In the whirling nebula, the solidifying gas spins around the sun as if the sun were the hub of a wheel. Multiple additional gravitational centers form, drawing smaller portions of gaseous (and eventually solid) materials into them. Through *accretion*—the process of particle collision and sticking together—solid objects grow in size. Each of these gravitational centers gradually enlarges, increasing its own mass, all while orbiting the sun. This is how planets form. This is how Earth came into existence.

---

1. Noam I. Libeskind and R. Brent Tully, "Our Place in the Cosmos," *Scientific American* 315, no. 1 (July 2016), 32–39, at 38.

The sun is our local star with eight planets orbiting. The Earth inhabits a "Goldilocks zone," just the right distance from the sun for life to flourish.

Two of the planets in our solar system, Mercury and Venus, have orbits much closer to the sun than Earth. Five other planets circle the sun in larger orbits: Mars, Jupiter, Saturn, Uranus, and Neptune. Another planetary body—Pluto—used to be considered a ninth planet, but Pluto is now seen as belonging to a group of *dwarf planets* orbiting the sun on the furthest perimeter scientists have discovered so far.[2] There are unconfirmed reports of another planet beyond the dwarf planet belt. We are still learning about the make-up of our solar system.

The inner four planets—Mercury, Venus, Earth, and Mars—contain silicate and iron compounds. They are rocky. The outer planets—Jupiter, Saturn, Uranus, and Neptune—consist mainly of lighter materials such as hydrogen, helium, and water in the form of ice. The outer planets are gas giants. The process of accretion continues to the present day, although by this time the gravitational centering of each planet has pretty well cleared its neighborhood of nebula gas and debris.

The principle of gravitational centering obtains on smaller scales too. The Moon orbits the Earth, as if the Earth were an axle and the Moon the rim of a wheel. Four moons similarly orbit Jupiter. Saturn is haloed by multiple moons and concentric rings of space debris. In short, we have orbiting systems within systems within our solar system.

The Earth itself is such a gravitational system. The densest mass is found in the center of our planet. The outer crust of our planet rotates around this center. If you stand still, every twenty-four hours you will find yourself once again in virtually the same relationship to the sun. In addition, the Earth orbits the sun

---

2. Pluto sports eleven-thousand-foot mountains of ice and exhibits very few craters, suggesting that it cannot be considered either a rocky planet or a gas giant. Because Pluto's gravity is unable to clear its orbital path of debris, it fails to qualify for the planet club.

about every 365 days, making up a year. The cycles of time with which we are so familiar are due to rotation and orbiting.

Let's get more precise. A rotational day is 23 hours and 56 minutes; and an orbital year is 365.24 days. A person standing on the Earth's surface at the equator is whizzing round at eighteen miles per second. But none of us feels this rotational movement because everything else in our environment is moving with us as a unit.

Early civilizations invented clocks and calendars to organize temporal passage in terms of cycles. Despite their inaccuracy, archaic peoples did a pretty good job when deciding that each day would be 24 hours and each year 365 days. What is important to observe about clocks and calendars is that they are based in nature, based on our experience with Earth's rotation and orbit. Clocks and calendars are natural.

Other time units are conventional, not natural. Weeks and months are based on symbols. The modern seven-day week derives from the creation account in Genesis, where God creates the cosmos in six days and then rests on the seventh. This symbolic seven-day week dovetails with a natural seven-day week in cultures that divide the lunar month of twenty-eight days into four weeks. (During the Soviet period, atheist Russian leaders tried to institute a ten-day week in order to eliminate any biblical influence on the calendar. This failed culturally. So the seven-day week continues, for theists and atheists.)

Almost every other time measurement is a multiple of twelve: 12 hours for daylight plus 12 hours for night produce a day of 24 hours. Hours are divided into 60 minutes, which is 5 X 12. Curiously, the number twelve pops up in various ancient cultures. The Babylonians divided the night sky into twelve constellations and the year into twelve months, bequeathing to us today the Zodiac. Egyptian sundials pre-dating Moses also relied on twelve daylight hours, as did later Chinese time metrics. Dividing time in the Bible is most likely based on the fact that Israel was divided into twelve tribes. Jesus followed suit with twelve disciples who became the twelve apostles. The number twelve seems conventional, yet, curiously it is nearly universal.

The importance of measuring time is that it represents one point of intersection between cultural convention and the natural world. The fundamental human experience is one of passage, and recurring natural cycles become a means by which our ancestors attempted to measure passage.

Planet Earth: Spheres within Spheres

Scientists call Earth a Goldilocks planet. In the German tale, recall, Goldilocks tastes the breakfast oatmeal prepared for the three bears and prefers Baby Bear's breakfast because "it's not too hot and it's not too cold; it's just right." The distance of Earth's orbit from the sun places it in the "Goldilocks zone" where it is not too hot and not too cold. It's just right for water to exist in frozen, liquid, and gaseous forms. Earth may be a Goldilocks planet now, but this was not always the case.

This third planet from the sun took its present shape about 4.5 billion years ago. It began in a hot molten state with considerable convulsing, erupting, and amalgamating. It might have looked like chaos, but this chaos was an open system, feeding off solar energy and leading eventually to a new form of order.

The mixing and comingling and compounding led to chemical differentiation. Heavier materials such as iron fell toward the Earth's center, while lighter materials floated closer to the planet's surface. Today, a dense inner core of iron centers Earth around an interior ball of sorts, an iron ball still in its hot molten state. As the planet's surface cooled, a rocky mantle formed like a larger ball surrounding the interior ball. This mantle consists of silicon, aluminum, calcium, sodium, potassium, magnesium, gold, lead, uranium, and, of course, more iron. Around the rocky mantle the Earth's crust formed, cooling sufficiently for life to develop. Occasionally, lighter metals rush through the mantle and crust toward the surface, erupting in dramatic and sometimes devastating volcanic blasts.

More specifically, our species lives only on Earth's crust, supported directly by the *lithosphere*. The lithosphere (*lith* connotes rock) provides the rocky bottom that contains the oceans like a swimming pool, and it provides the rocky foundation that supports mountains and valleys and riverbeds. The lithosphere, including the crust, is about sixty miles thick at most locations. Relative to the size of the planet, our lithosphere is about as thin as the green skin on a watermelon.

The next level below the lithosphere is the mantle, divided into the upper mantle and the lower mantle. The upper mantle is called the *asthenosphere*. At sixty miles (one hundred kilometers) below the Earth's crust, the temperature is so high that metals are partially molten. This molten metal is slippery. The lithosphere, which is cool enough to be solid, slips around on the surface of the asthenosphere like a sailboat on a lake. The Earth's crust may feel solid to you while jumping up and down, but in fact the crust and entire lithosphere are sailing.

The lower mantle is called the *mesosphere*. Because the mesosphere is deeper, it undergoes an increase in pressure. The increased pressure actually strengthens the rock structure and makes this layer a bit more rigid, despite the high temperatures of the more fluid asthenosphere above.

At the planet's center lies the outer core and the inner core. Each have slightly different properties. The *outer core*, approximately 1410 miles (2,260 kilometers) thick, flows somewhat like hot liquid. Here the liquid iron flows according to convective currents, and the unevenness of this flow is responsible for the magnetic field of Earth. Finally, at the very center is the *inner core*, which is approximately 754 miles (1,206 kilometers) thick. The inner core is relatively more rigid simply because the extreme pressure prevents movement.

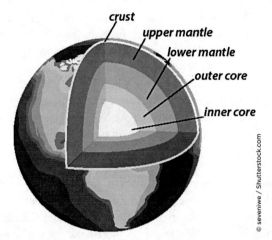

crust

upper mantle

lower mantle

outer core

inner core

© seveniwe / Shutterstock.com

As we dig down through the layers of the Earth, the temperature rises drastically. Continental drift occurs because the Earth's crust floats—and drifts—on the liquid mantel.

The Hadean Eon and Beyond

Right now the Earth's surface is just the right temperature to sustain life; but it did not begin this way, and it will not end this way. It came from Hades, and it will return to Hades.

In ancient Greek mythology, *Hades* referred to the underworld where the souls of the dead would end up. Christians associate Hades with hell, with fire and torment. Perhaps this is why scientists have named the first eon of Earth's history, the Hadean Eon.[3] The Hadean Eon was so hot and inhospitable, only the devil could feel at home.

The hot Earth gave birth to the moon long before it gave birth to life. While the proto-Earth was a large ball of molten material, a giant asteroid the size of Mars collided with it. The violent impact expelled a plume of vapor and liquid rock, which became trapped in a low orbit around Earth. The moon then cooled and grew in size due to its own accretion process. Over time the moon's orbit moved away from Earth; and it continues to move away from its mother planet by about two inches (five centimeters) per year.

Earth's crust shortly after the birth of the moon provided an environment quite different from what exists today. The temperature was too hot for water to exist in liquid form. The land was volcanic and molten. From the sky the Earth was daily getting bombed by comets and asteroids and meteors. The atmosphere

---

3. From 4.6 to 4.0 billion years ago. An alternative hypothesis suggests that during this early chapter in Earth's story a period of cold took place, and during this period life began. Maddie Stone, "Astronomers Might Have Just Solved a Key Mystery about the Origin of Life," Gizmodo, *http://gizmodo.com/astronomers-might-have-just-solved-a-key-mystery-about-1778095567.*

was so thick that the sun and the moon would appear in only dim outline. No free oxygen was available for breathing. Instead, the atmosphere consisted of 80 percent carbon dioxide plus methane, carbon monoxide, and nitrogen—gases poisonous to humans.

In almost a repeat of the cosmic big bang, Earth followed a course of cooling. When the temperature dropped sufficiently, the oceans became liquid. The atmosphere dropped its gaseous water in the form of acid rain, forming the first lakes and rivers. Accretion began to diminish as the number of hazardous asteroids and meteors in Earth's orbit were reduced.

Nothing about planet Earth is static. Nothing is permanent. Everything is in movement, even if it may not look like it on a daily basis. Nature is temporal, changeable, alterable. Recall that *history* is defined as the chronicle and interpretation of contingent events; history is both what happened and the story of what happened. Nature has a history in the former sense, even if humans were not present to record or interpret it.

The ecosphere of Planet Earth as we know it today is an emergent phenomenon. This explosive natural history led circuitously through long periods of time to creating a Goldilocks habitat for countless creatures. What will the future bring?

Conclusion

Cosmic History, like Big History, includes all that happened in the natural world before humans arrived. The universe is still expanding, still reeling from the big bang. Countless galaxies whirl and swirl to make stars, which in turn whirl and swirl to make planetary systems, which in turn whirl and swirl to make moons. The physical components to our cosmos are in constant movement.

The magnificence, unfathomability, and beauty of the cosmos give rise to the question of God as creator. The religion of Islam has tendered its answer to this question.

> God—Whom we know as Allah—has created the universe in all its diversity, richness and vitality: the stars, the sun and moon, the earth and all its communities of living beings. All these reflect and manifest the boundless glory and mercy of their Creator.[4]

The following chapters will turn such ancient answers into modern questions. Can the cosmos account for itself? Does the cosmos require a transcendent reality to bring it into existence and to guide its direction through natural history?

---

4. "Islamic Declaration on Global Climate Change (2015)," International Islamic Climate Change Symposium, *http://islamicclimatedeclaration.org/islamic-declaration-on-global-climate-change/*.

Review Questions

1. How do scientific cosmologists use the term "Goldilocks"?
2. What is the role of gravity in the formation of galaxies and planetary systems?
3. What are some ways that planet Earth is constantly moving and changing today?
4. Why do we measure time the way we do?

Discussion Questions

1. Retrieving the second law of thermodynamics (entropy) from the previous chapter, how can we account for the emergence of living creatures on our planet?
2. How do you think about time on a daily basis? In light of cosmic history and Earth's movements within the solar system, how does time relate to space?
3. Like a child who is born, lives, and dies, planet Earth has its birth, maturing process, and eventual demise. People today live during a single window of time—a Goldilocks time, so to speak. Eventually this Goldilocks window will close and all life on Earth will go extinct. In view of this prospect, what do you think is the meaning of historical life?
4. Does an Islamic interpretation of cosmos-as-creation add anything that cannot be gained from a scientific history of the universe?

Additional Resources

Print Sources

Christian, David, Cynthia Stokes Brown, and Craig Benjamin. *Big History: Between Nothing and Everything.* New York: McGraw Hill, 2014.

Chapter 2, "The Emergence of the Sun, the Solar System, and the Earth," provides a brief but informative story of the period from 4.6 to 3.8 billion years ago. This is a good place to obtain the basic facts and scientific vocabulary.

Davies, Paul. *The Goldilocks Enigma: Why Is the Universe Just Right for Life?* New York: Houghton Mifflin, 2006.

Paul Davies is the perhaps the number one writer describing the theological implications of natural science. His writing is always clear, thoughtful, and informative. The best.

Impey, Chris. *How It Ends: From You to the Universe*. New York: Norton, 2010.

Astrobiologist Impey is an extraordinary writer. He makes difficult concepts understandable. In order to get to the future end of the universe, in chapters 7–12 Impey tells us much that we need to know about Earth and our solar system.

Schulz, Kathryn. "The Really Big One." *The New Yorker* (July 20, 2015): 52–59.

This article explains why seismologists are forecasting a very large earthquake to hit the west coast of North America. Even though the San Andreas fault line in California is widely known, the Cascadia subduction zone may produce a far more powerful quake.

Web Sources

"How the Earth Was Made." The History Channel. *http://www.history.com/shows/how-the-earth-was-made*.

This documentary provides a narrated account of our planet's formation.

The Evolution of Living Creatures

A fire-mist and a planet—
　　A crystal and a cell,
A jelly fish and a saurian,
　　And caves where the cave men dwell;
Then a sense of law and beauty
　　And a face turned from the cold,—
Some call it Evolution,
　　And others call it God.

—William Herbert Carruth (1859–1924),
　　"Each in His Own Tongue"

arth is a Goldilocks planet: it's neither too hot nor too cold but just right for life. And it's just right in terms of both space and time. As it orbits the sun, Earth's spatial location permits water to appear in all three forms: liquid, gas, and ice. In terms of time, Earth is enjoying a Goldilocks era between its origin in the heat of Hades and its demise in the heat of the sun's expansion. The evolution and extinction of life on Earth will turn out to have been but a puff of animate existence in an otherwise ignored corner of material history.

We view Cosmic History geographically from our place on Earth and temporally during the twenty-first century. We cannot help but have a perspective, a way of looking at things, a context of meaning. There is but one history of the cosmos, to be sure; but we today on Earth are attempting to understand the big story in light of our little story. That little story includes almost four billion years of biological evolution.

The Big Bang Cosmos: Evolution		
EON	**ERA**	**PERIOD**
HADEAN 4.6 to 3.9 bya		
ARCHEOZOIC 3.9 to 2.5 bya		
PROTEROZOIC 2.5 bya to 540 mya		
PHANEROZOIC 540 mya through today	PALEOZOIC	Cambrian 540–485 mya Ordovician 485–438 mya Silurian 438–408 mya Devonian 408–360 mya Carboniferous 360–280 mya Permian 280–245 mya
	MESOZOIC	Triassic 245–208 mya Jurassic 208–146 mya Crestaceous 146–65 mya
	CENOZOIC	Paleogene 65–24 mya Neogene 24–1.8 mya Quarternary 1.8 mya–today

Life's Origin (3.9 Billion Years Ago)

"Life seems miraculous," write the big historians.[1] While the term *miraculous* is uncommon in both scientific and historical discourse, it is the case that to date no scientist knows how life first appeared on Earth. There is no widely accepted scientific account of the origin of life. Perhaps this is why big historians speak of life as miraculous.

How did the inorganic become organic? How did abiotic (non-living) material become biota (living entities). "The organic dimension," writes Paul Tillich, describing the leap to life's complexity, "is characterized by self-related,

---

1. David Christian, Cynthia Stokes Brown, and Craig Benjamin, *Big History: Between Nothing and Everything* (New York: McGraw-Hill, 2014), 56.

self-preserving, self-increasing, and self-continuing *Gestalten* (living wholes)."[2] Life adds something new to the history of the cosmos: self-relatedness.

In the face of not knowing, scientists lift up hypotheses regarding the origin of life. Perhaps the most popular hypothesis is that of the primordial soup. Just after the Hadean Eon (about 3.9 billion years ago), when crust temperatures had cooled sufficiently for water to exist in liquid form, a pond formed. This particular pond was rich in chemicals, making it a chemical soup of sorts. Some of these (non-living) chemicals were the very chemicals that are at work today in living cells. Chemistry alone does not explain life, yet living cells rely on the chemicals they process internally. In this primordial pond, the chemicals of life were present, but life itself had not yet appeared.

According to this scientific origin story, a bolt of lightning came down from the sky and shocked the pond. At this moment the so-called miracle happened. Suddenly the non-living chemicals became alive, and the long road of evolution to the development of humankind began.

The primordial pond is not the only origin story scientists tell. A second story begins in the primordial ocean, actually in the hydrothermal vents deep within the ocean. These vents blew exceptionally hot air from rumbling volcanoes into the water. Buildups of minerals containing iron, sulfur, and nickel jetted through the heated vents, forming small regions of carbon-bearing molecules. These molecules chemically changed into the first carbon atoms and, like Legos, they linked together to form more complex molecules. The volcanic jets provided both the chemicals necessary for life along with a supply of energy to fuel the chemistry of life. Primitive life eventually swam to the ocean's surface, walked onto land, and evolved into our ancestors. So goes this story of origin. Neither the primordial pond nor the ocean heat vent stories have been confirmed scientifically, yet they function as hypotheses to explain the so-called "miracle" of life.

These stories are hypotheses, not explanations. Even without an explanation for the origin of life, scientists agree that life does not spontaneously generate. It takes life to make more life. Louis Pasteur (1822–1895) gave us this principle now accepted by scientists: *Omne vivum ex vivo*, meaning life comes only from life. If this principle holds, then the implication is staggering: all life on Earth is the child of this one moment in the primordial pond or the underwater thermal vent. In that pond or vent the first cell with DNA (deoxyribonucleic acid) became the progenitor of all subsequent living things, including humans.

Life scientists have painted themselves into a corner of sorts. On the one hand, they say all life must come from prior life. On the other hand, they must account for the origin of life in the first place. Terrence Deacon, an evolutionary

---

2. Paul Tillich, *Systematic Theology*, 3 vols. (Chicago: University of Chicago Press, 1951–1963), 3:20.

theorist at the University of California at Berkeley, stresses that we need to acknowledge the severity of this dilemma. "The first organism wasn't a product of natural evolution," he says, because we must adhere to the "crucial and hard-won dogma of biology: the denial of spontaneous generation."[3] To say it another way, the theory of evolution cannot provide an explanation for the origin of life. We simply cannot set *omne vivum ex vivo* aside to say glibly that nonliving chemical elements evolved into living chemical elements because "the truth of the maxim 'only life begets life' is tested untold billions of times in the modern world."[4] Not only has the origin of life on Earth not been explained, what we are confident we know about life through evolutionary theory forbids such an explanation. We might call this "Deacon's dilemma."

Perhaps this dilemma could be solved with the panspermia theory. According to the panspermia theory, life did not evolve *de novo* ("from the beginning") on Earth. Rather, life was *imported* to Earth. Perhaps a wandering asteroid loaded with primitive life collided with Earth and deposited living microbes on our planet's surface. This may sound fantastical, but it is a respected theory, widely accepted at NASA. However, this does not solve Deacon's dilemma; it only puts the dilemma back a step. How did life originate on that life-bearing asteroid? The scientific community cannot avoid Deacon's dilemma.

What Is Life?

Pretend we are on the Earth 3.9 billion years ago watching lightning strike the pond where life originated. Immediately after the lightning strike, we dip into the water and find life in our dipping cup. But how do we know it's actually life? Curiously, no agreed-upon definition of life exists. A definition could exist only after scientists have an explanation, and as just mentioned, no explanation exists as of yet. So scientists try to *describe* life, even while they wait to *explain* life.

Distinguishing non-living things from living things is a challenge. One observation is that *living organisms exhibit centering*—that is, a living creature enjoys an interior system. A living creature is a whole organism, which cannot be reduced to its chemical parts. The chemicals of DNA are the same as all other chemicals, yet in the case of the microbial creature, they function as an internal system. The living creature exhibits emergent properties, properties that belong to life but had no precedent in the non-living chemicals that preceded it. These emergent properties require an organism to interact with the surrounding environment as a unit.

---

3. Terrence W. Deacon, *Incomplete Nature: How Mind Emerged from Matter* (New York: Norton, 2012), 430.

4. Ibid., 431.

Another observation is that *living organisms eat*; that is, each organism draws energy from the environment, synthesizes it, and expels waste. Humans draw energy from the environment by eating, drinking, and breathing. Plants draw energy directly from the sun's light (through photosynthesis, by changing light energy into chemical energy) and from water, soil minerals, and the air.

Living organisms reproduce; they make copies of themselves. Cells divide and make duplicates through asexual mitosis. Some plants reproduce asexually; that is, they duplicate themselves genetically. Other plants reproduce sexually; that is, the gametes of two plants fuse their genetic material. Humans make babies through sexual reproduction. Most living creatures reproduce either sexually or asexually.

Once life has originated, it *evolves*. Evolution is a part of any definition of life and requires a more precise description of reproduction. Organic reproduction differs from the copy-and-paste procedure we perform on the computer. The biological duplication process is not precise. Slight modifications happen in the reproduction process, so that offspring do not fully replicate their parents. Traits of offspring are contingent; they are not totally determined by their parents' traits. Charles Darwin noticed this and called it *inherited variation*. Slight variations in inheritance lead to large variations over long sequences of reproduction. New traits emerge, while previous traits disappear. Populations of living creatures undergo *descent with modification* when chronicled over long periods of time. This is how life evolves.

Bacteria, Archaea, Eukaryotes, and the Evolution of Life

Remarkably, the earliest microbial life scientists can find comes in three forms: bacteria, archaea, and eukaryotes. Bacteria and archaea—together called prokaryotes—carry DNA, but their cells lack a nucleus and membrane. Eukaryotic cells have a nucleus enclosed within a membrane (along with other characteristics). This suggests that the two types of prokaryotes appeared first, then the eukaryotes creatively synthesized the prokaryotes and produced a new life form, the cell. Some biologists employ the autogenous model: they surmise that eukaryotes self-generated. Others employ the chimera model: multiple archaea (more likely than bacteria) combined, synthesized, and produced a symbiotic merger.[5] Regardless of which model wins, life at this early stage was relatively simple. But it was simple in three ways, none of which are reducible to the others. If there were once a single common ancestor to all three, we've lost it in the sands of time.

---

5. Some transitional bacteria have been discovered, suggesting that bacteria may not be limited to only the prokaryote classification.

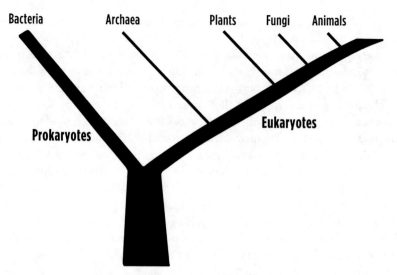

This figure shows a simplified tree of life with a single trunk representing the (unknown) last universal common ancestor (LUCA), which branched to form bacteria and archaea. Then archaea branched to form eukaryotes. Humans are complex eukaryotes.

Allegedly, the prokaryotes emerged from the primordial pond as single, protocelled organisms without a nucleus or membrane. Bacteria then as now eat organic compounds that contain carbon and excrete acids as waste in a process called *fermentation*. (Even today bacteria are used in the fermentation process to make cheese and wine.) Archaea then as now eat inorganic material such as sulfur, which they find in abundance in deep sea locations near volcanic heat vents. As these single-celled microorganisms evolved, they developed the process of *photosynthesis* by which they could eat light, so to speak, converting energy from sunlight to chemical compounds, and by which they could convert carbon dioxide into molecules used for making sugars. What was their waste product? Oxygen. Over two billion years, Earth's atmosphere underwent an increase in oxygen from 1 percent to 20 percent. Simple bacteria made it possible for more complex, oxygen-breathing life forms to evolve. The oxygen breathers added *respiration* to fermentation and photosynthesis on the list of metabolic processes employed by living creatures on Earth.

The eukaryotes emerged with a nucleus (containing DNA) and membranes to separate the distinct functioning structures within the cell, called organelles. Among the organelles we find mitochondria for respiration and chloroplasts for photosynthesis. The eukaryotic branch on the tree of life has sprouted plants, fungi, animals, and humans. Eukaryotic cells are much larger than prokaryotes—ten to a thousand times larger.

Curiously, the evolution of sex brought death. As long as primitive microbes reproduce through cell division, they are in their own way immortal. They don't die. But when sexual dimorphism appeared so that reproduction required mommies plus daddies, things changed. The mommies and daddies died so that their children could live to reproductive age and then pass on as well. Sex and death come together in evolution.

Today immortal bacteria and archaea together constitute half of the biomass (biological material) on the surface of the Earth. Even though humans are considered eukaryotic animals, a human body includes (in its intestines and elsewhere) a thousand species of microbes from the bacterial and archaeal branches of the tree of life. Each of us is a walking, talking embodiment of life's evolutionary history.

And Earth's atmosphere, which used to consist of only 1 percent oxygen, today consists of approximately 20 percent oxygen and 80 percent nitrogen, just right for human lungs. Or, to reverse it, human lungs evolved in correspondence to the oxygen content of the atmosphere. As life inherited its chemistry from Earth's surface, life in turn has altered the make-up of Earth's surface.

The Cambrian Explosion (540 Million Years Ago)

The evolution of complex life forms sped up under the oxygen-rich atmosphere. Scientists can trace a distinct movement from simplicity to complexity, even though the simpler structures such as bacteria and archaea never disappeared. They are still with us.

About 540 million years ago, an extraordinary burst of new and more complex life forms appeared. This period, called the Cambrian Explosion, lasted for 20 to 25 million years, a relatively short period of time in cosmic history. Initially, this evolutionary explosion took place in the sea, where new species drew oxygen from the water and developed vertebrae for bodily structure. Then teeth and claws made their appearance. About 400 million years ago some of the sea creatures ventured on to land, first as amphibians, then as reptiles, and finally as warm-blooded animals.

Mass Extinctions Alter the Course of Evolution

Periods of explosive evolutionary development were met with relatively sudden mass extinctions. While extinction is a normal part of the gradual process of evolution, the fossil history shows evidence of accelerated extinctions due to planet-wide cataclysmic events, such as drops in oxygen or huge asteroids crashing into the Earth. Since the Cambrian Explosion, mass extinctions have taken place four times. In the Permian extinction (about 250 million years ago), 96 percent of all species perished because of the acidification of the oceans.[6] But cockroaches survived and so did some small reptiles.

---

6. Eric Hand, "Acid Oceans Cited in Earth's Worst Die-Off," *Science* 348, no. 6231 (April 10, 2015): 165–66.

The surviving small reptiles evolved into dinosaurs, the largest of land creatures. Pangaea (the single land mass or supercontinent of that time) began to separate into today's seven continents about 200 million years ago, and the dinosaurs traveled with the tectonic plates. The dinosaurs ruled as the unchallenged kings of beasts for 150 million years.

The first dinosaurs to evolve were small, walking on two legs so as to free up the lungs for breathing in an atmosphere of low oxygen. The body plan of the first dinosaurs included bipedalism, elongated neck, grasping hands with a functioning thumb, and large pelvis muscles. Before the end of the Triassic period they split into two groups, one walking on two legs and the other on four. When the oxygen content of Earth's atmosphere jumped to 27 percent, so also did the population, body size, and variety of dinosaurs.

Then came a dark day; 65 million years ago, an asteroid almost ten kilometers in diameter smacked into our planet near the Yucatan Peninsula in the Gulf of Mexico. The explosion sent fiery debris up into the atmosphere, and a thick cloud of particulate matter covered the planet, blocking the sun's rays. The cloud may have lasted many years. Earth was engulfed in a deep chill. Plants died, animals died, and of course the dinosaurs died. All dinosaurs were wiped out. The cockroaches, however, made it through.

When the skies finally cleared and the bones of the dinosaurs were becoming fossilized, there was room for new species to evolve. The asteroid cataclysm had removed the dangerous dinosaur predators, providing ecological space for mammals to propagate.[7] Forty million years ago our planet was crawling with mammals that would eventually develop into whales and horses and wolves and humans. Brains and opposable thumbs and stereoscopic vision evolved, readying pre-human ancestors to give birth to *Homo sapiens*. And of course, all these developments were witnessed by the cockroaches.

What Is Evolution?

Evolution is a process of change over time that applies to species, not individuals. Individual organisms or individual persons do not evolve. Evolution means change, but not all change is evolution. What we will call *biological evolution* refers specifically to Charles Darwin's (1809–1882) theory originally put forth in his 1859 book, *On the Origin of Species by Natural Selection*. Note that Darwin's title applies evolution to species, not to individuals. Note also that Darwin specified the means of evolution: natural selection.

---

7. Recent fossil discoveries strongly suggest that mammals had begun to develop already during the dinosaur period and may have been better equipped to pass through the screen of natural selection. "Their sharp senses and fine-motor coordination (both enhanced by larger brain size), along with elevated metabolism, enabled them [mammals] to thrive in the cold and dark of the night." Stephan Bruzatte and Zhe-Xi Luo, "The Ascent of the Mammals," *Scientific American* 314, no. 6 (June 2016): 28–35, at 31.

As mentioned above, reproduction does not mean precise replication. What Darwin observed was inherited *variation*. Darwin observed that offspring produced by sexual reproduction differ slightly from their parents, but he had no scientific explanation for this difference. By a quirk of history, a contemporary to Darwin, a monk named Gregor Mendel living in an Augustinian monastery in what is now the Czech Republic, discovered the role played by dominant and recessive genes, formulating what we now know as the rules of Mendelian inheritance. Having read *Origin of Species*, Mendel knew he could provide Darwin with an explanation for inherited variation. However, he was too shy to visit the exalted master of evolutionary theory and tender his genetic theory. Darwin went to his grave thinking this mystery was unsolved.

Mendelian genetics gradually morphed into the new field of molecular biology; and molecular biologists devised an explanation for inherited variation: genetic mutation.[8] Inheritance comes in units called genes; frequently the chemical composition of these genes changes. Each gene is made up of a specific segment of DNA, and when DNA divides and recombines, alterations sneak in. DNA and the genes on DNA are not perfect replicators. Genetic change accounts for slight variations in inherited traits.

Natural selection determines which variations of inherited traits will endure and which will go extinct. For example, if a cat gives birth to a litter of kittens, each kitten (assuming there are no genetically identical twins) will have slightly different genes than the others. Genes express themselves in observable traits, such as fur color or intelligence or running speed. Some traits are more adaptive than others. If the kittens are born in the wild, predators will kill some of the kittens before they reach reproductive age. Perhaps a hawk will see the white kitten and kill it for lunch, but the brown kitten whose fur color matches the drying leaves in the environment will survive. Perhaps a coyote will kill the dull-witted kitten, whereas the kitten with greater intelligence will hide effectively and survive. Perhaps a large snake will devour the kitten that is slow of foot, whereas the speedy runner will escape the serpent and survive. The surviving kittens will grow to reproductive age and pass their genes on to the next generation of kittens. The genes of the non-surviving kittens will die out. Over many generations, the genetic make-up of cats will change. Cats as a species will adapt to their environment. This is called *natural selection* of surviving traits. Natural selection is the process by which new species evolve over time.

---

8. "Molecular biology, a discipline that emerged in the second half of the twentieth century, nearly one hundred years after the publication of the *Origin of Species*, undoubtedly provides the strongest evidence yet of the evolution of organisms." Francisco J. Ayala, "Molecular Biology: Darwin's Precious Gift," in *The Cambridge Encyclopedia of Darwin and Evolutionary Thought*, ed. Michael Ruse (Cambridge: Cambridge University Press, 2003), 397–404, at 397.

Darwin used the term *survival of the fittest* (which was coined by Herbert Spencer) interchangeably with *natural selection*. The term *fit* here does not refer to traits such as strength or intelligence belonging to an individual. To be fit does not refer to brawn or brains. Rather, it refers solely to reproduction. To be fit is to reproduce, to pass one's genes on to the next generation. It would be more precise to speak of the survival of the *reproductively* fit. When a species fails to become reproductively fit, it goes extinct. What we identify as extinct species are species that have been selected out or "de-selected," so to speak, by natural selection. The fossil record and the DNA record suggest that perhaps 95 percent of all species have gone extinct.

It must be emphasized that the term *survival of the fittest* within evolutionary theory refers to one and only one kind of fitness, reproductive fitness. It does not describe physical traits such as strength, speed, or intelligence. To be fit means, in short, to make more babies that survive to make more babies.

From Extinction to Petroleum

Where did those extinct species from millions of years ago go? Where did the bodies of the dead animals and plants go? They became oil. Actually, it's called *petroleum*, literally "rock oil." It's also called *crude oil* prior to refining. Petroleum or crude oil is the product of dead plants and animals after long periods of decomposition and pressure. When found under pressure beneath a rock formation, just above the petroleum reserve sits a layer of natural gas. Oil and gas mean power because, when burned, they produce heat. When we drive a car or cook dinner on a gas stove, we are benefitting from the death of formerly living creatures over billions of years.

In the struggle for existence, the species *Homo sapiens* has survived—so far, that is. Natural selection once selected us, but now, because of our technology, we as a species are altering nature in such a way as to enhance our continued survival. Whereas all previous species adapted to their respective environments, we human beings are adapting our environment to us. Will human beings survive for the foreseeable future, or will we add to the planet's petroleum deposit?

The Rise of *Homo Sapiens*

Perhaps seventy thousand years ago, *Homo sapiens* stood up on two legs and walked out of Africa to populate the world. Along their route they encountered other species in the genus *Homo*. They encountered Neanderthals in Western

Europe and Denisovans in Asia. These other species eventually went extinct. Only *Homo sapiens* lived on to conquer the Earth.[9]

Why did our hominin species alone survive? One theory is that a genetic mutation occurred that encoded a penchant for cooperation, and it was cooperation that conquered.[10] Other animals and even other representatives of *Homo* were individualistic, or had only limited loyalties within their immediate families. *Homo sapiens*, in contrast, created large groups of unrelated individuals who could cooperate in economics and in war. "The emergence of traits that made us, on the one hand, peerless collaborators and, on the other ruthless competitors best explains *H. sapiens'* sudden rise to world domination," writes paleoanthropologist Curtis Marean.[11] Evidently cooperation is reproductively adaptive and contributes to survival of the fittest.

The reproductive fitness enhanced by cooperation among hominins follows a precedent already established among prehuman creatures. Within the larger framework of competition, groups of primitive organisms already found cooperation could contribute to reproductive adaptation. Even eukaryotic cells must have formed a symbiosis with early types of procaryotic cells, contends biologist Lynn Margulis, so that both could survive. "The view of evolution as chronic bloody competition among individuals and species, a popular distortion of Darwin's notion of 'survival of the fittest,' dissolves before a new view of continual cooperation, strong interaction, and mutual dependence among life forms. Life did not take over the globe by combat, but by networking. Life forms multiplied and complexified by co-opting others, not just by killing them."[12]

Despite the probable accuracy of this contention, one dare not pit cooperation and competition against one another. It is not the case that one or the other exclusively accounts for species survival or extinction. Rather, it is most judicious to conclude that local cooperation within the larger matrix of global competition best describes the evolution of species. Our hominin ancestors most likely perfected cooperation better than their competitors, explaining why we are here and the Neanderthals are not.

This ability to cooperate is called *eusociality* by Edward O. Wilson, an influential scientist and expert on ants. Eusociality is more than merely getting

---

9. No one knows for certain how many hominin species existed. "It is possible that many human species once existed," write the editors of *Nature*; "but became extinct with such finality that even those few that were fossilized have since disappeared, leaving absolutely no trace." "Humanity's Forgotten Family," *Nature* 534, no. 7606 (June 9, 2016): 151.

10. It would be too simple to put cooperation on the shoulders of a single gene. If cooperation is in fact genetic, it is most likely the product of multiple genes working together. The important point is that evolution selected for cooperation.

11. Curtis W. Marean, "The Most Invasive Species of All," *Scientific American* 313, no. 2 (August 2015): 35.

12. Lynn Margulis and Dorion Sagan, *Microcosmos: Four Billion Years of Microbial Evolution* (Berkeley: University of California Press, 1986), 28–29.

along with others. In a colony of insects or crustaceans or mammals, it includes a division of labor, cooperative raising of the young, and lower castes giving up breeding on behalf of the dominant caste. For both ants and humans, "a eusocial colony has marked advantages over solitary individuals competing for the same niche."[13] How is it that one species survives while another goes extinct? War and genocide do the trick. "Wars and genocide have been universal and eternal."[14] To win the war and obliterate competing genomes takes eusocial cooperation within the in-group and competition against the out-group. Local cooperation leads to victory in global competition.[15]

The Triumph of *Homo Sapiens* over Neanderthals

A second theory augments the first to explain why Neanderthals went extinct while our ancestors adapted and survived. This second theory applies invasive biology to the account of *Homo sapiens* invading Eurasia, the home of the Neanderthals. An alien or invasive species is one that moves into a new geographic region where it has not previously lived, and frequently causes the extinction of one or more native species. When our human ancestors first invaded the Neanderthal homeland, the two species shared much in common: both were intelligent, large-bodied, hunters of large game, tool makers, and communal. Both existed at the apex of the food chain, that is, they both ate the large animals that also ate all other plants and animals. Two factors precipitated the fall of the Neanderthal and the reproductive success of *Homo sapiens:* climate change and the domestication of animals by the latter.

From forty thousand to thirty-five thousand years ago, the Neanderthal hunting grounds contracted due to dropping temperatures. The meat supply for all carnivore animals—wolves, large cats, and others right along with Neanderthals and modern humans—crashed. Our human ancestors adapted. Perhaps as early as thirty-six thousand years ago, *Homo sapiens* domesticated the wolf, who became the dog.[16] Dogs increased the efficiency of hunting. A pack of hunting

---

13. Edward O. Wilson, *The Social Conquest of Earth* (New York: Norton, 2012), 109.

14. Ibid., 65.

15. The human species is still evolving. Mutated genes—called "alleles"—can be selected for in a population and monitored by genetic researchers. Mutations "might increase height; those in another copy, or allele, might decrease it. If changing conditions favor, say, tallness, then tall people will have more offspring, and more copies of the variants that code for tallness will circulate in the population." Elizabeth Pennisi, "Tracking How Humans Evolve in Real Time," *Science* 352, no. 6288 (May 20, 2016): 876–77, at 876.

16. Dog DNA studies suggest that during one period between 15,000 and 12,500 years ago domestication of wolves may have taken place separately in Western Europe and East Asia. "Ancient Dog DNA Shows Dual Origins," *Nature* 534, no. 7606 (June 9, 2016): 155. To support the hypothesis that dogs aided *Homo sapiens* in surviving longer than the Neanderthals, one would need to date domestication much earlier.

dogs could quickly locate a large animal and hold it in place until the hunters arrived for the kill. In the struggle for survival, our eusocial dog-domesticating ancestors became selected.

Anthropologist Pat Shipman summarizes this second account: "I suggest the combination of climate change and the arrival of modern humans with new abilities acted together to cause Neanderthal extinctions."[17] She adds, "Humans are the most invasive species that has ever lived."[18] Like weeds taking over the garden, hominins are victors in the struggle for existence.

As historians chronicle past contingent events, evolutionary biologists try to explain why events in our biological past happened the way they did. Each evolutionary event must be explainable by the principle *survival of the fittest.*

Even though the story of evolution on Earth is relatively brief—only 3.9 billion years compared to the 13.82 billion years of cosmic history—it is decisive for our existence. It provides us modern humans with our pedigree.

Could Science Become Religious?

Darwinian theory has become more than just science. Like a slogan gone viral on the web, Darwinian evolution has spread from the laboratory to every aspect of modern culture. For example, the biology of evolution has become translated into social Darwinism, an ethical, social, economic, and political ideology. Social Darwinism encourages large businesses to survive and small businesses to go extinct. The retail giant, Amazon, say critics, fosters internally its own form of social Darwinism by ruthless competition. "Losers leave or are fired in annual culling of the staff—'purposeful Darwinism,'" a *New York Times* article reports.[19] Darwinian science expresses itself today as a business philosophy. The science of evolution has become a way of thinking morally about society.

Darwinism has also been enlisted to support the religious perspective we know as *naturalism.* "Essentially, naturalism is the idea that the world revealed to us by scientific investigation is the one true world," says Cal Tech physicist Sean Carroll.[20] "We are floating in a purposeless cosmos, confronting the inevitability of death, wondering what any of it means. . . . Our emergence has brought meaning and mattering into the world."[21] Today's naturalists feel gratitude

---

17. Pat Shipman, *The Invaders: How Humans and Their Dogs Drove Neanderthals to Extinction* (Cambridge, MA: Harvard University Press, 2015), 229.

18. Ibid., 2.

19. Jodi Kantor and David Streitfeld, "Inside Amazon: Wrestling Big Ideas in a Bruising Workplace," *New York Times* (August 15, 2015), http://www.nytimes.com/2015/08/16/technology/inside-amazon-wrestling-big-ideas-in-a-bruising-workplace.html?_r=0.

20. Sean Carroll, *The Big Picture: On the Origins of Life, Meaning, and the Universe Itself* (New York: Dutton, 2016), 20.

21. Ibid., 431.

toward Darwin for providing a worldview—what in a later chapter we will call a "myth"—that anchors religious depth within the natural realm.

The religious depth of the evolutionary worldview is expressed in culture, not in the laboratory. Tillich observes, "Religion is the substance of culture and culture the form of religion."[22] If a culture takes on meaning-giving power, then that culture is religious. Tillich's tenet, then, requires that we examine human culture, including the meaning-giving ideas of science. When science takes on meaning-giving power, it becomes scientism. What we see in the new naturalism is that evolution provides meaning-giving power for some among us. The science of evolution has become so absorbed into culture that evolutionary culture has begun to take on religious characteristics.

Here is an architectural example of the meaning-giving power attributed to science. Upon entering the gothic façade of the Natural History Museum in London, the first thing you see is a giant reconstruction of a sauropod, a dinosaur. Behind the dinosaur and sitting on a throne-like chair is a statue of Charles Darwin. Darwin is sitting where one would expect the bishop to sit in a cathedral. The *Kids Only* guidebook to the museum explicitly asks, "What makes the Museum look like a cathedral?"[23] We must ask, what is going on? How did evolutionary science take on religious form?

Michael Ruse, philosopher of science, writes about the impact of Darwinian evolution on modern consciousness.

> By and large, evolution became what one might call a "popular science"—respectable (more or less) but not cutting-edge science, more philosophical and background than anything else. In some hands, it became virtually a secular religion, an alternative suited for the industrial, urban world, to compensate for the perceived failure of the more conventional religions of the past. It is amusing how often the palaces of evolution, otherwise known as natural history museums, now being built in major city after major city, were so often modeled on medieval cathedrals. Instead of going to the Church of Christ on a Sunday morning, the family could go to the Church of Darwin on a Sunday afternoon.[24]

There is no question that Darwin's theory of evolution is solid science. Yet for many people the evolution story plays a role in culture that is powerfully religious. "Evolution . . . is a unifying myth," says historian John Herman Randall, because it provides a non-religious framework for connecting a variety of things.[25] What

---

22. Tillich, *Systematic Theology*, 3:248.

23. Natural Historical Museum, *Kids Only* (London: Natural History Museum, 2008), 2.

24. Michael Ruse, "Introduction," in *Cambridge Encyclopedia of Darwin*, ed. Michael Ruse, 20.

25. John Herman Randall Jr., *Nature and Historical Experience* (New York: Columbia University Press, 1958), 264.

Ruse and Randall are pointing out is that evolutionary history has become a scientized myth. Curiously, *the scientific concept of evolution has become an anti-religious religion in modern culture.*

The theory of evolution developing out of Charles Darwin's pioneering work is solid science. But at the level of culture we often see something added to the science, namely, religious and ethical claims. With the term *evolution*, naturalists refer to an inherent religious depth to nature that is pitted against institutional religion. Social Darwinists refer to an ethic that supports *laissez faire* capitalism. The student of Cosmic History must carefully distinguish between reliable science and religion in disguise.

Conclusion

Before life can evolve, it must originate. Scientists know a great deal about life's evolution, but they do not know how it began in the first place. Even if we think of life's origin as miraculous, the story of life's evolution over time is now well known. Life has a history, a chronicle of contingent modifications. Life's history on Earth is a decisive chapter in the more comprehensive Cosmic History.

The evolutionary history of life on Earth provokes a most puzzling yet astounding thought: Cosmic History achieves awareness of itself through human consciousness. Evolutionary biologist Simon Conway Morris ponders this phenomenon: "Evolution is the mechanism by which the Universe has become self-aware. In doing so, it has allowed us to enter previously unimagined worlds. Poetry unstrings our hearts, music ravishes us, myths inspire us."[26] These "previously unimagined worlds" transcend the everyday biology that has produced us. To what might these worlds be calling us?

This leads to the next question: does the history of biological evolution have meaning? Theologian Elizabeth Johnson wrestles with the meaning of death and extinction. "Considered in an evolutionary framework, pain, suffering, and death in the natural world do not fit into the common theological explanation . . . they are morally neutral."[27] How can death and extinction be dubbed morally neutral?

Does the history of evolution's past promise redemption in the future? This is not clear. The best Johnson can do is connect God with the unfit rather than the fit. She affirms "the compassionate presence of God in the midst of the shocking enormity of pain and death. The indwelling, empowering Creator Spirit abides amid the agony and loss."[28] The meaninglessness of evolution's

---

26. Simon Morris, *The Runes of Evolution: How the Universe Became Self-Aware* (West Conshohocken, PA: Templeton, 2015), 286.

27. Elizabeth A. Johnson, *Ask the Beasts: Darwin and the God of Love* (London: Bloomsbury, 2014), 185.

28. Ibid., 191.

story raises for Johnson the question of God, and she answers with a testimony to the God of compassion and grace.

The theologian would feel comforted if it could be shown via science that nature's evolution is directional, progressive, going somewhere transformative. But, alas, this is not the case.

Is there healing in evolution's future? According to the self-imposed limits of the scientific method, the answer must be negative: life's evolution has no direction, purpose, goal, meaning, or promise. Any meaning must come from beyond; it is not internal to physics or biology. Evolutionary biologist Jeffrey Schloss holds that "it may indeed make sense if the cosmos has purpose, though it does not make sense for science to provide the answer."[29] To put it another way, "there is purpose *for* evolution, but no discernible purpose *in* evolution."[30] For purpose, one needs subjectivity. Whose subjectivity provides the purpose *for* evolution? God's?

The meaning question leads directly to the God question: does evolution raise the question of God? Yes, indeed. Evolutionary history right along with its progenitor, Cosmic History, cannot account for itself. Those "previously unimagined worlds" demand a more comprehensive contextualizing, a home nesting, an ontological grounding. Could Cosmic History be asking the human race to raise the question of God? Is God the author of evolution's story? Or is evolution the author of its own story?

When asking the question of God, the historian notes that many previous answers are in conflict with one another. So the historian must chronicle the controversy over evolution. More heated controversy over the existence and nature of God is raised by evolutionary theory than by any other branch of natural science. As suggested by the architecture of a London natural history museum, belief in evolution sometimes replaces traditional religion.

Later chapters will take up the evolution controversy in detail. For the moment, note simply that Darwin's account of evolution belongs along with the big bang in the scientific story of origin as big historians tell it. Later chapters will consider alternative stories of origin, as well as ways in which the question of God becomes raised.

Review Questions

1. What distinguishes the *origin* of life from the *evolution* of life?
2. How does natural selection act on variation in inheritance?

29. Jeffrey P. Schloss, "Evolutionary Theory and Religious Belief," in *The Oxford Handbook of Religion and Science*, ed. Philip Clayton and Zachary Simpson (Oxford: Oxford University Press, 2006), 186–206, at 197.

30. Ibid., 201, italics in original.

3. What defines a "fit" species?

4. Why was it necessary for the dinosaurs to go extinct before humans could evolve?

Discussion Questions

1. If variation in inheritance is due to accidental mutations in the genome, does this suggest that evolution is guided by a progressive purpose? Explain.

2. We observe that advances in scientific knowledge and technological mastery exhibit progress. Do you believe human progress is rooted in a prior evolutionary progress?

3. If religion is the substance of culture, do you see meaning-making power exhibited in your cultural context?

4. How can science itself take on meaning-making power in modern Western culture?

Additional Resources

Print Sources

Christian, David, Cynthia Stokes Brown, and Craig Benjamin. *Big History: Between Nothing and Everything*. New York: McGraw Hill, 2014.

The role played by evolution in Big History is discussed especially in chapter 3. Note, for example, this quote from page 67: "We humans are connected to every living organism on Earth because we share with each one the same genetic code that has been maintaining and reproducing life since the first living cell emerged."

Darwin, Charles, *On the Origin of Species by Natural Selection*. 7th ed.

This edition is available from many sources. Consider reading it on disc, which is included in the paperbound edition of Ted Peters and Martinez Hewlett, *Theological and Scientific Commentary on Darwin's* Origin of Species (Nashville: Abingdon, 2009). Read especially chapter 4, on natural selection.

Moritz, Joshua M. *Science and Religion: Beyond Warfare and Toward Understanding*. Winona, MN: Anselm Academic, 2015.

Chapters 6 and 7 provide a lucid outline and analysis of the various issues surrounding human uniqueness in evolutionary history.

Morris, Simon Conway. *The Runes of Evolution: How the Universe Became Self-Aware*. West Conshohocken, PA: Templeton, 2015.

A heavy tome, this detailed argument from life's origin to human consciousness illustrates the value of convergent evolution for combating reductionism and opening the material world to visions of what might lie beyond. Morris is one of the world's leading contemporary theorists regarding biological evolution and its implications.

Web Resources

"Evolution." *The Scientist. http://www.the-scientist.com/?articles.list/categoryNo/2625 /category/The-Scientist/tagNo/8/tags/evolution/.*

A series of articles pertaining to evolution.

"Evolutionary Biology." *Scientific American. http://www.scientificamerican.com /evolutionary-biology/.*

Another series of articles on evolution.

Our Pre-Human and Human Ancestors

We are such little men when the stars come out!
Ah, God behind the stars, touch with your finger
This mite of meaningless dust and give it substance.
　　　　　—HERMAN HAGEDORN (1882–1964),
　　　　　　　　"STARRY NIGHT"

magine being invited to a family reunion. It's a summertime barbecue, and grandma and grandpa sit at the center table, with the rest of the family spread out on either side. Look around at all the relatives and notice the family resemblances: a similarly shaped nose, similar hair color or eye color. At the reunion there may be in-laws or adoptees who are not biologically related to the family, but each person *is* biologically related to the larger human family.

While the entire human race shares an ancestry, it's not yet known who should sit in the chairs of the matriarch and patriarch. Sitting around the table are our siblings, the Neanderthals, and among our cousins are the chimpanzees, bonobos, and gorillas. But who is the common progenitor?

Humans did not descend from apes. Rather, humans and apes descended from some other species, a common ancestor. Because 98.5 percent of the human genome overlaps with the chimpanzee genome, it's easy to surmise that our common ancestor does not go back very far.

Cosmic History does not ask only the God-question. It also asks the human-question. Who are we? Does looking at our family tree help tell us who we are?

The *Homo sapiens* family has a long pre-history. World history began with the first appearance of city-state societies around 4000 to 3000 BCE, maybe earlier. Let's say 6000 years ago as an estimate. Human pre-history lasted much longer, perhaps 200,000 years longer. Had a diary been written, it would have recorded the life of our forager, farmer, and citizen relatives. This chapter will draw upon archaeological evidence to assemble a picture of the life of our ancestors. The next chapter will look at their religious symbols and speculate on their spiritual sensibilities, noting how a continuity of mind binds us today with our pre-historic progenitors.

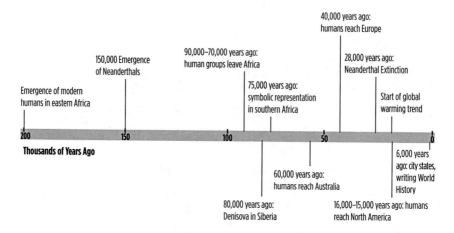

Our Common Ancestors

The term *hominin* refers to the inclusive category of human beings and other human ancestors. The category of hominin begins with the superfamily of *Hominoidea*, which includes both humans and all apes. Within this superfamily, the family of *Hominidae* is a little more specific. It includes chimpanzees, bonobos, gorillas, gibbons, and proto-humans.

Superfamily	Hominoidea
Family	Hominidae
Subfamily	Homininae
Tribe	Hominini
Genus	Homo
Species	Sapiens

Within this family we narrow the scope further to the subfamily of *Homininae*, limited to those who walk upright with a two-footed posture. This marks the split between the chimpanzee branch and the human branch on the family tree. Bipedalism—walking upright on two legs—began perhaps seven million years ago. Every species of human is bipedal. Within this subfamily we find the tribe *Hominini* and the genus *Homo*, which includes any bipedal primate with a brain larger than 800 cubic centimeters. This includes contemporary humans, with 1300 cubic centimeters or more of brain matter. Finally, the species *sapiens* refers to us, modern humans. We human beings belong to the species known to biologists as *Homo sapiens sapiens*. The Latin root for *sapien* means wisdom or, more generally, intelligence. Humans are smart hominins.

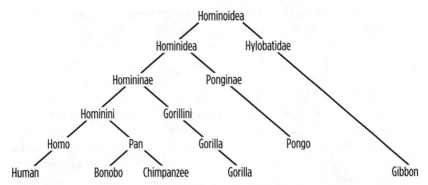

Humans—*Homos sapiens*—are "wise" Hominoidea. This family tree shows some of our closest relatives: bonobo, chimpanzee, gorilla, and gibbon. Humans did not descend from apes. Rather, humans and the great apes descended from a common ancestor.

Apes came down from the trees to forage on the land in eastern Africa some seven million years ago. The Rift Valley in Kenya and Tanzania is rich in fossils of *Homo erectus*, dating about 1.8 million years ago. These fossils help to tell us how the bipedal human branch separated from the proto-chimpanzee branch on our family tree. The proto-chimp branch led to the evolution of today's sub-branches such as the common chimp (*Pan troglodytes*) and the bonobo (*Pan panicus*). On the bipedal human branch perhaps eighteen different species evolved, lived, and went extinct. Only one species survives in the present day: us. Only after many fits and starts and extinctions has natural selection resulted in victory for *Homo sapiens* in the struggle for existence. *Homo sapiens* dominates the current geological period (termed the Anthropocene period). How long does *Homo sapiens* have before extinction? The answer is contingent—that is, it is yet to be determined.

When and where did *Homo sapiens* originate? The dominant view is the "out of Africa hypothesis." According to this widely accepted view, *Homo sapiens* evolved from *Homo erectus*. By 1.8 million years ago *Homo erectus* was standing on two legs and walking. *Homo sapiens* became a distinct species between 250,000 and 200,000 years ago while still in eastern Africa. Then between 90,000 and 70,000 years ago, *Homo sapiens* emigrated from Africa and began to colonize Europe, Asia, and the Americas.[1]

---

1. Chinese paleontologists claim they have found *Homo sapiens'* teeth in a cave that dates their arrival in China at 80,000 to 120,000 years ago. If this can be confirmed, it suggests our ancestors left Africa earlier than the consensus estimate. Ann Gibbons, "First Modern Humans in China," *Science* 350, no. 6258 (October 16, 2015): 264–65.

What appears to us today as racial differences are due to periods of repro-ductive isolation—that is, one group of *Homo sapiens* became geographically sep-arated from other groups for long periods of time, allowing for minor genetic changes. All human beings belong to a single species, however, because all can interbreed and reproduce regardless of race.

Our early ancestors shaped stones for tools, leading to the appellation the *Stone Age*, which lasted until bronze processing during the city-state period. Approximately fifty thousand years ago our progenitors developed a diver-sity of tools—harpoons, needles, knives, and such—from a variety of mate-rials, including rock but also ivory and bone. They deliberately built fires for warmth, to scare off predators, to illuminate dark caves, and to cook food. What we today consider technological development was underway. Some archaeologists refer to this period as the "revolution of the Upper Paleolithic." The concept of revolution within the Stone Age suggests a sudden change. Other archaeologists demure, describing the rise of technology as a slow and gradual process taking a hundred thousand years. In either case, by fifty thou-sand years ago our ancestors were recognizable as *our* ancestors: they looked like us and behaved like us.

At least eighteen other known species share our genus, *Homo*. "The truth is," writes popular historian Yuval Noah Harari, "that from about 2 million years ago until around 10,000 years ago, the world was home, at one and the same time, to several human species."[2]

In short, *Homo sapiens* is the only species among many that evolved from *Homo erectus* to survive until the modern world. None of the others, including Neanderthals, made it. They went extinct.

The case of the Neanderthal is especially puzzling. Between 150 thousand and 28 thousand years ago, Neanderthal hunter-gatherers roamed from Iraq to Belgium. They left behind tools, weapons, and cave art. Their brains were approximately the same size as *Homo sapiens'* brains, and some evidence sug-gests Neanderthals spoke in symbolic language. Exactly which Darwinian prin-ciple is responsible for Neanderthal extinction and *Homo sapiens* survival is not yet known. In a previous chapter we considered the dog theory: because *Homo sapiens* domesticated dogs they became much more effective hunters than *Homo neanderthalensis*, and this led the former to victory in the struggle for existence. Up until this separation, however, it appears that both species could speak. Per-haps they could even speak to each other. Because many modern humans today carry a small percentage of Neanderthal DNA, at least some of our ancestors must have carried on meaningful Neanderthal-human conversation. The place of language in human evolution is considered next.

---

2. Yuval Noah Harari, *Sapiens: A Brief History of Humankind* (New York: Harper, 2015), 8.

From Language to Symbolic Thinking and Co-Evolution

If *Homo sapiens* share so many characteristics with ancestral and parallel species, what qualities do human beings have that made it possible for them to rise to the top of the heap? The most widely agreed upon answer is *language*. According to Harari, "*Homo sapiens* conquered the world thanks above all to unique language."[3] Language marks a giant leap forward in human consciousness, but in itself language does not make human beings become something other than an animal. "While it is undeniable that humans are the most accomplished known users of language, many scientists have come to view the advanced linguistic ability of humans as a difference in degree rather than in kind from that of other animals," observes Joshua Moritz.[4]

Symbolic meaning refers to the human capacity to abstract from the concrete experience and construct symbolic systems of meaning; spoken or written *language* refers to one type of system within symbolic meaning. Not only do we speak to communicate, we think with language and structure our thoughts with language. An entire world of symbolic meaning foments constantly within our minds. Moreover, symbols provide the glue that binds us into social organizations. Spoken language is the first colossal leap in human consciousness.

Ursula Goodenough and Terrence Deacon, both evolutionary theorists, mark the emergence of symbolic thinking as a giant leap in human thinking. Symbolic thinking provides a feedback loop that influences the evolution of the human brain, which in turn influences the appearance of human culture and even the evolution of our terrestrial environment. "Symbolic cognition . . . precipitates a cascade of reorganizational cognitive and co-evolutionary events that eventually produce a brain with a capacity for the kind of mindfulness, intersubjective projection, aesthetic sensibility, and empathy that is now possible."[5] Because symbolic or linguistic thinking and communication contribute to the brain's development, we can speak of *co-evolution* of biology and culture. Human evolution has "entailed the co-evolution of three emergent modalities—brain, symbolic language, and culture—each feeding into and responding to the other two and hence generating particularly complex patterns and outcomes."[6] Note the spiral of growth. First, the brain makes it possible for the first experience with spoken language. Second, the development of language in turn influences

---

3. Ibid., 19.

4. Joshua M. Moritz, *Science and Religion: Beyond Warfare and Toward Understanding* (Winona, MN: Anselm Academic, 2015), 188.

5. Ursula Goodenough and Terrence W. Deacon, "The Sacred Emergence of Nature," in *The Oxford Handbook of Religion and Science*, ed. Philip Clayton and Zachary Simpson (Oxford and New York: Oxford University Press, 2006), 853–71, at 863.

6. Ibid.

the evolution of the brain; natural selection evidently favors linguistic capacity. Third, the cycle repeats itself over time, and our linguistic sophistication co-evolves with our brain. In short, cultural history influences biological evolution.

Because of symbolic communication, human knowledge can be collected and stored in shared memory. Knowledge can be accumulated, synthesized, expanded, and taught. Knowledge can grow. What one generation learns can be passed on to the next generation through schooling. This leads big historians to mark the transition from pre-history to history with the appearance of "collective learning."[7] Collective learning sets humans apart from the rest of nature and makes human history distinct from, yet still within, natural history. This leads world historians to flag the leap forward in social cooperation that language made possible.

> All animal species have ways of communicating, but language is another matter. Humans evolved an anatomical sound-making apparatus that could not only pronounce words—that is, individual sounds with meanings assigned to them—but also arrange words in complete clusters of meaning and transmit those meanings from one person to another at a fast rate. . . . Underlying the act of speaking is the capacity for symbolic thought, a talent that, as far as we know, only *Homo sapiens* has. . . . Equipped with language, hunters of 40,000 years ago could huddle together to plan tactics for trapping and slaughtering a herd of zebras. Mothers could explain and children understand why it would be dangerous to go near certain animals.[8]

How did our ancestors first come to speak? *Homo sapiens*, along with the Neanderthals, possess a gene called FOXP2, which may be responsible for language potential. Yet, like any potential, this potential needs to be actualized.[9] This gene needs to be expressed, that is, the gene needs to manufacture a protein that influences our phenotype, our body. Exactly what contingent event precipitated the language leap remains unknown to researchers.

This language leap remains a bit of a mystery because humans do not learn to speak unless first spoken to. An infant comes into the world with no language.

---

7. David Christian, Cynthia Stokes Brown, and Craig Benjamin, *Big History: Between Nothing and Everything* (New York: McGraw-Hill, 2014), 89.

8. Ross E. Dunn and Laura J. Mitchell, *Panorama: A World History* (New York: McGraw Hill, 2015), 31.

9. While both Neanderthals and *Homo sapiens* possess the FOXP2 gene, only the *Homo sapiens* genome includes CNTNAP2, which also contributes to linguistic capacity. Might this have distinguished the two species? See Kate Wong, "Neanderthal Minds," *Scientific American* 312, no. 2 (February 2015): 36–43, at 39. Even if FOXP2 is decisive, it is not alone responsible. It must coordinate with gene expression for other capacities such as vocalization.

In the baby's first months and years, he or she is bombarded daily with words and sentences from parents and siblings. When the infant finally responds with a word, the grownups' facial delight conveys to the infant that words and language are good things. This interaction elicits within the infant a desire to talk, to utter words, to formulate sentences. The infant speaks because he or she was first spoken to.

As the baby grows into a toddler and then a teenager, his or her larynx becomes physically structured according to the particular language he or she is learning. The brain, which continues to develop physically until age twenty-five, also takes on specific characteristics according to the language being spoken. If a person attempts to learn a foreign language later in life, he or she will likely have an accent because the larynx and brain are already formed for the mother tongue. Children who grow up in a bilingual environment will be able to speak multiple languages without accent because their larynx and brain co-develop to conform to their mother tongues.

What might this reveal about the origin of language in human history? Was it necessary for our ancestors to be spoken to before they could, in turn, speak to one another? From whence came the first word?

The Stone Age

During the Paleolithic and Neolithic Eras, our ancestors used stone for tools and weapons. The Paleolithic Era (from two hundred thousand to twelve thousand years ago) is commonly called the "Old Stone Age" and the Neolithic Era (from twelve thousand years ago to four or three thousand BCE) the "New Stone Age." The Stone Age ends when our ancestors in city-states discovered how to make tools and swords first from bronze and later from iron. Big historians argue that world history should begin with the Paleolithic Era because that was when our ancestors became much like us physically, socially, technologically, and linguistically.[10] Whether our Paleolithic ancestors belong to natural history or human history, they certainly belong within Cosmic History.

Life was not easy for our ancient ancestors due to their experience with climate change. Earth's climate has never been stable. During the Paleolithic Era our planet underwent two ice ages, periods of low temperatures and creeping glaciers. Colder temperatures dried even the non-glacial regions, turning forests into grasslands. People necessarily learned how to make warm clothes and heat their caves with fire. The most recent ice age ended only 11,500 years ago. Over the two millennia from 13,500 to 11,500 years ago, warmer temperatures increased atmospheric moisture, leading to reforestation and expansion of game.

---

10. Some world historians do include the Paleolithic Era in their history. Dunn and Mitchell, *Panorama*, provide an example.

The global population at the end of the most recent ice age was between five and fifteen million.

Paleolithic societies supported themselves with foraging. These were hunter-gatherer societies, hunting game and gathering roots, nuts, fruits, and berries. Cooperative teamwork developed in both berry-picking and animal-killing. Forager communities tended to be nomadic, moving from region to region in order to exploit seasonal changes in availability of edible plants and game.

Hunter-gatherers organized themselves into small societies, usually from a dozen to two dozen persons. These societies were families, as everyone was related. A foraging family may have had ties with other foraging families, making up a larger clan or still larger tribe. In the more inclusive tribe, when it came time to marry, a spouse would be selected from another family. Usually the bride left her home family and went to live with her husband and his family. Typically the hunters were men and the gatherers were women. Teamwork was necessary for survival. Justice and punishment were personal affairs. Foraging families tended to be small, closely knit, cooperative, and nomadic.

Foraging societies were also artistic. They carved figures or painted pictures on rocks, frequently the rock walls inside caves. In South Africa perhaps fifteen thousand rock art sites are ascribed to the San Bush people, dating back seventy-five thousand years. They depict hunting scenes. Similarly, Australian Aboriginal cave art dating back forty thousand years depicts crocodiles and fish and fauna. Small statues of pregnant women appeared in many locations in Eurasia about twenty-five thousand years ago. Paleontologists refer to these molded clay or carved women as "Venus figurines." In short, the human imagination had begun to copy in art what the eyes were seeing. The human propensity to mimesis—imitation—began to express itself during the Paleolithic Era.

Hunter-gatherer societies were predators, and they exerted considerable pressure on the environment. As they spread from Africa to other continents, they entered ecological niches that had not dealt with humans previously. The humans killed and killed and killed. In the Americas, it is thought that invading human beings led to the extinction of 75 percent of animal species weighing more than a hundred pounds. In Australia, humans eliminated 86 percent of the larger animals.[11]

Mammoths once roamed today's state of Kentucky, but they met their demise by coordinated teams of human hunters. When the last mammoth was slain only seven thousand years ago, the entire species went extinct. The popular New Age idea that our prehistoric ancestors lived in idyllic or Edenic harmony with surrounding nature is not supported by the known facts.

Twenty-first century humans have not forgotten how to hunt. For most people, hunting is no longer a survival necessity, but a recreational option, a

---

11. Charles C. Mann, *1491: New Revelations of the Americas before Columbus* (New York: Vintage Books, 2006), 174–92.

sport. But even sport hunting has an impact on the ecology. When a sport fisher tries to catch the "big one" or a hunter tries to shoot the trophy, they are culling mature animals capable of reproduction. According to a recent scientific study of predation, "humans function as an unsustainable *super-predator*, which—unless additionally constrained by managers—will continue to alter ecological and evolutionary processes globally."[12] It is obvious that *Homo sapiens* are winners in the battle for survival—so far, at least. Our evolutionary future is still contingent, unpredictable.

The Agricultural Revolution

Foraging families were nomadic. They followed the seasons or exhausted the resources of one region and moved on. Foraging turned out to be inefficient. Over time agriculture was discovered, and the family units became stationary. Berry picking and hunting did not cease, but the growing of crops was added and became the dominant source of food. Farming included planting, tending, and harvesting edible plants plus grazing domesticated animals.

In general, the men would go hunting while the women stayed near the village gathering berries, nuts, and roots. Perhaps these women discovered that they could grow their own vegetables and fruits. Perhaps it was the women who created and tended the first gardens. Once the principle of gardening was discovered, some twelve thousand years ago, it could be scaled up to the level of the farm. The hunting men then came home to plow the field, to grow wheat, barley, or corn. No written records confirm or refute this hypothesis, but it is plausible.

Expanding gardens were quickly accompanied by the domestication of animals. Wild goats became domesticated goats and yaks became cows to provide milk. Wolves became dogs. Oxen and horses were conscripted into pulling the plows. Bees were conscripted to pollinate crops and to supply honey.

Foraging did not come to an abrupt end the first day a garden was planted. The two methods of family sustenance overlapped for millennia. Initially, agriculture simply added wealth to subsistence foragers. Affluent foragers made their appearance in the Holocene epoch. The rudiments of a division of labor between hunters and farmers within a single clan or tribe was beginning to emerge. So also did new technology emerge, such as mortars and pestles for grinding grain.

With increased food production came increased population growth. Families expanded in size. Clans and tribes became larger with more complex memberships. During the hunter-gatherer era, families were streamlined for efficiency and mobility. Babies born with deformities who might not be able to walk or work were left to die, to be eaten by wild animals. Adult individuals

12. Chris T. Darimont, Caroline H. Fox, Heather M. Bryan, and Thomas E. Reimchen, "The Unique Ecology of Human Predators," *Science* 349, no. 6250 (August 21, 2015): 858–60, at 858.

crippled by an accident or seniors too old to work were similarly discarded and left to die in the wilderness. With the advent of stationary living after the rise of agriculture, these practices changed. Some infanticide continued, but euthanasia was reduced. With a stationary homestead, more children and infirm grown-ups could be housed and cared for. The population grew.

The human race began to experience crowding. Land for farming and grazing meat animals became limited, so efficiency in production became a priority. Breeding techniques in both plant strains and animal domestication grew in sophistication. Agricultural productivity rose. The creative potential of *Homo sapiens* was leading our ancestors into a period of rapid development and eventually to a new threshold: civilization.

This early agrarian era during the Holocene epoch saw the development of small villages of a few hundred people and increased trade; but the rise of cities would wait for thousands of years. In southwestern Asia, the Mediterranean Sea coast, and northern Africa this agrarian era lasted from perhaps eleven thousand to five thousand years ago. In China it lasted two thousand years longer. In central America it lasted still longer; it lasted almost into the common era. Agriculture never took hold in Australia; so when the Europeans arrived at the dawn of modernity they met aboriginal foragers. Global population grew to about fifty million during the early agrarian era.

Agrarian villages consisted of permanent homes with a growing division of labor. Although it is too early in human pre-history for politics—because one cannot have politics until one has a city, a *polis*—it is probable that agrarian villages experimented with pre-political forms of governance. Were governments consensual or coercive? Were villages ruled by bottom-up or top-down power structures? Archaeological evidence such as uniformity of house size suggests that these early village governments were consensual or bottom-up. In short, farming families banded together in villages to form cooperative social organization. Coercive or top-down politics would come later with the rise of the *polis*.

Banding together cooperatively in villages still required some form of leadership. Because villages were made up of extended families—made up of clans and tribes—rule by elders or even rule by chiefs developed. Egalitarianism remained the class structure, but division of labor led to consensual governance with designated leadership.

Growth of human population and growth in agricultural productivity together naturally had an impact on the biosphere. Large swaths of jungle and forest were burned in order to clear land for crops. Frequently, farmers pursued unsustainable agricultural practices, exhausting the mineral value of the soil. This over-farming along with overgrazing led to desertification. Excessive irrigation led to salinization (too much salt in the soil). Genetic modification through inbreeding of crops and animals led in some cases to greater susceptibility to blights and diseases. No science of environmental sustainability had been devised, therefore many of the regions of first farming are deserts today.

Conclusion

The study of history does more than retrieve information about the past. It contributes to our self-understanding. We look at our ancestors through scientific glasses, but, like mirrors, those glasses reflect our own image.

Through scientific lenses we can now see that our ancestors, the original *Homo sapiens*, did not suddenly appear. Ancient humans had their own ancestry, going back to a common ancestor shared with the great apes.

A definitive leap in evolutionary development took place when the language threshold was crossed. At some point our ancestors learned to speak and to understand themselves symbolically. In the leap to spoken language, humans surpassed the previous constrictions of biology and environment. With language our ancestors could abstract from the concrete, make generalizations, compare and contrast alternative futures, and coordinate group thinking. With language our ancestors became ready to explore what transcends the immediate human condition. With the advent of the word, the question of God began to dawn on human consciousness.

People, not genes, ask the question of God. Something other than genes alone must have led to this question being asked in human history. Axial theorist Robert Bellah delicately locates the God question within evolution. "Of particular importance are the behavioral and symbolic aspects of evolution, which build on genetic capacities but are themselves not genetically controlled, as it is there that we will probably find most of the resources for religion—cultural developments from biological beginnings."[13] Biological evolution launches culture, and culture is where the question of God dawns.

But before the dawn of God-consciousness, archaic awareness had to become ready. That readiness appears in the form of spiritual sensibilities. These spiritual sensibilities will be identified in the next chapter.

Review Questions

1. Our Paleolithic (Stone Age) ancestors shared a common ancestor with other extinct hominins as well as with today's chimpanzees, bonobos, gorillas, and orangutans. What do you think humans and apes share in common? What is distinctive about *Homo sapiens*?

13. Robert N. Bellah, *Religion in Human Evolution from the Paleolithic to the Axial Age* (Cambridge, MA: Harvard University Press, 2011), xii.

2. Symbolic communication through language marks a leap in human consciousness. What are the differences between pre-symbolic and symbolic communication?

3. How does language contribute to the evolution of a cooperative species?

4. What distinguishes foragers from farmers?

Discussion Questions

1. Can you imagine pre-linguistic consciousness? Can you practice a form of meditation in which you expel symbolic thought from your mind and immerse yourself in non-linguistic awareness? What do you experience?

2. Social cooperation among humans is far more complex than it is among most species. How do you describe the creative tension between your own individualization and your social participation?

3. What is co-evolution and how might it be operating today?

4. If today you could meet a Neanderthal person, what would you say?

Additional Resources

Print Sources

Cole-Turner, Ron. *The End of Adam and Eve*. Pittsburgh: Theology Plus, 2016.

This readable book is excellent for college students wishing to grapple with the tension between biblical literalism and scientific literacy. The author reinterprets the Christian message while taking on board evolution's version of human origins. See also Cole-Turner's website, *www.theologyplus.org/*.

Deacon, Terrence W. *Incomplete Nature: How Mind Emerged from Matter*. New York: W. W. Norton, 2012.

In this widely acclaimed work, Deacon exhibits the illuminating value of emergentist theory. He makes the case that language and symbolic thinking distinguish *Homo sapiens* in evolutionary development. Big historians rely upon Deacon for their own constructive work.

Dunn, Ross E., and Laura J. Mitchell. *Panorama: A World History*. New York: McGraw Hill, 2015.

Perhaps the best of the current genre of World History textbooks, this book by world historians includes the history of our paleolithic ancestors but does not include the big bang. "Part 1: Settling the Planet," provides a succinct and illuminating overview of the Holocene.

Harari, Yuval Noah. *Sapiens: A Brief History of Humankind.* New York: Harper, 2015.

Harari is a spritely and exciting writer. He nicely connects natural factors with human history and he recognizes the contingency in human events. His otherwise delightful chronicle is tarnished by an undisguised bias against religion and religious traditions. Despite this drawback, the book elicits an appreciation for the long and dramatic story that has led to *Homo sapiens.*

Mann, Charles C. *1491: New Revelations of the Americas before Columbus.* New York: Vintage Books, 2006.

Mann, Charles C. *1493: Uncovering the New World Columbus Created.* New York: Vintage Books, 2012.

These two works make for marvelous reading. *1491* vividly reports the extent of human population in the Americas before the arrival of the Europeans. *1493* demonstrates the impact of nature and natural resources on the pattern of colonization in the so-called new world and the role of global economics leading to the modern empires.

Tibayrenc, Michel, and Francisco J. Ayala, eds. *On Human Nature: Biology, Psychology, Ethics, Politics, and Religion.* Amsterdam: Elsevier, 2017.

Leading scientists present a history of humanity and draw out its implications for contemporary society, race relations, and religion.

Media Sources

Craynston, Bryan, narrator. *Big History.* 3 disc DVD set.

These fascinating and intriguing vignettes on how natural phenomena invisibly influenced the course of human history were originally broadcast on H2, the television history channel. The episode on salt is particularly interesting, because it shows how deer trails led to human roads all because of our biological need for salt. A genuinely delightful way to learn Big History.

6

Religious Symbols and Spiritual Sensibilities

The spacious firmament on high,
With all the blue ethereal sky,
And spangled heavens, a shining frame,
Their great Original proclaim.

—JOSEPH ADDISON (1672–1719), "ODE"

"Most of human history seems to be just one damn thing after another," says journalist and historian Gwynne Dyer.[1] Actually, this is not true. History as the historian interprets it is more than merely a collection of damn things. It's a collection of meaningful things strung together to tell a story. History is a narrative, and narratives attempt to turn one damn thing after another into a meaningful story.

This chapter will cross the bridge, so to speak, from pre-history to history. It will track the changes taking place when foragers and farmers first became citizens, and when our ancestors began to read and write. In common parlance the term, *pre-historical*, refers to the period before writing, while the term, *historical*, refers to the period where written records provide resources for historians. Here, in this book, both fit within Cosmic History; both the pre-historical and the historical belong to history. Nevertheless, the rise of symbolic thought and especially written language marks a decisive threshold in the development of human consciousness. To become a citizen who reads and writes, one must live in a city, a *polis*. Written history was born shortly after its two elder siblings were born, the city-state and war.

The rise of the polis or the city-state will be discussed in this chapter and again in a later chapter in regard to the Axial Age (the time when religions began to effect great change in cultures and civilizations). This chapter will identify the

---

1. Gwynne Dyer, *War* (New York: Crown, 1985), 30.

spiritual sensibilities among foragers, farmers, and pre-axial ancestors. These sensibilities were typically tied to the environment and to early culture. The larger concern is with the development of different stages of human consciousness over time, sometimes called the differentiation of human consciousness. This chapter will show how a pattern of religious or spiritual sensibilities appeared among our preliterate ancestors and will acknowledge the enduring role of these sensibilities in twenty-first century human consciousness.

Remember that an interpretive dynamic is at work in the study of history: when we learn the story of our ancestors, we also learn who we are. To ask about where things came from is to ask about our own identity. This is the mystery: studying the past objectively changes us subjectively.

The Polis, Politics, and Citizenship

The first leap in human consciousness reviewed here was the emergence of spoken language. The second was the emergence of written language. Writing began in fits and starts during the fourth or fifth millennium before the common era. Writing coincided roughly with the rise of a new form of human community, the city-state.

The city was called the *polis* in Greek, the root of the term *politics*. In Latin the term is *civitas*, root of the term *civilization*. To be civil is to be citified. Scholars typically use the adjective *archaic* to describe the sensibilities and accomplishments of early citizens.

The city-state became more than merely an overgrown village. The citizens of the polis came from a variety of locations in the countryside, not only from a single family, clan, or tribe. The city-state included strangers. This required an impersonal government, usually a top-down or coercive government. Instead of tapping tribal chiefs for leadership, the city-state crowned a king or queen. In the case of Athens, Greece, the city-state experimented with government by democracy. Most city-states relied on a single ruler, the king.

What made the city-state possible was increased agricultural productivity. Mayan farmers eighteen hundred years ago in what is now Mexico, for example, found they could grow enough food to feed their family in only ninety days per year. Crop production for the remaining two hundred seventy days yielded surplus value. For the emerging city-state, this meant that one farming family could feed three other families. The three other families could be trained in the crafts or the arts; and some could become full time soldiers. With the advent of city-states, a new economy emerged that made possible leaps in human eusociality (social cooperation) and creativity.

Nearly six thousand years ago, city-state economies began to appear in the Tigris and Euphrates river valleys, followed soon thereafter by upper and lower Egypt. About four thousand years ago the polis appeared independently in Crete and China. Soon the ancient Near East was strewn with city-states, many federated together within empires. The cities would engage each other in relentless warfare until an empire would be formed; the empire would either destroy the city or incorporate it into a larger political unit.

It was during the city-state era that transcendental awareness dawned on the consciousness of some—not all—of our ancestors. It was the "age of the emergence of the idea of transcendence," says sociologist Hans Joas.[2] It was this pivotal (or "axial") insight into transcendence that propelled human consciousness beyond parochialism into the realm of the universal. Eric Voegelin describes this axial insight: "A symbolism for the expression of true order was found which claimed to be scientifically valid for all [people]."[3] Later chapters in this book will look at this axial breakthrough in China, India, Greece, and Israel. Here the focus is on the pre-axial spirituality of foragers, farmers, and non-axial citizens.

In order to reach back in time to ask what our ancestral foragers and farmers were thinking, scholars must investigate the written records of the city-state citizenry and then extrapolate backward in time. This method seems to provide historians with considerable knowledge of human consciousness during the spoken and early written language periods. Today's historians of religion know enough to describe (at least partially) the spiritual sensibilities and religious symbols of our Stone Age ancestors.

The Spirituality of Foragers, Farmers, and Citizens

As we have noted, the pre-history of smart hominins begins with our human ancestors engaged in hunting and gathering to provide food and sustenance. At some later point hominins discovered agriculture, and this led to social and economic growth as well as population growth. Eventually farmers formed villages. This was followed by cities, and civilization began. How did the question of God arise during the city-state period? Could looking at the spiritual practices of prehistoric people help answer this question?

Some historians dismiss religious and spiritual practices during the Stone Age by labelling them *animism*, which suggests that pre-historic people mistakenly thought things in nature were enlivened by spirits. It may be true that foragers and farmers were animists, but the situation is much more complex. The spiritual presence that prehistoric people experienced in nature exhibited

---

2. Hans Joas, "The Axial Age Debate as Religious Discourse," in *The Axial Age and Its Consequences*, ed. Robert N. Bellah and Hans Joas (Cambridge, MA: Harvard University Press, 2012), 9–29, at 11.

3. Eric Voegelin, *Order and History*, 5 vols. (Baton Rouge: Louisiana State University Press, 1956–1987), 2:28.

a structure that expressed itself in symbolic form. Neither big historians nor world historians look into early religion in sufficient detail to apprehend just how our early ancestors structured their worldview and their psyches. This is an area where this book, *God in Cosmic History*, contributes what cannot be found in standard histories. The elements in this symbolic structure will be referred to here with the term *sensibility*.

The following discussion rests upon a set of assumptions. First, archaic *Homo sapiens* were fully human in the same sense that we today are human. Second, human beings are inherently religious. "*Homo sapiens* is also *Homo religiosus*," writes Karen Armstrong.[4] Third, it is possible to distinguish between intra-cosmic and supra-cosmic understandings of the divine: *intra-cosmic* consciousness pictures the gods as characters within the cosmos, whereas *supra-cosmic* consciousness believes that the divine transcends the cosmos. These assumptions allow scholars to presume that pre-literate and archaic societies exhibited the same spiritual or religious sensibilities we see at work in today's psyche and culture, even if their symbols might have been specific to their time and their context. Again, the same sensibilities are operative in both pre-axial and axial stages of consciousness, even if the concept of the divine changed drastically. Scholars get at the sensibilities by analyzing the symbol systems of a given people in a given period.

Some key terms require clarification. The term *sensibility* will refer to a generic category of human understanding that is expressed in specific symbols and myths. The term *symbol* will refer to the specific name or type of religious figure that appears in a spiritual or religious context. Sensibilities are categorical, whereas symbols are specific. The term *myth* will refer to a story or category of stories that are composed of symbols. The symbols and the myths of a specific historical group will differ from those of other historical groups, to be sure, but we will see that sets of symbols and myths exhibit a common sensibility structure.

Among the symbols are names of gods and goddesses. Tillich tells us that "gods are beings who transcend the realm of ordinary experience in power and meaning, with whom [people] have relations which surpass ordinary relations in intensity and significance."[5] The names of gods and goddesses within myths are symbolic because they are multivalent. *Multivalence* means that each god or goddess may be a character in a story but, in addition, each deity evokes one or another sensibility, and this in turn leads to multiple levels of meaning. Poseidon, for example, is more than merely a name for a god in a myth about the sea; Poseidon refers to the sea itself. Each symbol emits many levels of meaning. The

4. Karen Armstrong, *A History of God: The 4000 Year Quest of Judaism, Christianity, and Islam* (New York: Alfred A. Knopf, 1994), xix.

5. Paul Tillich, *Systematic Theology*, 3 vols. (Chicago: University of Chicago Press, 1951–1963), 1:212.

names of the gods and goddesses are less important than the levels of meaning that resonate with human sensibilities.

Sensibilities include the beyond, the intimate, the *axis mundi*, shamanism, and autochthony.[6] Each of these sensibilities took on symbolic form among Stone Age foragers, farmers, and citizens.

Sensing the Beyond

Archaic peoples experienced the power and magnificence of the sky, and they intuitively wondered if there might be something beyond the sky. People today are still struck with awe when they become aware of the reality of the beyond, the high, the incomprehensible, and even the transcendent.

The symbol systems of archaic foragers, farmers, and citizens included sky gods—divine figures associated with the sky—such as Marduk among the early Sumerians and later Babylonians, Indra among the Dravidians and Aryans living in the Indus River Valley, and Itzam Na among the Mayans in Central America. In these examples, the sky god was associated with thunder clouds roaring above and lightning bolts plummeting toward earth. In Egypt, the preeminent sky god was the sun, the source of all energy and power. Sky gods in archaic cultures tended to be male, masculine, strong. Sky gods were responsible for weather, climate, and military power when called upon to defend the tribe or village.

"Beholding the sky," writes Mircea Eliade, a revered scholar in the field of history of religions, our human ancestor "simultaneously discovers the divine incommensurability and his own situation in the cosmos. For the sky, *by its own mode of being*, reveals transcendence, force, eternity. It *exists absolutely* because it is *high, infinite, eternal, powerful*."[7] The sky itself is a physical phenomenon, to be sure; but the sky provokes within the human psyche a sense of beyondness, an awareness of possible transcendence.

For pre-differentiated or intra-cosmic consciousness prior to the Axial Period, sky gods communicated the sense of the beyond. For axial or supra-cosmic consciousness, the divine transcends the sky as well as all of reality. For the Qur'an declares,

> High above all is God,
> The King, the Truth! (Qur'an 20:114)

In both intra-cosmic and later supra-cosmic consciousness, the adjective *high* evokes the sense of the beyond. For modern people, outer space evokes the sense of the beyond, because outer space is beyond the sky.

---

6. Each of these concepts is discussed later in this chapter.

7. Mircea Eliade, *The Sacred and the Profane*, trans. William R. Trask (New York: Harcourt, Brace, and World, 1957), 119, italics in original.

At the level of differentiated consciousness in Christian theology, rational conceptions of God vibrate with the beyond sensibility. In the work of Saint Anselm of Canterbury (1033–1109), for example, "God is that, than which nothing greater can be conceived."[8] It would be impossible to conceive of a God beyond the final beyond. The geography of the sky has been translated into a mental geography of concepts, with "that, than which nothing greater can be conceived" becoming what is beyond the beyond.

This human capacity to be prompted by the sky to think about beyondness can be termed the *beyond sensibility*. When the perceived sky moves inside the mind and becomes conceptual, we will apply the philosophical term *transcendence* to human awareness. The beyond sensibility makes it possible for the human person to become aware of the possibility of a transcendent reality.

Sensing the Intimate

We experience intimacy at two levels. At the more superficial level, *intimate* refers to a personal need for daily sustenance: food, shelter, caring family, and such, what in evolutionary theory we would call "survival." At a deeper level, *intimate* refers to what happens within the self, within consciousness. In the pre-axial period, the God question was this: is what lies beyond us in power accompanied by a divine dimension that provides sustenance for the people? The compact symbolism with its intra-cosmic deities turns from the sky beyond toward the animals people hunt or to the soil people plow.

Let's start by looking at hunter-gatherer symbolism. In addition to the sky god representing the beyond, forager symbolism includes a second, semi-divine figure representing the intimate: the master of the animals, also called by scholars "the master of the hunt." The master of the animals is alleged to be the king of the animal species upon which the tribe of hunters depends for its sustenance. Among many Eskimo tribes, for example, the master of the animals is a giant caribou, the king of the caribou. The king of the caribou decides just how many individual animals the tribe may cull and kill during the hunting season. In pre-hunt rituals, the hunters placate the king of the caribou in dance; and they mimic slaying the animal in that dance. There is a suggestion of grace at work here, because the tribe responds in gratitude to the master of the animals, who has given what is needed for life.

A tribe may include many masters of the hunt in its symbol system. Native Amerindians may include rituals for hunting on behalf of the master of the salmon, the master of the bear, the master of the deer, and so on.

---

8. "Id quo nihil majus cogitari possit." Anselm of Canterbury, *Proslogium* 2, in *Saint Anselm: Basic Writings*, trans. S. N. Deane (LaSalle, IL: Open Court, 1966), 7.

Romulus and Remus, the founders of Rome, were said to have been raised in the wild by a mother wolf. The wolf figure may hearken back to the Master of the Hunt and the transition from foraging and farming to civilization.

Symbolism changes with the move from foraging to farming, even though the sensibilities are constant. Daily sustenance clearly comes now from one basic source, namely, the earth. The earth provides the soil, the impetus to grow, the harvest, and finally the food upon which human life itself depends. Women and soil are thought of together, perhaps because women discovered agriculture or because of a correspondence between the woman's ability to give birth to children with the soil's ability to give birth to crops. The result is that *Mother Earth* takes on feminine symbolism.

The ancient Greek poet Hesiod sets the leitmotif for religious sensibilities in general, namely, the mythical marriage of heaven and earth. Earth is named *Gaia* and heaven is named *Ouranos*.

> Earth [Gaia] bore first of all one equal to herself, starry heaven [Ouranos], so that he should cover her all about, to be a secure seat forever for the blessed gods.[9]

Note how in this myth Mother Earth, Gaia, creates her own husband, Ouranos, the sky. The power of creation lies primarily in the earth, only secondarily in the sky. Gaia marries her son, so to speak, and their progeny include the other gods and the human race. One of those progeny is Ceres (whose name we remember

---

9. Hesiod, *Theogony* 126. *Theogony and Works and Days*, trans. M. L. West (Oxford: Oxford University Press, 1988), 7.

when we eat breakfast cereal). Whereas the gods of the sky dominated in hunter-gatherer society, the divinity of earth dominates in agricultural society.

Earth mother symbolism was by no means restricted to Greece; it appears nearly everywhere during the early agricultural age. Hebat, sometimes called Khepat, the wife of the sky god Teshub, was widely worshipped among the Hittites. Among today's Navaho Amerindians, Yadilqil Hastqin is the sky-man and his wife is Nihosdzan Esdza, or earth woman. Such earth mother symbolism is not forgotten; it lives on in the modern world even though it has premodern origins. From the 1890s we inherit the moving testimony of an individual named Smohalla of the Umatilla tribe in North America. He appears to be resisting the forced transition from foraging to farming; so he forbids farming based upon feminine symbolism.

> You ask me to plough the ground? Shall I take a knife and tear my mother's bosom? Then when I die she will not take me to her bosom to rest. You ask me to dig for stone? Shall I dig under her skin for her bones? Then when I die I cannot enter her body to be born again. You ask me to cut grass and make hay and sell it, and be rich like the white men! But how dare I cut off my mother's hair?[10]

Even though this is a nineteenth-century source, it suggests what might also have been the case among our pre-historic ancestors.

Reliance on the earth as mother remains contemporary, not merely ancient. Pope Francis recalled his namesake, Francis of Assisi, when he wrote in 2015, "Everything is related, and we human beings are united as brothers and sisters on a wonderful pilgrimage, woven together by the love God has for each of his creatures and which also unites us in fond affection with brother sun, sister moon, brother river and mother earth."[11]

According to Eliade, because "the Great mother . . . [is] the foundation, in a sense, of the universe, the earth is endowed with manifold religious significance. It was adored because of its permanence, because all things came from it and all things return to it."[12] The master of the animals among hunter-gatherers and the earth mother among the farmers are two kinds of symbols that evoke the intimate sensibility.

As the transition takes place from foraging to farming, the predominantly male sky symbolism remains evocative but loses some of its potency. Curiously, the responsibility of the sky god increases while his stature decreases. The sky

---

10. Cited in Mircea Eliade, *Patterns in Comparative Religion*, trans. Rosemary Sheed (New York: World, 1963), 246.

11. Pope Francis, *Laudato si'*, no. 92, available at *http://w2.vatican.va/content/francesco/en/encyclicals/documents/papa-francesco_20150524_enciclica-laudato-si.html*.

12. Ibid., no. 240.

god becomes primarily responsible for rain, which is envisioned as cosmic semen needed by the earth mother to make the crops grow. This is a big responsibility. Even so, the sky god becomes less important, relatively speaking, because human homage is now focused on the earth mother who provides the villages with what they need to survive. Religious rituals frequently incorporate mimesis—that is, they imitate something from the myth. Ancient farmers incorporated sexual intercourse in their rituals to both imitate the relationship between sky and earth as well as encourage cosmic intercourse on the part of the gods to make crops grow. Village life for our early agricultural ancestors was dominated by feminine symbolism and fertility rituals.

Sensibilities of the beyond and the intimate can be compared. Whereas, for foragers, the sky god is removed from everyday affairs in the far-off sky, the master of the animals is terramorphic (earthly in location), living close to the tribe. The sky god is violent and somewhat impersonal, whereas the master of the animals cares for the tribe and provides its livelihood. For farmers, the earth mother goddess assumes many of the responsibilities formerly belonging to the master of the animals. Whereas the sky god elicits our sense of what is beyond, the master of the animals and the earth mother goddess elicit a sense of the intimate.

Intimate? Yes, intimate. The master of the animals and the earth mother goddess are about as close to spiritual intimacy as we could expect in the early archaic mind. As consciousness differentiated through history, the capacity of the individual soul deepened and became open to internalizing the manifestation of the divine. Spiritual symbolism intensified following the era of hunters and gatherers. Modern people are capable of enjoying a profound inner spiritual life made possible by the differentiation in consciousness that took place during the Axial Age in the first millennium BCE. Deep within, we human beings think, and we feel. We are a soul; or we are a self. What we will call the *axial insight* is the dawning awareness that the supra-cosmic beyondness of the divine creates within us a soul, a soul that constitutes our innermost self. Our "soul is endowed with translucent windows that open to the beyond," writes beloved Jewish theologian Abraham Joshua Heschel (1907–1972).[13]

God in Cosmic History assumes that whenever the question of ultimate reality arises the question of God also arises. To be ultimate is to be beyond the beyond, to be the reality beyond which there is no further beyond. Yet the very concept of God combines the beyond with the intimate. Jewish theologian Elliot Dorff makes this point clearly: "In the practice of religion, *God* signifies that the speaker is not just contemplating ultimate reality, but relating to it personally."[14]

13. Abraham Joshua Heschel, "God in Search of Man," in *Contemporary Jewish Theology*, ed. Elliot N. Dorff and Louis E. Newman (Oxford: Oxford University Press, 1999), 81–94, at 89.

14. Elliot N. Dorff, "Jewish Images of God," in *Models of God and Alternative Ultimate Realities*, ed. Jeanine Diller and Asa Kasher (Heidelberg: Springer, 2013), 111–24, at 119–120.

Unless both beyond and intimate sensibilities are evoked, it is not God that is being thought.

Sensing the *Axis Mundi*

The dialectic between the beyond and the intimate provides the generative dynamic at work in virtually all spiritual awareness. Yet other sensibilities also help structure both psyche and community in the religious dimension of culture. Three more will be briefly discussed: the *axis mundi*, shaminism, and autochthony. These three sensibilities rise to symbolic articulation most frequently within the intra-cosmic consciousness of foragers and farmers.

Axis mundi literally means "center of the earth," the phenomenal center of the land, the point around which human thinking and human community are organized. To center the habitable earth became a greater concern of our ancestral farmers, even though our nomadic foragers had previously sought to organize their communities around a cosmic center as well.

The center is sacred because it connects earth with heaven, the earth mother goddess with the sky god. Think of a pole that reaches upward from the ground as high as one can imagine. Eliade describes the sacred center of archaic religions as "a universal pillar, *axis mundi*, which . . . at once connects and supports heaven and earth . . . at the very center of the universe, for the whole of the habitable world extends around it."[15] The *axis mundi* is not necessarily an actual pillar—although, if one visits certain New Mexico pueblo villages today, one will find in the center of the village an actual pillar, like a telephone pole. On the top of the pole will be placed the first fruits of the harvest; during ceremonies young men will compete to see who can shinny up the pole the quickest.

The key to understanding the *axis mundi* is to realize that, by establishing the cosmic center, the village organizes itself around what is sacred. Human beings have a built-in thirst for reality, and the *axis mundi* orients members of tribes or villages around what seems to them to be ultimately real. The Achilpa clan, within the Arunta tribe of nomadic Australian aborigines, tell an origin myth of the sky god Numbakula creating the world. Numbakula took the trunk of a gum tree and fashioned a long pole, the *kauwa-auwa*, and then planted the pole in the ground, climbed to the top, and disappeared into the sky. The pole became for the Achilpa their *axis mundi*, the cosmic axis. During their nomadic wanderings, the Achilpa carried their pole and replanted it each time they set up camp or a new village. On one occasion in the 1920s, the pole broke. The Achilpa were overcome with consternation. They wandered about aimlessly for a time; finally they lay down to let death overtake them.[16]

---

15. Eliade, *Sacred and the Profane*, 36–37.

16. Ibid., 33.

For the most part, the *axis mundi* is thought of figuratively; it structures other religious symbols so as to geographically mark the spot where heaven and earth connect and where the sacred is established. For example, contemporary Chinese Buddhists will place a statue of the Buddha on a mountain top so that it can be seen for miles around. Armies plant flags over conquered territories. The ancient Babylonians built ziggurats, human-constructed mountains on the top of which the sky god is said to mate with the earth-mother goddess. Christians even today sometimes erect church-steeples so high they seem to touch the clouds.

Shamanism

The *axis mundi* can appear in human form. Shamans in many cultures claim that in a vision they fly to heaven, where they meet with the deities and learn the esoteric secrets of healing. Shaman symbolism typically includes feathers—feathers from the hawk or eagle that bears them from earth to heaven. In the person of the shaman, so to speak, heaven and earth are connected.

"The pre-eminently shamanic technique is the passage from one cosmic region to another—from earth to sky or from earth to the underworld," writes Eliade; "the universe in general is conceived as having three levels—sky, earth, underworld—connected by a central axis."[17] Breaking the plane of ordinary existence and entering other levels is something the shaman can do but the rest of the people cannot. Frequently the trip from one level to another takes place within a trance, within an ecstatic experience.

Shamans are usually healers. In their vision of heaven, they attend a medical school with sky deities as teachers. They learn which roots and berries have medicinal powers. Many shamans are known as root doctors. When a person falls ill in a forager or farmer society, he or she goes to the shaman as one today might go to the medical clinic. What the shaman offers is heavenly healing. "Shamanism is precisely one of the archaic techniques of ecstasy—at once mysticism, magic, and religion in the broadest sense of the term."[18]

Autochthony

Autochthony is the sense that we belong to the earth or to the land, the sense that we are indigenous. Those who grew up on a family farm will frequently tell their friends how many years—how many generations—have passed with their family on that land. The 1943 musical *Oklahoma*, by composer Richard Rogers and lyricist Oscar Hammerstein III, includes the memorable chorus, "We know we belong to the land, and the land we belong to is grand." When the late

---

17. Mircea Eliade, *Shamanism*, trans. Willard R. Trask (Princeton: Princeton University Press, 1964), 259.

18. Ibid., xix.

Pope John Paul II would travel abroad, he customarily exited his airplane and immediately prostrated himself. The Holy Father kissed the ground, showing reverence for the land he was visiting. The entire human race is autochthonous according to the Bible's creation account. "Then the LORD God formed man ['*adam*] from the dust of the ground ['*adamah*]" (Gen. 2:7).

Autochthony is much more important to farmers than foragers. Earth mother symbolism prompts the feelings of autochthony that dominated the agrarian era. These feelings have by no means disappeared, as vicious battles over land rights continue today in many locations in our world.

Astrology

Without a doubt the longest and largest religious tradition in human history is astrology. Astrology is not institutionalized. It has no churches. Yet it is powerful in the lives of people on every continent. The key to astrology's religious success is its marriage of the beyond with the intimate. Astrology's message is that the stars—the most beyond things the human eye can perceive—affect our daily life. Our destiny is tied to the stars.

"Astrology exists in most cultures at different levels," writes Nicholas Campion. "It assumes one or more of the following: (1) the celestial bodies are divine, (2) the stars and planets send messages (Latin: *omen* or "warning") on behalf of gods and goddesses, or God, (3) all things in the cosmos are interdependent, (4) the cosmos unfolds in a strict mathematical or geometrical order, and (5) different times have different qualities."[19] On the one hand, astrology evokes our beyond sensibility by drawing our attention to the magnificence

The Anatomical Zodiac (1412). The most widespread religion in human history is Astrology. The distant stars evoke the beyond sensibility, while the horoscope evokes the intimate sensibility.

of what we perceive in the night sky. Yet it also evokes our intimate sensibility,

---

19. Nicholas Campion, *Astrology and Cosmology in the World's Religions* (New York: New York University Press, 2012), 12.

because what happens in the sky becomes meaningful to our daily life. A person's daily horoscope mediates that meaning. "Astrology assumes there is a significant relationship between the stars or planets and affairs on earth."[20] This is the key: the stars in the beyond are intimately connected to your and my personal destiny.

Astrology is premodern. When modern astronomy triumphed five centuries ago, it kept astrology's mathematical ordering but removed the personal meaning associated with stars and planets. Today, astrology is considered pseudoscience by establishment science.[21]

Conclusion

The culture of foragers, farmers, and early citizens is characterized by compact consciousness, intra-cosmic consciousness. Even in the case of astrology, the stars belong within the ordered cosmos, within the worldview.

This means that all of reality is thought to exist on the same plane of existence. And the goal of life, in evolutionary terms, is at minimum survival and at maximum human flourishing. Compact consciousness is "embedded," to use the term of philosopher Charles Taylor. "Human agents are embedded in society, society in the cosmos, and the cosmos incorporates the divine."[22] All of reality is intra-cosmic for compact consciousness. Even the symbols resonating with the beyond sensibility referred to sky-gods—stars, sun, or storm—existing within the cosmic world.

We have been working with the assumption that religion is the depth of culture while culture is the form of religion. Listing spiritual sensibilities helps one to grasp the way in which religious sensibilities structure culture. We noted above that the religious symbolism of early hunter-gatherer societies is basically animistic with considerable respect for the power of the sky. The move to agriculture sees a growth in earth symbolism, including reliance upon an earth mother goddess responsible for making the crops grow. Frequently sky symbolism is combined with earth symbolism: the male sky god fertilizes the earth mother goddess with rain. The goal of this chapter has been to show a pattern of religious sensibilities developed among our prehistoric ancestors and to

---

20. Ibid., 11.

21. According to skeptics, "astrologers fail to recognize astrology's many problems. They refuse to accept that experience can be unreliable; they brush aside negative evidence; and they dismiss critics as close-minded by definition. As a result, astrologers are promoting both an illusion and a deceit. . . . Ultimately, the issue is a personal one—whether factual truth is to be more important than personal meaning." Geoffrey Dean, "Does Astrology Need to Be True?" *Skeptical Inquirer* 40, no. 4 (July/August 2016): 38–45, at 45.

22. Charles Taylor, "What Was the Axial Revolution?," in *The Axial Age and Its Consequences*, ed. Robert N. Bellah and Hans Joas (Cambridge, MA: Harvard University Press, 2012), 30–46, at 34.

acknowledge the enduring role of spiritual sensibilities still at work in human consciousness and culture.

It will be fitting here to invoke a key principle of Big History: the historian should demonstrate the influence of nature on human cultural developments. The need to hunt game and gather wild berries helped to define the religious symbolism of society during the forager stage. Similarly, the experience of watching the earth produce edible crops greatly influenced religious symbolism during the farmer stage. Our forager and farmer ancestors lived in a homogenous world where the gods and goddesses were intra-cosmic—that is, divine beings belonged to the realm of what people today call *nature*. Foragers and farmers as well as early citizens had no concept of either nature or religion; they simply described their world in terms of sky gods, animal masters, and the earth mother goddess.

The gods and goddesses of foragers and farmers were personifications of what modern people think of as impersonal nature. Yet one may wonder: did our ancestors experience an authentic insight into the beyond? An insight into the intimate? Did they undergo any experience of transcendence? Did they have an experience of the transcendent present within their inner soul? It appears that they did not.

Even so, Eliade suggests that the transcendental insight was already present, though in oblique form. "Life is not possible without an opening toward the transcendent," writes Eliade; "in other words, human beings cannot live in chaos."[23] The word *cosmos* here refers to an ordered world of meaning; it does not refer to big bang cosmogony. Did foragers and farmers order their cosmos around the *axis mundi* and the shaman? And, if so, would this constitute an awareness of transcendence? If this is the case, then at minimum our pre-civil ancestors sensed transcendent reality to the degree that their social structure could be organized around a sacred center. With a sacred center, their life became cosmos (ordered) rather than chaos (disordered). Did they need more transcendence than this?

Review Questions

1. Surplus food production among farmers made possible the rise of the polis, the city-state. How would the social order necessarily change for citizens?
2. How do religious or spiritual sensibilities—such as the beyond, the intimate, the *axis mundi*, shamans, and autochthony—structure a Stone Age culture?
3. What changes in social cooperation mark the transition to city-state citizenship?

---

23. Eliade, *Sacred and the Profane*, 34.

Discussion Questions

1. If survival-of-the-fittest characterizes all biological life, how might this be reflected in the religious symbolism of foragers and farmers?
2. Might any of the religious or spiritual sensibilities discussed in this chapter have had reproductive or survival advantages? Explain your view.
3. Identify examples of the religious or spiritual sensibilities discussed in this chapter at work in contemporary life.

Additional Resources

Print Sources

Bellah, Robert N. *Religion in Human Evolution from the Paleolithic to the Axial Age.* Cambridge, MA: Harvard University Press, 2011.

Bellah provides an illuminating description of the interaction between evolution and human religion. See especially chapters 2 and 3.

Eliade, Mircea. *The Sacred and the Profane.* Translated by William R. Trask. New York: Harcourt, Brace, and World, 1957.

Eliade was a prolific scholar in the history of religions school who compared and contrasted religious sensibilities and symbols from archaic cultures everywhere in the world.

Web Sources

Johanson, Donald. "Origins of Modern Humans: Multiregional or Out of Africa." Actionbioscience. *http://www.actionbioscience.org/evolution/johanson.html.*

One of the world's leading paleoanthropologists, Johanson compares two rival models for the evolution of *Homo sapiens.* Against the out of Africa model, he pits the multiregional model. According to the multiregional model, multiple species descended from *Homo erectus* in different regions of the world. Then genes from all proto-human populations flowed between different regions and, by mixing together, contributed to what we see today as fully modern humans. While this text relies on the out of Africa model, both models have supporting evidence.

Mythical Stories of Origin

The sun, the moon, the stars, the seas, the hills and the plains,
Are not these, O Soul, the Vision of Him who reigns?

—ALFRED LORD TENNYSON (1809–1892),
"THE HIGHER PANTHEISM"

Like virtually every small child, I used to ask "why?" *ad nauseam.* On one occasion I asked, "Mom, why do I have a belly button?"

"Everybody has a belly button," she answered.

"But, I wanna know why."

"Well, back when God was creating the human race he gave each one of us a belly button so we would have a place to put the dipping salt when eating celery in bed."

"But," I pressed, "I don't eat celery in bed."

"Well, when you do, you'll have a place for your salt."

What my mother was doing is what myth-tellers have been doing since pre-historic times, namely, telling stories of origin that explain why the world of today is the way it is. Big bang cosmology provides one such story—but it's only one of many. Modern global society tells so many stories of origin, it is impossible to Google them all. Just what is a story of origin and what function does it serve?

A story of origin—that is, a *cosmogony* or etiological narrative—usually takes the form of myth, a story about how the world was created in the beginning, which explains why things are the way they are today. Ancient myths were stories about symbolically important characters—gods—who define reality. Today's origin story eliminates the gods, but in every other respect the big bang functions as a myth. Effective history insures continuity between the way our ancestors thought and the way today's scientists think.

This point bears repeating. A scientific account of Cosmic History functions for today's civilization in much the same way that myth functioned for our ancestors. If we better understand our ancestors, we will better understand ourselves.

What Is Myth?

Of the various definitions of the word *myth*, three are important to our understanding of ourselves within Cosmic History:

1. A myth is a false story or mistaken belief; a myth should not be taken as literally true.
2. A myth is a story—a narrative—about how the gods created the world (or a part of the world) in the beginning—*in illo tempore*[1]—that explains why things are the way things are today.
3. A myth is a conceptual set, a worldview, a persistent framework for interpreting new experience.

1. Myth as False Story

According to the first definition, a myth is a story or a presumed fact that is false. Frequently scientists today use the term *myth* to refer to scientific beliefs that are misleading. For example, the widespread belief that screening for breast or prostate cancer catches the disease in its early stage—and this will help to save lives—is a myth. Even though this is widely believed by both patients and doctors, research scientists claim this is false. Annual mammograms do not reduce mortality because some tumors will lead to death irrespective of when they are detected and treated. Screening does not significantly reduce deaths due to prostate cancer either. Note how the term *myth* appears in this scientific discussion.

> This blind faith in cancer screening is an example of how ideas about human biology and behaviour can persist among people—including scientists—even though the scientific evidence shows the concepts to be false. . . . Scientists should work to discredit myths.[2]

In short, according to the first definition, a myth is a false belief that can be discredited with scientific evidence.

Big historians like this first definition of myth. Big historians believe a myth is a story of origin that is scientifically false. Or, more charitably, a myth is a story that we would not want to believe literally. Myths "resort to metaphors, stories, parables, to language that tries to convey more than can be conveyed in simple, direct prose. So, it is usually a mistake to take origin stories too literally," say the big historians.[3] Accordingly, poetic stories of origin cannot be true. Therefore, they must be replaced or at least supplemented with literally true stories.

---

1. Latin for "at that time."

2. Megan Scudellari, "Myths That Will Not Die," *Nature* 528, no. 7582 (December 17, 2015): 322–25, at 323.

3. David Christian, Cynthia Stokes Brown, and Craig Benjamin, *Big History: Between Nothing and Everything* (New York: McGraw-Hill, 2014), 12.

Big historians believe their own story of origin should be taken literally because it is based on science, while all other stories of origin should be taken as poetic and not literally true. The story told by big historians "offers a literal account of the origin of everything. . . . It is not simply a poetic attempt to make up for ignorance."[4] According to the big historians, myths are poetic origin stories made up by ignorant people, whereas scientific Big History is literally true (it describes reality as it literally is) and is not just one more myth. This first definition of myth, then, functions to distinguish the origin story based on science from false origin stories.

2. Myth as Story of Origin

Rather than this first use, this chapter will give special attention to the second definition of myth: a myth is a story about how the gods created the world (or a part of the world) in the beginning, *in illo tempore*, which explains why things are the way they are today. Our ancestors living in cultures during the premodern period understood their world—their ordered cosmos—in terms of the myths they told. Myths provided the worldviews through which our forbearers interpreted their experience.

This second definition fits with the kind of myth that world historians like. Historians should move away from the idea that if they get "all the facts" they will find "truth," observes Mark Welter. Instead, "truth lies in finding what is common amid diversity . . . a myth (tradition) that describes what people have together . . . a set of shared beliefs that rise above petty divisiveness." Historians should not focus only on narrow subjects and "wallow in detail that obscures the patterns," but should "concentrate on myths that rise above trivia and illustrate what a people have in common." Myths, accordingly, are "the motor of history."[5] To understand human history, the world historian attends to the motor which drives it. Whereas big historians prefer myth according to its first definition, world historians prefer the second.

Let us look more closely at ancient myths. The characters in a myth (usually ancient gods or godlike creatures) act *paradigmatically*. That is, these symbolic characters set a pattern that the social order follows. As a paradigm, the myth explains why things are the way they are today. A story of origin is set in the past, to be sure, but it is not merely about the past. It explains why today's world is the way it is. On this count, ancient myths and contemporary science share much in common.

Nevertheless, myth and science *are* quite different in other respects. The rise of science marks a significant leap in human consciousness. The modern

---

4. Ibid., 14.

5. Mark Welter, "William H. McNeill: Father of World History, 1917–2016," World History Association, *www.thewha.org/*.

scientific account represents a much more differentiated stage of consciousness than my mother's belly button story or the myths of ancient foragers and farmers. Yet some overlap between science and myth might be discernible.

Within the discussions of myth, history, and science that follow, two technical terms will be employed: *archonic* and *epigenetic*. The first is derived from the Greek term *archē*, which means both "origin" and "governance." As origin, it comes into English in words such as *archaeology*, the study of archaic things. As governance, it comes into English in words such as *monarchy*, rule by a single king or queen. In short, *archonic thinking* assumes that the way something begins governs its essential nature. Myths provide the preeminent example of archonic thinking.

The term *epigenesis* combines two Greek words, *genesis*, meaning "beginning," with the preposition, *epi*, meaning "on top of" or "again." The concept of epigenesis entails new genesis, unrepeatability, historicity, or the emergence of new properties.[6] Myth, according to the second definition, tends to be archonic, whereas history is epigenetic. Science is a mixture of the two. One of our tasks here is to compare and contrast ancient myth with modern science when telling a story of origin.

3. Myth as Conceptual Set

The third (and more abstract) definition of myth refers to a conceptual set, a set of presuppositions that frame the suppositions of a theoretical scheme. The myth frames data that reinforces an assumed worldview, perspective, or ideology. According to this third definition, myth is not a story per se. Rather, it's a commitment held at the level of presupposition rather than stated. Whereas the first definition of *myth* identifies a specific fact or belief that is false, the third definition deals with myth more broadly as a conceptual set within which facts and beliefs are contextualized.

People think out of one or another conceptual set or worldview. With the first definition in mind, scientists frequently contend that some assumed facts held by other scientists are myths. At the risk of oversimplification, one might trumpet, "My myth is true but your myth is false." But the third use of the term *myth* is larger in scope. A myth in its first use is a supposition, but in its third use a myth is a *pre*supposition. Myths are usually assumed, not debated. This book's discussion occasionally looks for myths, in the third sense, which are presupposed by scientists, big historians, and others that constitute a significant component in their worldview.

---

6. *Epigenesis* in molecular biology refers to non-genetic factors in gene expression. This is *not* the definition used here. Rather, *epigenesis* as the emergence of new properties was introduced in evolutionary biology by Jan C. Smuts, *Holism and Evolution* (New York: Macmillan, 1926; Cape Town, South Africa: N & S Press, 1987).

Here is an example of a debate regarding myth in the first and third senses: *science and religion are at war.* This may seem like a simple sentence, but it actually constitutes a myth, a conceptual set, a framework through which many people interpret what they learn about either science or religion. The idea of warfare applied to science and religion is a presupposition through which many people filter whatever they hear or learn or discuss. This presuppositional set connotes that religion is the enemy of science. In this case, the myth happens to be false, contends Joshua Moritz in his book, *Science and Religion: Beyond Warfare and Toward Understanding.* "This book illustrates how the narrative that science and religion are at war is a *myth* in two key senses of the word: it is foundational to a certain anti-religious worldview, and it is historically false."[7] The idea that science and religion are at war is a myth in both the third and first senses of the word, at least according to Moritz. The belief that science and religion are in an unavoidable war is a presumed fact to be corrected as well as a conceptual set that needs resetting. Even so, this myth is widely believed today and it influences the perspective of big historians. Because this myth influences big historians, it will be important to analyze it right along with ancient myths of origin.

Later in this book the most culturally potent myth in the third sense, scientism, will be subjected to analysis. In the present chapter, however, the second definition of myth will guide the exposition and interpretation of our ancestors' ways of thinking.

Marduk, Tiamat, and the King of Babylon

As we saw in the previous chapter, it was easy for our ancestors to think of the earth below their feet as feminine and the sky above as masculine. The earth below produces crops, food, and sustenance in a way that is analogous to a mother giving life to her children. The sky above provides sun and rain, which fertilize and nourish the growth of those crops. This is somewhat analogous to the way a father provides for a wife and family. The rain makes the crops grow on earth, as a father fertilizes the mother so she can conceive and make the children grow. In myth after myth, one finds male sky gods and female earth goddesses.

One persistent theme in Big History is that the constraints of the natural environment significantly affect the range of human activity, and these natural constraints influence the direction taken in human history. The big historian would rightly observe, therefore, that the ancient farmer's experience with nature influenced that farmer's religious symbols. Farmers experienced the fertility and productivity of both women and soil, so the symbolic association and religious

---

7. Joshua Moritz, *Science and Religion: Beyond Warfare and Toward Understanding* (Winona, MN: Anselm Academic, 2016), 8.

significance of the two is not surprising. The fertility symbols of farmers endured into the city-state era, largely because farming continued to provide the food for all the citizens of the body politic. A city could be a city only because it was supported by surrounding farms and, to a lesser extent, by surrounding foragers.

Beginning in Mesopotamia about 3500 BCE, one central myth started to get repeated in the sequence of empires that led from Sumer and Akkad to the later rise of Babylonia. With each empire, the myth changed slightly, to be sure, but the continuity is remarkable. This myth recounts the creation of the world as a battle between two divine forces, Marduk and Tiamat. In the course of the story, the female Tiamat comes to represent our earth while the male Maduk represents the sky and, importantly, the king. Here's the Babylonian story of origin, known by its opening phrase, *Enuma Elish*.

"When from on high," opens *Enuma Elish*. In this beginning before there was any time—what we call *in illo tempore*—nothing had names. Apsu, the god of fresh waters, and Tiamat, the goddess of the salt waters, were mingled together, giving birth to their child, Mummu, in the form of rising mist. In this time before there was time, there existed only undifferentiated yet chaotic unity.

Apsu and Tiamat gave birth to many children, and then grandchildren, and eventually to a large populace of gods and goddesses. Among these gods, Ea emerged as the clever one. Ea gained popularity, even leadership among the deities.

Because the gods were unruly and noisy, Apsu's primordial sleep was disturbed. He resolved to end the clamor by murdering all the deities. When Tiamat heard about Apsu's plan, she cried out in horror. She could not conceive of killing her own children and grandchildren. After telling Ea about her husband's plan, Ea decided to champion the cause of the gods and goddesses. He cast a spell on Apsu, pulled Apsu's crown from his head, and slew him. Ea then built his palace on Apsu's waters, and it was there that, with the goddess Damkina, he fathered Marduk, the four-eared, four-eyed giant who became the god of the rains and storms.

Ea's victory did not win the peace, however. The unresting deities went to Tiamat, complaining about Ea for slaying Apsu. Tiamat reacted, taking sides against Ea. She assembled an army of dragons and monsters. At the head of this army she appointed the god Kingu as general. Kingu had magical powers. Even the powerful Ea was at a loss on how to combat such an array of military might. So Ea called upon his son Marduk. Marduk gladly agreed to take on his father's battle, on the condition that he, Marduk, should he gain victory, would become ruler of the gods. Ea and the allied gods agreed. They crowned Marduk in advance of the battle at a banquet, where they gave him his royal robes and scepter.

Then the battle began. Marduk armed himself with a bow and arrows, a club, and a spear made of lightning. He marched forth in search of Tiamat and her monstrous army. He confronted her. Rolling his thunder and storms in front

Public Domain

In the Babylonian creation myth, *Enuma Elish*, Marduk defeats Tiamat, then fashions the heavens and the fertile earth from her body. The Babylonian king represented Marduk in ritual reenactments of the myth, ensuring a successful harvest.

of him, he attacked. Kingu's battle plan soon disintegrated. Tiamat was left alone to fight Marduk. She howled as they closed for battle. Adroit Marduk caught her in his nets. When she opened her mouth to devour him, he filled her lungs with a gale wind. When Tiamat could no longer close her mouth with this gale blasting in it, he shot an arrow down her throat. It split her heart, and Tiamat was slain.

Once Kingu's army had been routed, Marduk split Tiamat's water-laden body in half like a clam shell. One half he put in the sky to make the heavens. Across the heavens he appointed stations for the gods; these gods are visible as stars at night. Marduk also made the moon and set it forth on its schedule across the heavens. From the other half of Tiamat's body Marduk fashioned the land. He laid the land on top of Apsu's fresh waters, which now arise through the soil in wells and springs. From Tiamat's eyes he made flow the Tigris and Euphrates rivers. Marduk mapped out the land as pastures and fields, and he commanded the rains to fall and the seeds to grow. All life-giving power rises out of the body of Tiamat, the slain mother of us all.[8]

---

8. In the Babylonian worldview, the earth was thought to rest on water, water that could bubble up from wells or overrun the river banks. Tiamat's name has cognates. One variant of her name, *thalatth*, comes into Greek as *thalatta* or *thalassa*, meaning "sea." Another variant appears in the Hebrew word *tehom* (found in Gen. 1:2), meaning "the deep" or "the abyss." Only a portion of Tiamat's body provides the earth as soil, yet as both water and soil she symbolizes the life-force periodically threatened by watery chaos.

Marduk demanded that the now vanquished gods who had supported Tiamat be enlisted in agricultural labor. The deities complained about their forced labor, and rebelled. Marduk sympathized with the rebellious deities; he murdered the captured Kingu and took his blood, along with some soil and his own spittle, and fashioned a new creature. This new creature was a human being. Soon, humans populated the land. Marduk commanded the human race to serve the gods by maintaining the canals and boundary ditches, by seeding and harvesting, by raising farm animals, and by preparing the granaries for festivals such as the annual coronation festival.⁹ During this festival, the current king is given robes and a scepter just as Marduk in the myth. The archonic origin story told by *Enuma Elish* explains why Babylon has a king and why the populace works on the farms.¹⁰

Imagine people living in the Tigris and Euphrates region of ancient Mesopotamia, watching storm clouds encroach and close out the sun, then seeing sudden lightning flashes, hearing thunder claps, and watching torrents of water come down, flooding the plains. It would be understandable for people to tell a story about a great battle taking place in the heavens, a battle that will decide whether they live or die in the chaos of uncontrolled waters, whether they will or will not have fertile farmland to grow food. It would be appropriate for the people to believe that what they witnessed in the sky each year was Marduk and Tiamat fighting it out once again, and they would hope that Marduk would win again, just as he did at the beginning, the time before time. The beginning of a myth is *everywhen*, including now. The origin story explains what is happening right now, today.

The ancient Babylonians celebrated the origin of their world on the first day of spring, our March 21. At this special annual festival, the story of the battle between Marduk and Tiamat was retold. Actually, it was acted out. The king played the part of Marduk. Once the play had concluded, the king (like Marduk) got crowned (or re-crowned). Then he gave orders to the farmers of Babylonia to go about their tasks working in the fields and canals. This myth explains how the gods created the world in the beginning and it explains why agriculture and kingship are the way they are currently.

One of the Babylonian kings who worshipped Marduk and benefitted from the myth was Hammurabi (1810–1750 BCE). King Hammurabi is especially remembered by today's historians because of his attempt to rule the kingdom through law. A carved stele he had set up for all to see shows Hammurabi

---

9. Alexander Heidel, *The Babylonian Genesis*, 2nd ed. (Chicago: University of Chicago Press, 1952), 153. Available online at *http://www.gly.uga.edu/railsback/CS/CSMarduk.html*.

10. *Enuma Elish*, 78–85. *Enuma Elish* symbolizes the unity of heaven with earth in sustaining agricultural life. The text was discovered in the ruins of King Ashurbanipal's library at Nineveh, dating to the seventh century BCE. It may reflect prior variants of the myth going back to the First Babylonian Dynasty, 2050–1750 BCE, which includes the reign of King Hammurabi about 1900 BCE. Ibid., 85.

receiving the laws from a sky god, either Shamash or perhaps Marduk himself. The gods have commissioned the king to "cause justice to prevail in the land, to destroy the evil and the wicked, to prevent the strong from oppressing the weak," says the preamble. In the subsequent list of laws, number 195 reads, "If a son strike his father, they shall cut off his fingers."[11] The gods have decreed that sons who strike their fathers will get their fingers cut off as punishment. Evidently, the philosophy of law embraced by the gods was simple: "An eye for an eye, and a tooth for a tooth."[12] The king's executioners are commissioned to enforce on earth the laws of heaven.

Ziggurat as *Axis Mundi*

© THAER JEBUR / iStockphoto.com

The Babylonians along with their predecessors and successors—the Sumerians, Akkadians, Elamites, and Assyrians—built their own pyramid mountains to connect heaven and earth. These mountains were called *ziggurats*. Each took the form of a terraced step pyramid of successively receding stories or levels. The ancient Greek historian Herodotus, who visited Babylon, described a ritual that mimicked the descent of Marduk to the top of the ziggurat to lie on a ceremonial couch, a couch already occupied by a priestess. In this fertility ritual, the king played the role of Marduk. In sum, the ziggurat functioned as an *axis mundi*, a celestial pole marking the spot where the marriage of heaven and earth takes place.

---

11. "Hammurabi's Code of Laws," trans. L. W. King, *http://www.sacred-texts.com/ane/ham/ham06.htm*.

12. "The Early Middle East 4c, Hammurabi's Code: An Eye for an Eye," Ancient Civilizations, *http://www.ushistory.org/civ/4c.asp*.

During the farmer period prior to the rise of the city-state, it seems that creation myths tended to depict a sweet marriage between heaven and earth. With the rise of the city-state, the relationship between heaven and earth became more violent. In the city-state version, the sky god slays the goddess who will become our earth mother. The fertility of the soil then emerges from her slain body. Even so, the older marriage symbolism is not forgotten completely, as the sexual rite on the roof of the ziggurat indicates. Perhaps the violence of the sky god in subduing the earth mother in later myths connotes the warrior king in battle to extend the city-state into an empire.

Such a myth, like others fitting the second definition, takes the form of a story or narrative. Myth does not come in the form of a logical syllogism. Myth does not present a rational argument. "In mythic cultures," writes evolutionary psychologist Merlin Donald, "the governing ideas tend to be narrative constructs."[13] If one thinks mythically in the sense of our second definition, he or she thinks in narratives or stories.

History is not myth. Historians should report on myths but avoid myth-like thinking for themselves. "Myths tend to construct beginnings which the historian then feels summoned to deconstruct," avers Heidelberg Egyptologist Jan Assman.[14] The modern historian has moved from *mythos* to *logos*, from myth to reason. Even so, the cosmic historian must employ all tools to get at the cosmic story, and this may include analysis of cosmogonic myths.

The word *cosmos* can refer to two different things. *Cosmos* designates the universe as today's scientists describe it. This is the cosmos that originated with a big bang. In addition, the term *cosmos* refers to the world or worldview of our ancient ancestors who used myths to describe the ordered reality in which they lived. The gods and goddesses of the Babylonians were intra-cosmic, that is, they lived within the world as Babylonians perceived it. In Cosmic History, we look at both.

Is Big History a Modern Myth of Origin?

Today's big historians offer a story of origin based on modern science. "This is a creation story for our time," writes big historian Cynthia Stokes Brown.[15] Does

---

13. Merlin Donald, "An Evolutionary Approach to Culture: Implications for the Study of the Axial Age," in *The Axial Age and Its Consequences*, ed. Robert N. Bellah and Hans Joas (Cambridge, MA: Harvard University Press, 2012), 47–76, at 54.

14. Jan Assmann, "Cultural Memory and the Myth of the Axial Age," in *Axial Age*, ed. Bellah and Joas, 366–410, at 366. Assmann surmises that the very concept of the Axial Age is a myth in the third sense of our usage of that term. As an Egyptologist, Assmann deconstructs all myths of both the second and third types.

15. Cynthia Stokes Brown, *Big History from the Big Bang to the Present* (New York: New Press, 2007), xi.

Big History tell a myth like the myth of Marduk? Just how are Big History and ancient myth similar and dissimilar?

Big historians tell us that ancient myths "must resort to metaphors, stories, parables, to language that tries to convey more than can be conveyed in simple, direct prose." Put another way, ancient mythical stories of origin are "poetic."[16] The "modern origin story," say the big historians, is different. Rather than poetic, a science-based history is literal. The modern origin story "offers a literal account of the origin of everything. It expects to be taken seriously as a description of what actually happened beginning about 13.8 billion years ago. It is not simply a poetic attempt to make up for ignorance."[17] This implies that ancient myth-makers were ignorant, while today's big historians are knowledgeable. Big historians base their history on scientific knowledge, knowledge archaic peoples did not yet have. Whereas ancient myth-makers resorted to poetry, today's big historians can provide us with a "literal" account of what "actually happened." To be literal is superior to being poetic. The self-appointed task of the big historian is to provide a scientific story of origin that is literally true and sharply distinct from mythical stories of origin that are not.

But the matter is actually much more complicated. One big historian, David Christian, asks the discipline of Big History to play the same role played by a classic creation myth. The value of such a creation myth is that it does more than science alone can do. A myth can speak to deeply personal questions: Who am I? Where do I belong? What is the totality of which I am a part? And, of course, who is the king and how should the subjects obey the king? These questions ask about ultimate reality. They tap into religious and spiritual sensibilities.

By offering *memorable and authoritative* accounts of how everything began—from our own communities, to the animals, plants and landscapes around us, to the Earth, the Moon and skies, and even the universe itself—*creation myths* provide universal coordinates within which people can imagine their own existence and find a role in the larger scheme of things. *Creation myths* are powerful because they speak to our deep spiritual, psychic, and social need for a sense of place and a sense of belonging.[18]

This is what ancient creation myths did. Can today's Big History do this as well?

Dominican University Big History professor Harlan Stelmach says, no. He ponders the significance of what David Christian is saying here. "I would suggest

---

16. Christian, Brown, and Benjamin, *Big History*, 12.

17. Ibid., 14.

18. David Christian, *Maps of Time: An Introduction to Big History* (Berkeley: University of California Press, 2005), 2, italics added.

that Christian, with his shift to narrative and myth, has moved beyond science and into truth, meaning and identity. . . . Christian is certainly tying his new myth to the latest knowledge, but he is claiming more than what science as science can claim. . . . This is very much a religious stance."[19] Big History does not teach *about* history. Rather, it teaches *history as a worldview*, as the ground of life's meaning, as the fundamental truth, as a substitute for traditional religion. On the one hand, Big History claims to provide a *scientific* account of Cosmic History. But, on the other hand, it sets for itself a religious agenda.

A hole has opened up in the bottom of the Big History boat. On the one hand, the big historian wants to chronicle and interpret events selectively—scientifically—by leaving out claims of divine activity. Any purported scientific account of Big History would be meaningless, because that is the nature of all scientific accounts. On the other hand, after selecting out claims of divine action, this big historian still wants to capitalize on the religious and spiritual needs of those who claim to believe in the divine. David Christian wants science without God and also wants personal meaning for today's consumer of Big History. Can the big historian have it both ways?

In effect, Big History asks the question of God while denying it is asking the question of God. Cosmic History, in contrast to Big History, seeks to ask the question of God directly.

Conclusion

Looking at ancient myth is an important stopover during our tour through Cosmic History because it helps make the mind of the cosmic historian transparent. Even though the ancient Babylonian cosmology took the form of a classical myth and today's cosmology takes the form of a scientific story, we must honestly ask, what do they share in common?

Both ancient myth and the cosmogony of big historians tell a story of origin that purportedly explains why things are the way they are today. Neither is pure history in the sense of simply chronicling past events. Both attempt to provide human meaning by appealing to ultimate or final reality in a way that applies to our intimate self-understanding.

Yet there is a difference worth noting between a mythical cosmogony and the big bang cosmogony based on contemporary science. As we have demonstrated, ancient myth expresses the archonic mind of our ancestors. The origin explains everything. Not so for the scientific worldview. Because contemporary scientific accounts of the origin of our cosmos rely upon contingency at the subatomic level, the world of big bang cosmology can be perceived as dynamic by

19. Harlan Stelmach, "Teaching Big History or Teaching about Big History: A Religious Question?" Unpublished scholarly paper, 2015.

the epigenetic mind. Reality is changing. Reality is fundamentally historical; that is, reality is temporal, changing, and nonrepeating. In this important regard, both Big History and Cosmic History, which rely on science as science sees itself, depart from myth.

There is another dissimilarity. Stories of origin justify social power for the person or group telling the story. Ancient myths tended to validate kingship. In ancient Mesopotamia, the king along with his court priests had the privilege of telling a myth that validated their position of governance. In contrast, Big History supports no king. In fact, it supports no nation or ethnic group. Neither does World History. Perhaps we should ask, does anyone find himself or herself privileged because of Big History's story of origin or World History's stories?

Our question all the way through looks something like this: is God the author of cosmic history? Or does history author itself? Or might there be a co-authorship?

Review Questions

1. What did the ancient Babylonian myth, *Enuma Elish*, communicate?
2. Compare and contrast the three understandings of myth.
3. What is a story of origin? How does a story of origin illustrate archonic thinking?
4. What do myths tell us about the likely interactions between people and their environment?

Discussion Questions

1. How do myths illustrate religious sensibilities?
2. How does each element in the second definition of myth describe the relationship of a people to its physical environment?
3. Can you relate the second definition of myth to any other origin stories you are aware of?
4. Do people who live in the modern and emerging postmodern world within a pluralistic yet comprehensive global context still need origin stories?
5. Can you distinguish myth from history? If a myth is archonic, it tells how the origin of something determines its essential and unchanging nature. If a story is historical, it tells about an unrepeatable course of events; history indirectly opens us to an unpredictable future. Can you identify two common stories, one mythical and the other historical?

Additional Resources

Print Sources

Hamilton, Virginia, and Barry Moser. *In the Beginning: Creation Stories from Around the World.* New York: Harcourt, Brace, and Jovanovich, 1988.

This spritely collection of short renditions of ancient creation myths is delightful. Examples stretch from the cosmic egg in ancient China to Prometheus in ancient Greece. Very readable. Brief commentaries accompany each origin story.

Web Sources

Gawande, Atul. "The Mistrust of Science." California Institute of Technology Commencement Address, June 10, 2016. *http://www.newyorker.com/news/news-desk/the-mistrust-of-science?mbid=social_facebook.*

Mark, Joshua J. "Mythology." *Ancient History Encyclopedia. http://www.ancient.eu/mythology/.*

Mark explains why world historians are interested in myth in the second sense.

Peters, Ted. "Myth in the Heart of Science." *http://tedstimelytake.com/wp-content/uploads/2012/12/ETI-Myth-heart-of-science.pdf.*

A description of myth in the third sense—a conceptual set of presuppositions—as it manifests itself in scientific theory.

"What Are the Myths of Babylon? Definitions and Significance." Study.com. *http://study.com/academy/lesson/what-are-the-myths-of-babylon-definition-significance.html*

The Origin Story
in Genesis 1:1–2:4a

Beyond your limitless Space, before your measureless Time,
Ere Life or Death began was this changeless Essence sublime.
—Lewis Morris (1833–1907), "God Within Yet Above"

This book has been looking at stories of origin, beginning with the big bang. The big bang account of the beginning of the cosmos is the standard model universally accepted in today's scientific community. Retold by big historians, the big bang cosmology virtually constitutes the worldview of the modern world. The preceding chapter looked at an origin myth in ancient Babylon. The human psyche seems to feel compelled to explore origins, to go back to beginnings, to seek to ground reality in the source of all things. An archonic orientation apparently drives human thought backwards, in search of a story of origin that explains why things today are the way they are. It is widely assumed that the way something begins determines its essence.

Yet the archonic mind fails to acknowledge something significant about the reality within which we live, namely, that genuinely new things happen. Reality is historical. Events are contingent. Novel qualities emerge. Both nature and humanity are unpredictable. Tomorrow will be different from today. If this is the case, then no story of origin, whether scientific or mythical, will ever provide a satisfying account of human grounding or source.

This chapter continues the historical task of retrieving past moments when our ancestors asked the question of God and proposed various answers. One place where this occurs is the Bible, a book shared in part by adherents to multiple religions. We will give special attention to the first account of creation as it appears in Genesis 1:1–2:4a. In Judaism, Christianity, and Islam this biblical passage is associated with a decisive theological doctrine identified with its Latin phrase, *creatio ex nihilo*, meaning that the cosmos was drawn out of nothing. *Creatio ex nihilo* declares theologically that all physical reality is totally dependent on God, who is its creator.

"Your Lord is Allah," says the Qur'an, "who created the heavens and the earth in six days" (Yunus 31). Seyyed Hossein Nasr speaks for Islam when emphasizing how important this account is. "The Qur'an . . . insists on the ontological dependence of the world upon God and the fact that all the coherence, regularity, and harmony of the natural order is the result of the Creator and His Wisdom, which is reflected in His creation."[1] Most Jewish and Christian theologians are of the same mind.

Even though the Bible was written in the era when myths reigned in archaic consciousness, and even though the Bible's account, like myth, provides an etiology (an origin account), the concept of *creatio ex nihilo* marks it off as singular. Genesis 1:1–2:4a includes some overlap with the Babylonian Marduk myth; yet the God of ancient Israel exhibits a level of transcendence that exceeds such other mythical accounts. The gods in most myths are intra-cosmic, whereas the God of Genesis 1:1–2:4a seems to be supra-cosmic. And, curiously, cosmic creation in this biblical account exhibits features that make it surprisingly consonant with big bang cosmology.

Reading Genesis 1:1–2:4a

In the beginning, God created by uttering the divine word, according to the biblical text. Actually, God's word is not limited to the beginning. God's word is eternal. God keeps on speaking. When the God of ancient Israel first spoke, something new happened: the cosmos came into existence. When God speaks now, a new future opens up that cannot be reduced to what had existed in the past. *Creatio ex nihilo* in the past translates into renewal, transformation, and even redemption in the future. On the one hand, the book of Genesis provides an etiology; on the other hand, it provides a promise. Here is how the key text, Genesis 1:1–2:4a, opens.

> In the beginning when God (*Elohim*) created the heavens and the earth, the earth was a formless void and darkness covered the face of the deep (*tehom*, sea of chaos), while a wind from God swept over the face of the waters. Then God said, "Let there be light"; and there was light. And God saw that the light was good; and God separated the light from the darkness. (Gen. 1:1–4)

This passage is known as the primeval history, or the first creation account, or the Hebrew cosmogony. Biblical scholars refer to the unknown author of Genesis 1:1–2:4a as the Priestly source. "This text is a poetic narrative that likely was formed for liturgical usage," writes Old Testament scholar Walter

---

1. Seyyed Hossein Nasr, "The Question of Cosmogenesis—The Cosmos as a Subject of Scientific Study," *Islam and Science* 4, no. 1 (Summer 2006): 43–60, at 44–45.

Above the front door of the Washington Cathedral, this relief depicts the creation of the world from the waters of chaos. Creation entails both calling things into existence and establishing order.

Brueggemann. "It is commonly assigned to the Priestly tradition, which means that it is addressed to a community of exiles."[2] Specifically, the addressees were Hebrew exiles in Babylon. With this in mind, one would expect a contextual influence on the text reflecting Babylonian culture.

Like other ancient myths, Genesis 1:1–2:4a provides an origin story that explains why things are the way they are today. Our week of seven days, for example, is rooted in the original seven days God needed to create the cosmos. The original seven-day creation period fixed the paradigm, so to speak, so that every weekly cycle repeats and sanctifies the creation. When Jews and Christians worship on the Sabbath, they are reminding themselves of their transcendental ground in the divine source of all things.

Unlike most other ancient myths, however, God's creative work seems effortless. God simply speaks, and things happen. God's word is the ground and source of all reality. In contrast to the Babylonian myth of Marduk, there is no battle taking place. In fact, the biblical text may actually be related to the Babylonian *Enuma Elish* in Genesis 1:2, where the word translated "the deep," *tehom,* may be cognate to Tiamat, the water dragon slain by Marduk. If so, the author of Genesis 1:1–2:4a must have known *Enuma Elish* and is telling the reader that the Babylonians are mistaken in their account of creation. "The decisive difference between Genesis and the Babylonian account of creation is that creation in Genesis is not the result of a struggle: the dramatic element is missing," writes Old Testament scholar Claus Westermann.[3] The simple word of God brings

2. Walter Brueggemann, *Genesis*, Interpretation (Louisville: Westminster John Knox, 1982), 22.

3. Claus Westermann, *Genesis 1–11*, trans. John J. Scullion, SJ (Minneapolis: Fortress, 1974), 81.

creation out of nothing and marks the origin of all things, not a primordial war between gods in the sky.

Creation Out of Nothing or Out of Something?

The Hebrew phrasing of the opening verses of Genesis 1:1–2 is ambiguous. On the one hand, the text could read, "In the beginning, God created." Or the text could read, "When God began to create." Does God's creative work mark the beginning or not? On the second reading, one need not necessarily interpret this text to signify a beginning with *creatio ex nihilo*: "In the beginning when God created the heavens and the earth" (NRSV). The theological concept of creation out of nothing finds at best only equivocal textual support in Genesis 1:1–2:4a.

Could this mean that God manipulated preexisting matter in order to make our cosmos? Does God begin with nothingness, or does God begin with something already existing in a chaotic state? The tone of the text suggests that God is making order out of chaos. Chaos represents a "peculiar intermediate state between nothingness and creation," writes Old Testament scholar Gerhard von Rad.[4] After having granted the allusion to chaos in Genesis 1:1, von Rad adds that *creatio ex nihilo* is still supported by this text. "It would be false to say, however, that the idea of the *creatio ex nihilo* was not present here at all."[5]

It is not uncommon in the Hebrew scriptures to describe the God of Israel by analogy to a potter. Isaiah 64:8 says, "Yet, O LORD, you are our Father; we are the clay, and you are our potter; we are all the work of your hand." As the potter forms the clay, so also God forms the world. The potter does not create the clay out of nothing. Rather, the potter merely forms preexisting clay. Could this mean that the clay—in this case physical atoms and subatomic particles—is eternal? Does God necessarily live eternally with a physical world as a next door neighbor, even if that physical world is chaotic and without form? If so, would this imply tacitly that there are two eternal realities, God and the world? Could Genesis 1:1–2:4a support such a dualism?

Some feminist theologians embrace such dualism. They object to placing all the power of creation into the hands of an apparently masculine sky god such as the God of Israel. Drew University theologian Catherine Keller, for example, finds the creative potential not in God the potter but rather in the deep *tehom*,

---

4. Gerhard von Rad, *Genesis*, trans. John Marks (Louisville: Westminster John Knox, 1961), 48.

5. Ibid., 49. Von Rad is importing the theological commitment to *creatio ex nihilo* in order to interpret this ambiguous text. Von Rad's student, Westermann, disagrees with his teacher on this point. Westermann wants to draw a conclusion directly from the text, not superimpose a theological conclusion. "Von Rad's method of argument puts us in too great a danger of determining the meaning of the text from convictions already held. One can maintain this objection even if one agrees with von Rad's conclusion. . . . Theological arguments alone cannot decide the problem." Westermann, *Genesis 1–11*, 96.

which plays a role equivalent to the clay that the potter merely forms. The power of creation is found in the chaotic deep waters identified with the feminine Tiamat, not in Marduk's victory and not in the ordering command of the divine word. "Ocean of divinity, womb and place-holder of beginnings, it is not Elohim but the first place or *capacity* of genesis."[6] The clay of creation is more than clay; it's a virtual ocean of chaos and creativity, according to Keller.

Keller complains that traditional interpretations of this passage in terms of *creatio ex nihilo* are inauthentic to the Hebrew scripture and represent an infection coming from Greek dualism, especially Plato's dualism.[7] Christian theologians have "locked into a dogma a clean and simple form of Hellenistic dualism."[8] On the one hand, Keller creates a dualism that makes both God and the stuff of the world eternal. On the other hand, Keller complains against Jewish and Christian interpreters of the Bible who embrace a Greek dualism between eternal spirit and temporal matter.

Old Testament scholar Ian McFarland finds Keller inconsistent. On the one hand, she debases Greek dualism for contaminating the Bible. On the other hand, her own interpretation posits an eternal dualism including both a creator deity plus the creative matrix of the *tehom*. This is "baffling," writes McFarland, "given that dualism (viz., the affirmation of two ontologically ultimate principles) is precisely what creation from nothing was formulated to oppose."[9] In sum, Keller contradicts herself by first dismissing dualism and then reaffirming dualism.

The conceptual framework of the Hebrew language did not lead early biblical writers to work with the concept of nothingness, which is needed for *creatio ex nihilo* to make sense. The idea of nothingness as such does not appear in Genesis. The dialectic between being and non-being was imported from Greece, as Keller rightly notes, especially the post-axial metaphysics of Plato's philosophy. When Jewish scholars three centuries before Jesus translated their Hebrew writings into Greek—into the version known as the *Septuagint*—they adopted not only the Greek language but also the Greek way of thinking. Genesis 1:1 eliminates any ambiguity by stating clearly that God created heaven and earth "in the beginning." God did not start with something, but with nothing. With this precedent, the Hebrew understanding of creation gradually became *creatio ex nihilo* for Greek-speaking Jews. This tells us that Genesis 1:1–2:4a was already being interpreted to teach creation out of nothing before New Testament times. Thus it was natural for Saint Paul to write that God "gives life to the dead and

---

6. Catherine Keller, *Face of the Deep: A Theology of Becoming* (London and New York: Routledge, 2003), 231, italics in original.

7. Greek and Hellenistic thought will be discussed in later chapters.

8. Keller, *Face of the Deep*, 48.

9. Ian A. McFarland, *From Nothing: A Theology of Creation* (Louisville: Westminster John Knox, 2014), 19, n. 65.

calls into existence the things that do not exist" (Rom. 4:17). New Testament and post-New Testament writers joined their Jewish colleagues in affirming the doctrine of creation out of nothing.

A century and a half after Jesus, Christian theologian Theophilus of Antioch wrote, "All things God has made out of things that were not into things that are."[10] Theophilus based his view not only on Genesis but also on the rational implications of understanding the God of Genesis. McFarland draws out the ancient and contemporary reasoning: "If God is to be confessed as Lord without qualification, then everything that is not God must depend on God for its existence without qualification. Otherwise, whatever realities existed independently of God would constitute a limit on God's ability to realize God's will in creation, in the same way that the properties of wood constrain the creative possibilities open to the carpenter. Because Theophilus refused to acknowledge any such limits, he concluded that creation cannot be thought of as God reshaping some preexisting material in the manner of a human artisan who, in making a pot from clay or bread from flour, creates *from something else*. Instead, God brings into being the very stuff of which the universe is made. In short, God creates *from nothing*."[11] Even though Genesis 1:1–2:4a may be ambiguous, theological interpretation proceeds to take on board the concept of *creatio ex nihilo*.

Contemporary Roman Catholic theologian Anne Clifford emphasizes, "*Creatio ex nihilo* is a doctrine about God who freely chose to create and of the dependence on God for existence."[12] Similarly, contemporary Muslim scholar Nasr would concede no ground to Keller's revival of fertile chaos: "In the Islamic perspective, God is the absolute and sole Creator, the sole giver of existence to the cosmos. . . . God alone is the giver of existence and of forms."[13]

The Ancient Bible and Modern Science

Jews, Christians, and Muslims employ the term *creation* when speaking about the relationship of the natural world to God. Pope Francis, who is both a trained scientist and a theologian, says, "In the Judaeo-Christian tradition, the word *creation* has a broader meaning than *nature*, for it has to do with God's loving plan in which every creature has its own value and significance. Nature is usually seen as a system which can be studied, understood and controlled, whereas creation

---

10. Theophilus of Antioch, *To Autolycus* 1.4, in *The Ante-Nicene Fathers: The Writings of the Fathers down to A.D. 325*, ed. Alexander Roberts and James Donaldson, trans. Marcus Dods, 9 vols. (Buffalo: The Christian Literature Publishing Company, 1886; Grand Rapids: Eerdmans, 1954), 1:90.

11. McFarland, *From Nothing*, 2.

12. Anne M. Clifford, "Creation," in *Systematic Theology: Roman Catholic Perspectives*, ed. Francis Schüssler Fiorenza and John P. Galvin, 2nd ed. (Minneapolis: Fortress, 2011), 201–54, at 231.

13. Nasr, "Question of Cosmogenesis," 53.

can only be understood as a gift from the outstretched hand of the Father of all, and as a reality illuminated by the love which calls us together into universal communion."[14] *Nature* may be a scientific term, but *creation* is not. So, it is worth asking, what is the relationship between Genesis and science?

When looking at the relationship between Genesis and science, some scholars suggest that Genesis 1:1–2:4a is neither myth nor science. Brueggemann avers that the Genesis writers "break with the mythological perception of reality which assumes that all the real action is with the gods and creation of itself has no significant value. On the other hand, they resist a scientific view of creation which assumes that the world contains its own mysteries and can be understood in terms of itself without any transcendent referent."[15] Genesis is not myth because it's not polytheistic, says Brueggemann; but Genesis is not science because it's not naturalistic.

"Judaeo-Christian thought demythologized nature," writes Pope Francis. "While continuing to admire its grandeur and immensity, it no longer saw nature as divine."[16] Demythologize? How does Genesis 1:1–2:4a differ from myth? The priestly author of this biblical story avoids in part the battle between the gods one finds in *Enuma Elish*, to be sure, and the Genesis origin story suggests a radical beginning by declaring that creation took place once and only once, in the beginning. In the beginning, the world was new. And yet, Genesis 1:1–2:4a includes an archonic dimension when it explains how the week was established at the world's founding. The seven-day week was established *in illo tempore*, therefore each Sabbath day of rest recapitulates the creation, so to speak. Archonic thinking is a feature belonging to myth. We might conclude, then, that the biblical creation story is at least quasi-mythical.

However, Genesis 1:1–2:4a could not count as modern science. What modern people understand to be science is very recent; a scientific account of the world's origin was not an option for any of the ancient scriptures. Even so, *creatio ex nihilo* along with unrepeatable historicity and openness to what is new are ideas that are still with us and are, to some degree, integrated into the scientific origin story.

Another Bible commentator, E. A. Speiser, places the Hebrew creation account in the context of "Babylonian science." The biblical tradition "aligned itself with the traditional tenets of Babylonia's science," he writes. "In ancient times, however, science often blended into religion; and the two could not be separated in such issues as cosmogony and the origin of man."[17] Speiser is misleading. Science and religion did not blend in the ancient world because no such thing as modern science existed then; neither did religion, for that matter. What

---

14. *Laudato si*, no. 76.

15. Brueggemann, *Genesis*, 12.

16. *Laudato si*, no. 78.

17. E. A. Speiser, *Genesis*, Anchor Bible (Garden City, NY: Doubleday, 1964), 11.

existed was culture. Babylonian culture replete with its *Enuma Elish* provided a contextual influence on what appears in the early chapters of the Hebrew Scriptures. But within Babylonian culture, science and religion had not yet differentiated themselves from within compact consciousness. Over the subsequent millennia, compact consciousness differentiated. New distinctions could be made. Differentiation in consciousness was a gradual process that continues today. At the birth of modernity only five centuries ago, Western culture distinguished science from religion. Today, this split is taken for granted. Neither *Enuma Elish* nor the Priestly author of Genesis would have had any understanding of this split between religion and science.

Today the biblical texts must be interpreted in the modern and emerging postmodern context. This context includes science—in large doses. Just as the Hebrew writers of Genesis probably interpreted the story of creation in light of the Babylonian story of *Enuma Elish*, so also do Jewish and Christian believers feel obligated today to interpret creation in light of big bang cosmogony and evolutionary biology.[18]

In the context of modern science and Darwin's theory of evolution, evolutionary history plays the role for us that the earth mother did for the ancient farmers. This could imply that evolutionary biology is a natural process that similarly obeys the command of the creator God to "bring forth living creatures of every kind." In short, the creation was created to be creative, avers Joshua Moritz.

> Among ancient creation accounts, the Bible is distinct in viewing the created cosmos as a historical entity and in describing how divine will has shaped creation from the time when everything was formless, void, and dark—before the stars, sun, Earth, or moon existed—to the time when the created world could be inhabited by plants, animals, and human beings. The central theme of the Genesis creation account is that God formed the cosmos in order that he might fill it with life. Included in these central affirmations unique to the biblical faith are the convictions that there is only one God and that God is the sole Creator; that God's creative activity is voluntary, rational, and effortless; that the world was created out of nothing; that the Creator is distinct from the created world; that creation is characterized by law-like order rather than chaos; and that creation is created to be creative.[19]

---

18. McFarland disappointingly fails to separate the theological answer from the scientific question: "To put it in a nutshell, it is my contention that while the Christian confession of the lordship of Christ is inseparable from the doctrine of creation from nothing, it is completely unaffected by the scientific question of whether or not (let alone when) the world had a temporal beginning." McFarland, *From Nothing*, xiv–xv. McFarland notwithstanding, it would seem that the scientific account of big bang and related stories of origin beg for theological questioning.

19. Joshua M. Moritz, *Science and Religion: Beyond Warfare and Toward Understanding* (Winona, MN: Anselm Academic), 135.

This means, among other things, that no twenty-first-century Bible reader needs to choose between science and faith. No opposition is necessary. "When I'm talking about God," writes popular religious author Rob Bell, "I'm talking about the source of *all* truth, whatever labels it wears, whoever says it, and wherever it is found—from a lab to a cathedral to a pub to Mars."[20]

Foretelling the Future of Creation

It's time to return to the question, is Genesis 1:1–2:4a an archonic myth? It certainly looks like it. However, if it is the case, as Brueggemann contends, that the biblical creation account is neither myth nor science, then we must ask, is it history? If it is history, it is not a chronicle of contingent events in the same sense that either World History or Big History is. Genesis 1:1–2:4a does fit within the big bang chronicle (some uncanny correspondences will be pointed out momentarily). The relationship of this creation story with modern views of time, especially the present and the future, deserves some attention.

Might a person interpret Genesis 1:1–2:4a epigenetically? Could biblical readers see the newness of God's creative activity at work here? Can biblical readers see God's promise that, in the future, there will be a Sabbath coming?

Is it possible to think of the opening account of creation in Genesis 1:1–2:4a as describing not merely a beginning but also the present time? Could one think of the creation week of seven days as inclusive of the entire history of creation from big bang to whatever will become of the universe in the future? Could evolutionary history constitute one small episode in the divine epic of creation, "Let the earth bring forth living creatures" (Gen. 1:24)? Could an interpreter today be standing between the initial moment when God opened his divine mouth to say, "Let there be . . ." and the final moment when God declares that, behold, it is "very good"? Could one look forward to the Sabbath day, to God's first day of rest, still in the future?

In the fourth century, Saint Augustine nearly approached such a schematization when wrestling with the question, does creation out of nothing take place in time or in eternity? Regardless of his answer, the tantalizing thought raised by this question is that God's eternal word might be inclusive of the entire scope of evolutionary and even Cosmic History. God's "word is spoken eternally, and by it all things are uttered eternally. It is not the case that what was being said comes to an end, and something else is then said, so that everything is uttered in a succession with a conclusion, but everything is said in the simultaneity of eternity. Otherwise time and change would already exist, and there would not be

---

20. Rob Bell, *What We Talk about When We Talk about God* (New York: Harper, 2013), 75, italics in original.

a true eternity and true immortality."[21] In Augustine's view, the word by which God drew being from nonbeing—drew a physical world out of a nothing that preceded it—is the very same word by which all of reality is presently sustained and will be consummated. Perhaps today's interpreter of Genesis 1:1–2:4a might consider that future consummation will be the crowning conclusion of creation; the entire history of creation is a single inclusive divine act whereby what comes into existence is perfected in its existence. If so, then the present generation stands in the middle of this yet-to-be completed story of creation.

In sum, Genesis 1:1–2:4a need not be a story about a single week of past history that occurred once upon a time many years ago. Rather, in story form it describes the entire history of the cosmos, including the present moment. It is a story that is not yet over. It is ongoing. Today's generation finds itself in the middle of this story, looking back at the beginning and forward to its future climax. The story of Genesis 1:1–2:4a will not become an archonic myth until the story is complete, until the creation has been called into God's promised new creation.

Conclusion

Questions presuppose answers. When one asks the question of God today, one begins by taking a look at past answers. *Enuma Elish* provides one answer. Geneis 1:1–2:ba provides another answer. For us today, we turn these answers back into a question: does Cosmic History lead us to ask about God?

Review Questions

1. How is Genesis 1:1–2:4a similar to *Enuma Elish*? How is it different?
2. When interpreting Genesis 1:1–2:4a, why does the doctrine of *creatio ex nihilo* attract Jewish, Christian, and Muslim theologians?
3. How might a feminist theologian argue against *creatio ex nihilo*?
4. Distinguish compact consciousness from differentiated consciousness on the distinction between science and religion.

Discussion Questions

1. Why might we think of *Enuma Elish* and Genesis 1:1–2:4a as prescientific?
2. What spiritual sensibilities resonate with the biblical story of origin?

---

21. Augustine, *Confessions* 11.7.9; translation from Augustine, *Confessions*, trans. Henry Chadwick (Oxford and New York: Oxford University Press, 1991), 226.

3. Think about the seven-day week. What alternative ways of measuring time might one consider?

4. How can a story set in the past actually illuminate present reality?

Additional Resources

Print Sources

Brueggemann, Walter. *Genesis.* Interpretation. Louisville: Westminster John Knox, 1982.

> Brueggemann provides the most lucid exposition of the Hebrew Scriptures among today's scholars.

Clifford, Anne M. "Creation." In *Systematic Theology: Roman Catholic Perspectives*, edited by Francis Schüssler Fiorenza and John P. Galvin, 201–54. 2nd ed. Minneapolis: Fortress, 2011.

> Professor Clifford offers a gratifyingly comprehensive historical and systematic presentation of the Christian understanding of creation with special attention to big bang cosmology and evolution.

Keller, Catherine. *Face of the Deep: A Theology of Becoming.* New York: Routledge, 2003.

> Keller is a genius and an unorthodox interpreter of the Bible. She identifies creation less with God's word and more with the deep or chaotic material that is ordered by the divine word. Indirectly she revives the intimate sensibilities at work in the feminine symbolism of prehistoric farmers.

McFarland, Ian A. *From Nothing: A Theology of Creation.* Louisville: Westminster John Knox, 2014.

> McFarland connects our interpretation of Genesis with the theological concept of *creatio ex nihilo.* He demonstrates the conceptual importance of the theological commitment to creation out of nothing.

Nasr, Seyyed Hossein. "The Question of Cosmogenesis—the Cosmos as a Subject of Scientific Study," *Islam and Science* 4, no. 1 (Summer 2006): 43–60.

> One of America's premier Muslim intellectuals offers this clear and succinct exposition of the doctrine of creation in light of the big bang and related scientific cosmological thinking. Nasr makes the point that the materialist assumptions of modern science fail to take into account the whole of reality, especially spiritual reality.

9

CHAPTER

The Origin Story
in Genesis 2:4b–3:24

Tiger! Tiger! burning bright
In the forests of the night,
What immortal hand or eye
Could frame thy fearful symmetry?
—WILLIAM BLAKE (1757–1827),
"TIGER"

By examining big bang theory plus creation myths in ancient cultures, earlier chapters have shown how both contemporary scientists and our premodern ancestors constructed their *cosmogonies*, accounts of the origin of the cosmos. Genesis 1:1–2:4a provides the Bible with its most comprehensive cosmogony, accounting for the existence of God and the world. But every cosmogony also needs to account for human nature. Just how did *Homo sapiens* come to be the way they are? Genesis 2:4b–3:24 offers an *anthropogony*, a story of human origin that describes the human condition as people experience it in every generation.

Adam and Eve

The story of Adam and Eve in the garden of Eden is an origin story, an archonic story, an etiological narrative with intra-cosmic characters. The Eden story describes the human condition as people experience it every day. The story is placed in the past, as are most myths, but it describes what has been true of human beings throughout history and for the foreseeable future.

The garden of Eden—*paradise* in the Persian language—is located in what we today call Iraq, between the Tigris and Euphrates rivers. Nevertheless, this story is intended to describe all people of all times and all places, including you, the reader, and me, the author. We all live daily in this garden, or perhaps in the field of weeds just east of Eden.

According to the Eden story, here is what human beings do: each of us tries to draw a line between good and evil, and then we place ourselves on the good side of the line. That is to say, a person's first reflex in a moment of anxiety is to justify himself or herself. This causes a problem. By declaring ourselves good, we estrange ourselves from the true source of the good, namely, God. In addition, by declaring ourselves good, we justify becoming violent toward other people whom we dub less good or even evil. We blind ourselves into committing acts of violence in the name of the good. This is the universal human condition described in this simple story.

The Genesis anthropogony begins by telling us about the origin of human beings *in illo tempore*.[1] From their very origin, humans have a built-in tension, a double identity that slings them between soil and spirit. This tension fills them with anxiety.

> The LORD God (*Yahweh Elohim*) formed man ('*adam*) from the dust of the ground ('*adamah*), and breathed into his nostrils the breath of life; and the man became a living being (*nephesh*). (Gen. 2:7)

One the one hand, the first human being is clay, soil, earth, dust—'*adamah* in Hebrew. Like a potter, God builds a clay doll. Then God blows divine breath into the doll and it becomes a human person, an '*adam*. Note that '*adam* is not first of all a name. Rather, it refers to a human being.[2]

Later in the text, the noun '*adam* becomes a name, *Adam*. Symbolically, this indicates that *Homo sapiens* are more than merely products of the earth. With the breath of God, they find themselves situated in a tension between the animal and the divine, between what is natural and what is supranatural, between humility and dignity, between what is temporal and what is eternal. Humans are not in themselves divine, to be sure; but their earthiness is restless, yearning for heaven.

Genesis further indicates that their very existence is a gift of God, a gift of divine grace. Will the human race thank God for its existence, or will the human race attempt to replace God with some sort of substitute ultimate? To replace God with oneself as ultimate is what the Greek myths called *hubris* and what the Latin Christians called *pride*.

As the story continues, Eve is given to Adam as his wife, partner, and helper. Adam and Eve are depicted as the paradigm for a wholesome human marriage. Within this setting, Eve engages in conversation with a serpent in the garden.

---

1. Latin for "at that time." See chapter 7 for the use of this phrase in connection with cosmogonies.

2. "The person as a living being is to be understood as a whole and any idea that one is made up of body and soul is ruled out." Claus Westermann, *Genesis 1–11*, trans. John J. Scullion, SJ (Minneapolis: Fortress, 1974), 207.

> Now the serpent was more crafty than any other wild animal that the LORD God had made. He said to the woman, "Did God say, 'You shall not eat from any tree in the garden'?" The woman said to the serpent, "We may eat of the fruit of the trees in the garden; but God said, 'You shall not eat of the fruit of the tree that is in the middle of the garden, nor shall you touch it, or you shall die.'" But the serpent said to the woman, "You will not die; for God knows that when you eat of it your eyes will be opened, and you will be like God, knowing good and evil." So when the woman saw that the tree was good for food, and that it was a delight to the eyes, and that the tree was to be desired to make one wise, she took of its fruit and ate; and she also gave some to her husband, who was with her, and he ate. Then the eyes of both were opened, and they knew that they were naked; and they sewed fig leaves together and made loincloths for themselves. (Gen. 3:1–7)

When Eve looks at the tree of knowledge bearing the forbidden fruit, she likes what she sees. It appears "good" to eat. One thing this indicates is that human beings are naturally attracted to what is good. This is healthy, to be sure. The human condition, however, is plagued by a conflict between competing good things. There is no abject evil in this story, only competition between a variety of good things.

The serpent lists other good things that will happen: "You will not die, for God knows that when you eat of it your eyes will be opened, and you will be like God, knowing good and evil" (Gen. 2:4–5). Eve becomes suspicious that God might be pulling the wool over her eyes. The serpent suggests she remove the wool to see more clearly. To have one's eyes opened, to gain enlightenment, to gain knowledge, sounds attractive. It sounds like the goal of virtually everyone's spiritual quest. To be like God? How could one turn down such an opportunity? Eating the forbidden fruit on the tree of knowledge would appear to be a good thing to do. At least, it appears good on Eve's scale of values.

After eating the forbidden fruit, the woman shares it with her man. Both human creatures gain something from this: the knowledge of good and evil. Their eyes do become opened, figuratively speaking. Nevertheless, this new knowing involves some collateral damage. Suddenly they become aware of something they had not noticed before: they are not wearing any clothes. So they quickly sew together leaves from plants to cover up their private places. Physically, the man and woman learn how to cover up their bodies. Symbolically, they are learning how to cover up their guilt, how to hide the truth, how to present a false front. Open eyes make deceit possible. Open eyes make a new form of blindness possible. Even without telling falsehoods, they could present themselves with half-truths, misleading half-truths.

But the LORD God called to the man, and said to him, "Where are you?" He said, "I heard the sound of you in the garden, and I was afraid, because I was naked; and I hid myself." He said, "Who told you that you were naked? Have you eaten from the tree of which I commanded you not to eat?" The man said, "The woman whom you gave to be with me, she gave me fruit from the tree, and I ate." Then the LORD God said to the woman, "What is this that you have done?" The woman said, "The serpent tricked me, and I ate." (Gen. 3:10–13)

This three-cornered conversation presents a chain of self-justification. When God inquires about eating the forbidden fruit, Adam and Eve respond with an admission of guilt, but they also try to shift the blame. Adam says, in effect, "It's not my fault. Blame the woman you gave me. It's your fault, God." Eve follows, "It's not my fault. Blame the serpent who beguiled me. And, God, while we're at it, who made the serpent?" God, she implies, is guilty for creating a serpent who talks in the garden of Eden. It is God's fault for prohibiting the man and woman from eating of the tree of knowledge, so God is really the guilty party. Adam and Eve have drawn a line between good and evil, and they have placed one another, the serpent, and even God on the evil side.[3]

"Adam wanted to appear innocent, he passed on his guilt from himself to God, who had given him his wife. Eve also tries to excuse herself and accuses the serpent, which was also a creature of God," comments Reformation theologian Martin Luther. "Here Adam is presented as a typical instance of all sinners and of such who despair because of their sin. They cannot do otherwise than accuse God and excuse themselves."[4] Adam and Eve drew a line between good and evil, and they placed God on the evil side of that line.

Placing God on the evil side of the line is a lie, of course. "The lie is the specific evil which [humanity] has introduced into nature," said Jewish existentialist Martin Buber (1878–1965).[5] Why would anyone want to tell such a lie? Curiously, it is a lie that human beings regularly tell themselves. There is self-deception involved. Eyes open to the difference between good and evil lead to the lie, to a new form of blindness. Why does this happen?

Post-axial human beings work with the assumption that goodness is eternal. Becoming eternal attracts the human self. The goodness of eternity especially

---

3. "The story is a theological critique of anxiety," comments Brueggemann. "Overcoming of God is thought to lead to the nullification of anxiety about the self. But the story teaches otherwise. It is only God, the one who calls, permits and prohibits, who can deal with the anxiety among us." Walter Brueggemann, *Genesis*, Interpretation (Louisville: Westminster John Knox, 1982), 53.

4. Martin Luther, "Lectures on Genesis," in *Luther's Works*, American ed., vols. 1–30 ed. Jaroslav Pelikan (St. Louis: Concordia, 1955–1967); vols. 31–55 ed. Helmut T. Lehmann (Minneapolis: Fortress, 1955–1986), 1:178–79.

5. Martin Buber, *Good and Evil* (New York: Charles Scribners' Sons, 1952), 7.

attracts the self. It is difficult for people to admit that they fall short of the good, that they are less than what the eternal good requires. So desperate are human beings to identify themselves with what is good that they will vilify God if necessary in order to do so. They will condemn God for placing evil into the creation. They will judge God by a criterion that they foolishly believe transcends God.

Knowledge of good and evil makes people tenaciously fight to be good, and this leads to violence against others. Adam and Eve gave birth to two sons, Cain and Abel. One murdered the other. "Cain rose up against his brother Abel, and killed him" (Gen. 4:8). Since this first murder, killing has not ceased. How does one get from pursuing the good to murder?

It is not unusual for a person to desire the good and to covet the goods that others have. People are tempted to steal other's goods in order to make themselves better or best. Archaic city-states pursued the goods of others through war, genocide, and pillage. Today's nation-states use economic pressure, terrorism, and war to obtain access to petroleum. Large businesses contribute obscene amounts of cash to political candidates in order to get legislation that favors low labor costs and expanded markets. Teen gangs in large cities covet the turf of rival gangs, and through fighting take control.

Both nations and individuals excuse their thefts verbally through self-justification, through ideologies that identify themselves or their cause with the good; and they identify the cause of the victim with what is evil. A nation will justify going to war on the grounds that it stands for freedom while its enemy stands for tyranny. A government will deny social services to the poor on the grounds that the poor are lazy. One race will justify discrimination against another on the grounds that the victimized race is primitive, stupid, and inferior. Atheists describe themselves as moral while alleging that violence in the world is due to immoral religion. Human beings both individually and in groups identify themselves with what is good, identifying outsiders—including God when necessary—with what is evil. The Adam and Eve story communicates that human beings try to steal goodness for themselves, even if they must steal it from God.

With an angel holding a fiery sword to prevent their return to the garden of Eden, Adam and Eve found themselves expelled and cut off from the tree of the knowledge of good and evil. They were also cut off from the tree of life. Because they had not eaten fruit of the tree of life, they would die. Human beings cannot live forever. Death is the inescapable human lot east of Eden.

Christians often refer to the Adam and Eve story as the *Fall into sin and death*. The story begins in paradise and ends with human expulsion from paradise. The human race finds itself today east of Eden, yearning for paradise lost. As a result, human beings today live in a state called *sin*, which some Christians call *original sin*. This means each person is born into a state of sin, even if that person does not initiate sin.

Is the Eden story historical in the sense that it took place in one time and location? Only the most conservative believers think so. Given the evolutionary version of human history, it appears that violence and all that is called *sin* has no datable origin; it was always there. The non-historicity of the Eden story upsets some American evangelicals who feel the need to anchor the Fall within history. Even without a moment in history, however, the doctrine of original sin is still fitting, according to evangelical theologian Karl Giberson: "Regardless of how it originated, or whether it even had an origin, something appropriately called *sin* remains a deeply rooted part of human nature and, given that we are born this way, original sin is not a bad name for it."[6]

In "The Fall" (1479), by Hugo van der Goes, the serpent tempts Adam and Eve to eat the forbidden fruit. Subsequently, Adam blames Eve, while Eve blames the serpent and, because the serpent was created by God, indirectly blames God.

Even though Cosmic History cannot locate a specific point on the calendar when the Fall took place, the yearning virtually all people feel for a transcendent healing of the ills of historical existence warrants the continued use of the terms *Fall*, *sin*, and *original sin*. "Theology must clearly and unambiguously represent the Fall as a symbol for the human situation universally, not as the story of an event that happened once upon a time," says Tillich.[7]

Redemption for the Fallen

The human race lives in estrangement from its divine creator, subject to relentless violence leading to death for both the perpetrators and victims. Estrangement and death are the destiny of all human beings. Can human beings hope

6. Karl W. Giberson, *Saving the Original Sinner* (Boston: Beacon, 2015), 176.

7. Paul Tillich, *Systematic Theology*, 3 vols. (Chicago: University of Chicago Press, 1951–1963), 2:29.

for redemption? Will this estrangement be overcome? Will the anxious human heart find healing? Is there reason for hope?

Hope in Islam comes from resolving to do God's will. Obedience to Allah will prepare each person for Judgment Day and, after passing through judgment, paradise will be the reward. In making this promise, the deceit of Adam and Eve prompts almost no attention. When the Qur'an picks up the Eden account with the eating of the forbidden fruit, its emphasis is less on the cover-up and more on the disobedience per se. Human disobedience requires punishment in the form of expulsion from paradise, as the Genesis story reports. However, after the couple has left the garden, Allah, in his mercy, offers the sinners guidance. This guidance will lead the sinners through a future judgment and back into paradise.

> [God] turned to him [Adam], and gave him guidance. . . . "Whosoever follows My guidance, will not lose his way, nor fall into misery. But whosoever turns away from my message, verily for him is a life narrowed down, and We shall raise him up blind on the Day of Judgment." (Qur'an, 20:122–24)

If Adam and Eve represent the entire human race, then every individual is enjoined by God to follow divine guidance or else find rejection on Judgment Day. Obedience to Allah's will is the key to salvation.

The Christian interpretation is different. Here, redemption is a gift of God's grace delivered to an estranged creation through the historical event of Jesus Christ. When Jesus was crucified on the cross on Good Friday, he was the victim of human violence, the victim of human self-justification. The Romans who actually put Jesus to death did so in the name of something good, namely, protecting Roman sovereignty from sedition. The Jewish leaders who requested the death penalty did so for a good reason, namely, to rid the community of a blasphemer. Jesus' claim to speak for God as the Son of God, thought the Jewish leaders, was *prima facie* evidence that he was committing blasphemy. Both Roman and Jewish leaders believed they were justified in hanging Jesus on the cross until death. Everyone who conspired in putting Jesus to death was pursuing one or another good thing. The problem with such violence is that self-deception accompanies self-justification.

The Christian tradition reports that, while dying on the cross, Jesus said, "Father, forgive them; for they do not know what they are doing" (Luke 23:34). The killers had thought of themselves as doing good, so they could not know that they were doing evil. To know the difference between good and evil is to find devious ways to deceive oneself into believing one is good in every circumstance. The only way to overcome self-deception is through revelation. In the cross of Jesus, say Christians, God was revealing just what kind of sin has been contaminating the human race since Adam and Eve. By raising Jesus from the dead, God was declaring divine forgiveness for human sinning despite the fact that humans "do not know what they are doing." By promising future resurrection into the new creation for those who through faith accept God's forgiveness, Christians say that God is acting to effect salvation for the entire cosmos. "Sin is estrangement; grace is reconciliation."[8]

The symbol of this salvation is the New Jerusalem.

> And I saw the holy city, the new Jerusalem, coming down out of heaven from God, prepared as a bride adorned for her husband. And I heard a loud voice from the throne saying, "See, the home of God is among mortals. He will dwell with them; they will be his peoples, and God himself will be with them; he will wipe every tear from their eyes. Death will be no more; mourning and crying and pain will be no more, for the first things have passed away." (Rev. 21:2–4)

The New Jerusalem is not a literal city descending from the sky. Rather, it symbolizes the redeemed social order, the perfected city-state, the kingdom of God, the new creation.

In the New Jerusalem, all estrangement will be overcome. The gulf that separates God from creation will be bridged. Wounds will be healed. Death will die. The Resurrection of Jesus on Easter is God's promise of a corresponding transformation of the cosmos. This transformation will turn the present creation into the garden of Eden. In the symbolism of the New Jerusalem, one can find the garden of Eden as a park in the middle of the city.

> Then the angel showed me the river of the water of life, bright as crystal, flowing from the throne of God and of the Lamb through the middle of the street of the city. On either side of the river is the tree of life. (Rev. 22:1–2)

Downtown in the New Jerusalem are located the same river of life and tree of life found in Genesis 2:4b–3:24. When one walks through the gates into the center of New Jerusalem, one walks into the very garden of Eden that humankind had left after the Fall. For the New Testament, paradise belongs to the future; it does not represent a return to the past.

The story of the Fall accompanied by the human desire to return to paradise lost is not merely a charming story some religions tell. It is intended to describe the human condition universally. Voegelin makes this point: "the fall from the order of being and the return to it is the fundamental problem in human existence."[9]

---

8. Ibid., 2:57.

9. Eric Voegelin, *Order and History*, 5 vols. (Baton Rouge: Louisiana State University Press, 1956–1987), 1:299.

Conclusion

For Muslims, Christians, and Jews, the children of Adam today live in an estranged situation east of Eden. According to the Qur'an, those who respond to Allah through obedience will, at death, pass through the Day of Judgment into God's paradise. According to the New Testament, those who in faith receive God's forgiveness of sins will pass through the judgment into God's new creation.

The cosmic historian is not likely to locate the garden of Eden on a map or a calendar. Yet it stands in transcendental judgment against ordinary daily life, condemning human deceit, violence, and war. Paradise also provides a gracious promise that the future does not have to be what the past was or the present is. The story of origin in Genesis 2:4b–3:34 explains the human condition as experienced today while yearning for a transformation tomorrow.

Review Questions

1. How do *cosmogony* and *anthropogony* connect?
2. What is the relation between *'adam* and *'adamah*?
3. What is the tension in the nature of the human being?
4. What kind of knowledge does the tree of knowledge offer?

Discussion Questions

1. Remind yourself: in Genesis, just what did the serpent say to Eve? What did Adam and Eve say to God? Why?
2. What features of a myth of origin do you find in the Eden story?
3. Can you identify any ways in which God behaves graciously in this story?
4. Compare and contrast Muslim and Christian interpretations of the story of Adam and Eve.

Additional Resources

Print Sources

Brueggemann, Walter. *Genesis*. Interpretation. Louisville: Westminster John Knox, 1982.

In a very readable fashion, Brueggemann places God's demand on the human race prior to the Fall in threefold form: the human race has (1) a *vocation*, a calling to till the garden and care for the earth; (2) a *permission* to eat all that earth produces and to enjoy the beauty of creation; and (3) a *prohibition* against eating the forbidden fruit on the tree of knowledge of good and evil. Despite the Fall, human beings today are still under this divine mandate. See pp. 40–53.

Buber, Martin. *Good and Evil.* New York: Charles Scribners' Sons, 1952.

In this classic by a beloved existentialist philosopher and Jewish theologian, Martin Buber describes the human Fall into sin in a lucid and compelling fashion. He also describes a gracious and loving God.

Luther, Martin. *Luther's Works.* American ed. Vols. 1–30. Edited by Jaroslav Pelikan. St. Louis: Concordia, 1955–1967. Vols. 31–55. Edited by Helmut T. Lehmann. Minneapolis: Fortress, 1955–1986.

The first volume, *Lectures on Genesis*, provides the interpretation of the Eden story cited in this chapter.

Peters, Ted. *Sin Boldly! Justifying Faith for Fragile and Broken Souls.* Minneapolis: Fortress, 2015.

This treatment of Christian spirituality analyzes extensively the phenomenon of self-justification in the Bible, society, and the individual. It takes up the further task of comparing and contrasting Roman Catholics, Lutherans, Reformed, and Methodists on justification and reconciliation.

10

CHAPTER

Critical Thinking about Cosmic History

Perplext in faith, but pure in deeds,
  At last he beat his music out.
  There lives more faith in honest doubt,
Believe me, than in half the creeds.

—ALFRED LORD TENNYSON (1809–1892)
"IN MEMORIAM"

What does it mean to think critically? It means one has the ability to hold in mind two or more thoughts at the same time. More importantly, the different thoughts may not cohere with one another. In some cases, two thoughts might even contradict one another. In the mind, one can think in the abstract, measure in the abstract, evaluate in the abstract, and make a decision based on this evaluation.

A critical thinker can postpone making an evaluation until sufficient evidence has been mustered. To think critically, one must suspend judgment temporarily while examining each alternative and measuring it for its characteristics, its plusses and minuses.

Sometimes the alternatives are not obvious. Sometimes in conversation only one idea is being expressed. If this is the case, then a critical thinker must devise an alternative way of looking at the matter and insert it into the existing conversation. News reporters attempt to exercise critical thinking by conducting interviews in which they ask "tough questions." A tough question is one in which two or more alternative ways of looking at things come to the surface. When historians are examining ancient texts or archaeological artifacts, they ask tough questions even though nobody from the ancient world is there to answer.

Critical consciousness marks the leap in differentiation taken by the modern mind. Even though certain premodern individuals distinguished themselves with their critical minds, only in modernity has critical thinking become a cultural norm. The differentiation in consciousness leading to critical thinking was seeded in the Axial Period, and the modern period has brought it to full blossom.

Terms such as *critical reflexivity* or *reflexive consciousness* indicate "the ability to use reason to transcend the immediately given," notes Uppsala University professor Björn Wittrock.[1] Twenty-five hundred years or so ago intellectual giants popped their heads up above the fog of compact consciousness: Laozi, Confucius, Buddha, Zoroaster, Plato, Aristotle, and Isaiah. They are remembered as influential minds. What distinguishes today's modernity is that critical consciousness has spread throughout the wider culture. Everyone with a university education is expected to think critically, especially scientists and theologians. Those who disregard their own critical capacities risk regressing into packaged ideologies and other forms of group think.

We must apply critical thinking to Big History on two fronts, both the history itself and the historian. What the big historian reports is one thing. The mind of the big historian is another. For us to be critical means we look carefully at both.

This chapter introduces the concept of critical realism, a disciplined form of critical thinking. *Critical realism* describes the mindset of the natural scientist when he or she is studying the world of nature. A scientist must hold two things in mind at one time: the evidence and the reality toward which that evidence points. This is challenging because the scientist can perceive the evidence but frequently cannot perceive the reality. Therefore, the scientist must construct a mental model of what is invisible yet believed to be real. In the case of the big bang, for example, no scientist today can perceive the big bang, so he or she must create a mental model of it based upon the evidence.

The scientist uses imagination to construct conceptual models of nature. Even though these concepts are constructed by the imagination, the scientist believes they refer to what is real. Scientific models are both imaginary and real at the same time. Scientists begin with presuppositions, with a worldview within which these imaginary models will fit. These presuppositions derive from larger more inclusive models. Our discussion of critical realism will be nested within a larger set of four presupposed inclusive models for thinking about nature: an enchanted view of nature; a dualistic view of nature; a mechanistic view of nature; and a contingent view of nature (referring to quantum contingency).

When theologians raise the question of God, they must decide which conceptual model of nature serves as the most fitting jumping off point for this question. In pre-modern society, belief in the divine dimension felt quite at home in both the enchanted view of nature and the dualistic view of nature. But belief in God appeared to be systematically removed from nature in the third model, the mechanistic view of nature. With the discovery of quantum physics,

---

1. Björn Wittrock, "The Axial Age in Global History: Cultural Crystallizations and Societal Transformatins," in *The Axial Age and Its Consequences*, ed. Robert N. Bellah and Hans Joas (Cambridge, MA: Harvard University Press, 2012), 102–25, at 108.

however, the question of God pops up once again in the fourth model, the contingent view of nature.

Four Models of Nature

In this book, *God in Cosmic History*, the history of human consciousness is divided into three eras: premodern, modern, and postmodern. The first era, the premodern, is itself divided into periods of differentiating human consciousness: spoken language, written language, and the axial breakthrough. In previous chapters we traced the movement among our ancestors to spoken and written language. In future chapters we will turn to the premodern axial insight into transcendence.

The modern era characterized by critical consciousness will be divided into two periods: the rational and the relative. The postmodern era has only begun. The term *postmodern* refers to three not-necessarily compatible concerns, namely, quantum contingency in physics, holistic interpretations of emergence in evolution and society, and deconstructing the power dynamics within specific social contexts. This last version of postmodernism, deconstructionism, extends the logic of the doctrine of cultural relativity, which developed during the modern period.

Big historians today work out of the modern rational mindset, whereas world historians work out of the modern relative mindset. In this book the cosmic historian will work out of both the rational and the relative with an eye to the postmodern era.

Premodern, Modern, and Postmodern Consciousness

ERAS	PERIODS	TYPES OF CONSCIOUSNESS	VIEW OF NATURE
Premodern 200,000 years ago	1. spoken language 2. written language	compact	enchanted
	3. axial	differentiated	dualistic
Modern 1650 CE to present	1. rational (1650–present) 2. relativistic (1800–present)	critical	mechanistic
Post-Modern 1900 CE to present	1. quest for meaning of quantum contingency (1920–present) 2. quest for holism (1920–present) 3. quest for deconstructionist relativity (1970–present)	post-critical	quantum contingency

Enchanted View of Nature

For our earliest ancestors during the Paleolithic Era and Holocene epoch, the world appeared enchanted. Foragers, farmers, and citizens perceived the world around them to be alive with spiritual forces. Thunder and lightning were personified in myths as sky gods. Plant and animal species were thought to be animated by spirits that transcended individuals. Perhaps men and women caught up by romantic passions felt they were being driven by the whims of the love goddess, Aphrodite or Venus. Good fortune or ruinous disaster conveyed meaning to life. Some world historians and big historians apply the term *animism* to describe the enchanted world of Stone Age hominins. Our ancestors saw themselves as embedded in a single textured reality, in which the physical and the spiritual were woven together in compact consciousness, intra-cosmic consciousness.

The enchanted worldview was completely intra-cosmic, but it included both the natural and the supernatural.[2] It included miracles, angels, demons, fairies, trolls, and the uncanny. At the intersection of the natural and the supernatural, stories would be told, narratives that placed human life in an awesome cosmos.

Dualistic View of Nature

Eventually, compact consciousness differentiated. One product of this differentiation was dualism. The dualistic view of nature differentiated the physical and spiritual dimensions. Dualists believe reality is divided into two substances, matter and spirit. The split between matter and spirit accounts for the split between body and soul, the earthly and the heavenly, the temporal and the eternal.

During the first millennium prior to the common era, some city-state citizens experienced a breakthrough in consciousness, discovering a transcendent dimension that seemed to be more real than their everyday world. Some philosophers refer to this as the axial breakthrough, and refer to the axial worldview as the perennial philosophy. Some Islamic, Jewish, and Christian theologians have incorporated perennialism into classical theism. Hindu and some Buddhist philosophers have incorporated perennialism into mysticism. The perennial philosophy is characterized primarily by substance dualism, a dualism between the material and the spiritual, between body and soul; the physical world is but a shadow of the much more real divine realm. What people experience in the physical world is temporal, ephemeral, corruptible, and subject to death. Beyond the shadow of the physical world is the transcendent realm of spirit, which is eternal, immutable, incorruptible, and life-giving. In the everyday realm, human minds are subject to distortion and even falsehood, but to be attuned to the realm of spiritual light is to live in the truth, to live in the realm of God.

---

2. *Supranatural* designates realities that are above nature. This term is preferable to *supernatural*, which could mean simply a greatly exaggerated or enhanced version of nature.

This transcendental insight dawned on selected individuals during the Axial Period and gave rise to what was later called the *higher religions*: Hinduism, Buddhism, Daoism, Confucianism, Judaism, Christianity, and eventually Islam. Although most higher religions state that the ultimate truth is eternal and unchanging, each historical religion adapts this truth to its own specific symbol system. Religion, says perennial philosopher Huston Smith, is "the human relationship to a realm that is invisible and powerful and good, those three qualities combined."[3]

The windows to transcendent or supra-cosmic reality are closed to the scientist or the historian trying to pursue objective knowledge. Ultimate reality can be known only inwardly, only by a person whose soul is open, whose heart is loving. "The ultimate Reality is not clearly and immediately apprehended, except by those who have made themselves loving, pure in heart, and poor in spirit," writes Aldous Huxley.[4] In sum, the natural realm—including the historical realm—exists as but a shadow of a second realm, the ultimate yet transcendent ground of all reality.

Mechanistic View of Nature

The worldviews of enchantment and dualism dominated culture until only five centuries ago. Then a third model captivated the emerging Western mind: the mechanistic view of nature. Even though reason was inherited from the Axial Period, modernity took the understanding of nature further into a mechanistic conceptual model, which holds that the physical world runs like a machine. The idea of the machine came from the building of mechanical clocks in medieval times. The impressive mechanical clock that adorned the cathedral at Strasbourg provided the mental model from which European scientists extrapolated: "The whole universe runs like this clock," they concluded. The laws of nature govern the way the gears mesh and grind. Every event is the effect of a prior cause. This mental model became extremely fertile, leading to experiment after experiment, producing an ever growing cache of scientific knowledge. This is the value of a conceptual model: it suggests fertile directions for future research. One cannot say this too strongly, the mechanistic model of nature enabled science and technology to revolutionize modern society.

At the dayspring of the modern age, nearly all research scientists were Christian or Jewish theologians. For them, God was conceived as the clockmaker and the world the clock. This led to the doctrine of the *two books*, both of which reveal God. The Bible is one book, revealing God as redeemer. The

---

3. Huston Smith, *The Way Things Are: Conversations with Huston Smith on the Spiritual Life*, ed. Phil Cousineau (Berkeley: University of California Press, 2003), 137.

4. Aldous Huxley, *The Perennial Philosophy* (New York: Collins Fantana, 1946, 1958), 12.

second is the book of nature, revealing God as creator. The two books reveal one God. The priest interprets the Bible while the scientist interprets nature. At the time, the priest and the scientist were often the same person. No split between faith and reason—between faith and science—existed until the West was well into the Enlightenment.

Isaac Newton (1642–1727) established *classical physics* or *classical mechanics* (also called the *Newtonian worldview*). Newton read both books, the book of nature and the Bible. Newton found in the mechanistic model a treasure chest of new knowledge about nature, both small and large, in optics, the laws of motion, fluid dynamics, universal gravitation, the paths of comets, the timing of tides, and other phenomena. Although he wrote more pages of theology than science, his major work, published in 1687, *Philosophiae Naturalis Principia Mathematica* (*Mathematical Principles of Natural Philosophy*) continues to provide the definitive interpretation of the natural world to the present day. Even in his own time he was recognized as a genius. Alexander Pope (1688–1744) penned a poetic quip about Newton.

Nature and nature's laws
　　Lay hid in night;
God said, "Let Newton be,"
　　And all was light.

Newton's science began by trusting the transcendental ground for reason, God. The scientist can trust that the laws of nature will be discoverable because God guarantees that reason will produce results. At the turn of the nineteenth century, a more secular generation of scientists decided to delete God from their world picture. What they ended up with was a clockwork world with no clockmaker, a designed cosmos but no designer. The English word *scientist* was coined by William Whewell in 1831 after the break from theology had occurred, perhaps contributing to the present association of science with what is non-religious.

The mechanistic worldview that gradually came to dominate science found no need to appeal to angels, demons, miracles, or even the will of God to explain natural phenomena. God lost his job, so to speak. The nineteenth century disenchanted nature and replaced perennial dualism with materialism, the view that reality is solely and finally material in nature. This became (and still is) unacceptable to many, who fear that the modern view of nature has lost the sense of the sacred. Seyyed Nasr, whom we cited earlier, fights against modernity by advocating a retrieval of the perennial philosophy. He advocates "the resacralization of nature, not in the sense of bestowing sacredness upon nature, which is beyond the power of [a human], but of lifting aside the veils of ignorance and pride that have hidden the sacredness of nature from the view of a whole segment of humanity."[5] In Nasr's view, the problem of the mechanistic model is that it hides the presence of the sacred.

Although Oxford's notorious materialist Richard Dawkins would never consider a resacralization of nature, he still regrets the loss of enchantment. In the enchanted worldview, miracles could happen, but in the mechanistic worldview that limits all events to natural cause and effect no miracles can be acknowledged. "The very idea of a supernatural miracle is nonsense," he writes.[6] And yet he misses the idea of miracle, so he brings it back. Dawkins ascribes the miraculous to reality as science sees reality. "The real world, as understood scientifically, has a magic of its own—the kind I call poetic magic: an inspiring beauty which is all the more magical because it is real and because we can understand how it works."[7] Both Nasr and Dawkins in their respective ways regret the expulsion of the supranatural (or supernatural) from the natural required by the mechanistic model of nature.

One more important thing. In addition to the removal of God from the mechanistic nexus of cause and effect, something else happened at the turn of the nineteenth century, namely, the discovery of historical relativism. Armed with critical consciousness, western historians could demonstrate that human meaning is culture-specific; that is, worldviews change over time. The modern world differs from the premodern world, they could observe, and these differences were said to be due to differing contexts. The doctrine of historical relativism sprouted and grew over time to become what is known today as *cultural relativism* or, for short, *pluralism*.

A difference between the world of the scientist and the world of the historian began to open up. Two types of truth emerged, one scientific and the other historical. Scientific truth is based on necessity, based on the mechanistic model. Historical truth, in contrast, is based on contingency; the historian describes without explaining the course of events in light of natural necessity. Philosopher Stephen Pepper notes the difference: "There is no necessity in historical truths. The historian describes events as they have occurred. . . . The scientist, on the other hand, is primarily interested in the laws of nature, and attends to events only because they exemplify the laws."[8] This distinction led two centuries ago to the division in Western universities between the natural sciences (*Wissenschaften*) and the humanities or historical sciences (*Geisteswissenschaften*). English language universities customarily include a college of sciences and a college of humanities, even if they add other professional schools or departments.

---

5. Seyyed Hosssein Nasr, *Religion and the Order of Nature* (Oxford: Oxford University Press, 1996), 7.

6. Richard Dawkins, *The Magic of Reality* (New York: Free Press, 2015), 256.

7. Ibid., 31.

8. Stephen C. Pepper, *World Hypotheses* (Berkeley: University of California Press, 1966), 182.

Among the postmodernists, the deconstructionist school has pressed the principle of relativity to such an extreme that the principle of universal reason becomes sacrificed. All reason is contextual, making all science contextual. Furthermore, scientific reason is accused of invisibly supporting the power position of the colonizers over against the colonized. By relativizing reason, deconstructionist postmodernists believe they are undercutting the foundation of Western power in geopolitics. The method is to lift up non-dominant knowledges (in the plural) as rebel knowledges. French deconstructionist Michael Foucault, for example, anticipates the "insurrection of subjugated knowledges."[9] By multiplying types of knowledge, the postmodernist can deconstruct the dominant mechanistic model.

Today's world historians may not be postmodern deconstructionists, but they have sharply separated themselves from their rationalist colleagues in the natural sciences.[10] Rationalist scientists think they can render explanatory judgments about the laws of nature that apply to the world clock for all times and all places, while relativist historians limit their judgments to specific cultural times in specific locations. Rational universalism and relative pluralism are two sisters within the single modern family.

Contingent View of Nature

The fourth and final model of nature is focused on the atom and what is inside the atom. Subatomic particles do not behave like gears in a clock. The mechanistic model must be abandoned by physicists when researching fundamental reality. Subatomic events cannot be exhaustively explained by antecedent causes. Fundamental physical processes do not obey laws of nature, at least not the laws that were formulated during the Newtonian era.

Photons or electrons within atoms are not individually predictable. They do not behave in a deterministic fashion, at least not individually. They do not behave like gears in a machine or hands on a clock. Statistically, however, over time and in large numbers, their behavior becomes predictable. For this reason,

---

9. Michel Foucault, *Power/Knowledge: Selected Interviews and Other Writings: 1972–1977*, ed. Colin Gordon (New York: Pantheon Books, 1980), 81.

10. Even though world historians recognize contextualization, relativity, and cultural diversity, they seek to sweep up diversity into a grand worldwide narrative. "Although it is important for students of world history to have a deep and nuanced understanding of each of the various cultures, states, and other entities that have been part of the vast mosaic of human history, the world historian stands back from these individual elements. . . . The world historian studies phenomena that transcend single states, regions, and cultures, such as cultural contact and exchange and movements that have had a global or at least a transregional impact. The world historian also often engages in comparative history, and in that respect might be thought of as a historical anthropologist." "What Is World History?" World History Association, *http://www.thewha.org/about-wha/what-is-world-history/*.

quantum physicists think of subatomic activity with the analogy of a wave rather than a particle. What they track is a quantity of particles in wave form. The term *quantum*, from the Latin *quantus* suggesting quantity, indicates that subatomic measurements take a probabilistic rather than a deterministic form. The specific behavior of a specific particle is contingent, so to speak, even if what the wave of many particles does is more predictable. We can only know in advance what quanta do, not what individuals do. In short, at the most fundamental level of physical reality, many scientists believe nature is contingent and not deterministic.

There is mystery at the quantum level. This is no license for prematurely re-enchanting nature, however. Mystery does not automatically translate into mysticism, even though some new spiritualities try to claim quantum mechanics as scientific confirmation of enchantment or even perennial dualism. Fearing an invasion of what some call "woo," many scientists take a defensive stance against roving bands of alleged pseudoscientists. "Quantum mechanics is a favorite subject of all varieties of pseudoscience. It is portrayed with a halo of mysticism that bears the signature of Qi, Daoism, Aryuveda, Karma, and many of the other Eastern mystical concepts that the promoters of woo can concoct," writes scientist Sadri Hassani at Illinois State University. He continues, "With mathematical precision, we can conclude that all particles—including atoms, subatomic particles, *and* (massless) photons—are material, and any science that studies them is, by its very nature, materialistic."[11] Note the final word, "materialistic." Is more than strict science going on here?

Materialism, naturalism, mysticism, and such are ideologies painted over the science; they are not science itself. The critical thinker keeps this distinction in mind. A scientific explanation tells us what happens within the material world, to be sure; but such a scientific explanation is insufficient reason to conclude that a materialist ideology is true. Such an "ism" constitutes a myth, according to the third definition. Of particular concern in this book will be the distinction between *science* and *scientism*, which will be given detailed attention in later chapters. For the time being, simply treat with critical suspicion any "ism."

At the observable level, such as waterfalls or erosion, Newton's mechanics still obtain. At the unobservable subatomic level, however, quantum contingency reigns. And although atoms may be small, they're everywhere. This means that at the unseen level, the physical world is contingent. (Later chapters will return to quantum contingency.) For the moment, the important point is that quantum physics attempts to study scientifically a reality that is invisible.

---

11. Sadri Hassani, "Post-Materialist Science? A Smokescreen for Woo," *Skeptical Inquirer* 39, no. 5 (September/October 2015): 38–41, at 41.

Naive Realism versus Critical Realism

Imagine sitting quietly on the seashore watching the sun set. It can be quite dramatic, even breathtaking. The white clouds turn orange, then pink. The Western sky lights up like a celestial fire. If you keep your eyes focused on the sun, the shining orb simply drops down behind the ocean's horizon. One moment you see it. The next, you don't. What happened to the sun? It appears to have fallen out of the sky! The fire-bright colors in the clouds remain for a few minutes, and fade away.

Our word for this phenomenon is *sunset*. To say the sun sets presupposes naive realism. The sun is real. When we say it sets, we are reporting exactly what we saw. What we saw truly happened. We can easily verify the accuracy of our claim by asking numerous other witnesses who watched exactly the same sunset. When we say, "I just saw the sun drop into the ocean," we mean the sun literally dropped into the ocean.

But we can also think about the sunset critically. After Copernicus discovered that the Earth orbits the sun and rotates on its axis, it became inaccurate to say that the sun sets. The Earth simply rotates so that the sun ceases to be in our field of vision. The sun does not exactly set. Rather, our western horizon moves in such a way as to hide the sun. Despite what we see, we know it is not factually true that the sun sets.

We do not actually perceive the Earth rotating on its axis, however. We know that it rotates only because someone taught us or because we participated in a science experiment that proved this to be the case. In our minds we can imagine the Earth rotating. We imagine that this rotation hides the sun from us. Furthermore, the physicists and our science teachers tell us this is a fact. If we believe the purported fact that the Earth rotates even though we see the sun set, then we are engaging in critical realism. If we are critical thinkers, we believe what we think rather than what we see. This is very important: *the critical realist believes what is thought rather than what is perceived.* It is this divorce from empirical perception toward mental conception that is the hallmark of contemporary science.

If thinking trumps perceiving, how then does a scientist proceed to perform empirical research? The scientist proceeds by constructing conceptual models. Such model construction relies on the assumptions of *critical realism*. According to Ian G. Barbour, "*Critical realism* must acknowledge both the creativity of [the human] mind and the existence of patterns in events that are not created by [a human's] mind. . . . Scientific language does not provide a replica of nature but a symbolic system that is abstract and selective and deals with limited aspects of the situation for particular purposes."[12] This approach to scientific knowing

---

12. Ian G. Barbour, *Issues in Science and Religion* (Englewood Cliffs, NJ: Prentice Hall, 1966), 172.

includes two significant assumptions: first, that an objective physical world exists independently from human subjectivity and, second, that human subjectivity constructs the picture of that world to hold in the mind. Perhaps this combination is inconsistent or unverifiable. Yet critical realism appears to provide the operative faith that propels the zeal of scientific researchers who are attempting to turn nature's mysteries into knowledge.

Scientists claim that their craft is empirical. But if one limits empirical knowledge to what is perceived by the five senses—sight, hearing, smell, touch, and taste—then it is apparent that this is not how scientists actually apply their craft. Sense knowledge is naive knowledge, belonging to compact consciousness. By interpreting sense experience through the filter of a conceptual model, scientists actually rely on critical realism to gain further knowledge. We have just reviewed how today's scientists work from one or both modern inclusive models of nature, Newtonian or classical mechanics and quantum contingency.

There is room for both naive realism and critical realism in daily life. There is no need to stop using the word "sunset" just because one has become a critical realist. One merely needs to remember that those scientists working behind telescopes or behind computer screens or in their laboratories are critical realists.

The Faith of the Scientist

The critical realist must proceed with faith that the real world exists and is rational. Once this faith commitment has been made, then he or she can face frustrations or discouragements while trusting that this unseen truth still holds. Without a basic faith in reason, the research scientist cannot proceed. Nobel Prize winning physicist Charles Townes does not shy away from labeling this scientific disposition faith. "Faith is necessary for the scientist even to get started . . . because he [or she] must have confidence that there is order in the universe, and that the human mind—in fact [one's] own mind—has a good chance of understanding this order. . . . In fact, it is just this faith in an orderly universe, understandable to [humankind], which allowed the basic change from an age of superstition to an age of science."[13] In short, science in general and critical realism in particular are built on faith in something unseen.

Yet that faith in something unseen can itself be subject to critical review. A healthy skepticism applies not only to scientific reasoning but to the foundations of such reasoning. "Skepticism is thus an essential component of inquiry and a necessary aspect of critical intelligence," says skeptic Paul Kurtz. "Without it, science and the development of human knowledge would not be possible. It is

---

13. Charles H. Townes, "The Convergence of Science and Religion," *Think* 32, no. 2 (March/April 1966): 2–7, at 4, available at *http://www.templetonprize.org/pdfs/THINK.pdf*.

both positive and creative."[14] The acceptance on faith of what is given alternates with skeptical self-criticism in a continuing spiral.

Openness to Transcendent Reality

"Sooner or later we all have to accept something as given," writes physicist Paul Davies, "whether it be God, or logic, or a set of laws, or some other foundation for existence. Thus ultimate questions will always lie beyond the scope of empirical science."[15] That is to say, natural science cannot ground itself. At the level of assumption or at the level of the first faith, the scientific method must recognize an openness to ultimacy that transcends it.

Critical consciousness in the human mind is evoked by the experience of transcendence. The term *transcendence* is used frequently in this book. On the one hand, it refers to a dimension in human consciousness that propels the human mind to go beyond, to search after what is beyond. On the other hand, the term *transcendence* refers also to what the human mind finds in this search. Or, to reverse it, some persons experience transcendent reality coming to them. A visit from transcendent reality may be shocking; but it reorients one's psyche and one's vision of what both the soul and the social order should be.

In itself, what the seeker of the beyond finds is not one object among others. Rather, transendent reality is non-objectifiable. It lies beyond the split between the subject and the object. An adequate anthropology must acknowledge that one characteristic of the human self is that it is open to what is beyond the self. We as human persons are fundamentally inclined to seek what is transcendent, a moral universe included. "Therefore we say: human beings are bodily creatures who have a fundamentally unlimited transcendentality and unlimited openness to being as such in knowledge and freedom," observes theologian Karl Rahner.[16]

An experience with transcendent mystery shocks human consciousness sufficiently to reorient one's view of history and the truth of history. According to Voegelin, "Truth is not a body of propositions about a world-immanent object; it is the world-transcendent *summum bonum* [ultimate good], experienced as an orienting force in the soul, about which we can speak only in analogical symbols."[17] When an individual person consciously opens himself or herself to

14. Paul Kurtz, *Transcendental Temptation: A Critique of Religion and the Paranormal* (Buffalo: Prometheus, 1984), 35.

15. Paul Davies, *The Mind of God: The Scientific Basis for a Rational World* (New York: Simon and Schuster, 1992), 15.

16. Karl Rahner, *Theological Investigations*, 22 vols. (London: Darton, Longman, and Todd, 1961–1976; New York: Seabury, 1974–1976; New York: Crossroad, 1976–1988), 21:42.

17. Eric Voegelin, *Order and History*, 5 vols. (Baton Rouge: Louisiana State University Press, 1956–1987), 3:363.

transcendental truth, he or she is already living in that truth. He or she is living in a religious version of critical consciousness.

Some Words about Words

In light of what has just been said, some comments about the use of certain words in forthcoming chapters are in order. The term *critical thinker* will, for the most part, refer to you, the reader, along with the mindset of the modern scientist, which carefully weighs alternatives—two or more thoughts at one time—before rendering a judgment. The word *axialist* will refer to one or more ancient sages or seers or other intellectual leaders during the first millennium BCE who exhibit a differentiation in consciousness because of a purported experience with transcendence. Some axialists exhibited critical thinking and, thereby, have directly contributed to modern thinking. The term *axial theorist* will refer to contemporary scholars who analyze the Axial Period, such as Karl Jaspers, Robert Bellah, Eric Voegelin, and Karen Armstrong. The term *perennialist* will refer to contemporaries who believe the *perennial philosophy*, a form of dualistic metaphysics based on the religion of the axialists. Perennialists include Aldous Huxley, Seyyed Hossein Nasr, and Huston Smith.

Conclusion

Why include this chapter on critical thinking? First, doing so helps to incorporate into this work of Cosmic History the sub-history of differentiation in human consciousness. Critical thinking in the modern era is decisive in this sub-history. Second, a review of critical thinking helps to show how the two periods within the modern era—the rational and the relative—combine to establish critical realism in the scientific method. Third, this excursus demonstrates that, because of critical realism, scientists do not make literal statements about realities they cannot perceive. What scientists say about physical reality is the product of the particular conceptual model that generates hypotheses, gathers evidence, and draws conclusions. Consequently, it would be premature for big historians to describe the history they construct as "literal." If science is not literal, then history based on that science cannot be literal either. The Big History that big historians construct is relative, just as any world historian or postmodern deconstructionist might have said in the first place.

Big History is itself contextual. Big historians represent one perspective among many. The Big History constructed by big historians is based on a set of presuppositions—a conceptual set or *myth* in the third use of the term—that does not include openness to transcendence. When people and cultures that claim an experience of transcendence become the object of the big historian's inquiry, the possibility of actual transcendence is tacitly ruled out in advance as an explanation. The invisibility of transcendent reality in Big History is due in large part to the conceptual presuppositions out of which the big historian works. In order to deal fairly with ancient or contemporary claims involving transcendence, the cosmic historian will have to interrogate history more critically than big historians do.

Critical thinking is a tool. Like other tools, it is used best when employed in building something of value or beauty. In this case, critical thinking is a tool to be used in building a human life characterized by integrity, thoughtfulness, and caring. Educators at the Carnegie Foundation place critical thinking within the larger framework of student formation. "So *a life of the mind for practice* means the cultivation of reflection and criticism, such as advocates of critical thinking promote, but not for the sake of reflecting and criticizing alone. Rather, the point of such cultivation is that students must learn to deliberate about their possibilities for a life well lived, including their responsibility to contribute to the life of their times."[18]

With critical thinking in mind, the next chapter returns to the big bang beginning of Cosmic History. It will look at the disagreements that lead to intellectual combat over the assumptions that make up the conceptual model of the big bang. It will become apparent that within the scientific discussion there is a war between those who wish to raise the question of God and those who wish to squelch it. The war is fought at the level of critical realism and the assumptions that structure the conceptual model. The next chapter will provide a critical analysis of big bang science and will ask how this story of origin could contribute to an honest, healthy, and meaningful worldview.

Review Questions

1. Before reading this chapter, what had been your understanding of *critical thinking*?
2. How did the mechanistic model of nature facilitate the rise of modern science?
3. Define critical thinking. How does it differ from other thinking?
4. Distinguish everyday naive realism from critical realism in science.

---

18. William M. Sullivan and Matthew S. Rosen, "Preface," in *A New Agenda for Higher Education: Shaping a Life of the Mind for Practics*, ed. William M. Sullivan and Matthew S. Rosen (San Francisco: Jossey-Bass, 2008), xvi.

Discussion Questions

1. How do you employ critical thinking in your academic study? How do you employ it elsewhere in your daily life?
2. If scientists operating within the quantum contingency model of nature are unable to perceive the objects of their study, how does reliance on critical realism prompt new research?
3. Given that subatomic phenomena such as electrons or photons are individually unpredictable yet still behave statistically in predictable patterns, ought one to think of nature as fundamentally deterministic? Indeterministic?
4. Speculate about human free will. Do you think indeterminism at the quantum level has any influence on what human beings experience as freedom?

Additional Resources

Print Sources

Barbour, Ian G. *Religion and Science: Historical and Contemporary Issues.* New York: Harper, 1997.

> The late Ian Barbour was the dean of the emerging field of science and religion. Barbour carefully delineates the historical and conceptual connections between the worldview of modern science and theological adaptations and critiques.

Huxley, Aldous. *The Perennial Philosophy.* London and Glasgow: Collins, 1946.

> This is the classic exposition of the perennial philosophy, a nickname applied to the transcendental insights rising out of the axial breakthrough. According to perennialists, a dualism between matter and spirit underlies all of the so-called higher religions. To say it another way, each religious tradition is allegedly a historically specific expression of a single underlying philosophy.

Murphy, Nancey C. *Reasoning and Rhetoric in Religion.* Valley Forge, PA: Trinity, 1994.

> Murphy, a professor of philosophical theology, brings the standards of rational thought to bear on religious reasoning. Chapter 9, "Reasoning in History," and chapter 10, "Reasoning in Biblical Studies," are especially pertinent.

Murphy, Nancey C., and George F. R. Ellis. *On the Moral Nature of the Universe: Theology, Cosmology, and Ethics.* Minneapolis: Fortress, 1996.

> This eye-opening treatment of cosmology grounds an ethic of love and passivism in the natural world as God is creating it. The key concept is *kenosis,*

referring to self-emptying love. See especially chapter 8, "Ethics and Theories of God."

Nasr, Seyyed Hossein. *Religion and the Order of Nature.* Oxford: Oxford University Press, 1996.

Nasr offers a critique of the mechanistic model of nature that dominates modern science from the perspective of a perennialist philosopher within Islam. Clearly and forcefully written. Most illuminating.

Peters, Ted, and Carl Peterson. "The Higgs Boson: An Adventure in Critical Realism," *Theology and Science* 11, no. 3 (August 2013): 185–207.

This article traces the discovery of the Higgs Boson as an example of critical realism at work in science.

Smith, Huston. *Beyond the Post-Modern Mind.* New York: Crossroad, 1982.

Smith expands on the perennial philosophy and argues that the mechanical model of modernity unnecessarily sacrifices the insights of religious dualism. The coming post-modern mind, Smith hopes, will retrieve the dualism lost by post-Newtonian physics.

Web Sources

"Defining Critical Thinking." The Critical Thinking Community. *http://www.criticalthinking.org/pages/defining-critical-thinking/766.*

A definition of critical thinking as the intellectually disciplined process of conceptualizing, applying, analyzing, synthesizing, and evaluating information as a guide to belief and action.

Gawande, Atul. "The Mistrust of Science." California Institute of Technology Commencement Address, June 10, 2016. *http://www.newyorker.com/news/news-desk/the-mistrust-of-science?mbid=social_facebook.*

In this address, Gawande defends what he believes to be genuine science against pseudo-science. To be a critical thinker is to look at each subject—to look at science itself—and entertain two or more perspectives before rendering a judgment.

11

CHAPTER

Fine Tuning, the Anthropic Principle, and the Multiverse

This is a place too fair

To be the child of Chance, and not of Care.

No atoms casually together hurl'd

Could e'er produce so beautiful a world.

—JOHN DRYDEN (1631–1700), "DESIGN"

Physicist Michio Kaku opens his new book, *The Future of the Mind*, with a near aphoristic statement: "The two greatest mysteries in all of nature are the mind and the universe." At this point Kaku turns to what big historians call the "big questions." Kaku adds: "Ever since our ancestors first gasped at the splendor of the starry sky, we have puzzled over those eternal questions: Where did it all come from? What does it all mean?"[1]

Recall that the cosmic historian asks the question of God in two modes. The first is to chronicle past events when cultures raised the question of God and suggested their own answers. Previous chapters discussed the ways foragers and farmers and early citizens identified divine powers with what modern people think of as natural forces. The second mode in which the historian addresses the question of God begins by asking, what is the ground of history? Is history all there is? Or is history grounded in a reality more fundamental, more ultimate? If so, then is this ultimate reality divine or not?

The second mode will occupy this chapter, which turns again to the story of the big bang. According to the big historian, the big bang belongs to nature's history. But locating the big bang within natural history does not in itself confront the fundamental question of existence: why is there something and not nothing? Why does this particular universe exist? What accounts for the physical reality within which human history takes place? Is the material universe ultimate, or penultimate?

---

1. Michio Kaku, *The Future of the Mind: The Scientific Quest to Understand, Enhance, and Empower the Mind* (New York: Doubleday, 2014), 1.

Many people in the present generation ask questions such as these: Why am I here? What is the meaning or purpose of my life in light of the history of an apparently impersonal cosmos? These are existential questions because they deal with the alternatives between existing and not existing or, as Hamlet put it, "To be or not to be? That is the question."

This chapter will approach such deeply personal and profoundly existential questions in the context of physical cosmology. By attempting to understand human beings in light of Cosmic History, the present chapter will pose the question of what lies beyond physical existence and will show how contingent history unavoidably raises the question of a necessary God. In this chapter, the theme of the book as a whole will be delineated.

The Anthropic Principle

Why are we on Earth at all? Was it inevitable from the time of the big bang that cosmic evolution would lead to biological evolution and eventually produce our species, *Homo sapiens*? Or was our arrival an accident? Did the universe at the beginning know we living creatures would be coming? Or are we human beings intruders of sorts in an otherwise impersonal or even hostile physical world? Does evolution have a built-in direction, purpose, *telos*, or endpoint?

What astounds physical cosmologists are the initial conditions framing the big bang already in the first seconds of cosmic expansion. The big bang appears to be finely tuned in such a way as to invite the formation of galaxies, stars, planets, and eventually people. This fine tuning has been called by physical cosmologists *the anthropic (cosmological) principle*. They key word here, *anthropos*, is Greek for human being. In short, the anthropic principle suggests that way back when the big bang banged the universe was preparing for us.

Logically, the anthropic principle can take two forms, a weak and a strong form. According to the weak anthropic principle, the initial conditions at the big bang made the eventual evolution of life *possible*, but not inevitable. According to the strong anthropic principle, the initial conditions at the big bang made the eventual evolution of life *inevitable*. It is important to note that the idea of weak and strong anthropic principles came from physical scientists, not theologians or mystics or New Age practitioners.

The anthropic principle in either its weak or strong form suggests that some intelligence designed the universe before it began. Could that designer be God? Some scientists are motivated to explain away both the weak and the strong anthropic principles so as to eliminate the question of God. Because the question of God arises from within the science of physical cosmology, the theologian should feel obligated to complement the science and address this question. Before doing so, it is necessary to detail the finely tuned initial conditions that give rise to the very concept of the anthropic principle.

When the big bang banged some 13.8 billion years ago, it had a starting point with specific initial conditions, the original parameters that would structure the universe. What is so significant here is that these initial conditions did not have to be what they were. They could have been otherwise. They were themselves contingent. Had even the slightest change in one of numerous initial conditions been different, then the history of the universe would have been different and unable to support the evolution of life or the emergence of intelligence, mind, and civilization. In other words, even the most modest alteration in the big bang would have meant that people would not be here to study the big bang.

For example, if gravity had been stronger or weaker by 1 part in 10^{30}, then life-sustaining stars such as the sun could not exist, making life impossible. Or if the initial explosion of the big bang had differed in strength by as little as 1 part in 10^{66}, the universe would have either collapsed or expanded too rapidly for stars to form; in either case, life would have been impossible. If the mass of neutrinos were 5×10^{-34} kg instead of 5×10^{-35} kg, then the additional gravitational mass would have resulted in a contracting rather than an expanding universe, making life impossible. The list of "accidents" or "convenient coincidences" goes on and on.

Numbers such as these astound scientists, who grasp their profound implications. "If gravity were stronger, stars would burn faster and die younger. . . . If electromagnetism were stronger, the electrical repulsion between protons would be greater, threatening the stability of atomic nuclei," speculates physicist Paul Davies,[2] who also compares the mass of neutrons with other particles. The ratio of the mass of the neutron to the mass of the proton is just slightly over one: 1.0013784170. Yet this tiny fraction makes the difference between life and no life. "The fact that the neutron's mass is coincidentally just a little bit more than the combined mass of the proton, electron, and neutrino is what enables free neutrons to decay. If the neutron were even *very* slightly lighter, it could not decay without an energy input of some sort . . . with disastrous consequences for life."[3] Princeton physicist Freeman Dyson is remembered widely for having opined, "As we look out into the universe and identify the many accidents of physics and astronomy that have worked together to our benefit, it almost seems as if the universe must in some sense have known we were coming."[4]

2. Paul Davies, *The Goldilocks Enigma* (Boston: Houghton Mifflin, 2006), 143.

3. Ibid., 145. The concept of the anthropic principle has been developed by Brandon Carter, "Large Number Coincidences and the Anthropic Principle in Cosmology," in *Confrontation of Cosmological Theories with Observational Data*, ed. M. S. Longair, IAU Symposia 63 (Dortrecht, Netherlands: Reidel, 1974); and by John Barrow and Frank J. Tipler, *The Anthropic Cosmological Principles* (Oxford: Oxford University Press, 1986). Actually, there are multiple variants. The strong anthropic principle holds that the initial conditions require that life eventually evolve. The weak anthropic principle holds that the initial conditions merely make it possible for life to eventually evolve. Davies embraces the weak anthropic principle but not the strong anthropic principle.

4. Freeman Dyson, *Disturbing the Universe* (New York: Harper, 1979), 250.

This looks like design. Who would be the designer? Did God engineer the initial conditions of the universe so that the big bang would lead from nothing to everything, including the Earth and human beings? Oxford University theologian Alister McGrath provides an affirmative answer: "God, then, unquestionably represents a plausible explanation of anthropic phenomena."[5]

Scientific questions leading to theological answers arise first from within physical cosmology. If a scientist would remain strictly within the conceptual set or myth of materialism and naturalism, the most he or she could say scientifically is that the initial conditions were contingent. That is, the initial conditions were a lucky accident that made our particular natural history possible and the evolution of life possible. The initial conditions were due to happenstance, randomness, luck. Despite this demur, these anthropic *physical* observations provide the empirical data that give rise to the question of teleology, to the question of meaning.

The Battle over Divine Design

"No design is possible!" trumpet defensive naturalists. No teleology or direction or meaning is allowed inside the cosmological door of science! There must be another explanation, a scientific explanation that would eliminate design. Multiverse theory provides that alternative explanation.

Martin Rees, renowned British physical cosmologist, illustrates the logic at work here. Rees can list the lucky coincidences that lead to the anthropic principle. But, even though the anthropic principle raises the question of God from within science, Rees wants to sidestep the God question. He offers a substitute explanation, called the *many worlds interpretation* version of multiverse theory.

Faced with the facts describing the role of the anthropic principle in making our universe biophilic,[6] Rees considers three alternative explanations: happenstance, God, or the multiverse. Rees says he finds the first option unreasonable and the second one unnecessarily religious, so he opts for the third. "We can conjecture that our universe is a specially favored domain in a still vaster multiverse."[7] In Rees's logic, happenstance or chance cannot provide an explanation;

5. Alister E. McGrath, *A Fine-Tuned Universe: The Quest for God in Science and Theology*, 2009 Gifford Lectures (Louisville: Westminster John Knox, 2009), 121.

6. That is, tending toward life.

7. Martin J. Rees, "Living in a Multiverse," in *The Far Future Universe: Eschatology from a Cosmic Perspective*, ed. George F. R. Ellis (Philadelphia: Templeton, 2002), 65–85, at 66. Baylor physicist Gerald Cleaver, in an unpublished talk, disconnects multiverse theory from M theory, if M theory means M(embrane) theory. The two are not equivalent. Multiverses are a prediction of other theories besides M(embrane) theory. See discussion of M theory in the work of Stephen Hawking below. Cleaver goes on: "For me, the key aspect is these three explanations are not mutually exclusive. Rees is using erroneous logic in doing so. It's not either A or B or C; just as we now accept that it's not *either God or evolution*, but instead is *God and evolution as method of creation*. I think to accept the

either would be unreasonable. Happenstance only dramatizes the contingency, while a scientific explanation looks for an antecedent cause. Could God provide that antecedent cause? No. The idea of God's design leads one from physics to metaphysics, so this must be rejected because it connotes religion. Therefore, he argues, we have to look for another explanation for the anthropic principle. The idea of the multiverse provides a specifically scientific candidate for explanation. But, we ask here: is the multiverse really scientific?

The basic idea of a multiverse was not developed simply as an anti-religious device to rid us of a unique universe. The concept of the multiverse has made good sense to cosmologists trying to describe what happened during the period of inflation.[8] Yet multiverse theory provides opportunity to eliminate the God hypothesis. What is significant here is this: the anthropic principle within physics compels the cosmologist to ask the question of God. The God question arises naturally from within scientific discussion. Now, let us look at bit more closely at the negative answer.

The Principle of Plenitude versus the Principle of Contingency

The postulation of multiple universes is based on a philosophical assumption that denies the finality of contingent events for defining nature. This assumption is built on the *principle of plenitude*. Basically, the principle of plenitude says

---

claim that the three are exclusive conditions plays into the hands of the New Atheists. I also see happenstance as something that depends on perspective. Looking from within creation forces us to base occurrences on probabilities, which may at times suggest happenstance, but a sense of happenstance should likely disappear from a transcendent view."

8. Lawrence M. Krauss at Arizona State University claims there is evidence of the multiverse. Interpreting the BICEP2 (Background Imaging of Extragalactic Polarization 2) experiment, Kraus contends that during inflation (prior to 380,000 years after the big bang) quantum fluctuations in the gravitational field would have been amplified into gravitational waves, rippling the fabric of space-time. The effect would be a polarization of the CMB (Cosmic Microwave Background produced at 380,000 years); and evidence of this polarization can be found in BICEP2. According to Krauss, this opens the possibility of Andre Linde's concept of "eternal inflation" plus the ongoing creation of many universes. Feeling the need to write off the anthropic principle as "pompously . . . abhorrent," he says one of the results of BICEP2 "may be that the inflationary transition producing our observed universe requires Linde's eternal inflation. In this case, while we may never be able to directly observe other universes, we will be as confident of their existence as our predecessors in the early 20th century were of the existence of atoms." Lawrence M. Krauss, "A Beacon from the Big Bang," *Scientific American* 311, no. 4 (October 2014): 59–67, at 67. In short, no empirical evidence of a second or third universe exists, yet Kraus may be confident that they exist if one remembers the theory of the atom and if one finds the anthropic principle pompously abhorrent. As it turns out, the BICEP2 has been discredited. The reported gravity waves allegedly supporting wild inflation turned out to be cosmic dust. The data was fine, but the interpretation was wrong. Bob Berman, "Multiverses: Science or Science Fiction," *Astronomy* 43, no. 9 (September 2015): 28–33, at 33. The abhorrent anthropic principle may still be viable.

that every potential becomes actualized. If hikers in a forest come to a fork in the path, they have a choice. They can take the one on the left or the one on the right. If they take one and not the other, this action is contingent on a free decision. According to the principle of plenitude, in contrast, the one group of hikers takes both. In one universe they take the left fork. In another universe they take the right one. By multiplying universes so that every potential gets actualized, the scientist can eliminate contingency and happenstance right along with design. Everything looks causally determined, in this view. Everything fits the mechanical model and avoids the quantum contingency model. Does multiverse theory sound like science fiction? Some scientists take the idea of many universes quite seriously.

Translated into contemporary physical cosmology, the resulting multiverse hypothesis posits that all mathematically possible universes become actualized. Wherever a potential event is found, it happens. If every potential does not get actualized within our universe, then there must exist another universe or an array of universes where this actualization takes place. So goes the logic of multiverse theory.

The multiverse idea is uncompromisingly mechanistic and deterministic, expelling the idea that contingency could be real. If multiple universes follow one another in sequence or parallel one another in time, then there is room for every potential to get actualized. In many of the parallel universes there exists another you and another me, but with slightly different traits. This undercuts the idea that we are special or lucky or blessed or even unique.

Oddly, the principle of plenitude is a discarded medieval theological axiom. Some medieval theologians believed that God actualizes every divine potential.[9] Curiously, in science, this long-outdated, premodern religious idea has been dusted off and silently invoked in secular circles to support multiverse theory.

What motivates multiverse theorists is the desire to import Newton's mechanistic model into both the atom and the cosmic singularity and, thereby, rid themselves of the pesky problem of quantum contingency. One of the reasons the theologians had previously dumped the principle of plenitude was that it raised the specter of determinism and took away human freedom. With multiverse theory, determinism is back and human freedom becomes a delusion.

Thus there are two principles at issue. The *principle of plenitude* asserts that every potential becomes actualized, eventually if not immediately. Applied to the anthropic principle, the potential for living creatures on a Goldilocks planet will eventually get actualized just as the potential for an impersonal or hostile physical universe will also get actualized, but in a universe separate from ours. The *principle of contingency*, in contrast, assumes that some potentials become actualized but others do not. If one affirms the principle of contingency, one

9. Most theologians today discard the principle of plenitude and embrace contingency, however.

affirms that what actually exists in our universe is only one possibility among other unactualized possibilities. The way things are is the product of past contingent actual events. Things could have happened differently, but they happened this way; and this accounts for the actual universe in which we live. This warrants treating nature as historical.

Today's big historians and cosmic historians along with world historians rely on the principle of contingency, according to which every historical event is a one-time-only contingent event. One who affirms the principle of plenitude is a *determinist*. One who affirms the principle of contingency is an *indeterminist*. Note that both principles—plenitude and contingency—are philosophical principles that inform science but, in themselves, are not the conclusions of science. They are assumptions at work before scientific theorizing is pursued. It appears that Rees and his colleagues affirm multiverse theory in order to support their prior philosophical commitment to determinism.

If a scientist desires to postulate determinism to describe reality, then contingency must be eschewed and something like the principle of plenitude invoked. This extra-scientific commitment provides the basis for the theory of multiple universes. The logic goes like this: because each potential pathway of a subatomic particle is taken, and because only one of these paths is taken in our universe, it follows that there must exist other universes where the other potentials get actualized. The collection of all of these universes is called the *multiverse*. As one might imagine, this number of universes within the multiverse would be very large. This number would have to be enormous if every potential for every historical event becomes actualized.

Proponents of string or M theory (variants on the multiverse theory) believe they are assembling evidence to support the multiverse idea, even if as yet their argument has not proven persuasive. Like Rees, Cambridge physicist Stephen Hawking enthusiastically embraces M-Theory. We might ask: just what is M-Theory? "No one seems to know what the 'M' stands for," writes Hawking; "but it may be 'master,' 'miracle,' or 'mystery.' It seems to be all three."[10] After this

---

10. Stephen Hawking and Leonard Mlodinow, *The Grand Design* (New York: Bantam, 2010), 117. In contrast to Hawking's suggestions, in searching for the origin of the term "M-Theory," it appears that within the string/M-Theory community (which originated the term) "M" stands for membrane. Mary-Jane Rubenstein asserts that, configured *spatially*, an infinite number of different worlds would be "separated either by gargantuan expanses of ordinary space-time or by a rapidly expanding sea of energy." Configured *temporally*, one universe or a part of a universe collapses in order to form a new universe, "a process repeated throughout infinite time." The many-worlds interpretation configuration is based on quantum mechanics, "which suggests that the universe separates into different branches every time a subatomic particle decides on a position." Mary-Jane Rubenstein, *Worlds without End: The Many Lives of the Universe* (New York: Columbia University Press, 2104), 6. According to Rubenstein, M-Theory represents "the merging of scientific developments and philosophical expedience . . . a way out of the fine-tuning problem" (p. 17). The many-worlds interpretation configuration most directly relies upon the principle of plenitude, a deterministic view holding that every potential must become actualized.

somewhat confusing introduction, Hawking proceeds to assert that "the Laws of M-Theory therefore allow for *different universes* with different apparent laws."[11]

Hawking supports the philosophical position identified above as determinism. He explicitly advocates what he calls "scientific determinism" this way: "Given the state of the universe at one time, a complete set of laws fully determines both the future and the past. This would exclude the possibility of miracles or an active role for God. . . . A scientific law is not a scientific law if it holds only when some supernatural being decides not to intervene."[12] The cosmic determinism espoused by Hawking applies to the earliest big bang universe as well as to everyday mental activity. It derives not from scientific evidence but rather from Hawking's conceptual set, what we earlier dubbed a "myth." Must such a deterministic interpretation of physics reign unchallenged?

If we could demythologize or deconstruct the science here, then we would discover consonance between the anthropic principle and a biblical understanding of God as creator. "For the theist," observes McGrath, "unsurprisingly these observations point to the inherent potentiality with which the Creator has endowed creation."[13]

The God question arises spontaneously out of cosmology because appeal to a divine designer makes sense in light of the anthropic principle. But this appeal to a divine designer relies to a large extent on the idea that our universe is contingent, unique, or one of a kind. By positing many universes each with its own deterministic laws, the uniqueness of our universe goes away and so does the awe many people feel in response to the idea of finely tuned initial conditions.

Determinism versus Free Will

More difficulties challenge the deterministic model of our cosmos. What most humans experience every day simply does not fit the deterministic universe described by Rees or Hawking. Most humans experience themselves as sentient human persons with a lively interior life. Each person enjoys subjectivity, an inner mental and emotional self-understanding. In addition, individuals experience human freedom. What is called *freedom* is a combination of deliberation, decision, and action. When we deliberate, we think through alternatives. When we decide, we choose to actualize one potential and let the other options go. When we act, the course of history is affected. One's action changes things. At the level of everyday human freedom, it is obvious that the world includes contingency plus freely willed action. Without contingency and free will, there would be no history.

---

11. Hawking and Mlodinow, *Grand Design*, 118.

12. Ibid., 30.

13. McGrath, *Fine-Tuned Universe*, 120.

Just who deliberates, decides, and acts? You and I do. Each of us is a person. Each of us is a self. What we know as our daily freedom is a form of self-determination. We are not totally predetermined by external physical processes. As a self, we become a determiner. We add self-determination to the big history of the universe. Did fine tuning at the big bang make our daily freedom possible according to the weak anthropic principle? Did it make freedom inevitable, according to the strong anthropic principle? Is our human free will a gift from a contingent cosmic evolution?

One's free action is in principle unpredictable by an external viewer. Nevertheless, this free activity is embedded in human experience. Does this daily experience of freedom fit into the determined universe described by Rees and Hawking? If the determinists win this argument, then the freedom you and I experience will become a mere delusion.

How one views the original big bang and how one views daily free decision-making come together in a single package, a single reality begging for an explanation. The impact of Cosmic History is felt within our very psyche.

Determinism versus Contingency

Not every physical cosmologist accepts M-Theory or its determinism. According to George Ellis, mathematician, cosmologist, and co-author with Hawking in scientific research, we live in an *underdetermined* world.[14] Our daily life is not totally contingent, to be sure; we don't live in chaos. Yet our universe is underdetermined in the sense that some—not all—events resist being explained exhaustively by their antecedent causes. Some events exhibit contingency, randomness, chance. "Irreducible randomness occurs in physics at the quantum level, thereby influencing cosmology and the existence of life on Earth. If it were not for this randomness, we would be stuck in the vice of determinism and outcomes would be limited and uninteresting. But it is there, as part of the design of the universe."[15] Randomness, says Ellis, insures that the physical universe escapes the vice grip of the exhaustive determinism implied in the Newtonian model.

For Ellis, three kinds of causation characterize the universe in its micro (sub-atomic) and macro (big bang, galaxies) scope: necessity, purpose, and chance. *Necessity* identifies the constants, the non-contingent dimension of reality. Necessity "has an inexorable impersonal quality. It is the heart of physics and

14. George F. R. Ellis and Stephen S. Hawking, *The Large Scale Structure of Space-Time* (Cambridge, UK: Cambridge University Press, 1973).

15. George F. R. Ellis, "Necessity, Purpose, and Chance: The Role of Randomness and Indeterminism in Nature from Complex Macroscopic Systems to Relativistic Cosmology," in *The Providence of God in the Randomness of Nature: Scientific and Theological Perspectives*, ed. Robert John Russell and Joshua M. Moritz (Philadelphia: Templeton, 2017), forthcoming.

chemistry. It can be successfully described by mathematical equations." At the human level, we experience more than necessity; we experience a partially open future to be filled with purposive action. *Purpose* "is the core of human being, as well indeed of all life. All living entities embody some kind of purpose or function in their structure and actions." Finally, *chance* "embodies the idea of randomness, implying a lack of purpose or meaning. Things just happen that way, not because it's inevitable, but because it's possible, and maybe probable. It is prevalent in the real universe because of the large number of unrelated causes that influence events, and in particular because of the vast numbers of micro-events that underlie all macroscopic outcomes. All three kinds of causation occur in an intricate interplay in the real universe."[16] The universe is partially determined, to be sure; but some level of contingency is operative all the way from subatomic quantum physics to free human decision-making.

What happens at the subatomic or quantum level and what happened at the big bang both prepare the physical stage for the drama of meaning in our experience of human subjectivity. Ellis writes, "There is much evidence that molecular machinery in biology is designed to use that randomness to attain its desired results. . . . This is true also in terms of macro levels of behaviour, and in particular as regards how the brain functions. . . . Randomness is harnessed through the process of adaptive selection, which allows higher levels of order and meaning to emerge. It is then a virtue, not a vice; it allows purpose to be an active agent by selecting desired outcomes from a range of possibilities."[17] In sum, selected outcomes by a thinking self take advantage of quantum randomness, and the thinking self is thereby prepared to interpret meaning at the subjective level. In other words, our brain activity includes subatomic quantum activity, which is indeterministic. This indeterminism in our physical substrate makes possible freedom within our subjectivity.

In human freedom, the person or the centered self determines which potentials get actualized. The range of potentials is constrained, to be sure, by physical conditions. One cannot decide to fly without wings, for example, but one can decide whether to walk or run. A range of potentials becomes options for the self's deliberation and decision.

The freedom we experience on a daily basis appears to follow a pattern: deliberation, decision, and action. What we call *freedom* is in fact *self-determination*. What the self decides determines what will take place in the physical world. What the self determines becomes the stuff of history. Rather than simply carrying out the orders of a predetermined causal sequence, the self freely makes decisions and takes actions, which in turn determine the course of events. The self determines; this is what *human freedom* means.

---

16. Ibid.
17. Ibid.

University of California at Berkeley physicist Henry Stapp centers free human decision-making in the organism, in what this chapter has called the *person* or the *self.* "The intricate interplay of chance and determinism instituted by quantum mechanics effectively frees the organism to pursue, in an optimal way, its own goals based on its own values, which have themselves been created, from a wealth of open possibilities, by its own earlier actions."[18] Placing choices within a scale of the organism's values provides the garden within which meaning grows; and this garden was first planted by quantum physical principles. The key is that some individual events are not predetermined, even if they are determined by the action of a free self.

Has Cosmic Evolution Determined That We Would Be Free?

Why must one go back to the big bang or to subatomic physics to look for contingency? Because physical contingency is a precursor to human freedom. "The contingency of events may be the basic reality of nature," comments theologian Wolfhart Pannenberg.[19] Contingency in nature makes human freedom possible. Does it make human freedom inevitable? If we opt for the strong anthropic principle, then we might say that *cosmic evolution determined that we would be free.* Is this an unavoidable paradox?

The alternative is to deny both contingency in nature and free will in human life. Denying contingency at the physical level turns freedom at the human level into an illusion, at least according to Hawking. "The molecular basis of biology shows that biological processes are governed by the laws of physics and chemistry and therefore are as determined as the orbits of the planets. Recent experiments in neuroscience support the view that it is our physical brain, following the known laws of science, that determines our actions, and not some agency that exists outside those laws. . . . It is hard to imagine how free will can operate if our behavior is determined by physical law, so it seems that we are no more than biological machines and that free will is just an illusion."[20] Hawking here wants to appeal to physical or chemical laws that predetermine what an individual human subjectivity would decide, thereby making self-determination into an illusion. What is hard for Hawking to imagine is that there exists such a thing as subjectivity, a human self, an act of self-determination. Even though it is hard

---

18. Henry P. Stapp, "The Hard Problem: A Quantum Approach," in *Explaining Consciousness: The Hard Problem*, ed. Jonathan Shear (Cambridge, MA: MIT Press, 1997), 197–216, at 211.

19. Wolfhart Pannenberg, "Contributions from Systematic Theology," in *The Oxford Handbook of Religion and Science*, ed. Philip Clayton and Zachary Simpson (Oxford: Oxford University Press, 2006), 359–71, at 361.

20. Hawking and Mlodinow, *Grand Design*, 32.

for Hawking to imagine, this is what we experience every day as an indisputable datum within our subjective apperception of reality.

In summary, contingency in the physical world is a necessary condition for free will in the human world. Without contingency and indeterminism at the physical level, we could not experience freedom as self-determination at the human level. Nevertheless, contingency is not a sufficient condition for explaining all the complexities that make up our human situation. At this point scientists are unable to trace all the steps from subatomic indeterminate electron movement up to the biosphere, then to the mind, then to our daily subjective experience. Emergent properties at the human level have not to date been explained on the basis of previous causes. One evolutionary emergent is human subjectivity, the human self that deliberates, decides, and takes action. Though emergent, human subjectivity remains grounded in the fundamental physical processes of our natural and historical world going all the way back to the initial conditions present at the big bang. Yes, it appears that the big bang somehow knew we were coming.

The Big Bang Asks the Question of God

Jewish theologian Daniel Matt poses the question we ask here: "Does the big bang, which serves as the scientific creation myth of our culture, have anything to do with God?"[21] The God question arises out of the science like water and steam arise from Old Faithful in Yellowstone Park.

This chapter has reviewed a number of unsettled controversies within big bang science: the weak anthropic principle versus the strong anthropic principle, determinism versus indeterminism, one contingent universe versus a determined multiverse, happenstance versus design, and meaning versus meaninglessness. It is not necessary for the theologian asking the question of God to decide which side of each scientific controversy should win. All the theologian needs to show is that various scientific pictures of the early universe leave room to include the question of divine action in the natural world. The concept of God as creator is consonant with the natural world as science describes it, at least most of the time. Because various scientific models gain ground or fall behind as research progresses, adroit theologians should not base their theology on just one scientific theory.

Rees and other physical cosmologists recognize that the question of God is raised side-by-side with happenstance and multiverse theories as a possible explanation for the origin of our cosmos. This is the take-away point: asking the question of God makes scientific sense within big bang theory. Affirming God as creator is plausible. It is so plausible that some physical cosmologists go to

21. Daniel C. Matt, *God and the Big Bang*, 2nd ed. (Woodstock, VT: Jewish Lights, 2016), xi.

exaggerated lengths just to exclude the divine explanation. For some scientists and their disciples among the big historians, positing the theory of the multiverse provides an alternative to addressing the God question. The God question in part generates the anti-God theory of the multiverse. This being the case, perhaps Cosmic History should address the God question without compunction.

How should Cosmic History approach the question of God? Should cosmic historians ask, did a divine engineer design the initial conditions? In effect, did God light the fuse on the big bang? The problem with formulating the question of God this way is that these formulations are partially oblique. They presuppose that God is one physical cause among others. Asking whether God is one cause among others within the universe might divert us down a blind alley. God's action in the natural world does not routinely take the form of one physical cause among others. This leads Cambridge physicist-theologian John Polkinghorne to aver, "The question of the significance of the anthropic principle is a scientific *metaquestion;* that is to say it arises from the insights of scientific cosmology but goes beyond what science alone is competent to discuss."[22] In other words, even if God is responsible for the big bang, God should not be thought of as one deterministic cause among others.

The Cosmological Argument for God's Existence

Such discussions regarding the big bang and the anthropic principle provide modern people with an opportunity to engage in a persisting premodern argument regarding the existence of God. One version born in early Islam, the *kalam* argument, has matured and been taken up by a contemporary Christian apologist, William Lane Craig. Here is the argument in a nutshell:[23]

1. Whatever begins to exist has a cause
2. The universe began to exist.
3. Therefore, the universe has a cause.
   This cause is God.

How might this premodern argument fit with the big bang and the anthropic principle? Does big bang cosmology require appeal to the existence of God as a cosmic first cause to be coherent?

It appears that the first premise—everything that begins has a cause—relies on an assumption shared by Newtonian mechanics, namely, every effect has a

---

22. John Polkinghorne, *Beyond Science: The Wider Human Context* (Cambridge, UK: Cambridge University Press, 1996), 89.

23. William Lane Craig, "The Kalam Cosmological Argument," Reasonable Faith with William Lane Craig, *http://www.reasonablefaith.org/transcript-kalam-cosmological-argument.*

cause. Philosophers refer to this assumption as the *causal principle* or sometimes as the *principle of sufficient reason*. This is an assumption, not a conclusion based upon science, even if scientists appeal to it.

The second premise—the universe has a beginning—seems to be corroborated with the big bang story of origin, including the anthropic principle regarding initial conditions at the big bang. Even if some physical scientists rail and flail against the argument's conclusion, they recognize that the God question arises here. So it appears fair in the *kalam* argument to ask, what caused the initial conditions and who lit the fuse on the big bang? Does appeal to a divine engineer make the big bang story coherent?

If the first two premises obtain, then the conclusion regarding a creator God is soundly argued. But what if the universe is viewed through the lenses of quantum contingency rather than the mechanistic lens?

The contingency principle refuses to permit the principle of sufficient reason to explain certain events, especially subatomic events. Actual events are underdetermined, that is, their causal past only partially explains why these particular events occur. For the *kalam* argument to be sound, it must interpolate an amendment to the first premise: contingent events are exhaustively determined by their causal past. The problem with such an amendment, however, is that it would undercut the very nature of contingency. It would replace contingency with determinism. It would reduce quantum contingency to Newtonian mechanics. If quantum contingency is observable in the physics laboratory, it must remain standing as a feature of our physical universe. Quantum contingency rightfully belongs as a premise in the cosmological argument, not a closed determinism.

In sum, the *kalam* argument to explain the big bang story of origin by appeal to a creator God works much better within the Newtonian mechanistic model than it would in the quantum contingency model of nature. When one takes quantum contingency into consideration, the *kalam* argument becomes oblique; that is, by treating God as one cause among others, it misformulates the question of God.

What is a better way to formulate the question of God? A theory of divine action that works within a quantum framework would not require God to intervene in nature as one cause among others. Rather, God could work in, with, and through quantum processes without breaking the cause-effect nexus. Because quantum processes are everywhere, any action God takes at the quantum level affects physical reality everywhere. God could act at the quantum level and influence the course of physical events without functioning as one cause among others or without breaking any laws of nature.

Here is why this discussion is important: if one works from within the quantum model then the concept of divine creation could be rendered consonant with the multiverse as easily as with the big bang. According to astronomer Carr, it is not necessary for "the existence of a multiverse to preclude God since there is no reason why a Creator should not act through the multiverse."[24] Although the big bang theory immediately appears to be consonant with a biblical view of divine creation, this does not preclude consonance between multiverse theory and divine action. In either case, the question of God becomes reasonable to ask.

Criticism of the Cosmological Argument

Physicist Paul Davies asserts that the traditional cosmological argument—the *kalam* argument—falls short of proving that appeal to God is necessary to explain the big bang, the anthropic principle, or other events in the history of the universe.

> Even granted the cosmological argument so far—that the universe must have a cause—there is a logical difficulty in attributing that cause to God, for it could then be asked 'What caused God?' The response is usually "God does not need a cause. He is a *necessary* being, whose cause is to be found within himself.' But the cosmological argument is founded on the assumption that everything requires a cause, yet ends in the conclusion that at least one thing (god) does not require a cause. The argument seems to be self-contradictory.[25]

To ask what caused God only pushes the question of the necessary first cause back a stage. This is strictly a logical move on Davies part. It does not acknowledge a relevant premise, namely, empirical knowledge of the past stops at the big bang. So it is the necessary ground of the big bang that is being asked about here, not the abstract logic of an infinite regress of "What caused . . . ?" questions. In short, Davies's rhetorical question is a bit of a cheap shot. The cosmological argument is not self-contradictory. What the cosmological argument successfully provides is a plausible warrant for a necessary being to set the initial conditions of a Newtonian cosmos.

Whether the argument is self-contradictory or not, the appeal to God is plausible. It is plausible to nominate God as the necessary being needed to ground the contingent existence of the cosmos, in the first place, as well as contingency within Cosmic History, in the second place. The question of God has arisen within the context of physical cosmology, as the preceding review of the discussion among physicists has shown. The existence of a creator God is consonant with what else we know about the big bang and its initial conditions. A big bang cosmogony with God as the big banger would be coherent, given the data.

24. Bernard Carr, "Cosmology and Religion," in *The Oxford Handbook of Religion and Science*, ed. Clayton and Simpson (Oxford: Oxford University Press, 2006), 139–55, at 153.

25. Paul Davies, *God and the New Physics* (New York: Simon and Schuster, 1983), 37.

Does this mean the cosmological argument has successfully proven the existence of God? No, not quite. What the cosmological argument does accomplish, however, is to demonstrate consonance between belief in God and affirmation of big bang cosmology.

Anne Clifford, cited in an earlier chapter, adds one additional caution, namely, it might be unwise for any theologian to tie *creatio ex nihilo* too tightly to a specific scientific theory regarding the origin of the universe. Even if scientific theories change, which they do regularly, the concept of God as creator remains constant. "It is unwise for the church or its theologians to equate any scientific theory of the universe's beginning with the ancient doctrine of creation *ex nihilo*. . . . *Creatio ex nihilo* is a doctrine about God who freely chose to create and of the dependence on God for existence."[26] Even though attributing the big bang to a divine creative act is scientifically plausible, the doctrine of *creatio ex nihilo* derives solely from divine revelation and theological reflection. The big bang cosmogony may very well raise the question of God, but appeal to special revelation would be necessary to answer it.

Conclusion

Philosopher of Religion Mary-Jane Rubenstein nicely sums up the point of this chapter: "Modern multiverse theorists proclaim an infinite number of worlds in part to avoid the conclusion that this world somehow was designed for us. . . . In short, the multiverse does away with the need for a creator-god."[27] Physical cosmologists have been compelled by the evidence to ask the question of God, and they have elected to say, "No." But the question of God has been unavoidable, even within science. The cosmic historian has good reason to raise the God question.

If big bang cosmology is to contribute to a healthy, robust, and meaningful worldview for modern and postmodern culture, it is necessary to ask disciples of anti-God scientism to withdraw their patent application for exclusive knowledge regarding cosmic beginnings. Whether atheists like it or not, they must share this cosmos with the religious family next door. Can materialists be persuaded to make room for honestly asking the God question?

Review Questions

1. Why do the initial conditions at the big bang astound today's scientists?
2. What is the relationship between quantum contingency and human freedom?

---

26. Anne M. Clifford, "Creation," in *Systematic Theology: Roman Catholic Perspectives*, ed. Francis Schüssler Fiorenza and John P. Galvin, 2nd ed. (Minneapolis: Fortress, 2011), 201–53, at 231.

27. Rubenstein, *Worlds without End*, 207.

3. What is the logic behind positing the existence of multiple universes?

4. How do these terms relate: *determinism* and *contingency?*

Discussion Questions

1. How does the question of God raised by the anthropic cosmological principle spark a fight between two models of nature, the mechanistic model and the quantum contingency model?

2. Does the question of God raised by the anthropic cosmological principle resonate with any of your religious or spiritual sensibilities?

3. Do you find the determinism of the multiverse theory credible? Satisfying? Necessary?

4. Do you think religious believers should pay any attention to these discussions within science? Why, or why not?

Additional Resources

Print Sources

Berman, Bob. "Multiverses: Science or Science Fiction." *Astronomy* 43, no. 9 (September 2015): 28–33.

> In this winsome and clearly written article, Berman catalogs versions of the multiverse fad in physics: inflations versions, the many worlds interpretation, string theory, BICEP2, and others. "A big problem many critics cite," notes Berman, "is that multiverse models don't predict anything, and thus they allow everything." Good reading.

Davies, Paul. *The Mind of God: The Scientific Basis for a Rational World.* New York: Simon and Schuster, 1992.

> Davies is one of the most lucid interpreters of contemporary physics in light of philosophical and theological questions. He provides an insightful analysis of the cosmological argument in light of the anthropoic principle and quantum contingency (pp. 200–205).

Hawking, Stephen, and Leonard Mlodinow. *The Grand Design.* New York: Bantam, 2010.

> Hawking is perhaps the world's most celebrated theoretical physicist. In this accessible book, Hawking expands on the idea of the multiverse and touts its virtues. He illustrates the passion some scientists exhibit when pursuing a deterministic, even Newtonian, model of nature.

Moritz, Joshua M. *Science and Religion: Beyond Warfare and Toward Understanding.* Winona, MN: Anselm Academic, 2015.

In chapter 5, "Creation and the Cosmos," Moritz provides a thorough and informative analysis of the anthropic principle debate as well as other implications of scientific cosmology for religious belief.

Russell, Robert John. *Cosmology from Alpha to Omega.* Minneapolis: Fortress, 2008.

Russell offers the most thorough examination of quantum contingency in both subatomic physics and the big bang, and he draws out implications for divine action in the material world. Russell contends that God acts in, with, and through quantum dynamics without breaking any laws of nature. His position is dubbed *non-interventionist objective divine action*, or NIODA.

Web Sources

"Cosmological Argument." *Stanford Encyclopedia of Philosophy* (2012). *http:// plato.stanford.edu/entries/cosmological-argument/.*

This article by a most reputable source provides a history and analysis of the cosmological argument, including the *kalam* version of the argument.

Woit, Peter. "Not Even Wrong." *http://www.math.columbia.edu/~woit/wordpress /?cat=10.*

Check out this blog and follow the physicists as they debate the multiverse model. This will keep the reader up to date.

PART TWO

The Axial Question of God and the Future of Life on Earth

We have been asking a set of questions to orient this book: Is God the author of cosmic history? Or does history author itself? Or might there be a co-authorship?

In part 1, we began with a more basic question: does a strictly scientific account of natural history and human history require that we raise the question of God? We found that a strictly scientific interpretation of either nature or humanity cannot on its own render a full account of reality. The God question sprouts up like wild flowers after a spring rain.

Part 2 will turn to the other mode in which the God question arises within Cosmic History. This section will look at selected chapters within World History where our ancestors posed the question of God and offered their answers. Previous answers to the God question will be collected, so to speak. Then those answers will be examined in light of contemporary challenges such as sharing our universe with extraterrestrial neighbors and enhancing the life-giving health of planet Earth.

This section will begin by assembling reports made by our ancestors during the axial age, claims that they had experienced a reality that transcends the physical and temporal plane of existence. This transcendent awareness led in some cases to belief in a personal divinity, and in other cases to a more impersonal oneness of all disparate things. In all axial cases, everyday temporal passage became swept up into an eternal healing.

Transcendental awareness dawned on human consciousness during the city-state period of human history two and a half millennia ago. Awareness of an ulti-mate healing beyond the mundane everyday world led to a sense of judgment, a condemnation of injustice, violence, and war. When measured over against the divine order, the human order we live in was judged to be futile. Human history gained a new interpretation in light of the axial insight; now human history came to be viewed as the search for a final ordering of life that would establish eternal justice, peace, and unity.

If it turns out that God is the author of Cosmic History, one might hypothesize that God shocked human consciousness with a revelation during the Axial Age, and this divine shock prompted our ancestors to embrace a new self-understanding. Today's advocates of perennialism like this explanation, because it suggests a dualism in which the eternal spiritual realm is said to be more real than the temporal physical realm. If it turns out that no God exists and that nature alone is responsible for the course of historical events, then at best we will deem the axial insight to be an emergent property of human complexity. There is a third option, namely, the co-authorship hypothesis. The co-authorship hypothesis combines revelation with emergence. One form of the co-authorship hypothesis is raised by today's religious naturalists: God is being created via human construction as evolution becomes self-aware through human consciousness. Another version of the third option contends that the ontological shock of the axial insight constitutes a divine revelation, while the symbolic interpretation and formulation of it constitutes the historical forms that have been taken by differentiating consciousness. We might summarize these three explanatory options: (a) emergence; (b) revelation; or (c) a combination of revelation and emergence.

To clarify, *God in Cosmic History* began by asking, what is ultimate reality? During the Axial Age, a profound awareness of transcendence emerged and insightful seers asked this very question in different ways: what is ultimate reality? In some cases, they answered that God is ultimate. In other cases, they did not. As this study proceeds, it will identify those axial cases where God became the answer along with those cases where a different answer was given. In both sets of cases, axial seers determined that history does not author itself and history cannot be considered ultimate reality.

Is God Missing in Big History?

Chronicling the history of the Axial Period raises an important methodological question: why is the question of God missing in the Big History curriculum? Why is it present in Cosmic History? Regardless of how it gets answered, the question of God represents a profound factor in the story of human consciousness. To select this fact out of the story told by the big historian is to construct an ideology.

Asking the question of God within any study of history should include, among other items, chronicling attempts by religious believers to offer their respective answers to the question, what is ultimate reality? The problem is that some historians deem religion of such negligible importance that it hardly makes the index let alone the table of contents. The answer to the God question in Brahmanism and Daoism—a comprehensive divine unity that transcends all personal deities—folds history into a supra-historical eternity. The answer to the God question provided by Moses and his heirs in Judaism, Christianity, and Islam is twofold: yes, God exists and history gains its eternal meaning from its interaction with God. Perhaps even more importantly, the God of Moses is gracious. If any of these axial claims would turn out to be true, it could be historically significant, because it would affect the very nature of history itself. And, if any axial claim is historically significant, one would expect a historian to chronicle it, study it, probe it, quiz it, and interpret it.

History, recall, is the chronicling and interpreting of contingent events. When interpreting, each historian will take a perspective. This perspective will influence what gets chronicled. Here is a transparent example. Israeli historian Yuval Noah Harari divides human history into three revolutionary thresholds.

> Three important revolutions shaped the course of history: the Cognitive Revolution kick-started history about 70,000 years ago. The Agricultural Revolution sped it up about 12,000 years ago. The Scientific Revolution, which got under way only 500 years ago, may well end history and start something completely different.[1]

What is missing in this list of three revolutions? Omitted by Harari is the revolution in the late city-state era that formed modern human life as we know it today. Karl Jaspers referred to this transformation in human consciousness as the "deepcut" in human history. This revolution took place during the first millennium before the common era and included, among other precedents, the axial breakthrough and the rise of the higher religions. The rise of the higher religions—including Daoism, Confucianism, Hinduism, Buddhism, Judaism, Christianity, Islam—does not count as a human advance in Harari's calculus. The critical reader will want to ask, what does Harari presuppose?

Elsewhere in his volume, Harari does briefly take up the history of religion. Foragers were animists and farmers were polytheists, he reports. Polytheism gave birth to monotheism, and monotheism gave birth to global waves of violence and bloodshed. Monotheism kills. "Monotheists have tended to be far more fanatical and missionary than polytheists," he writes.[2] The Christians have been the worst. "Christians slaughtered Christians by the millions to defend slightly different interpretations of the religion of love and compassion."[3] The word *axial* does not appear in Harari's index.

---

1. Yuval Noah Harari, *Sapiens: A Brief History of Humankind* (New York: Harper, 2015), 3.

2. Ibid., 218.

3. Ibid., 216.

Harari's disdain is built into his definition of religion. Religion can "be defined as *a system of human norms and values that is founded on a belief in a super-human order.*"[4] This is not inaccurate, but it is misleading. It fails to respect what axial spokespersons say of themselves. Note his phrase, "human norms and values." In all axial cases the "norms and values" are not human but rather supra-human. In Hinduism and Buddhism, karma and dharma are immortal even if not eternal. In Judaism and Islam along with Christianity the norms and values are eternal because they come from God. In Plato, justice and its standards are eternal. Even if Harari repudiates these beliefs, as a historian he should feel obligated to report accurately what our ancestors thought and believed.

The revolutionary threshold crossed by axial pioneers, discussed in subsequent chapters, includes three identifying markers. First, axial experiencers discovered that ultimate reality is mysterious, divine, and supra-cosmic. Second, axial seers lifted up a transcendent vision of a just and peaceful social order that judges the historical social order as deficient, estranged, and self-destructive. Third, axial philosophers cultivated the inner life of the soul; they discovered immediate access to the transcendent mystery and to the vision of a just society. By no means should this three-point model become a one-size-fits-all dress for archaic cultures, which took so many different shapes. Yet any account of human history that blatantly ignores these monumental threshold crossings should give us pause.

Admittedly, it is quite possible for the axial theory of history to be wrong. Recall the three explanatory options: emergence, revelation, or a combination. Suppose it could be shown by a historian that the phenomenon called the axial insight is merely an emergent insight built up by the accretion of new ideas over centuries of cultural development. Like so many advances achieved by our ancestors, the axial insight could be listed along with architecture, writing, the government of city-states, and organized armies with empires. The emergence explanation is reasonable. In fact, each of the three options warrants further inquiry.

One would expect, then, that a big historian or a world historian would investigate to discern which of the explanations is most adequate. Many of the chronicles of today's historians, however, simply delete this chapter in the human story.

What Is Coming?

This second section of the book will chronicle examples of axial insight as it appeared in ancient China, India, Greece, and Israel. It will then report on the rise of scientism, a myth-like (in the third sense of the term *myth*) ideology or

---

4. Ibid., 210, italics in original.

worldview superimposed on science and on everything else. The myth of scientism makes all reality look monistic, merely material or physical. Finally, this book will report on salient cases where historical understanding has become subservient to the modern myth of scientism. If the historian operates out of the myth of scientism, then we can expect the deletion of the question of God from his or her chronicles.

Modern science is a treasure that virtually everyone values. Curiously, modern science is a child of the Axial Age. Even more curiously, scientism is a grandchild of the Axial Age, and a rebellious grandchild at that. To understand modern and emerging postmodern global culture, one must grasp the interaction between science and scientism.

The next chapters turn to what some call the *axial breakthrough* in ancient Asia, Israel, and Greece. It will appear that the various axial seers share an important contextual factor: war. Before turning to visions of a heavenly city of peace and justice, it is necessary to consider the historical city in which humans actually live, a city at war.

12

War

History is a bath of blood.

—WILLIAM JAMES[1]

H istorians are obsessed by war. The midwives at the birth of the very concept of history—Herodotus and Thucydides in Greece and Simi Qian in China—assumed that history is the chronicle of war. Why?

The propensity for violence runs deep in human nature. Anthropologists find Stone Age human skeletons with arrowheads lodged between ribs, skulls smashed by blunt objects, and weapons of all sorts piled in graves. All are silent testimony to human brutality in the Paleolithic Age. Daily life for our forager and farmer ancestors must have been frightful, never knowing when an attack might come that would end one's life. With the advent of city-states, violence became organized. The polis and war were born as twins, but only after a long and violent pregnancy.

When historians first began to chronicle events during the city-state period, they used the term *army* to refer to an organized gang of bandits who would raid a town, pillage it for its valuables, murder the men, and carry the women off into slavery. The murderers and robbers came to be known as heroes. Little if any sympathy for those who suffered was registered by early historians let alone the soldiers. Obliteration became the fate for the losers. When big bullies began to build empires, they would present each city with an ultimatum: capitulate and live in the empire or watch your city turn into rubble. If the concept of history includes both what happened and the story of what happened, we should ask, why do historians select war to chronicle? Why does war seem so important to historians?

In the history of the differentiation in human consciousness, it rarely dawned on our ancestors that human life could be different, that life could be interesting and fulfilling even without war. Mayhem, violence, warfare, and genocide seemed to be so taken for granted that this became the very stuff of human

---

1. William James, "The Moral Equivalent of War" (1910), in William James, *Pragmatism and Other Essays* (New York: Pocket Books, 1973), 289–301, at 290.

history. Even when axial seers envisioned a transcendent social order governed by an ideal standard of peace and justice, everyone continued to take war for granted. Culture applauded the soldier for courage rather than condemn him for murder.

"Each battle was a matter of life and death, with the whole future seeming to hang in the balance," writes Gwynne Dyer, making clear that historical events are contingent. "From the historian's point of view, empires rise and fall, whole peoples appear and disappear, and borders fluctuate like droplets of rain running down the windowpane as the centuries flicker past."[2] Previous wars fade into the background as new wars draw the historian's attention.

Why a chapter on war in a book on Cosmic History? The gods and goddesses of

Classical Greek culture celebrated warfare in plays, histories, epic poetry, and civil observances. They were not alone; to the present day, civilization and warfare go hand in hand.

ancient foragers and farmers and citizens looked just like human beings. Gods and goddesses were warlike too. During the Axial Period, however, a shining sliver of transcendent light shown in the darkness. This light hinted that there might be another reality, a social order replete with peace and felicity. Due to effective history influencing us today, modern people are now double-minded about war. On the one hand, contemporary audiences love to watch violence and death on movie screens, television, and video games. Killing and dying violently provide entertainment. On the other hand, modern people weep at the sight of flag-draped caskets on the runways of military bases. For two and a half millennia now, a still small voice has begun to whisper in the human conscience: maybe the human race could live without war. Where does that voice come from? How will humanity respond?

Recall that the study of past contingent events such as wars is tied inescapably to interpretations that include self-understanding today. What we report about our ancestors indirectly becomes a mirror in which modern and postmodern people can look to see themselves.

---

2. Gwynne Dyer, *War* (New York: Crown, 1985), 26.

The War against War

Western, educated, industrialized, rich and democratic young people, people living in modern and emerging postmodern society, have generally embraced sympathy and empathy as noble cultural tropes. They do not believe they must express a deep inner thirst for violence or hunger for war. They want peace. Is the desire for peace realistic?

A revolution of sorts is taking place right now among historical thinkers. A new hypothesis is being entertained. In the words of Stanford University archaeologist Ian Morris, "War is now putting itself out of business."[3] How can this be? Because big and powerful governments find that the reduction in violence both domestic and foreign leads to prosperity. In order to protect economic growth, a government provides a domestic police force and an international military force to keep the peace. Paradoxically, history shows that past victories in war have led to strong states; and strong states in turn have led to increased peace. "The whole ten-thousand-year-long story of war since the end of the last ice age is in fact a single narrative leading up to this point, in which war has been the major factor in making today's world safer and richer than ever before."[4] Does war leads to peace?

In ancient city-states, soldiers would kill their enemies so they could become rich by plundering their enemies' possessions. In today's globalized economy, governments who hire soldiers want to keep their enemies alive so they can become new markets and eventually buy goods. Less violence is better for business.

Here is the logic of modern peace: only the government has the right to be violent. Citizens within a governed society lose the right to kill. The government assumes the right to kill in police actions, military actions, and executions. Nobody else does. Virtually nobody envisions eliminating violence totally. Apparently the total peace option contradicts human nature so completely that most people would dub it a fantasy.

Few of us in the modern world would approve let alone want to perpetrate violence, and yet violence persists. Is there a biological or cultural disposition in our inherited human nature that, under certain circumstances, leads to war, bloodshed, and genocide? The cosmic historian must pause to ask, who are we as human beings?

Genes and Genocide

Long before *Homo sapiens* declared war on one another, nature was already engaged in an arms race. "The coevolutionary development of offensive weapons by predators (better claws, teeth, gas attack, even poison-tipped barbs to catch

---

3. Ian Morris, *War! What Is It Good For?* (New York: Basic Books, 2014), 9.

4. Ibid., 10.

and kill food species) caused equally rapid countermeasures in the predators' prey, including better body armor, speed, hiding ability, and sometimes defensive weapons as well—all of which is technically called the biological arms race."[5] Human history only extends a pattern of conflict we have inherited from our pre-human ancestors. Is human violence genetic? Do *Homo sapiens* add something to conflict that goes beyond mere survival, beyond what our genes require? Yes: genocide.

Do genes cause genocide? Jared Diamond would say, yes. He observes, "Of all our human hallmarks . . . the one that has been derived most straightforwardly from animal precursors is genocide. Common chimps already carried out planned killings, extermination of neighboring bands, wars of territorial conquest, and abduction of young nubile females. If chimps were given spears and some instruction in their use, their killings would undoubtedly begin to approach ours in efficiency."[6] What Diamond provides here is an analogy between chimp and human behavior. There is no causative relationship. If we surmise that both chimps and humans share a common ancestor, however, it is reasonable to consider whether human beings have inherited an inborn propensity for genocide. That would explain why genocides continue to occur.

Critics of the Diamond diatribe are quick to point out that chimps may be violent but bonobos are not. In both chimp society and bonobo society females mate with a variety of males many times per day, but in bonobo society sex becomes a substitute for fighting, not its complement. Whereas chimps are violent, bonobos are peaceful. Both species of ape are our cousins in the larger family of apes. Does this mean that not every child of our common ancestor inherited the same genocidal gene?[7]

What evidence is there that the human propensity for murder, war, and destruction of the enemy is a trait *Homo sapiens* inherited from our pre-hominin evolutionary past? Morris observes, "Violence is overwhelmingly the preserve of young males. . . . Primatologists tell us that males commit well over 90 percent of assaults among chimpanzees, and policemen tell us that the human statistics are very similar. Young males (human or chimpanzee) will fight over almost anything, with sex and prestige as the major flash points and material goods a rather distant third, and they are most likely to turn homicidal when they get together in gangs that outnumber their opponents."[8] This observation leads to a

---

5. Peter Ward and Joe Kirschvink, *A New History of Life* (New York: Bloomsbury, 2015), 2–3.

6. Jared Diamond, *The Third Chimpanzee: The Evolution and Future of the Human Animal* (New York: Harper, 1993), 294.

7. "Asking whether our species is *naturally* peaceful or warlike, generous or possessive, free-loving or jealous, is like asking whether H$_2$O is *naturally* a solid, liquid, or gas. The only meaningful answer to such a question is: It depends." Christopher Ryan and Cacilda Jethá, *Sex at Dawn* (New York: Harper, 2010), 198, italics in original.

8. Morris, *War!*, 10.

hypothesis: "Our own violence, like that of other creatures, must be an evolutionary adaptation, descended with modification from the habits of ancestors millions of years ago."[9] If the gene is inherited, it is probably on the Y chromosome.

How might this evolutionary hypothesis be turned into an explanation for human violence? One candidate for explanation is the field of sociobiology, founded in the 1970s by Harvard entomologist Edward O. Wilson and Oxford science educator Richard Dawkins.[10] It has become nicknamed the *selfish gene* theory of evolution. According to the selfish gene theory, the driving force of evolutionary history is the driving desire of DNA to replicate itself. The incessant and aggressive advance of intact DNA sequences provides the explanatory principle for the history of life on our planet, for the behavior of all organisms, and for human culture, ethics, and religion. It is the DNA sequence (or gene in the loose sense of the word), which employs reproduction for the purposes of its own perpetuation into future individuals and gaining protection through the establishment of new species that will carry on this particular genetic code. The adjective *selfish* applied to *gene* indicates the hegemony over biological development exercised by DNA self-replication. The fact that this has to do with DNA replication, not modification, will be explored later.

The organism is DNA's way of making more DNA, according to the sociobiologists. One might think that an egg is a chicken's way of making more chickens, but the reverse is the case: a chicken is an egg's way of making more eggs. Organisms and populations of organisms are transport vehicles for DNA sequences to attain their own immortality through replication. "We, and all other animals, are machines created by our genes," writes Richard Dawkins.[11]

Reproductive fitness is the goal of genes in making machine vehicles, such as us. "Successful genes are genes that, in the environment influenced by all the other genes in a shared embryo, have beneficial effects on that embryo. Beneficial means that they make the embryo likely to develop into a successful adult, an adult likely to reproduce and pass those very same genes on to future generations."[12] Survival of the fittest means specifically *reproductive fitness*, indicating that the genes have made it through one body into the next generation.

And not only the genes of the individual count. What counts are the genes of the family, most of which are shared with a few variations between brothers

---

9. Ibid., 298.

10. More recently, E. O. Wilson has adopted "group selection" theory that relies upon "reciprocal altruism" and "eusociality" in support of the idea that multiple genomes become selected together, not merely the genomes of closely allied kin. Dawkins continues to support "kin selection," which ascribes greater influence to the "selfish gene." See Vanessa Thorpe, "Richard Dawkins in Furious Row with E. O. Wilson over Theory of Evolution," *The Guardian* (June 23, 2012), *http://www.theguardian.com/science/2012/jun/24/battle-of-the-professors*.

11. Richard Dawkins, *The Selfish Gene*, 2nd ed. (Oxford and New York: Oxford University Press, 1989), 2.

12. Ibid., 235.

and sisters. The term *inclusive fitness* refers to the genome of the individual organism combined with the genomes of next of kin, all of which together conspire for their own immortality at the expense of competing genomes.

Here is where the selfish gene theory approaches the question regarding human violence: DNA sequences compete with one another for immortality. "Genes are immortals, or rather, they are defined as genetic entities that come close to deserving the title."[13] The concept of survival of the fittest, coming from Herbert Spencer and Charles Darwin is now applied to the fittest DNA sequence, not to the organisms or species that live longer. Reproductive fitness now refers to the achievement of a particular genetic code to produce organisms that reach reproductive age, produce their own babies, and thereby perpetuate their genetic code into immortality. Organisms die, but the selfish genes live on. When human beings commit murder, they murder persons who are genetically different from their own families, according to the selfish gene theory. If organisms compete with one another, and if one population decimates a competitor, then the genes of the victor live on. The winning genes will have defined themselves as more reproductively fit.

Human genocide now has a purportedly scientific explanation: the selfish gene is responsible for genocide. The genes within human beings use human beings to kill off competing genes in other people. Once other people with competing genes are dead, then only those genes remaining in the reproductively fit will be passed on to future generations. In sum, human violence leading to war and genocide is genetically determined.

To be clear, sociobiologists do not identify a specific gene for genocide. Rather, they say that all genes lead to genocide because all genes seek immortality through the reproductive success of their host species. It does not matter what an individual gene or a configuration of genes code for; what matters is that all genes seek their own immortality and conscript the body into serving their purposes. Each of us as a human person is conscripted to serve the reproductive plot of our DNA sequence. Does this count as genetic determinism?

According to molecular biologists, human beings are not genetically determined, only predisposed. According to sociobiologists, however, that predisposition looks a lot like determinism. Wilson writes, "Human beings are strongly predisposed to respond with unreasoning hatred to external threats and to escalate their hostility sufficiently to overwhelm the source of threat by a respectable wide margin of safety. Our brains do appear to be programmed to the following extent: we are inclined to partition other people into friends and aliens."[14] It is the selfish gene that programs human brains. It is the selfish gene that programs human beings for cooperation within a tribe and military action against those

---

13. Ibid., 34.

14. Edward O. Wilson, *On Human Nature* (New York: Bantam Books, 1978), 122.

outside the tribe. It is the selfish gene that is responsible for murdering outsiders and fostering eusociality within the family, clan, and tribe.

This creates considerable consternation for religious believers. Religious believers who think that God is gracious affirm respect for the other, hospitality toward the stranger, compassion toward the weak, care for the sick, and love for one's enemies. These religious values are so contradictory to sociobiological principles that attempts to explain religion by appeal to evolution shipwreck themselves. Nature simply cannot endorse these religious values. "Much as we wish to believe otherwise," comments Dawkins, "universal love and the welfare of the species as a whole are concepts that simply do not make evolutionary sense."[15] Any command to love one's enemy simply does "not make evolutionary sense."

What does this imply for the question regarding humanity's inherited propensity toward war and genocide? Is this a viable scientific explanation for human violence?

Weaknesses in the Selfish Gene Theory

The selfish gene theory is weak on more than one count. The first weakness is that the selfish gene theory is not Darwinian. Oh yes, sociobiologists declare they are Darwin's disciples, but a closer look is needed.

Darwin emphasized *variation* in inheritance, that is, descent with *modification*. The sociobiologists, in contrast, emphasize genetic continuity without variation. They nominate descent without modification as the driving force of evolution. This makes sociobiological theory incompatible with Darwinian theory. This incompatibility makes sociobiology suspect because, as noted earlier, Darwinian theory has demonstrated scientific fertility. To date, the selfish gene theory has generated no fertile research programs in the study of human beings. In short, the selfish gene theory does not represent the best science.

A second weakness in the selfish gene theory is that it fails to explain why human beings murder close relatives. War may be declared against foreigners, obviously, but there is plenty of murder close to home as well. Brothers kill each other, beginning with Cain and Abel in the Bible. Domestic violence, including murder, is pervasive in homes. Princes murder one another when competing for their father's throne. When one murders a family member with similar genes, it would appear that the selfish gene is acting contrary to its own best interest.

The third and most decisive weakness is that the selfish gene theory cannot justify a social order in which the strong care for the weak or universal love is held up as a noble value. If one wishes to turn the selfish gene theory into a

---

15. Dawkins, *Selfish Gene*, 2.

social ethic such as we find in eugenics or social Darwinism (treated in a future chapter), this ethical agenda would be incompatible with liberal democratic commitments such as treating all members of society equally. It would also be incompatible with religious commitments such as love for one's enemy. In order to hold such values, a human society would have to defy its genes and repudiate its evolutionary inheritance.

According to Dawkins, we are able to defy our genes. We can lift our cultural values off from their original biological substrate. "We, alone on earth, can rebel against the tyranny of the selfish replicators."[16] This implies that religion, which is a form of culture, is capable of successfully promoting liberal values applicable to the universal human race. Liberal values defy genetic determinism, allegedly. "But," a critic must ask, "how could such defiance take place if the selfish genes are responsible for human social behavior?" The sociobiological argument is self-contradictory: if the selfish gene determines human culture, then how can human culture turn around and defy the selfish gene?

Even an appeal to brute survival of the fittest falls short of an evolutionary explanation. No doubt some thievery and some wars are fought for resources, for land to grow food and such. But once a nation or an empire has secured what resources it needs for survival, the drive to conquer continues unabated. The desire for power is insatiable. What sociobiologists fail to insert into their calculus is mimetic desire.[17] *Homo sapiens* characteristically desire much more than is merely required for survival; they desire what others have simply because others have it. Human beings covet certain things, not because they are needed, but solely because somebody else desires them. Greed outstrips need. Is there a gene for greed? Can human beings defy the greed gene?

In short, the selfish gene theory of the sociobiologist fails to explain the obvious propensity of *Homo sapiens* for gratuitous violence, that is, violence not in the service of reproductive fitness. The selfish gene theory also fails to explain why some people strive to love their enemies. To date, sociobiology has failed to account for the most noble and enviable virtues of the human race.

"The roots of all evil can be seen in natural selection, and are expressed (along with much that is good) in human nature. The enemy of justice and decency does indeed lie in our genes," says science writer Robert Wright.[18] If this claim of genetic determinism is even partially confirmed by actual empirical research, the product will be a scientific theory that looks a great deal like the theological doctrine of original sin. Theologian Gregory Peterson makes obvious the turn to theology. "In sociobiology, original sin becomes

16. Ibid., 201.

17. The most insightful analysis of mimetic desire has been carried out by French literary critic René Girard, formerly of Stanford University. See René Girard, *The One by Whom Scandal Comes* (East Lansing, MI: Michigan State University Press, 2014).

18. Robert Wright, *The Moral Animal* (New York: Pantheon, 1994), 151.

naturalized, providing both an origins story and an account of human behavior."[19] Even if sociobiology fails, the search for the biological roots of human behavior may bear fruit.

In the meantime, there is a dilemma. On the one hand, some want to think that the human propensity toward violence is an inherited physical propensity, biologically determined. On the other hand, some want to think that people can stop war through moral rhetoric and religious persuasion. Religious idealists and political leaders assume free will raises human beings above biological determinism and makes world peace possible. If world peace is possible, genetic determinism cannot be exhaustive.

War as Spiritual

War can feel spiritual. "War is an archetypal force that creates a larger-than-life arena into which we are irresistibly pulled," writes Edward Tick, who counsels soldiers with PTSD (post-traumatic stress disorder). "In war we embody and wrestle with god powers. The politics and hostilities of warfare rise from the gut of the war god. War evokes in us an altered state of consciousness. Odin, Ares, the Lord of Hosts, Lord Krishna, possess us. We are their servants."[20] War is so overwhelming to the individual psyche that the individual feels determined. What force determines war? Evolution? The gods? Human free will?

War is organized murder. In our post-axial era we sugar-coat organized murder with complex moral self-justification. The most common moral principle that justifies war, curiously, is denying personhood to the enemy. Killing is justified if the enemy is pictured as an animal, as inhuman. "What we conventionally call inhumanity is simply humanity under pressure," observes philosopher Michael Walzer. "War strips away our civilized adornments and reveals our nakedness. . . . [We human beings are] fearful, self-concerned, driven, murderous."[21] This applies to both our own nation and to our enemy. To recognize this purported fact of human nature allegedly qualifies one as realistic. If in fact war is sponsored by our genes, then we could congratulate ourselves for being realistic in acknowledging genetic determinism as it applies to both friends and foes alike. When preparing for war, the patriot could say that genetic determinism is the reality that justifies going to war. "I can't help it. My genes made me do it!"

This leads to "*the moral reality of war*—that is, all those experiences of which moral language is descriptive or within which it is necessarily employed."[22]

---

19. Gregory R. Peterson, "Falling Up: Evolution and Original Sin," in *Evolution and Ethics*, ed. Philip Clayton and Jeffrey Schloss (Grand Rapids: Eerdmans, 2004), 273.

20. Edward Tick, *War and the Soul* (Wheaton, IL: Quest, 2005), 41.

21. Michael Walzer, *Just and Unjust Wars*, 5th ed. (New York: Basic Books, 2015), 4.

22. Ibid., 15.

Moral realism relies on the assumption that, since human history is so permeated with war, any dream of a peaceful humanity is unrealistic. To be realistic is to subordinate morality to war, to justify one's particular role in war.

In ancient China, war needed no justification. War was a given. The only issue was whether one could carry out warfare in a superior manner. Sun Tzu (594–496 BCE) provided a pre-axial manual of sorts, *The Art of War*, in which he collected wisdom and strategy. He quotes Zhang Yu, saying, "The siege of cities and butchering of towns not only ages the army and wastes resources, it also has a lot of casualties, so it is the lowest form of attack."[23] Human butchery is condemned here not on the basis of a transcendental standard of justice but because it wastes resources.

Over a period of 295 years, according to big historian Ken Baskin, warfare in China "reduced the number of competing states from 170 to seven. . . . Partly as a result, the central theme of China's Axial Age was the movement from fragmentation to unity, from chaos to order."[24] A future chapter will look at the rise of axial consciousness and the question of how order can be drawn out of the chaos of relentless war.

In Greece, the logic of Sun Tzu's so-called realism seems to guide Thucydides's (460–395 BCE) history of the Peloponnesian War. As two Athenian generals, Cleomedes and Tisias, are negotiating with representatives of the city-state, Melos, the logic of realism surfaces. Athens plans to conquer Melos to shore up a large alliance against their main enemy, Sparta. The generals deliver to Melos the ultimatum: join Athens or suffer destruction. The generals admit they are setting aside what is right or what one might think of as justice. "Since you know as well as we do that right, as the world goes, is only in question between equals in power, while the strong do what they can and the weak suffer what they must."[25] What is just or right may adjudicate a difference between equals, but when power is asymmetrical then the strong win and the weak suffer. That's realism.

The Peloponnesian Wars devastated Greek civilization. Axial thinkers began to look toward a better future, a peaceful future. "Having lived through the devastation of the Peloponnesian Wars," comments Baskin, "Plato knew first hand that human-induced chaos had to be controlled. . . . Plato replaced the heroic leaders of Homer with his *theoros*, the philosopher who loves the spectacle of truth."[26] Frustration with war contributed to a phase transition—a

---

23. Sun Tzu, *The Art of War*, trans. Thomas Cleary (Boston and London: Shambala, 2005), 38–39.

24. Ken Baskin, "The Dynamics of Evolution: What Complexity Theory Suggests for Big History's Approach to Biological and Cultural Evolution," in *Teaching and Researching Big History: Exploring a New Scholarly Field*, ed. Leonid Grinin, David Baker, Esther Quaedackers, and Audrey Korotayev (Volgograd, Russia: Uchitel, 2014), 220–47, at 232.

25. Thucydides, *The Peloponnesian War*, book 5, in *The Landmark Thucydides: A Comprehensive Guide to the Peloponnesian War*, ed. Robert B. Strassler (New York: Free Press, 1996), 352.

26. Baskin, "The Dynamics of Evolution," 233.

differentiation in human consciousness—that began the still continuing search for a redeemed social order.

A future chapter will return to this purported military realism when Thrasymachus, in Plato's *Republic*, defines justice as the interest of the stronger. To affirm that "might makes right" is, allegedly, to be realistic. This realism morally justifies war.

Some people choose to be deliberately and self-consciously unrealistic by believing that war is less real than peace. They believe that peace is eternal while war is temporary. Since the Axial Age, the ideal of peace along with justice and felicity has been upheld as a divinely revealed standard by which to measure the historical actuality. The historical actuality, sadly, is that *peace* refers only to what a society does between wars. Eternal or everlasting peace as envisioned in symbols such as Zoroaster's paradise or the biblical kingdom of God seem to the realists to be an unreachable ideal.

Playing War

To be realistic, there will be no time in the foreseeable future when war will cease. As soon as a child is able to press an icon, he or she becomes part of the modern war culture. The young people playing video games today will become the snipers and bombers of tomorrow.

To be sure, most young males and some females appear to be genetically programmed to like things that go bang. Little boys love the loud noises made by trucks, trains, and bombs. This generates an enormous market for video game makers. It also generates an enormous recruitment pool for the U.S. military. *America's Army* official website[27] and video games—paid for with taxpayer dollars—provide youth with entertainment free of charge. They do so "for the purpose of military brand enhancement and recruitment," notes theologian Kelly Denton-Borhaug.[28]

Whereas Ian Morris is forecasting the end of war, Denton-Borhaug forecasts war's indefinite perpetuation because of the enormous profiteering that is supported by the wider culture. She defines American *war culture* as "the normalized interpenetration of the institutions, ethos and practices of war with ever-increasing facets of daily human life in the United States, including the economy, education, diverse cultural sites, patterns of labor and consumption, and even the capacity for imagination."[29] If Denton-Borhaug is accurate, we are witnessing an all-out war against peace.

---

27. *Http://www.americasarmy.com/*.

28. Kelly Denton-Borhaug, *U.S. War-Culture, Sacrifice, and Salvation* (London: Routledge, 2011), 32–33.

29. Ibid., 15.

Conclusion

The war-is-going-out-of-business hypothesis holds that history shows how past victories in war have led to strong states, and strong states in turn have led to increased peace. How well does that analysis agree with human history from the city-state period to the current planetary period? On each typical day, there are no less than fifty wars being fought around the world.

As noted previously, the early city-states were quickly eclipsed by military conquerors who established empires. Each polis was confronted with an ultimatum: either capitulate or be reduced to rubble. Many early cities were reduced to rubble. Almost the same phenomenon recurs today. In August 2015 the Islamic State in Iraq and Syria (ISIS) bombed and destroyed the city of Palmyra in Syria. Within the city was a Roman temple, which included among other things an altar to the Canaanite Baal, which had stood since BCE 17. The historic temple was destroyed by ISIS, who like the ruthless armies of the past is bent on establishing an empire, a worldwide Islamic caliphate. If this military movement continues, not only cities but entire nations will be given the same ultimatum our ancestors received five thousand years ago. Nothing in human nature seems to have changed during this period of history.

This treatment of war readies us for the axial breakthrough. The frustrating helplessness we feel in the face of war after war yearns for a message from beyond the human condition, a message of peace and justice and harmony. During the Axial Period a transcendental vision was born, a vision of eternal peace, justice, and harmony guaranteed by an eternal reality.

Review Questions

1. Foragers and farmers engaged in human violence. How did this change with city-states?
2. How does the theory of the selfish gene claim to provide an explanation for genocide?
3. How do selfish gene theorists justify a liberal ethic for modern civilization?
4. Do you think we human beings can defy our genes?

Discussion Questions

1. If war is in the genes, do you believe there is any reason to hope for world peace?
2. Review speeches you select from ISIS leaders or U.S. politicians that justify violence. What do you discern?

3. Why do you think historians give so much attention to wars?

4. With so many nuclear weapons now available in the world, what do you forecast for the future of war?

Additional Resources

Print Sources

Denton-Borhaug, Kelly. *U.S. War-Culture, Sacrifice, and Salvation.* London: Routledge, 2011.

In this most insightful study of culture and the military, Kelly Denton-Borhaug provides an analysis of the relationship between disguised religious beliefs in sacrifice and salvation to the government's justification of the military-industrial complex.

Morris, Ian. *War! What Is It Good For? Conflict and the Progress of Civilization from Primates to Robots.* New York: Picador, 2014.

This book provides a historical account of human conflict with a strong central thesis: war is becoming obsolete. The obsolescence of war is due to the rise of large and powerful empires that find that maintaining peace better serves prosperity. Morris speculates about our planet's future in light of the current American empire.

Peters, Ted. *Sin Boldly! Justifying Faith for Fragile and Broken Souls.* Minneapolis: Fortress, 2015.

This treatment of sin and grace analyzes the story of Adam and Eve in the garden of Eden and the cycle of self-justification and violence in political rhetoric. Give special attention to chapters 3 to 9.

Ryan, Christopher, and Cacilda Jethá. *Sex at Dawn: How We Mate, Why We Stray, and What It Means for Modern Relationships.* New York: Harper, 2010.

In this nicely written book, which covers a virtual encyclopedia of topics, the authors strive to retrieve the culture of our forager ancestors. They ask, what is natural? How has modern civilization repressed what is natural within us?

Tick, Edward. *War and the Soul: Healing Our Nation's Veterans from Post-Traumatic Stress Disorder.* Wheaton, IL: Quest, 2005.

Although this book does not deal with the evolution question, it is very valuable for understanding human violence and justification of violence. This dramatic and intriguing book deals directly with a huge human tragedy: PTSD and moral injury among U.S. soldiers returning from the battlefield. The book also reflects on war in history and its significance for understanding human nature.

Web Sources

"Peace and Security." United Nations *http://www.un.org/en/globalissues/peacesecurity/*. This site provides information about the United Nations' efforts to foster peace and security.

The Axial Breakthrough in China
Daoism and Confucianism

Always without desire we must be found,
If its deep mystery we would sound;
But if desire always within us be,
Its outer fringe is all that we shall see.

—Daodejing 1.3[1]

The defining trait of the axial insight is the belief in a transcendent order, an order of justice grounded in ultimate reality. The insight regarding what lies beyond history only takes place within history. In this chapter we will remind ourselves of just what history is. This will be followed by a description of the axial insight that appeared independently in numerous ancient cultures. This will be followed, in turn, by a brief look at two axial seers in ancient China, Laozi (Lao Tzu) and Confucius. From within history we may catch a fleeting glimpse of a reality that transcends history.

The Axial Age within History

In *God in Cosmic History*, the term *history* has been assigned four meanings. First, history as *events* refers to what happened. Second, history as *narrative* refers to what historians do, chronicling and interpreting past contingent events. Third, history as *the awareness of our finitude and mortality* implies a developing insight into a reality that transcends events. According to the fourth meaning, *effective*

---

1. *Dao* can be translated as "reason," or "way," or "guiding direction." Scholars debate the proper transliteration of this Chinese character; variations include *Tao, Tau, Dao, dao,* or *tau.* Alan Levinovitz recommends *dao* without the stative capital D. "Dao with a Capital D? A Study in the Significance of Capitalization," *Journal of the American Academy of Religion* 83, no. 3 (September 2015): 780–807. This text will generally employ *Dao,* the most common English rendering. Quotations from the *Daodejing* are drawn from *The Texts of Daoism,* trans. James Legge, 2 vols. (New York: Dover, 1891, 1962); audio version by Gutenberg, *http://www.gutenberg.org/ebooks/23974.*

history refers to the life of the past still living inside our consciousness within the horizon of the unsaid.

Taking history as the chronicle and interpretation of contingent events, this and the following chapters will attend to those contingent events that involve leaps in human consciousness. In the face of transcendent reality, history—historicity—in this third sense connotes the story of human subjectivity searching for ultimate meaning. The cosmic historian asks the question of the God of ultimate meaning.

Previous chapters have looked at big bang cosmology, the evolution of life on Earth, and the sensibilities of foragers, farmers, and early city-state citizens. Big History has been joined with World History. Because of the brevity of this book, it is necessary to be selective regarding the events to be chronicled and interpreted. Events taking place during the Axial Age on the eve of the common era are of particular importance to historians asking the God question.

The Axial Leap in Human Consciousness

The hypothesis that lies behind these chapters is that something extraordinary took place in three separate areas of the world—China, India, and the Mesopotamian-Mediterranean region—between 800 and 200 BCE. What occurred in each place was a leap in human consciousness, what philosopher Karl Jaspers calls the *axial insight*. In China the axial insight dawned on Laozi and Confucius along with their students. In India the axial insight erupted in the mystical queries of the Upanishads and the Buddha. In Iran Zoroaster reconceived human history as a cosmic struggle between good and evil, culminating in an apocalypse in which good would triumph.[2] Not far from Iran, the axial insight penetrated the Greek mind with philosophy and the Hebrew mind with prophecy. In all these cases reality became restructured so as to orient self, society, and cosmos toward a transcendent ground.

"What is new about this age, in all three areas of the world, is that [the human race] becomes conscious of Being as a whole," writes German philosopher Karl Jaspers, who coined the term *Axial Age* (*Achenzeit*). Our ancestors became profoundly aware of their finitude, limitations, and powerlessness in relation to an incomprehensible yet comprehensive mystery. This insight prompted the asking of "radical questions. Face to face with the void [the human race] strives for liberation and redemption. . . . [Humanity] experiences absoluteness in the depths of selfhood and in the lucidity of transcendence. . . . In this age were born the fundamental categories within which we still think today."[3]

---

2. Zoroaster will not be treated here.

3. Karl Jaspers, *The Origin and Goal of History*, trans. Michael Bullock (London: Routledge, 1953, 2010), 2.

Jaspers claims that the modern world we know today was born two and a half millennia ago.

The legacy of the axial breakthrough remains alive and well today in the so-called *higher religions* such as Daoism, Confucianism, Hinduism, Buddhism, Judaism, Christianity, and Islam, and in Greek philosophy. Jasper's deep cut diverted the stream of human history so that it now floods the human soul with the flow of transcendent mystery.

What is called the *Axial Age* exhibits three defining characteristics. First, ultimate reality is mysterious, divine, and supra-cosmic. Second, a transcendent model of a just and peaceful social order judges the historical social order in which we live as deficient, estranged, and self-destructive. Third, a deepened sense of the individual self produces an inner soul with immediate access to the transcendent mystery and to the vision of a just society. Did such a leap in human consciousness occur as axial theorists claim? Does axial thinking raise the question of God as the answer to the human search for ultimate reality? Is God's role in Cosmic History to shock human consciousness into envisioning what lies beyond cosmic history?

Many Cultures with One Axial Breakthrough?

For philosopher Jaspers it was an article of faith that the whole of humanity shares a common origin and a common goal. The peoples of Earth are divided into many distinct cultural traditions, but the historian would like to think that the human race is also somehow united. How? "Origin and goal are unknown to us, utterly unknown by any kind of knowledge," Jaspers says. "They can only be felt in the glimmer of ambiguous symbols."[4] Jaspers did not expect to identify the origin and goal that unites all people scientifically or literally. Yet, he surmised, the origin and goal of history may poke through symbolic discourse with hints, glimpses, and suggestions.

Axial theorist Jaspers had a social location, namely, Western culture. He was fully aware that in the Western world the Christian religion founded the philosophy of history. "But the Christian faith is only one faith, not the faith of mankind," he observed. This creates a conundrum: any concept of universal history arising from this one religious tradition would apply only to this tradition, not to the whole of humankind. So how can we move conceptually to a universal notion of history? As we saw earlier, Jaspers says we need to search for "the most deepcut dividing line in history," which marks the transition from prehistory to the humanity we have come to know today. This deepcut he called the *axis*, the transition from *Homo sapiens* to *Homo sapiens axialis*. This axis does double duty: it is both the *turning point* of history as well as the *connecting link* between

---

4. Ibid., xv.

all cultures. "The axis of world history, if such a thing exists, would have to be discovered *empirically*, as a fact capable of being accepted as such by all [people], Christians included."[5] Jaspers began with the Christian answer, and then he returned to the underlying question.

What this twentieth-century philosopher was trying to do was to escape his own contextual situation in order to speak universally. Jaspers engaged in a "search for an understanding of history that did not take the European experience as the self-evident vantage point or the Christian idea of the birth of Jesus Christ as the only important turning point in history," comments Björn Wittrock.[6] Is such an escape from Eurocentrism possible?

The attempted escape from Eurocentrism uncovers an inescapable paradox of the modern mind. On the one hand, each individual belongs inescapably to a cultural context, a specific social location, an ethnic tradition, a worldview with its own vested interests. Yet, on the other hand, we wish to think and speak universally. We wish to transcend our context. This wish to transcend our context becomes the pedagogical objective of both World History and Big History. Even if escape from one's own context is impossible, certainly the study of cultures in other places and other times broadens one's horizons. What Jaspers was attempting belongs squarely within the agenda of this book. We will treat his concept of the Axial Age as a hypothesis: approximately 2500 years ago some of our ancestors experienced a breakthrough of supra-cosmic transcendence that has led to a profoundly new sense of divinity and mystery. Whether Jaspers is correct or not regarding the breakthrough of the Axial Period, an examination of his hypothesis will shed light on the effective history that structures our consciousness today.

Granting that a development in human consciousness occurred during the Axial Period, how do we explain it? Two types of explanation are possible. First is the *emergence* option, according to which the axial advance in consciousness emerges as a natural development within a conflictual context. Because the axial insight evolved slowly, we would think of it as a baby step rather than a leap. Wittrock articulates the emergence explanation: "Recurring strains and tensions . . . in themselves tended to engender conditions that were propitious for the kind of deep-seated transformation the Axial transformations involved."[7] Egyptologist Jan Assmann affirms the emergence option while sharply criticizing the idea that a leap occurred. "Jaspers appears as a teller of myths, narrating about beginnings where they [historians] see slow developments, continuities,

---

5. Ibid., 1, italics in original.

6. Björn Wittrock, "The Axial Age in Global History: Cultural Crystallizations and Societal Transformations," in *The Axial Age and Its Consequences*, ed. Robert N. Bellah and Hans Joas (Cambridge, MA: Harvard University Press, 2012), 102–25, at 102.

7. Ibid., 111.

discontinuities, revisions, and recourses."[8] In short, the emergence explanation acknowledges that a breakthrough occurred but explains it as a natural evolution of human ideas.

Second is the *revelation* option, according to which transcendent reality breaks into compact consciousness from beyond, shocking human awareness and precipitating the leap to a new and unprecedented view of self, society, and cosmos. Axial philosopher Eric Voegelin elects the revelation option: "Revelation is not a piece of information, arbitrarily thrown out by some supernatural force, to be carried home as a possession, but the movement of response to an eruption of the divine in the psyche."[9] It is important to note that the concept of revelation at work here does not entail a transfer of knowledge from heaven to earth as in shamanism; rather, revelation consists of a divine shock to the soul that provokes a differentiation in consciousness. The divine revelation so shocked the human soul that it began to look for ultimate reality beyond the cosmos rather than within it.

There might be a third option, which combines the first and second. We might call it the *divine emergent* or *combination* explanation. Accordingly, the axial insight incorporates previous human knowing but adds a new level of transcendent awareness to it, and this emergence is guided by a divine actor who works within historical processes. The divine would work from within to guide the differentiation of human consciousness. In what follows it may not be possible to decide sharply between these three options; each option enjoys a level of respect for its applicability and coherence.

The Leap in Human Consciousness in Ancient China

The historical narrative describing city-state China cannot avoid acknowledging the sudden appearance of new ways of thinking. China during the later Zhou Dynasty (772–481 BCE) and the Warring States Period (450–221 BCE) provides the context for the following discussion. Whereas the early Zhou Empire had for some centuries (1045–771 BCE) maintained political control over the villages and city-states, the grip of the centralized monarchy was beginning to loosen. Independence-minded princes and kings were exerting their local power, leaving for the Zhou monarchy a mere ceremonial role in defining China as China. Axial seers rose up to ask, does there exist a transcendent moral order that eternally defines human selfhood and human society? Could such a moral

---

8. Jan Assmann, "Cultural Memory and the Myth of the Axial Age," in *Axial Age*, ed. Bellah and Joas, 366–410, at 366–67.

9. Eric Voegelin, *Order and History*, 5 vols. (Baton Rouge: Louisiana State University Press, 1956–1987), 4:232.

order provide warring peoples with a criterion of judgment and a vision of the proper social order to guide transformation? Two intellectual giants answered in the affirmative: Laozi and Confucius.

In terms of the symbols and myths Laozi and Confucius inherited, the reigning creation account took the form of the cosmic egg. According to this myth, *in illo tempore*[10] Phan Ku broke the shell from the inside, burst forth, and grew into a giant. Phan Ku separated earth, called, *yin*, from heaven, called *yang*. Phan Ku dug out valleys and river beds, using the removed dirt to make the mountains. Into the heavens he put the sun, moon, and stars. When Phan Ku died, the building work was completed. The dome of the sky was held in place by his skull, and the earth's soil was formed from his body. Today, we can hear his voice in the thunder and see his breath in the clouds. Rain falls from his sweat. It was painful for Phan Ku to sacrifice himself in creating this world, and human beings today continue to experience the pain built into the creation from the beginning.

The human race was created when lice from Phan Ku's hair fell to earth. People are vermin. Humans cannot claim much dignity from this myth.[11]

This was the creation myth accepted by many in China before Laozi and Confucius appeared on the scene. The combination of rain and soil reflect the farmer stage of Chinese history. This intra-cosmic worldview was the agricultural inheritance of Chinese culture on the eve of the Axial Period. With the rise of city-states, such creation myths were not lost, but they were supplemented with axial philosophy. Laozi and Confucius founded the first two of the three new religious traditions in Chinese history, the *three teachings* of China: Daoism (or Taoism), Confucianism, and Buddhism.[12]

Laozi's *Daodejing*

Chinese thinking during the first millennium BCE was characterized largely by its practicality in political affairs and its emphasis on personal virtue and filial piety (family loyalty). Compact consciousness in ancient China did not inherit a linguistic tradition influenced by metaphysics or related forms of abstract reflection. For the idea of transcendent reality to crack open compact consciousness and evoke differentiation, insightful seers and philosophers had to stretch and twist and bend their language by use of similes, metaphors, and parables. In order to open a window to transcendence, they had to break holes in the walls of their inherited ways of thinking.

---

10. Latin for "at that time." See chapter 7 for the use of this phrase in conjunction with creation myths.

11. Virginia Hamilton and Barry Moser, *In the Beginning: Creation Stories from Around the World* (New York: Harcourt, Brace, and Jovanovich, 1988), 20–23.

12. Buddhism will be covered in the chapter on India.

Confucius (551–479 BCE) referred to Laozi (571–531 BCE), his senior, as "the old philosopher."[13] How frequently the two master teachers met is unknown to historians. These two are remembered in large part because they accelerated two traditions of wisdom that have endured to the present. They are deemed important because they mark the axial breakthrough that led to a leap in human consciousness.

Perhaps the defining trait of the axial insight is the emerging belief in a transcendent order, an order of justice grounded in ultimate reality. The empirical reality of everyday living comes to be thought of as only a shadow or imperfect image of the transcendent order. Because everyday language is embedded in everyday experience, seers and nascent philosophers struggled to stretch words so as to point people toward the transcendent, the ineffable, the eternal.

How does Laozi deal with the limits and opportunities that language supplies? He opens his treatise, the *Daodejing*, the principal work of Daoism, by asserting that the Dao is beyond naming. To name anything is to distinguish it from everything else that has a different name. By denying a name to the Dao, Laozi asserts that the Dao is inclusive of all that is real. "The Dao, considered unchanging, has no name" (*Daodejing* 32.1), he writes. The Dao is "formless, standing alone, and undergoing no change, reaching everywhere and in no danger (of being exhausted). . . . I do not know its name, and I give it the designation of the Dao (the Way or Course). . . . I call it The Great'" (*Daodejing* 25.1, 2). Despite its formlessness, some words of some sort must be employed, so Laozi elects to describe the Dao metaphorically as the mother of all things. "It may be regarded as the Mother of all things" (*Daodejing* 25.2). Literally, the Dao has no name. Metaphorically, the Dao is our mother. Conceptually, "*Tao* is the *way of ultimate reality*," comments the renowned scholar of world religions, Huston Smith.[14]

On some occasions this seer would place the eternal order in time, in the past, in the archonic beginning of things. On other occasions, Laozi would place the eternal order in space, in heaven above. Whether in time or space, the transcendent order eludes the grasp of everyday thinking while it stands in judgment over everything that falls short of its standards.

When placing the transcendent order in time, Laozi describes the equivalent of a golden age or garden of Eden in the past. In fact, this originating age belongs at the beginning of all things. It defines all things. This primordial or archonic era embodied all the virtues of the perfect city-state. In fact, it was the perfect city-state, relegating all historical city-states to the status of impure facsimiles. In the perfect city or empire, sometimes called a "kingdom" by Laozi,

---

13. Fung Yu-Lan at Beijing University dates Laozi much later than Confucius. *A Short History of Chinese Philosophy*, trans. Derk Bodde (New York: Free Press, 1948), 93.

14. Huston Smith, *The World's Religions* (New York: Harper, 1991), 198.

all citizens shared a feeling of unity, community, and an egalitarian bond without the knowledge of class divisions, competition, or war. Then the human race fell from this blissful state into history, into a progressively deteriorating temporal chronicle. The fall came in stages of defection by the people from harmony with their political rulers.

> In the highest antiquity, (the people) did not know that there were rul- ers. In the next age they loved them and praised them. In the next they feared them; and in the next they despised them. Thus it was that when faith (in the Dao) was deficient in the rulers a want of faith in them ensued. . . . There ensued great hypocrisy. (*Daodejing* 17.1; 18.1)

In sum, citizens living in the transcendent city-state experienced harmony with Dao and within the human community. In contrast, the historical (located in time and space) city-state within which people live their daily lives is beset with rivalry, misrule, and sedition. The eternal ideal expressed in this myth of origin judges what is actual and temporal.

Metaphors of space duplicate this temporal pattern. For Laozi, the eternal order is located in heaven, while the historical or fallen order is located on earth. What happens here on earth either conforms to or violates the will of heaven, the way of Dao.

> [Humanity] takes [the] law from the Earth; the Earth takes its law from Heaven; Heaven takes its law from the Dao. The law of the Dao is its being what it is. (*Daodejing* 25.4)

> Heaven which by it is bright and pure;
> Earth rendered thereby firm and sure; . . .
> All creatures through it do live;
> Princes and kings who from it get
> The model which to all they give. (*Daodejing* 39.1)

Recall in the Phan Ku myth how heaven was associated with *yang* and earth with *yin*. Rain from heaven along with soil from earth are required for human life. In Laozi the heavenly model renders judgment against greedy rulers on earth. They "may be called robbers and boasters. This is contrary to the Dao, surely!" (*Daodejing* 53.3).

Despite the fall of humanity from the paradise of the past or the fall from the will of heaven above, Laozi believes redemption is possible. Redemption would come in the form of individual and social virtue, especially the virtues of humility and moderation. With curious logic, the *Daodejing* recommends evac- uating oneself of one's self and doing nothing (*wuwei*) and letting the cosmic Dao take its course. If an individual embodies Dao in the form of moderation in

This statue at Hangu Pass, Henan, China, depicts Laozi (571–531 BCE). Known as "the old philosopher," Laozi located the just and harmonious social order in the archonic past; the present political system is fallen from its primordial perfection.

life-style, others will gather around and benefit. Perhaps the *Daodejing* is relying on an emanation or radiation or infection theory of virtue, according to which the populace catches it from the single virtuous individual.

> To him who holds in his hands the Great Image (of the invisible Dao), the whole world repairs. [Other people] resort to him, and receive no hurt, but (find) rest, peace, and the feeling of ease. (*Daodejing* 35.1)

> It is only by this moderation that there is effected an early return [to humanity's normal state]. That early return is what I call the repeated accumulation of the attributes (of the Dao). (*Daodejing* 59.2)

Note that the "normal state" of humankind is the perfect state, the state from which we have fallen and become estranged. However, the Dao never went away. It sleeps within us, just waiting to be awakened. In order to retrieve the original or normal state, the individual needs to de-educate himself or herself and allow the primordial Dao to rise up and manifest itself. Serenity of mind allows the Dao to manifest itself within us.

To allow the Dao to repair one's estrangement requires a spiritual disposition of humility, calmness, quiet, and receptivity. Very much like Buddhist self-renunciation or Stoic virtue, Laozi identifies life's stress with the frustration of unfulfilled desire. By ridding oneself of desire, then no frustration can occur.

If we avoid coveting what others possess, we avoid disappointment. This is the secret to serenity of mind, the way of Dao.

Consider the political logic of Daoism: do nothing and let nature take its course. Can ceasing to take action lead to social healing? Might a critic contend that this prescription is based on a misunderstanding of the social order? When virtuous people withdraw from taking action, what fills the void is not Edenic or primordial harmony. Rather, what fills the void is political anarchy caused by selfishness, violence, and destruction. Practically speaking, anarchy can be arrested by tyranny. It is not surprising that legalism—what in contemporary politics is known as "law and order"—arose in China as an alternative to Daoism. The legalists took control, established peace, and punished mercilessly those who would violate the peace. Tyranny through law enforcement became the preferred political option. Having lost socially, Daoism had to withdraw into the safe psyche of the individual on personal retreat. Rather than a political philosophy, Daoism ended up offering a private if not mystical relationship between the self and the Dao.

One of the baffling dimensions of the Daoist belief complex is that life is meaningless, or at least graceless. "Heaven and earth do not act from the (impulse of) any wish to be benevolent" (*Daodejing* 5.1). Ultimate reality is neither friend nor foe to humanity in its plight.

No deity constitutes ultimate reality in Daoism. No cosmic egg or Phan Ku. No god is ultimate. Dao is ultimate. Yet it would be a mistake to equate the Dao with what modern Westerners call *nature*. The Dao is natural, to be sure; but it is unmistakably transcendent. As transcendent, it is everywhere immanent as well. The concept of the Dao resonates with both beyond and intimate sensibilities.

Confucius and the Will of Heaven

The word *Confucius* is the Latinized version of *Kung Fu-tzu*, meaning "Master Kung" in Chinese. When the young Confucius looked at his surroundings, he saw a hundred city-states in competition with one another, bickering, skirmishing, and making war. The Zhou Empire was weak, unable to govern and keep peace. Disorder, violence, and even regicide blanketed the political landscape. Confucius set about the task of establishing a peaceful order in the empire.

Confucius's prescription for healing was virtue. His word for virtue was *jen* (sometimes rendered *ren*), a vision of an ideal human being responsible to the larger society. *Jen* could be translated as goodness, benevolence, or love; but mostly it is rendered "humanity" in English. "Variously translated as goodness, man-to-man-ness, benevolence, and love, it is perhaps best rendered as human-heartedness," comments Smith.[15] To be truly human-hearted is to obey

---

15. Ibid., 172.

the law of reciprocity, what Western culture knows as the Golden Rule. "Do not do to others what you would not want others to do to you" (*Analects* 15.23). Confucius, according to one interpreter, capitalizes on "*timeless*, basic human needs and aspirations."[16]

Jen comes from *Tian*, heaven. Heaven, for Master Kung, was not the home where a pantheon of deities frolic. Rather, heaven functions as a guiding providence. Although literally heaven is above earth, metaphorically the concept of heaven represents transcendent order, ultimate reality. The will of heaven provides a transcendent moral law, a law destined to be inscribed within the hearts of human individuals and within the structure of the perfect kingdom. A person "who sins against Heaven has none to whom he can pray" (*Analects* 3.13). Confucius's answer to the question of God was not God. Rather, Confucius nominated the will of heaven to be ultimate, and the will of heaven was devoid of the personal traits of a gracious God.

For Confucius (551–479 BCE), just and harmonious social order was situated in heaven; earthly political systems are fallen from the heavenly model. Virtue consists of doing the will of heaven.

Heavenly *jen* is ultimate. This means it transcends death. It is better to die with *jen* than to live prosperously without it. "The resolute scholar and the humane person will under no circumstances seek life at the expense of humanity (*jen*). On occasion they will sacrifice their lives to preserve their humanity (*jen*)" (*Analects* 15.8).

Circulating in the Chinese culture of the day were stories of ancient forebears and proper rites (*li*) that recalled allegedly glorious times of the archonic past. Confucius proclaimed that historical disorders were caused by failure to honor the ancestors and to rightly perform the rites. He retold stories of ancient heroes who embodied the virtues that his contemporary society needed for renewal. Renewal consisted of returning to the past, the idealized past as Confucius described it. "I am a transmitter and not a creator," said Confucius; "I

---

16. Heiner Roetz, "The Axial Age Theory: A Challenge to Historicism or an Explanatory Device of Civilization Analysis? With a Look at the Normative Discourse in Axial Age China," in *Axial Age*, ed. Bellah and Joas, 248–73, at 263. Italics in original.

believe in and have a passion for the ancients" (*Analects* 7.1). A return to the past would be a return to *jen*. Confucius presupposed an archonic view of reality, where essence belongs to the past and the present historical moment represents a fall, a defect. Historical transformation, then, consists of a retrieval of the essential past.

The path to the past and to virtue would be paved by education, thought Confucius and his followers. "By nature [people] are pretty much alike," he said; "it is learning and practice that sets them apart" (*Analects* 17.2). Learning should become the goal of China's elite leadership. It would be the task of the political leader, Confucius taught, to become educated by learning the traditions of China and practicing the ancient rites correctly. Through education Confucius sought to overcome four enemies to the ordered soul and the ordered society: a biased mind, arbitrary judgments, obstinacy, and egotism (*Analects* 9.4). Whereas Laozi sought renewal through de-education; Confucius sought renewal through education.

Education, as far as historians know, was aimed at future male leaders of Chinese society—not women. The ideally educated person would be called *junz*, the equivalent of a "gentleman." Confucius wrote, "The gentleman understands what is right; the inferior man understands what is profitable" (*Analects* 4.16). There is no sign here of egalitarianism; nor is there a pre-cursor to democracy. Even in redemption, Confucius assumes the social order will be hierarchical, male-dominated, and ruled by those who are educated.

One of Confucius's students, Mo Tzu, however, saw the implication of viewing all human persons together as under the one will of heaven, *t'ien-hsia*. He extrapolated his master's teachings into a doctrine of universal love. Heaven, according to Mo Tzu (470–391 BCE), is an active force eliciting a reverence and respect for all persons regardless of class. "What is the will of Heaven that we should all obey? It is to love all [people] universally" (*The Will of Heaven* 28.3).[17] Despite Mo Tzu's breakthrough insight—that the corollary to universal love is the affirmation of a universal humanity made up of equal persons—human equality failed to become the dominant societal value in Chinese culture.

Education would provide redemption from the fallen state of Chinese society, and only some, not all, persons could become educated. What Confucius and Mo Tzu sensed in everyday life was estrangement. The historical human condition is a fallen one, estranged temporally from the idealized past and spatially from the will of heaven. "If the Way (Dao) prevailed in the world, I should not be trying to alter things" (*Analects* 18:6), Confucius said, echoing Laozi. Redemption could come only from education, thought Confucius and his followers.

---

17. Cited by William Theodore De Bary, *Sources of Chinese Tradition*, 2 vols. (New York: Columbia University Press, 1960), 1:46.

Both Laozi and Confucius believed an educated person should shoulder responsibility in the political order, and both sought peace rather than war, but their methods were different. Laozi recommended doing nothing and undoing something in order to yield to Dao, to yield to natural processes. Confucius, in contrast, recommended active pursuit of social betterment. Reforming society in light of the will of heaven is the political task according to Confucius.

Contemporary scholar, Fung Yu-Lan in the Peoples Republic of China, prefers Confucius over Laozi. He criticizes Daoism, saying that the Daoists "abandoned entirely the idea of an intelligent and purposeful Heaven, and sought instead for mystical union with an undifferentiated whole."[18] The will of heaven provides a blueprint for social justice, whereas the sublime Dao lies beyond morality and justice. In the effective history that followed the Axial Period, benevolent political leaders followed Confucius on the job and followed Laozi when on annual retreat. When busy, it's Confucius. When on retreat, it's Laozi.

Master Kung's many students compiled Confucius's teachings along with the observations of his students into a volume, the *Analects*, which has been passed down for two and a half millennia. In his own era, Confucius seemed to be ignored. Only gradually did Master Kung's teachings become the law of the land. Sinologist William Theodore de Bary provides a summary assessment.

> He and his school are responsible for the pedagogic tradition which characterizes all of later Chinese history, for the optimistic belief in the perfectibility of [humanity] through learning, and for the reverence for the scholar and the [person] of letters so pronounced in Chinese society. . . . Confucius was given the title "Supreme Sage and Foremost Teacher" and his tomb and temple in Ch'ü-fu in Shantung became a kind of Mecca for all educated Chinese.[19]

Conclusions

The answer to the question of God in axial China was not God. The Dao or the will of heaven became functionally ultimate in the systems of Daoism and Confucianism. Interaction with a personal deity was not thought to be ultimate or final. Gods, goddesses, and elevated heroes abound in Chinese traditions, but such divine personalities are subordinate to a supra-personal reality. Gods are penultimate; Dao is ultimate. One decisive characteristic of both the Dao and the will of heaven is that they provide a path to peace, a path away from war.

---

18. Fung Yu-Lan, *Short History*, 47.
19. De Bary, *Sources of Chinese Tradition*, 1:19.

War in the world of city-states was common, prompting Sun-Tzu to write *The Art of War*. "The Way (Dao) means humanness and justice," according to Du Mu, whom Sun-Tzu cites. Zhang Yu adds advice for the king: "If the people are treated with benevolence, faithfulness, and justice, then they will be of one mind, and will be glad to serve. The *I Ching* says, 'Joyful in difficulty, the people forget about their death.'"[20] Accordingly, justice is transcendentally grounded in the Dao. In addition, justice has the advantage of keeping the ruler in power because the populace is satisfied.

The vocabulary of neither Laozi nor Confucius employs abstract terms to refer to transcendent reality. Rather, they employ the term heaven—*yang* in pre-axial myth—to symbolize the supra-cosmic reality that renders judgment on intra-cosmic life.

Significantly, neither Laozi nor Confucius advocated polytheism, henotheism, or monotheism. Ultimate reality for these two thinkers, though transcendent and eternal, is not personal. Nevertheless, the question of ultimate reality in its transcendent dimension was raised, subordinating temporal history to an eternal reality.

Review Questions

1. What is Dao (Tao)?
2. What is the will of heaven?
3. What is the Axial Period?
4. What is the difference between emergence and revelation?

Discussion Questions

1. Why does Laozi place the transcendent moral order in an Edenic or paradise-like past or in heaven?
2. Why does Confucius place the transcendent moral order into a space above, in heaven?
3. Does the government of your country look daily at options for war? What is there about human nature that keeps warfare perpetual?
4. Why is it that some seers yearn for peace, promote cooperation, and present visions of human harmony?

---

20. Sun Tzu, *The Art of War*, trans. Thomas Cleary (Boston and London: Shambala, 2005), 4.

Additional Resources

Print Sources

Bellah, Robert N. *Religion in Human Evolution from the Paleolithic to the Axial Age.* Cambridge, MA: Harvard University Press, 2011.

Bellah's chapter 8, "Axial Age III: China in the Late First Millennium BCE," provides a lucid historical overview with explication and commentary on China's great intellectual leaders.

Jaspers, Karl. *The Origin and Goal of History.* Translated by Michael Bullock. London: Routledge, 1953, 2010.

This book lit the fuse that touched off the explosion of axialist thinking in the middle of the twentieth century. Eric Voegelin and Robert Bellah follow in Jasper's footsteps.

Roetz, Heiner. "The Axial Age Theory: A Challenge to Historicism or an Explanatory Device of Civilization Analysis? With a Look at the Normative Discourse in Axial Age China." In *The Axial Age and Its Consequences*, edited by Robert N. Bellah and Hans Joas, 248–73. Cambridge, MA: Harvard University Press, 2012.

Roetz offers a thorough critique of Jasper's Axial Age theory. He then proceeds to map Axial Age theory on ancient Chinese thought. Roetz contends that the axial experience in different cultural contexts produced different variants of the axial insight. "Jaspers' disputed theory of the age of transcendence may even itself be transcended. For Jaspers himself adheres to an ideology of origin that is not consistent with Axial Age consciousness. It is only against the Axial Age that one can think with it. The axis is wherever there is enlightened thought" (p. 267).

Smith, Huston. *The World's Religions.* New York: Harper, 1991.

This is the most popular textbook on the religions of the world. It is clearly written. Both novices and veterans will find themselves identifying with the spiritual quest of each tradition. See especially chapters 4 and 5, on Confucianism and Daoism.

Voegelin, Eric. *Order and History.* 5 Vols. Baton Rouge: Louisiana State University Press, 1956–1987.

Voegelin masters history with more erudition than seems possible for a human mind. In this detailed and profound five-volume work, the Austrian philosopher of history provides uncanny insight into the ancient and modern minds. Voegelin is not for the beginner.

Web Sources

"The 'Axial Age': 600–400 BCE." *World History Chronology. http://www.then again.info/WebChron/World/Axial.html.*

A series of hyperlinked chronologies and historical articles.

"Axial Age Thought: 900–200 BCE." *The Human Journey. http://www.human journey.us/axialintro.html.*

A brief introduction to Axial Age thought.

"Daoism." BBC. *http://www.bbc.co.uk/religion/religions/taoism/.*

A guide to Daoism's history, practices, ethics, and martial arts.

Mayer, John D. "The Significance of the Axial Age (the Great Transformation)." *Psychology Today* (May 25, 2009). *https://www.psychologytoday.com/blog /the-personality-analyst/200905/the-significance-the-axial-age-the-great -transformation.*

This article explores the question, did a new level of consciousness evolve in 550 BCE?

14
CHAPTER

The Axial Breakthrough in India
Hinduism and Buddhism

I am without alterations, without form
[Yet] I am everywhere, and within everything, underlying all sensory
    phenomena
And I am neither attached to anything [in the world] nor to liberation
    [from the world]
My true form is that of the bliss of Pure Consciousness, I am Shiva,
    I am Shiva.

—SHANKARA, *Nirvana Shatakam*[1]

The beginning of Brahmanism is a matter of dispute among today's historians. One historical theory is that nearly four thousand years ago, native Dravidian foragers, farmers, and citizens lived in the Indus River valley in what is now India. Most likely their religious beliefs and ceremonies included versions of the master of the animals and the earth mother goddess. During the second millennium BCE, the indigenous Dravidians entertained visitors, visitors who came to stay. The visitors—actually invaders—arrived with armies of Aryans sweeping into the Indus valley on horseback, most likely from the Iranian plateau. Whether the invasion came gradually as a migration or as a single military invasion is unknown. Nevertheless, once the invaders had established hegemony, they settled down, intermarried, and created what we now know as the Indo-Aryan culture. The product of the synthesis of the invading conquerors and the indigenous conquered is known as Brahmanism.

A second historical theory posits that Indian prehistory begins in India, not Iran. Indigenous developments in cultural complexity included an urbanization process leading to innovation and axial insight. India was the original home for

---

1. Translation by Rita Sherma, unpublished.

émigrés who departed to become the Iranians and Indo-Ayrans. In sum, what we will call Brahmanism is *sui generis* to India.[2]

A postmodern deconstructionist might review these two theories and conclude that theory one is colonial while theory two is reverse colonial. Theory one presupposes that innovation was imported from the Aryans, while theory two presupposes that innovation was indigenous to India and later exported to the Aryans. This competition between theories serves as a reminder that *history* refers both to what happened and to the historical story of what happened. Regardless of which theory wins, something wondrous happened beginning with the *Rigveda*.

Written texts became sacred scriptures three thousand years ago. In addition to the first text, the *Rigveda*, other Vedas appeared along with Upanishads. The Vedic tradition has come to be known as Brahmanism. Like a large tree trunk with two main branches, Brahmanism branched into Buddhism and Hinduism. Buddhism branched first, perhaps five centuries prior to the common era. With the final publication of the *Bhagavad Gita* in the fourth century CE, Hinduism took its present form. The Hindu branch included nests of multiple pre-axial traditions, becoming a single religion with an immense variety of expressions.[3] Hinduism is virtually a federation of previously distinct traditions that is today tied closely to Indian culture and politics.

Brahmanism was India's contribution to axial thinking, as described by big historian, Cynthia Stokes Brown.

> During the thousand years of the period 800 BCE to 200 BCE, Afro-Eurasia witnessed a notable creative outpouring of religious thought. All of the major world faiths of today appeared in this period, if one counts Christianity and Islam as developments of the prophetic stream of Hebrew life. . . . The new prophets and sages stressed how to gain salvation, release, or nirvana, how to achieve a better life after this one, or how to return to a better incarnation. In part, they were working out ethical systems that would motivate people to the behavior needed for living in the density of growing cities.[4]

---

2. "Thus the Iranians lived in the region of Sapta-Sindhu of the Rigveda before going to Iran. This gives us sufficient evidence that India was the original home of Iranians and also Indo-Aryans. Avestan also refers to Airyana Vaeja, which means the original land of the Aryans; this indicates that Iran was not their original home and thus indirectly shows that India was their original home." Satya Swarup Misra, "The date of the Rigveda and the Aryan Migration: Fresh Linguistic Evidence," in *The Indo-Aryan Controversy: Evidence and Inference in Indian History*, ed. Edwin Bryant and Laurie Patton (New York: Routledge, 2005), 211.

3. "Brahminism, though extremely diverse in thought and devotional practice, was the earliest belief system to exhibit at least some characteristics of a world religion. . . . That is, Brahminism was not limited to a group claiming a particular ethnic identity. [It follows that] we should not . . . equate the Brahmanic tradition with Hinduism." Ross E. Dunn and Laura J. Mitchell, *Panorama: A World History* (New York: McGraw Hill Education, 2015), 155.

4. David Christian, Cynthia Stokes Brown, and Craig Benjamin, *Big History: Between Nothing and Everything* (New York: McGraw-Hill, 2014), 124–25.

In chronicling the axial insight occurring in different cultures in different areas of the world during the city-state era, it would be a mistake to assume that all of the world's religions are the same or that all religious traditions can be reduced to a single deep structure. It is safer to assume that religions relate to one another asymptotically, that is, two religions are like two lines that approach one another but do not intersect. The comparisons made here in this book focus on the closest point of approach, the point of greatest similarity at the axial intersection. After this, they branch away in dissimilarities.

The question of God is asked in two modes in this book. The first mode is to chronicle moments in history when individuals or cultures posed their questions regarding the divine—ultimate reality with or without God—and provided their specific answers. This is history in the chronicle mode. The second mode subjects the very concept of history to critical analysis. It asks whether history is self-explanatory or whether it requires transcendental grounding in a reality more ultimate. The Axial Age requires the historian's attention to both modes. This chapter considers the quest for ultimate reality among India's archaic seers during the Axial Age.

The Wonder That Was India

Of the magnificent literature that arose in India, the Vedas and the Upanishads readied the ancient Indian mind for a leap in consciousness. The early Vedas began as poetry and hymnody, memorized and passed down from generation to generation orally. The earliest and most revered of the Vedas, the *Rigveda* (*Rig Veda* or *Rgveda*), likely composed between 1500 and 1000 BCE, may not have been written down until a thousand years later. The context discernible from the text is that of foragers, farmers, and early citizens with ox-drawn wagons, horse-drawn chariots, and weapons of bronze.

The *Rigveda* is structured around many myths of origin. The cosmic constitution, as we have seen in so many agricultural societies, is based on a male heaven with a female earth, together the parents of the human race.

> May Heaven and Earth swell our nourishment, the two who are father and mother, all-knowing, doing wondrous work. Communicative and wholesome unto all, may Heaven and Earth bring unto us gain, reward, and riches. (*Rigveda* 6.70)[5]

Note the task of the gods: to provide gain, reward, and riches. Presumed here is an intra-cosmic worldview within compact consciousness.

---

5. Wendy Doniger, *Hindu Myths: A Sourcebook: Translated from the Sanskrit* (New York: Penguin Books, 1975), 74–75.

In one creation myth, the male sky god, Indra, engages in a heavenly battle. Indra uses lightening—the *vajra* or thunder-bolt—as his spear to gain victory. Indra destroys Vritra the dragon, who had shut off the rain; that is, Indra overcame drought to provide rain for the crops.

> I will tell the heroic deeds of Indra, those which the Wielder of the Thunderbolt first accomplished. He slew the dragon and released the waters; he split open the bellies of the mountain. . . . The gliding waters have flowed straight down to the ocean. (*Rigveda* 1:32)[6]

Like so many mythical stories of origin, Indra creates by bringing order to chaos. University of Chicago Indologist Wendy Doniger observes, "The Hindu universe is a closed system, a world-egg with a rigid shell, so that nothing is ever created *ex nihilo*; rather, things are constantly rearranged, each put in its proper place, and by doing this—propping apart heaven and earth, distinguishing male from female, separating the classes of mankind on earth—ordered life emerges out of lifeless chaos."[7]

Even though this myth provides a story placed in the beginning, *in illo tempore*,[8] which explains why there is rain to grow crops today, theory one historians suggest the myth may harbor a second meaning. This myth may derive from the Aryan invasion. Indra could be a personification of the Aryan army, with Vritra representing the defeated Dravidians. In this preliterate age, suggest some Indologists, the Aryan (*arya* means noble) victory was remembered in verse form. This interpretation is rejected by theory two historians. What can be safely said is that the Vedas emerged from the experience of Sanskrit-speaking peoples who referred to themselves as *arya*.

Evidence mustered in behalf of the invasion/migration theory is the introduction of the caste system in the *Rigveda*. The Sanskrit word for caste, *varna*, means color. Human society is divided into four colors, with the lightest skin on top and the darkest on the bottom: (1) Brahmans sat on top of the social order; like shamans they became the priests and teachers who connect heaven with earth (the term, *Brahmanism*, derives from this caste); (2) Kshatriyas, second in rank, provided government and nobility along with kings and soldiers; (3) Vaishyas formed the class of landowners and merchants; while (4) Shudras became the workers, artisans, and serfs. A fifth group, originally known as Outcastes, are today called Pachamas or Dalits. After intermarriage between dark-skinned Dravidians and light-skinned Aryans, so the theory goes, the Indian social order became rigidly organized around an ontology of race that was justified by the most ancient of pre-axial myths.

---

6. Ibid., 75.

7. Ibid., 13.

8. Latin for "at that time." See chapter 7 for the use of this phrase in reference to ancient creation myths.

In an earlier chapter we saw how *Enuma Elish* provided an origin story to justify kingship in Babylonia. Perhaps in the case of India, the *Rigveda* provides divine sanction for the social structure, one that favors the fair-skinned invaders. When the victors compose the myths, it is no surprise that they come out looking good. "Vedic religious practices and beliefs reinforced the social and political order," observe world historians.[9]

The Vedic social order, which has persisted through the millennia into modern times, is racist and oppressive when measured by the United Nations Declaration of Human Rights of 1948. However, this is the case for virtually every social order in the archaic world. "India has no monopoly on the history of oppression," argues Robert Bellah. Every human society, as far as a historian can tell, has been oppressive toward significant portions of the population. Among foragers and farmers, certainly women and children were subordinated to their dominating males. Democracy and slavery went together in democracy's two great exemplars, ancient Athens and modern America, Bellah complains. "Caste is simply the form oppression takes in India."[10] The awakening from compact consciousness and the realization that each individual human person has dignity requires a transformation of consciousness, and that transformation began with the axial insight.

The Fullness of Reality

The *Rigveda* readies the psyche for the insight. It retells the myth of Indra in such a manner that the distinction between being and non-being pokes through. Prior to the activity of the gods, a primordial chaos cried out for ordering. Note the double valence of water symbolization: water is both chaos as in a flood but also the life-force as in fertility.

> Neither not-being nor being was there at that time; there was no air-filled space nor was there the sky which is beyond it. What enveloped all? . . . What was the unfathomable deep water? . . . In the beginning there was darkness concealed in darkness; all this was an indistinguishable flood of water. That, which possessing life-force, was enclosed by the vacuum, the One. . . . The gods appeared only later—after the creation of the world. (*Rigveda* 10.129)[11]

What we see here is an ancient Indian speculation regarding the unity of all things, the One, inclusive of being and non-being, chaos and order, matter and

9. Bonnie G. Smith, Mark Van De Mieroop, Richard Von Glahn, and Kris Lane, *Crossroads and Cultures: A History of the World's Peoples* (Boston: Bedford/St. Martin's, 2012), 89.

10. Robert N. Bellah, *Religion in Human Evolution from the Paleolithic to the Axial Age* (Cambridge, MA: Harvard University Press, 2011), 524.

11. Doniger, *Hindu Myths*, 75.

mind. Might the window to supra-cosmic transcendence have opened just a crack? "The world of *brahman*," says Doniger, "is a world of monism (which assumes that all living things are elements of a single universal being)."[12] Bellah employs a kind of hybrid term, *mythospeculation*, when the text "has raised the question of a higher order of ultimate reality than the gods."[13] Ordinarily, we distinguish sharply between myth and speculation. But Bellah perceives the emergence of speculation already within the myth. The *Rigveda* provides the first step on the ladder that the seers of the later Upanishads will climb on their way to the axial insight.

Brahman and Atman

In the Upanishads, a collection of books that interpret the Vedas transcribed still prior to the Common Era, this question about the unity of all things became a driving passion. The Upanishadic sages asserted that, indeed, all things are only one thing. That one thing is *Brahman*. Actually, Brahman is not a thing. To be a thing, a thing has to be distinguishable from other things. But Brahman is not distinguishable from anything. Rather, it is the underlying reality that makes thinghood possible. Brahman is fullness, the unity underlying all plurality.

The everyday world in which human consciousness operates is riddled with distinctions, separations, multiplicity, and the cause-effect interaction between things. Human consciousness perceives one's self to be distinguishable from everything else in the world. A human person thinks of himself or herself as a *self* (*atman* in Sanskrit), an independent entity existing over against all other selves and against objects in the world. But, announced the Brahman seers, this is all a delusion.

Maya is the name given to this delusory tendency. Maya obstructs our human ability to know ourselves as truly Brahman. Brahman alone is real. If we fail to realize our oneness with Brahman, we live in delusion.

History is a delusion. To chronicle events especially if they are related according to cause and effect, is to lead human consciousness in a detour away from ultimate reality. History is temporal. Ultimate reality, the fullness of reality or Brahman, is eternal. For human consciousness to devote itself to history is to miss the mark, so to speak. To be conscious only of the cause and effect events within history is to deny oneness with Brahman. It is to live in delusion, failing to grasp a more ultimate oneness of reality.

Living in the delusion of cause and effect does not end at death. Actions in this life precipitate reactions in the next life. If a human person in this life engages in causative action of a moral nature, the causal nexus insures that its effects will

---

12. Wendy Doniger, *The Hindus: An Alternative History* (New York: Penguin, 2009), 174.

13. Bellah, *Religion in Human Evolution*, 494.

return to its initiator. This is the law of *karma*, a law that remains intact beyond death. A causal event in this incarnation may reach through with an effect in the next incarnation. The law of karma determines what happens in the cycle of rebirth; but when the self jumps off the cycle of rebirth the law of karma ceases. Karma may be immortal, but it is not eternal. Only Brahman is eternal.

Rita is the invisible order of life and the universe. *Dharma* is the immortal moral order—the principle of right conduct that attunes one's human life to Rita—that distinguishes good from bad karma. Living according to Dharma will lead to a positive effect in one's next incarnation, while violating Dharma will lead to a negative effect.

To repeat, according to the law of karma, immoral actions in this life will result in punishment in the next life. Positive moral actions in this life will result in rewards granted in the next life. Negative karma results in rebirth in a lower caste, whereas positive karma results in rebirth in a higher caste. The object of Brahmanic spirituality is to ascend to the highest caste via a series of incarnations, and then to jump off the wheel of rebirth into an eternal unity with Brahman. Called moksha, this salvation is thought to be the atman's liberation from the world of delusion, liberation from the law of karma, liberation from the self as a distinct and separate entity.

Living daily in the domain of delusion is the product of ignorance, of not knowing the truth about the oneness of all things. Moksha is gained through knowledge that overcomes ignorance, gained by a light that overcomes darkness. But the kind of knowledge Brahmanism fosters is not what happens in school. It is not the product of Confucius's education. Instead, moksha requires inner knowledge, yogic knowledge, a genuine knowing of one's inner relationship to ultimate reality. The key to saving knowledge is the full realization of a single truth, namely, atman *is* Brahman; and Brahman *is* atman.

> All this is Brahman; in tranquility, let one meditate closely upon It as *tajjalān* (Brahman as That which births all things, into which all things dissolve, and in which they breathe/have their existence). . . . That whose creation is this cosmos, who values all desires, who contains all scents, who is bestowed with all flavors, who includes all this, who is still and without yearning—This is my Self within the heart, This is that Brahman. When I shall leave hereafter I shall certainly reach Him. (*Chandagya Upanishad* 3.14.1–4)[14]

The Self (*atman*), who is free from evil, free from old age, free from death, free from grief, free from hunger, free from thirst, whose desire is the Real (*Brahman*), is what the disciple of Brahmanism and Hinduism should seek.

---

14. Translation from Rita Sherma, *Hinduism and the Divine: An Introduction to Hindu Theology* (London: IB Tauris, 2017), forthcoming.

The simple relationship between self, society, and cosmos in the compact consciousness of the *Rigveda* is gradually becoming explicated if not revised. As consciousness differentiates in the Upanishads, the self and the ultimate reality beyond the cosmos become united. When the self and Brahman unite directly, the historical social order becomes marginalized. The social order now belongs to the realm of delusion. The spiritual goal of the self, the atman, is to escape historical existence and enter the timeless non-existence of Brahman.

Compact consciousness is differentiating into axial consciousness during this period. According to Bellah, what is happening here is "a move beyond mythospeculation . . . beyond narrative into conceptual thinking."[15] Conceptual thinking constitutes a level of differentiation beyond that of narrative, story, or myth. It represents a leap in human consciousness.

The term *Brahman* can refer to three different things. First, if when pronouncing it one emphasizes the final syllable, *Brahmán*, it refers to the ground of all reality. Second, if when pronouncing it one emphasizes the first syllable, *Bráhman*, it refers to a human person, a member of the priestly caste. Third, by deleting the final 'n', *Brahma* is the name of one of the gods who manifests *Brahmán* in the historical order. Actually, Brahma can be thought of as the creating god who manifests Brahman in time and space. Sometimes the god Brahma is placed next to Shiva and Vishnu to form what is misleadingly labeled *the Hindu Trinity*.

Brahman and the Gods

Hinduism is awash with gods, goddesses, myths, legends, and symbols. No one individual is expected to get the full picture. Each individual Hindu picks a favorite divine figure, either a god (*deva*), goddess (*devī*), or group (*devatā*, meaning luminous ones), on which to focus devotion. The preferred, tutelary, favorite deity (*iṣṭa-devatā*) becomes the chosen form through which to access the supreme divine reality, Brahman. The key to unlocking the complicated Hindu worldview is to see that the *devatā* are penultimate; they mediate a more ultimate reality, Brahman.

Contemporary Hindu theologian, Rita Sherma, observes that supreme divinity is most importantly manifested in three divine figures: Shiva, Vishnu, and Mahadevi. Three yes, but not the so-called Hindu Trinity. Each of these three principal deities have their own overlapping traditions, with Vishnu and Mahadevi also having multiple incarnations. Shiva and Vishnu are male figures with consorts or wives, while Mhadevi is said to be the divine mother of the cosmos. These divine figures are not facets, powers, or emanations of Brahman;

---

15. Bellah, *Religion in Human Evolution*, 513.

Images of Brahma, Vishnu, and Shiva are carved into walls of an ancient Hindu cave temple near Aurangabad, India. Sometimes misleadingly termed "the Hindu Trinity," these three divine figures manifest the ultimate unifying reality, Brahman.

they embody it, incarnate it. This distinguishes Hindu polytheism from what one might find in ancient Babylonia or Greece.[16]

Shankara: "I am Brahman"

"I am Brahman" (*aham Brahmasmi*), said the Advaita philosopher, Sri Shanka-racharya (788–820 CE), commonly known as Shankara, within the Hindu tra-dition a thousand years after the Upanishads had been transcribed. Shankara deepened the axial insight that realizes the unity of the soul with ultimate reality. "I am Brahman," *aham Brahmasi*, points to the ultimate and essential oneness of individual self and of Supreme Self (*atman*), and the comprehensive reality behind them both, *Brahman*.

Interestingly, within Shankara's Advaita (non-dualism) tradition, two ver-sions of Brahman have appeared: *nirguna Brahman*, the sublime divine reality so transcendent that it stands beyond all attributes, and *saguna Brahman*, a concept of the divine that includes attributes similar to the personal God of theism. Of these two, Shankara ranks nirguna Brahman higher. The divine at the ultimate level is twofold with the higher formless Brahman inclusive of the lower saguna Brahman, which becomes an active principle responsible for creating the world. As a non-dualist, Shankara insists that the lower Brahman is not imaginary

---

16. Sherma, *Hinduism and the Divine*.

but real, simply a less real expression of what is ultimately real, namely, nirguna Brahman. The god Shiva becomes Shankara's symbol for this movement within the divine that makes the pure consciousness of Brahman available to us humans within the domain of Maya. Despite myriads of gods and goddesses in Hindu polytheistic practice, nirguna Brahman has become the dominant Hindu concept of ultimate reality, of the truly divine. Brahman is India's axial answer to the question of God.

Perennialists like to place Upanishadic Brahmanism and Hindu Shankara among the dualists. Dualism posits two substances or two realities, a supernal spiritual reality and a subordinate physical or mundane reality. We must ask, is Brahmanism fully dualistic in the sense of positing two substances, one physical and the other spiritual? In its own way, the point of the Advaita form of Brahmanism is anti-dualistic. Ultimate reality differs from mundane everyday reality, to be sure, but the very distinction is a delusion. Shankara named his school of thought *Advaita Vedanta*, meaning non-dualism, just to emphasize this point. To say, "I am Brahman," is to realize oneness with the whole of reality. This is still dualism, but it is not a dualism of two separate substances. Rather, it is a dualism distinguishing an underlying integrated substance versus a surface pluralism, which is a delusion. Advaita is a dualism distinguishing ultimate being from a surface confusion in which material things are wrongly thought to be ultimate.

There is one more nuance worth exploring: is ultimate reality personal or impersonal? Ramanuja (1017–1137 CE)[17] reversed Shankara's ordering of ultimates. Whereas Shankara placed impersonal Brahman on top and all personhood lower on the ladder of reality, Ramanuja advocated a form of spirituality that presumed the personal dimension of the divine to be highest. Rejecting Shankara's Advaita (non-dualism), Ramanuja advocated what he called Vishista-Advaita (qualified monism); and he cultivated a form of spirituality previously known as Bhakti, or personal devotion to the god Vishnu. The Bhakti path to Brahman is through the god Vishnu, an avatar of saguna Brahman. Whereas Shankara's symbol for Brahman's dynamism is the god Shiva, Vishnu plays this role for Ramanuja. The gods may differ, but Brahman is ultimate for both Hindu philosophers. Both Shankara and Ramanuja are children of the axial breakthrough; they extend the axial insight into transcendent unity through their debate regarding the relative rank of the personal and the impersonal.

The Indian mind deliberating over Brahman evinces some similarities with the mind of the modern physical cosmologist. In an uncanny way, both are looking for the relationship of the one to the many. The cosmologist finds oneness in the archonic past, in the singularity prior to the big bang. The Indian philosopher finds oneness in Brahman, the eternal unity out of which physical plurality differentiates.

---

17. Ramanuja is reputed to have lived 120 years.

To risk oversimplification, one might summarize the Indian axial insight by saying that Brahman is the answer to the God question. As the unity of all things, Brahman surpasses and incorporates all that is personal, raising all multiplicities up into an undifferentiated impersonal unity. Human fulfillment will be found by realizing this oneness of all things in Brahman.

Buddha, Non-Self, and Nirvana

Siddhartha Gautama the Sakyamuni (ca. 563–483 BCE), who became the Buddha (that is, the "enlightened one") asked a fundamental question: how can we escape suffering and gain serenity of mind? Suffering is caused by unsatisfied craving, he said in his first sermon; by eliminating this craving, one can eliminate suffering. This is the hinge on which everything in Buddhist thinking swings.

The Buddhist door to enlightenment had been opened by Upanishadic speculation. Gautama walked through and then turned Brahman logic on its head. Instead of beginning with fullness, the Buddha began with emptiness. Instead of affirming the atman, he substituted the opposite, the non-self, *anatman* in Sanskrit and *anattā* in Pali. Neither Brahman nor atman have any essential substance. This reduces the Upanishadic equation, $1 = 1$, to the Buddhist equation, $0 = 0$. Once one realizes that he or she is a non-self rather than a self, then no longer will one utter phrases such as "I am" or "This is mine." This logical reversal provides the ontology that underlies the Buddhist spirituality that overcomes the problem of human suffering.

Hindu dharma (Sanskrit) becomes *dhamma* (Pali) as the disciples remember and pass on the teachings of the Buddha. The core Buddhist insight begins with the Four Noble Truths.

1. All of life is suffering (*dukkha*).
2. Suffering is the result of craving (*tanha*, desire, coveting), unsatisfied craving.
3. Suffering will cease when craving ceases.
4. The Eightfold Path is the way to stop craving.

The Eightfold Path is the path to knowledge, saving knowledge. By following this path, one transforms one's self into a non-self; as a non-self, one ceases to crave anything for the self. This douses the flames of desire and passion. This also counts as liberation from suffering because it sponsors liberation from the self, who is the subject of suffering. To gain liberation, Buddha's disciples must follow the Eightfold Path:

1. Right view—view reality as it is and not merely as one wants to see it.
2. Right intention—pursue self-renunciation.
3. Right speech—speak truthfully but not hurtfully.

4. Right action—avoid harming other life.
5. Right livelihood—earn a living that avoids harm to others.
6. Right effort—strive to improve.
7. Right mindfulness—pursue awareness of self and world, heightened consciousness.[18]
8. Right concentration—correct meditation.

Mindfulness and meditative consciousness lead to a state of awareness wherein the self is bracketed and one experiences fullness or, better, emptiness. Fullness without discrimination is logically the equivalent of emptiness. The self and all of reality realize a oneness, a oneness that paradoxically is both full and empty.

If the self suffers, the cure is to eliminate either the source of suffering or the self. Buddhists elect the latter. According to the Dalai Lama in the twenty-first century, "As we recognize that the basis of misery is this mistaken perception, this mistaken grasping at a nonexistent self, we see that suffering can be eliminated. Once we remove the mistaken perception, we shall no longer be troubled by suffering."[19] To penetrate the misperception and realize the non-existence of one's self leads to *nirvana,* to the healing experience of emptiness.

The Buddhist equivalent of Brahmanism's *moksha* is *nirvana.* The serenity of mind Gautama had sought is found in *nirvana,* the imperturbable stillness after the fires of craving, desire, coveting, and delusion have been extinguished. Nirvana is the state of egoless bliss, free from suffering.

With this ontology of emptiness combined with a spirituality that seeks nirvana, any transcendentally grounded model for the social order evaporates. There can be no equivalent of Israel's Ten Commandments or Plato's intuition regarding cosmic justice in the Buddhist system of thought. In addition, there can be no transcendental justification for the caste system. The Buddha himself drew out this implication. His own doctrine eliminated caste distinctions, because no structure in ultimate being justifies such social discrimination. *Nirvana* implies that in human history all persons are equal. Buddhist ontology implies human equality. In a Buddhist society, equality should be the moral norm, just as it should have been for Brahman society. "It is part of the definition of the axial age that it was then that a universally egalitarian ethic first appeared," observes Bellah.[20] Even so, no Buddhist society to date has produced an egalitarian political entity.

---

18. Mindfulness is "keeping one's consciousness alive to the present reality," writes the popular Vietnamese Zen teacher Thich Nhat Hanh, in *The Miracle of Mindfulness,* trans. Mobi Ho, rev. ed. (Boston: Beacon, 1987), 11.

19. Dalai Lama, *An Open Heart* (Boston: Little Brown and Company, 2001), 102.

20. Bellah, *Religion in Human Evolution,* 573.

This giant statue in Boghagaya, India, represents Siddhartha Gautama the Sakyamuni (ca. 563–483 BCE), the Buddha. Whereas Brahmanism saw ultimate reality as fullness, Buddhism saw ultimate reality as emptiness.

Escape from History

History loses all ontological grounding in Buddhism, just as it did in Brahminism and Hinduism. In Buddhism the historical nexus of material events is not exactly declared a delusion, but what reality history does possess becomes a barrier to individual enlightenment. One must transcend history to realize pure consciousness or pure emptiness beyond history.

The intersecting nexus of physical causes that constitutes history is dubbed *pratītyasamutpāda* or co-dependent co-arising. The finite universe is all around us, but it is ephemeral and, therefore, empty (*sunyata*). Reality is like a pancake with *pratītyasamutpāda* on the top and *sunyata* on the bottom.

Even though it is at bottom empty, the upper nexus of codependent co-arising is violent. The early Buddhists observed what Charles Darwin later noted: to live is to be violent. The chief ethical principle became for Buddhists *ahimsa*, non-violence. Commitment to *ahimsa* readies one to perceive underlying reality as it is.

If one fails to perceive reality as it is, one will continue living a deluded life—a frustrated life—because no person can have permanence, let alone possess every item he or she craves, covets, desires, or demands. The only way to avoid suffering is to avoid craving; and the only way to avoid craving is to rid oneself of self and thereby avoid the nexus of codependent co-arising.

Once one internally realizes this truth, then the cravings of the self become recognized as epiphenomenal, as avoidable. Once one has reoriented the self to a reality beyond the self, no longer is there a self to crave or to feel the pain of experiencing unmet cravings. The self will have become extinguished. One will have realized no-self, *anatman*. Renunciation and devotion through meditation is the path that leads to this ecstasy, to this moment of self-transcendence, to Nirvana, to extinguishment, to eternal peace.[21]

The Fourteenth Dalai Lama (Tenzin Gyatso) says that "Buddhism can be defined as a sort of combination of spiritual path and philosophical system. . . . Greater emphasis is given to reason and intelligence than faith. . . . The testimony of Buddha is not taken simply on blind faith just because he is the Buddha, but rather because Buddha's word has been proven reliable in the context of phenomena and topics that are amenable to logical reason and understanding."[22] Buddhism rests on reason and meditative discipline, not faith.

India Asks the Question of God

Even if gods and goddesses or spiritual heroes are tolerated in various Buddhist or Hindu traditions, they cannot claim ultimacy. At best, divine figures become transparent to what transcends them. Buddhist belief, like Hindu spirituality, passes through any deities on the way to an intimate realization of what lies beyond them. If we assume that the God-question is the question regarding ultimate reality, then in India that question is answered with a supra-personal oneness as either fulfillment or emptiness.

Brahman in India is more akin to the Dao in China than to Confucius's will of heaven. The will of heaven lodged the just social structure in a transcendent ideal. But Dao and Brahman lie beyond any structure, beyond morality or justice. All human souls stand equally in the face of the mystery of Dao or Brahman.

Whether as fulfillment or emptiness, India's axial reality cannot structure human society. The beyond cannot be responsible for the caste system, racism, patriarchy, militarism, or any of the kind of human inequalities we find in so many historical social orders. By absence, ultimate reality refuses to be co-opted by historical monarchs to justify oppression and injustice.

---

21. Buddhists affirm that "Nirvana is permanent, stable, imperishable, immovable, ageless, deathless, unborn, and unbecoming, that it is power, bliss, happiness, the secure refuge, the shelter, and the place of unassailable safety; that it is the real Truth and the supreme Reality; that it is the Good, the supreme goal and the one and only consummation of our life, the eternal, hidden, and incomprehensible Peace." Edward Conze, *Buddhism: Its Essence and Development* (New York: Philosophical Library, 1951), 40.

22. The Dalai Lama, "Compassion in Action," in *Healing Our Planet: Healing Our Selves*, ed. Dawson Church and Geralyn Gendreau (Santa Rosa, CA: Elite, 2005), 65.

Conclusion

Renowned philosopher of religion John Hick observes, "Each of the post-axial religions acknowledges, indeed stresses, our human finitude, suffering, mortality, and our inveterate tendency to injure one another both individually and collectively; and each affirms the real possibility and availability of a limitlessly better existence, to which it knows the way."[23] This certainly describes the path followed by the early Brahmans through Buddhism and Hinduism toward the modern world. Regardless of which explanation for the axial insight finally obtains—emergence, revelation, or a combination—the intellectual history of ancient India is wondrous.

Whether or not ancient Brahmanism, Buddhism, or modern Hinduism fit precisely the model formulated by axial theorists is beside the point. What is clear is that insightful seers in ancient India discovered a transcendent dimension to reality, a supra-historical dimension. At the same time, they realized that knowledge of the transcendent occurs only within the depths of the human soul, within the self or non-self, as the case may be. Beyond and intimate sensibilities converge in this most profound of transformative spiritual practices.

The question of God raised in this book does not appear with full force in the myths of origin such as found in the *Rigveda* or similar works. It appears more forcefully in the speculative quest for ultimacy, in the search for the transcendental ground of daily events and the vicissitudes of human history. Perhaps the question leading to God is the same in both the compact consciousness of myth and the differentiated consciousness of speculation, but the way it is asked in the latter comes closer to our own modern and emerging postmodern experience. Both Brahmanism and Buddhism raise the question of ultimacy, but neither answers with the idea of a personal deity. Gods and goddesses abound in traditional Hinduism and even in some expressions of Buddhism, but these deities were imported from pre-axial traditions through cultural accretion. The plurality of gods and goddesses is historical and intra-cosmic, from an Indian point of view, whereas the ultimate reality is eternal and supra-cosmic.

In short, the question of God raised in axial India does not give a personal deity as the answer, at least for the most part. For Ramanuja, of course, saguna Brahman manifest in Vishnu is both personal and ultimate. But for the larger axial tradition, including Buddha and Shankara, either an emptiness or a fullness of reality transcends revelatory avatars such as Vishnu or Shiva or Mahadevi. Anything historical, including the dimension of the personal, is taken up and tacitly obliterated in the eternal oneness that is ultimate.

It is disappointing to some interpreters of our ancestors' achievements that a full egalitarian ethic replete with human rights and universal compassion did not sweep over the Asian subcontinent. There are two ways to ground an

---

23. John Hick, *The New Frontier of Religion and Science: Religious Experience, Neuroscience and the Transcendent* (New York: Palgrave, 2006), 150.

egalitarian social order. The first is to find a map of the social order in ultimate reality, the ideal social order depicted symbolically as the kingdom of God or cosmic justice. The second reverses the logic. If the transcendent order provides no map for the historical order to copy, then no transcendental justification exists for class hierarchy, racism, discrimination against women, and other social inequities. Brahmanism prompted this second method for undercutting unjust social hierarchy. Brahmanism set out on the track toward human equality, but it became quickly derailed.

Even though Brahman alone is eternal for the Hindu, Rita along with Dharma are still immortal. Can one ask Rita and Dharma to help right the injustices in the social order? Unfortunately, no. In order to pursue justice within history, one would necessarily invoke Rita or Dharma, but these penultimate standards do not support the kind of historical equality post-axial modern culture demands. Must one then go above the head of Rita or Dharma, so to speak, and talk to the boss, Brahman? Brahman does not answer in ways that guide social architects.

Be that as it may, one can still conclude that any attempt to justify social repression fails to find support in the ultimate order of things, in the Dao, in Brahman, or in Buddhist emptiness. That is, the being of the world in which we live does not justify a social structure of inequality according to axial theorists.

Review Questions

1. How do daily consciousness (Maya) and pure consciousness (Brahman) compare?
2. How do Indra and Marduk (see chapter 7) compare?
3. How do *moksha* and *nirvana* compare?
4. What is the Buddhist logic for overcoming suffering?

Discussion Questions

1. According to the Upanishads, what is the relationship between Brahman and human history?
2. What kind of knowledge is required to realize the oneness of atman with Brahman?
3. What kind of knowledge is required to realize anatman?
4. How can a worldview consisting of self-society-cosmos morally justify human equality or inequality?

Additional Resources

Print Sources

Beck, Roger B., Linda Beck, Larry S. Krieger, Phillip C. Naylor, and Dahia Ibo Shabaka. *World History: Patterns of Interaction.* New York: Houghton Mifflin, McDougal Littel, 2007.

This world history text provides a brief yet accurate historical treatment of early Hinduism and Buddhism (pp. 66–71).

Bellah, Robert N. *Religion in Human Evolution from the Paleolithic to the Axial Age.* Cambridge, MA: Harvard University Press, 2011.

Bellah's chapter 9, "Axial Age IV: Ancient India," provides the best overview of Brahmanism, Hinduism, and Buddhism for discerning the axial elements.

The Dalai Lama. "Compassion in Action." In *Healing our Planet; Healing Our Selves,* ed. Dawson Church and Geralyn Gendreau. Santa Rosa, CA: Elite Books, 2005.

This collection of the Dalai Lama's thoughts provides a mood-setting compilation of insights into human nature and the pursuit of serenity of mind.

De Bary, William Theodore, ed. *Sources of Indian Tradition.* 2 Vols. New York: Columbia University Press, 1958.

This two-volume set provides extensive selections of original texts plus historical explication and commentary.

Doniger, Wendy. *Hindu Myths: A Sourcebook: Translated from the Sanskrit.* New York: Penguin, 1975.

This very readable sourcebook provides myths from the Vedic age right through their commentaries into existing Hindu tradition. Doniger points out that one connecting theme in the diverse myths is cosmic incest, an immoral primeval act that brought the current cosmos into existence. This suggest that for the Hindu mind, the physical cosmos from which we must wrest a daily living is somehow fallen, estranged.

Sherma, Rita. *Hinduism and the Divine: An Introduction to Hindu Theology.* London: IB Tauris, 2017.

At this writing, Sherma's treatment of Hindu theology is forthcoming. It should provide the most readable and accessible treatment of Hindu gods and goddesses in relationship to the all-encompassing reality, Brahman.

Web Sources

"Buddhism." BBC. *http://www.bbc.co.uk/religion/religions/buddhism/.*

A guide to Buddhism, including its beliefs, ethics, customs, history, and holy days.

"Hinduism." BBC. *http://www.bbc.co.uk/religion/religions/hinduism/.*

A guide to Hinduism, including its deities, ethics, history, texts, and worship.

15

CHAPTER

The Axial Breakthrough in Greece

Philosophy

Or let my lamp at midnight hour
Be seen in some high lonely tower,
Where I may oft out-watch the Bear
With thrice-great Hermes, or unsphere
the spirit of Plato, to unfold
What worlds or what vast regions hold
The immortal mind that hath forsook
Her mansion in this fleshly nook.

—John Milton (1608–1674), "Il Penseroso"

Socrates (470–399 BCE) was found guilty of atheism and executed. Although Socrates believed in God in the monotheistic sense, his rejection of polytheism (*asebeia*, impiety) was judged to be a capital crime in his city-state, Athens. With Socrates's execution, the Axial Age took a giant step forward.

Baby steps toward axial thinking had begun before Socrates. Citizens in the polis called Athens had inherited myths replete with an almost countless array of immortal beings. They inherited a pantheon with Zeus ruling from the top, sometimes called "king" and other times called "father." Athens had no king, but the gods did. In other myth-oriented societies such as ancient Babylonia, the heavenly king became

An artist's reconstruction shows the probable appearance of the massive statue of Zeus that once stood at Olympia. As, polytheists, the ancient Greeks believed in multiple gods that were very much a part of this world, not transcendent.

© duncan1890 / iStockphoto.com

the model and the authority for the earthly king. Not so in Athens. It was in Athens that politics was invented, where the leaders had to share their authority with a growing democratic spirit.

In this book we are asking the question of God. One method is to look at previous answers. Ancient Athens provides answers that help us to formulate the question more precisely.

Critical Consciousness in Ancient Athens

The poets who told the myths anticipated the axial insight. Hesiod (ca. 700 BCE) interpreted the inherited stories of the gods and goddesses in such a way that the question of transcendent justice poked through. We are watching the transition from myth (*mythos*) to reason (*logos*).

> But those who give straight verdicts and follow justice (*dikē*),
>
> both when fellow citizens and strangers are on trial,
>
> live in a city that blossoms, a city that prospers.[1]

In this passage from Hesiod's *Works and Days*, justice as fairness treats both insiders and outsiders equally. In addition, a just city is a thriving city. Justice stands as a supra-cosmic criterion that provides a vision for the social order and a criterion of judgment when the social order falls short. Modern civilization can take this for granted only because the concept of transcendental justice pressed itself into human consciousness at some point in the past sequence of contingent historical events.

Once a transcendental criterion for justice had entered the Greek mind, this criterion could be used in judgment against the historical social order, and even against the mythical gods. The passions and affairs and violence among the immortals atop Mount Olympus became repugnant to those imbibing a new and higher standard of morality. The moral life and a just social order stood like a mirror, condemning the gods of Homer and the myths of the Greek ancestors.

It was in this moment that the projection theory of religion was born. According to this theory, heaven becomes an imaginary screen onto which humans project their emotions and ideals and pretend they belong to the deities. Xenophanes of Colophon (ca. 570–475 BCE) attacked the anthropomorphism of the gods found commonly in myths. "The Ethiopians say their gods are snub-nosed and black, the Thracians that theirs have light blue eyes and red hair," and, if "horses and cattle" could draw pictures of the gods, they would look like

---

1. Hesiod, *Works and Days*, trans. Apostolos N. Athanassakis (Baltimore: Johns Hopkins University Press, 2004), 225.

"horses and cattle."[2] Xenophanes criticized mythical belief in the Olympian deities, asserting that it is absurd to believe the gods look like ourselves or behave like humans do. Xenophanes's consciousness was differentiating here, because he could bring a supra-cosmic or transcendent perspective to bear on an intra-cosmic worldview. Therefore, the stories the myths tell could not be true. It was in this moment—the transition from narrative myth (*mythos*) to rational theory (*logos*)—that the idea of myth as a false story was born.

The Birth of Axial Monotheism

God, according to Xenophanes, could not be in any "way similar to mortals in body or thought. . . . All of him [God] sees, all thinks, and all hears."[3] A new insight is here trying to break through, to penetrate human consciousness. It is by no means mature, but its birth process has begun.

Socrates (470–399 BCE), followed by Plato (428–348 BCE) and Aristotle (384–322 BCE), nourished this nascent notion of the divine to axial maturity. Socrates remained in the oral tradition, whereas Plato and Aristotle wrote multiple books. Socrates turned the key, so to speak, that opened the door from mythological polytheism to rational monotheism.

According to Socrates, the one God is supra-cosmic and reigns with an authority that transcends the political order of Athens. When he was standing trial accused of atheism, Socrates was asked to recant his beliefs. He refused. "I shall obey God rather than you," said Socrates. The accused prisoner went on to offer consolation to the judges who would be committing evil by condemning him. "I do nothing but go about persuading you all, old and young alike, not to take thought for your persons or your properties, but first and chiefly to care about the greatest improvement of the soul."[4] Note the double role of transcendence here. First, God is transcendent to both the gods of polytheism and to the social order represented by the court. Second, God has an immediate relationship to the soul. To give attention to the relationship each person has with God within the soul is paramount for Socrates.

According to Plato, the eternal God is the creator of the cosmos. God creates by making order out of chaos, the same order that people study with their rational minds. What God creates is good; evil is not something God created. Included in God's creative work is the human soul or mind (*psychē*, coming into English in *psychology*). Human beings' rational minds are the product of their

---

2. Xenophanes of Colophon, in *The Presocratic Philosophers*, ed. G. S. Kirk and J. E. Raven (Cambridge, UK: Cambridge University Press, 1960), 169.

3. Ibid.

4. Plato, *Apology* 29–30, in *The Dialogues of Plato*, trans. B. Jowett, 2 vols. (New York: Random House, 1892), 1:412–13. Subsequent quotations of Plato are from this edition.

immortal souls belonging to God. However, in everyday life, the immortal soul finds itself in tension with another soul, a mortal soul belonging to the mortal body. "When all things were in disorder God created in each thing in relation to itself, and in all things in relation to each other, all the measures and harmonies which they could possibly receive. . . . And they, imitating him, received from him the immortal principle of the soul; and around this they proceeded to fashion a mortal body."[5] The transcendentally grounded soul (mind) has immediate access to God and God's mind; and this, in turn, provides the mind with what is needed to understand the natural world.

According to Aristotle, Plato's prize student, the one God is the prime mover, the first mover. If the natural world is defined by its sequence of cause and effect, there must be a first cause, an uncaused cause that begins the entire history of cause and effect. That first cause is God.

> The first mover, then, exists of necessity. . . . On such a principle, then, depend the heavens and the world of nature. . . . We say therefore that God is a living being, eternal, most good, so that life and duration continues and eternally belong to God; for this *is* God.[6]

This cosmological argument for the existence of God was cited in an earlier chapter dealing with the anthropic principle. Aristotle's argument has been shepherded through effective history by Jews, Christians, and Muslims.

The heavens and the world of nature depend on God, according to Aristotle, even though God does not exactly create them. Aristotle's philosophy heavily influenced Jewish, Christian, and Muslim theologians in the later development of classical theism; but this particular belief of Aristotle's did not get passed on. Philosopher Michael Olson offers an interpretation that makes this point.

> Similar to Aristotle's divine *nous* [mind], the God of subsequent classical monotheism is an inviolable reality, indivisible and one, separate from the natural things and thus having transcendent being. . . . Aristotle's God is distinct from the God of most other monotheisms [Judaism, Christianity, Islam] in that Aristotle's divine *nous* does not create. God is not responsible for imbuing the natural order with design according to his divine wisdom.[7]

On the one hand, Aristotle seems to depict God as the prime mover, the first cause of the world. On the other hand, the eternal God transcends the temporal

---

5. Plato, *Timaeus* 69.

6. Aristotle, *Metaphysics* 1072, in *The Basic Works of Aristotle*, trans. Richard McKeon (New York: Random House, 1941), 880.

7. R. Michael Olson, "Aristotle on God: Divine *Nous* as Unmoved Modern," in *Models of God and Alternative Ultimate Realities*, ed. Jeanine Diller and Asa Kasher (Heidelberg: Springer, 2013), 101–9, at 107.

world and ought not to be thought of as one sequential cause among others. Medieval Roman Catholics incorporated Aristotle's thinking neatly by designating God the *primary cause* while the sequence of events within history is the job of *secondary causes*.

Even if Aristotle's God is not the creator, a breakthrough to a rationality of watershed significance occurred in Greece. The mundane world of nature is now said to be governed by the law of cause and effect. Further, the scientific mind is so structured that it can grasp what goes on in the world of cause and effect. God, who is responsible for the natural world, is beyond cause and effect yet still responsible for cause and effect. History is not a delusion. History is real, even if God is supra-historical. This is the core of what axial theorists wish to dub the axial insight.

For axial theorists such as Robert Bellah, the axial insight makes possible theoretical thinking. The compact consciousness of pre-axial thinking expressed itself in narrative. Every human expression came in the form of story. With the axial breakthrough came analytical and critical thinking. "Theoretic culture," observes Bellah, "is the ability to think analytically rather than narratively, to construct theories that can be criticized logically and empirically."[8] This giant step in the differentiation of consciousness took the ancient Athenians from *mythos* to *logos*.

Recall that critical thinking involves entertaining two or more thoughts at the same time. This doublethink permits comparative analysis. Critical thinking is the product of a historical event, the axial event. According to Bellah, "The emergence of second-order thinking, the idea that there are alternatives that have to be argued for, that marks the axial age."[9] It also marks an indispensable ingredient to modern thinking. Perhaps this is why modern axial theorists like to celebrate their axial ancestors.

Bully Justice in the Temporal Social Order

"Plato's work is a shoreless sea," comments Bellah.[10] Plato's mind was encyclopedic, writing on every subject a person in the ancient world could imagine. The one subject that will be discussed here is justice. Key to the axial insight is that there exists in eternity an ideal social order, an ideal polis or kingdom that guides and judges the actual historical order in which people live. Just how one is to access this transcendent justice becomes one of Plato's most vexing questions. In his work, *The Republic*, Plato offers an answer.

---

8. Robert N. Bellah, *Religion in Human Evolution from the Paleolithic to the Axial Age* (Cambridge, MA: Harvard University Press, 2011), 274.

9. Ibid., 279.

10. Ibid., 387.

Consider the everyday experience of bullies. Should a state be governed by bullies? The bully view of justice justifies the strong when they pick on the weak. It justifies powerful nations invading and conquering weak nations. It justifies the thievery of armed robbers who steal from unarmed storekeepers. It justifies tax structures that favor the rich while making the working class pay.

In Plato's dialog in *The Republic*, one character, named Thrasymachus, tries on the bully theory of justice to see if it fits. Thrasymachus says, "I proclaim that justice is nothing else than the interest of the stronger"—or, in Alain Badiou's translation, "Listen, listen very carefully. I say that justice is not and cannot be anything but the interest of the stronger."[11]

Socrates objects to the bully view. He asserts that justice is "absolute and eternal and immutable," making both the weak and the strong equal in relation to absolute justice.[12] According to Socrates, eternal justice stands in judgment over every historical social order. Bully justice is fake justice. Had Thrasymachus lived to read Charles Darwin's *Origin of Species*, he would have been pleased. According to Darwinian theory, variations in inheritance are acted upon by natural selection. The species that survive this selection are called *fit*, reproductively fit. Our common phrase, "survival of the fittest," has become synonymous with natural selection. Translated into social ethics, "survival of the fittest" justifies, according to social Darwinists, letting the

Note that Lady Justice is blindfolded. With the blindfold, she cannot see human differences. She becomes impartial as she exacts fairness equally. Only a transcendent vision of a just social order could be blind to differences between hierarchies, ranks, classes, and individuals, and stand in judgment over the actual historical social orders within society.

poor die by the wayside while favoring the rich, the healthy, the powerful classes. If one would like to deny the eternal and universal principles of justice, then one

---

11. Plato, *Republic* 1.338; Alain Badiou, *Plato's Republic: A Dialogue in Sixteen Chapters*, trans. Susan Spitzer (New York: Columbia University Press, 2012), 17.

12. Ibid., 5.479.

could try to ground social ethics in nature. What does nature do? Nature in the form of evolution favors the strong over the weak. Nature teaches what Thrasymachus teaches, namely, justice is "nothing else than the interest of the stronger."

The modern sensibility intuitively rejects this view, asserting that what happens in nature is not good enough. Whatever justice is, it is not exemplified in the killing of the wildebeest by the lion or the gobbling up of small businesses by large corporations. The concept of justice provides social leverage, leverage to judge what happens in nature, society, and even in one's own soul. Justice must be transcendent. Justice must be more than merely the interest of the stronger.

"Justice is not defined in the abstract but in opposition to the concrete forms which injustice assumes," comments Voegelin on *The Republic*. "The right order of the polis is not presented as an ideal state, but the elements of right order are developed in concrete opposition to the elements of disorder in the surrounding society."[13] Voegelin's observation is both correct and incorrect. It is correct to say that, through the mouth of Socrates, Plato judges Athens as falling short of ideal justice. Nevertheless, it is incorrect to deny that Plato's ideal republic provides a positive guide for the polis, an image of a just social order toward which people should strive. Plato's ideal republic stands in judgment against the historical republics in Greek city-states.

Justice in the Soul and in the Cosmos

Modern people require a moral universe—a meaningful world structured justly—in order to enjoy an integrated self. The self or the soul orients itself around the good, the ultimate good. "Symmetrically," begins philosopher Charles Taylor, "the assurance that I am turned towards this good gives me a sense of wholeness, of fullness of being, as a person or self, that nothing else can."[14] Human subjectivity requires organization around an objective ground of value, a good, a reliable moral universe. Without the good, the self loses its center and disintegrates. In order for the self to be a self, people rely upon a cosmos ordered toward what is good, just, and true.

But is there a grounding for goodness or justice that transcends what actually happens every day in nature and society? Justice must be more than just an ephemeral good. It must be eternal. If one's deepest inner self—one's soul—can be grafted onto the eternal trunk of justice, then one can share in its eternal flowering. Do the principles of justice transcend this life? Do they remain in effect beyond our death? Plato, speaking through the mouth of Socrates, would

13. Eric Voegelin, *Order and History*, 5 vols. (Baton Rouge: Louisiana State University Press, 1956–1987), 3:63.

14. Charles Taylor, *Sources of the Self: The Making of the Modern Identity* (Cambridge, MA: Harvard University Press, 1989), 63.

answer affirmatively: justice is eternal, and we will experience justice in our soul both in this life and beyond death.

In *Gorgias*, the Athenian philosopher affirms that "communion and friendship and orderliness and temperance and justice bind together heaven and earth and gods and [humans], and that this universe is therefore called Cosmos or order."[15] The cosmic order is invisibly structured according to ideal justice; the temporal attempts of human beings at just living are but short-lived shadows. The just (*dikaia*) ideal provides the blueprint for ordering the soul and for ordering society. Only if one's soul is well ordered can it be called lawful (*nominos*); and only if one's soul has the right order (*nomos*) is it capable of entering into authentic community (*koinōnia*).

In order to get clear on this relationship of supra-cosmic justice (*dikē*) to the soul, Plato asks which is better: perpetrating injustice or suffering injustice? If one perpetrates injustice as a bully, one may become wealthy, powerful, dominant, revered, glorified. If one suffers injustice, one may become unhealthy, marginalized, despised, imprisoned, or even dead before your time. Which is better? Which is worse? Socrates, Plato tells us, answers that it is better to be a victim of injustice than to perpetrate it. Of "these two evils, the doing injustice and the suffering injustice . . . we affirm that to do injustice is a greater [evil], and to suffer injustice a lesser evil."[16]

On what grounds does Socrates contend that the lot of the victim is preferable to the lot of the victimizer? The answer has to do with the formation of the soul. To perpetrate injustice deforms the soul. Perpetrating injustice estranges or alienates the soul from supra-cosmic order. It is better to face death with one's soul in order than in disorder. The soul deformed by injustice will be unable to find attunement with supra-cosmic order beyond death. It is imperative that one become justified (*dikaios*) within this life in order to find unity with what is eternal in the next life.

Socrates declares, "He who has lived all his life in justice and holiness shall go, when he is dead, to the Islands of the Blessed [*the island of Makarios*], and dwell there in perfect happiness out of the reach of evil; but . . . he who has lived unjustly and impiously shall go to the house of vengeance and punishment, which is called Tartarus."[17] Voegelin comments, "The order of the soul as revealed in Socrates has, indeed, become the new order of relations between God and [humanity]."[18]

In Plato's *Gorgias*, justice has gained the status of an ideal belonging in eternity right along with God. Justice as an ideal is actually more real than the bully

---

15. Plato, *Gorgias* 508.

16. Ibid., 509.

17. Ibid., 522.

18. Voegelin, *Order and History*, 3:43.

justice people frequently experience in the historical social order. Citizens may now appeal to ideal justice to guide the polis and to judge the polis on its short-comings. The eternal guides and judges the temporal. This belongs to the core of the axial insight achieved by the Greek philosophers.

Greece Asks the Question of God

What today we know as monotheism or classical theism derives in part from ancient Athens in Greece. During the Axial Period, God came to be viewed as the ultimate reality. God became the guarantor of justice. Eternal justice came to lure history toward its ideal while providing judgment against historical injustice. This Greek answer to the question of God becomes for us today a new question: can we rely upon this answer to be true or not? Regardless of how we answer this, we must acknowledge that the effective history of this ancient answer continues to inspire modern civilization to pursue justice in ever newer applications.

Conclusion

The question of God arose in ancient Athens, and God was given as one Greek answer. God is the ultimate reality, according to Socrates and his students. This was important because God provides a transcendent ground for the things we most value, such as truth, beauty, and justice. God also deepens the human soul. God eternalizes the soul, so to speak.

Three options could explain such an axial insight: emergence, revelation, or a combination of emergence and revelation. On the one hand, the breakthrough seen in Socrates built on a pre-history of ideas that was already breaking the grip of *mythos* on the Greek mind. *Logos* or reason was already poised to advance. This tends to support the emergence explanation. In the mind of axial theorist Eric Voegelin, however, the leap in human consciousness is so great that the revelation option appears stronger to him.

God acted in the Greek mind, Voegelin thinks. The effect of this divine revelation was a new and more profound understanding of the human soul. "When in this life the soul strives for justice for its own sake, it follows that gleam of immortality toward a more perfect order."[19] The ordering of the human soul according to the transcendental vision of eternal justice becomes an option in human spirituality today because of what took place in ancient Athens. A break-through occurred, which led to a threshold differentiation in human consciousness. The very thought processes available to us moderns is a gift to us from

---

19. Ibid., 3:130.

the axial insight of Socrates and his disciples. You the reader and I the author are today rethinking many of the very thoughts first appearing in the mind of Socrates.

Voegelin believes this differentiation in consciousness opened the human soul to the truth of history, a truth that both transcends and qualifies history. "By *historicity of Truth* we mean that transcendental reality, precisely because it is not an object of world-immanent knowledge, has a history of experience and symbolization. . . . The field of history is the soul of [humanity]."[20] Voegelin is using the third meaning of history, namely, history of mortals under judgment.

One might also say that Voegelin tacitly embraces the third of the three attempts to explain the axial insight, namely, the combination of revelation and emergence. That is, Voegelin holds that the shock of divine revelation in ancient Athens is still reverberating through history due to subsequent applications of the awareness of transcendence in pursuit of social justice. If the original axial insight is like a newly cut fir tree, then effective history has decorated it so that now it lights up as a Christmas tree. The axial breakthrough combines a revelation with emergence.

The gift of Greece to the future of the world was philosophy. No one unwraps this gift better than Voegelin. "Philosophy is the love of being through the love of divine Being as the source of its order."[21]

Review Questions

1. Just why might the Athenian court think Socrates was impious?
2. What is justice according to Thrasymachus? Socrates?
3. What is the connection between eternal justice and the human soul?
4. Compare *Makarios* with *Tartarus*.

Discussion Questions

1. Do you ever see Thrasymachus's view of justice in pure form? What does it look like in disguised form?
2. In your intuition, do you lean more toward Thrasymachus or more toward Socrates on the nature of justice?
3. When you criticize the current social order, do you appeal to a transcendent order of justice or to some other criterion?

---

20. Ibid., 3:363.
21. Ibid., 1:xiv.

4. When Greek philosophy appeared, belief in one God (monotheism) was inextricably tied to reason. Do you think belief in one God today is rational or mythical?

Additional Resources

Print Sources

Bellah, Robert N. *Religion in Human Evolution from the Paleolithic to the Axial Age.* Cambridge, MA: Harvard University Press, 2011.

In chapter 7, Bellah discusses the history of the Greek polis and its philosophical developments. Bellah is more concerned about the social order, while Voegelin is more concerned about the axial insight; nevertheless, Bellah and Voegelin together provide an indispensable reinterpretation of the West's Hellenic heritage.

Peters, Ted. *Sin Boldly: Justifying Faith for Fragile and Broken Souls.* Minneapolis: Fortress, 2015.

Chapters 3 through 6 show the dynamic interaction between cosmic justice and justice within the human soul. This is a contemporary treatment, not a review of axial consciousness. Socrates's insight into transcendent justice is alive and well in our psyches and our culture today.

Smith, Bonnie G., Mark Van De Mieroop, Richard Von Glahn, and Kris Lane. *Crossroads and Cultures: A History of the World's Peoples.* Boston: Bedford/St. Martin's, 2012.

This world history text provides a brief yet accurate timeline for archaic Greek history (pp. 142–63), which places the philosophical achievements within social and political context.

Voegelin, Eric. *Order and History.* 5 Vols. Baton Rouge: Louisiana State University Press, 1956–1987. See volume 2, *The World of the Polis*, and volume 3, *Plato and Aristotle.*

No one provides a more thorough reading than Voegelin of the ancient Greek documents that led to the axial breakthrough in the Hellenic world. Fascinating expositions and interpretations of Homer, Hesiod, Plato, and Aristotle.

Web Sources

"Aristotle (384–322 BCE)." *Internet Encyclopedia of Philosophy.* http://www.iep.utm.edu/aristotl/.

"Plato (427–347 BCE)." *Internet Encyclopedia of Philosophy.* http://www.iep.utm.edu/plato/.

The Axial Breakthrough in Israel

Judaism, Christianity, and Islam

This is the mysterious paradox of Biblical faith: *God is pursuing* [*humanity*].

—ABRAHAM JOSHUA HESCHEL[1]

Three contemporary religious traditions belong to the effective history of Moses in ancient Israel: Judaism, Christianity, and Islam. One distinguishing characteristic of the axial experience in ancient Israel is the birth of historical consciousness. Of course Israel shares with Greece and China the appearance of historians who write about what happened, who tell war stories. Like the others, Israel's history is recorded in writing. In the case of Israel, however, something gets added. For Israel, what happens is the product of an interaction between God and history. History becomes more than merely a series of contingent events; it becomes the promise of a transcendent God to bring history to fulfillment in the kingdom of God. History becomes meaningful in an eternal sense.

We have seen how in ancient Greece the axial breakthrough rode the transition from *mythos* (myth, story, narrative) to *logos* (reason, critical thinking). This is not the case in ancient Israel, where the axial insight remains embedded within the narrative. Israel's narrative is not myth, however; it is historical narrative.

This chapter turns to ancient Israel and the moment of transcendental shock: Moses standing before the burning bush. Moses' shocking experience belongs within the context of the ancient Hebrew people who were telling their own story. The Hebrew story lives on today in effective history among three children of the Hebrews: the Jews, the Christians, and the Muslims. Despite their many distinctions, Jews, Christians, and Muslims share a single Hebrew parentage and still draw their spiritual power from a single axial insight into divine transcendence.

---

1. Abraham Joshua Heschel, "God in Search of Man," in *Contemporary Jewish Theology*, ed. Elliot N. Dorff and Louis E. Newman (Oxford: Oxford University Press, 1999), 81–94, at 87, italics in original.

Moses and the Burning Bush

According to the book of Exodus, Moses had grown up as a prince in the royal house of Egypt, a Hebrew living among the Egyptian nobility. But when Moses decided to take the side of his kinsmen, he was forced to flee from Egypt. Eventually Moses led a revolt to free the slaves, successfully leading the Hebrews out of Egypt to the land that would become Israel. Moses was enabled to perform this miraculous feat after receiving a transcendental shock, by receiving a covenant promise from God.

While in the wilderness near Mount Sinai (sometimes called Mount Horeb), Moses sees a burning bush. Though on fire, this bush is not being consumed. He is puzzled. Out of the bush comes a voice. The voice commissions Moses to become a prophet who will lead the enslaved Hebrew people out of Egypt into liberty. This is Moses' call vision, the moment when he gets his vocation. The modern English word *vocation* means literally "a calling" (as in *vocal*). Moses' calling is to mediate the Sinai Covenant between God and the people of Israel.

Moses considers accepting his call, which includes returning to Egypt and leading the Hebrew people. But Moses does not quite get the picture immediately. Somewhat awkwardly, he quizzes the strange voice in the bush: "If I come to the Israelites and say to them, 'The God of your ancestors has sent me to you,' and they ask me, 'What is his name?' what shall I say to them?" (Exod. 3:13).

This is a dramatic moment, far more dramatic than most modern readers of the Bible at first realize. In the ancient world, people believed far more than modern people do in the power of words. Words and realities belonged together for our ancestors. To know the name of something was to have power over it. This is why witches and sorcerers were thought to have power; they could pronounce curses and devastating results would happen.

In the biblical era, to pronounce the name of a god in a liturgy was to gain power over the god. Priests, like sorcerers, could make the gods do human bidding, it was assumed. So Moses asking the one speaking in the bush for a name constitutes a threshold moment. If the voice gives Moses a name, then Moses, like a sorcerer, will gain power over the voice.

The voice in the bush responds very cleverly. The voice says, *'ehyeh 'asher 'ehyeh* (Exod. 3:14). This is typically translated "I am who I am" or "I will be who I will be." At root here is the Hebrew verb "to be." If one renders this verb in the third person imperfect causative intensive form, one gets what has been called the *tetragrammaton* (four letter word) *YHWH*, pronounced *Yahweh* (or sometimes *Jehovah*), which is treated in the Hebrew Bible as the divine name (Exod. 3:15). The point is that the word sometimes used for God's name, *Yahweh*, is a verb, and it means "God is" or "God will be what God will be" or "God will cause to be whatever will be." Since it is not a name in the usual sense, Moses will have no power over the voice. The voice will remain mysterious and elusive. This voice comes from a source beyond the cosmos, not from within the cosmos.

The voice goes on to tell Moses that the tetragrammaton is okay to use when identifying the sovereign God of Israel. "This is my name for ever, and this is my title for all generations" (Exod. 3:15). In a later century, the prophet Ezekiel reports God saying repeatedly, "And they will know that I am Yahweh." But *Yahweh* is more like a cipher than a name: a place holder, a title, an identifying word. In the final analysis, the God of Israel does not have a name in the same way that a person has a name.[2]

The constructive significance of this is that no individual, nor any creature in creation, can get power over the Holy One of Israel. Contemporary Jewish scholar Daniel Matt invokes the term, *Ein Sof* for God, which translates literally as "there is no end." For Matt, "*Ein Sof* is the Infinite, the God beyond God."[3] Christian theologians have gone on to describe God with the Latin phrase, *a se*, as being-unto-itself, or totally and utterly independent. In constructive theology, this is known as God's *aseity*.

Michelangelo's statue of Moses stands in the Church of San Pietro in Vincoli in Rome. The voice speaking to Moses in the burning bush would not give a name in the conventional sense; this God remains transcendent.

© Danilo Ascione / Shutterstock.com

Today's theologians like to speak of God in contrasting terms, as *transcendent*, meaning beyond human reach or understanding, plus *immanent*, meaning God is present within the domain or realm of humans as creatures. Notice how transcendence elicits the beyond sensibility while immanence elicits the intimate sensibility. The dynamism of the God of the Bible's symbolic speech is that the transcendent and incomprehensible God becomes an immanent partner with the covenant people of Israel.

The result of the Moses story is that one refers to the God of Israel with titles rather than names. One refers to God or addresses God as Lord, Father,

---

2. Among the divine names, none "exhausts" God or "offers the grasp or hold of a comprehension of him. The divine names have strictly no other function than to manifest this impossibility." Jean-Luc Marion, *God without Being*, trans. by Thomas A. Carlson (Chicago and London: University of Chicago Press, 1991), 106.

3. Daniel C. Matt, *God and the Big Bang* (Woodstock, VT: Jewish Lights, 2016), 22.

Holy One, and such. Even the English word *God* is not a name. It is the equivalent of the Greek noun, *theos*, which simply refers to the gods of the ancient Greek pantheon. God remains nameless even for modern Jews, Christians, and Muslims. The use of titles rather than a name preserves in human understanding the mystery and power of the God who transcends the cosmos yet calls humanity into covenant. It helps guard against conceptual idolatry, against imagining what God looks like in one's mind. It heeds Xenophanes's warning against projecting our image onto heaven, against creating our own godlet, our own idol.

Not everyone believes that the Moses story happened, nor do they believe in the truth of Moses' claim about God. Skeptic Paul Kurtz, for example, argues that "it is probable that he [Moses] neither spoke to God nor received a revelation from on high, and he clearly used cunning and deceit to make his followers believe that he had a supernatural role to fulfill."[4] Kurtz advises contemporary Jews to give up their faith, because their belief that they are the "chosen people" draws ire in the form of anti-Semitism. "Today it is important that religious Jews reexamine critically the origin of their biblical faith, for their devotion to Judaism is based upon cultural practice, ethnic and genetic loyalty, not divine grounds."[5] In short, ethnic Judaism should survive while religious Judaism should disappear. For our purposes here in this book, the accuracy or inaccuracy of the Exodus texts is less important than Moses' role in the differentiation of human consciousness and effective history. From a historical point of view, one cannot get around the fact that an enduringly powerful saltation is marked by this narrative.

El and Allah

The Exodus account indicates that before Moses received the tetragrammaton, God was known by the name *El*. Actually, *El* was a name ascribed to the sky-god of Canaan. It was used by the Hebrews along with everybody else in the region. *El* could be qualified for the sake of specificity; so, for example, *El-Elyon* identified God as most high and *El-Shaddai* referred to the god of the mountain. *Elohim* among the Canaanites was the name of the entire pantheon, including the sky-god (Baal), an earth-mother goddess, plus other nature deities. Biblical Hebrews seemed to have mixed the vocabulary together, sometimes referring to the God of Israel as *Yahweh Elohim*.

El became *Allah* in Islam. In both the Qur'an and subsequent Islamic tradition, Allah is said to have ninety-nine names. Having many names means, in

---

4. Paul Kurtz, *Transcendental Temptation: A Critique of Religion and the Paranormal* (Buffalo: Prometheus, 1984), 200.

5. Ibid., 201.

effect, no name. No one of these names permits the human speaker to grasp God's essence or to gain control of divinity. Allah is independent, *a se*, transcendent, ultimately mysterious. No completely agreed upon list of these names exists, even in the Qur'an. In effect, the divine holiness Moses sensed in the burning bush is reflected in the Islamic reverence and awe for Allah.

In ancient Israel, Yahweh Elohim was assumed to be sexless. Previous symbolism of the marriage of heaven with earth persisted in the biblical language, but Israel's deity has no consort. The use of the masculine pronoun in Scripture is most likely a holdover from the association of *El* with the previous male sky-god. "Yahweh has no consort and does not sire Israelite sons and daughters but creates a people by adoption," writes Norman Gottwald in his Marxist interpretation of ancient Israel. "Nevertheless, Yahweh's asexuality was apparently *not* invoked to challenge or to shatter male dominance in the Israelite society as a whole. . . . The overthrow of class dominion in early Israel had the indirect effect of improving the status of women relative to their status in Canaanite society, but there was no formal assault in Israel on several forms of feminine subordination."[6] In short, the patriarchal structure of Hebrew society, like that of Canaanite society, felt precious little impact from Moses' burning bush experience with the transcendent God. One might expect an experience with the axial God to result in social equality. One might expect an end to slavery and an affirmation of equality between women and men. But such social equality took centuries if not millennia to come about.

Law as Torah and as the Ten Commandments

After leading the Israelites out of Egypt, Moses returned to Sinai. On his second trip he brought his newly liberated Hebrew nation, actually a federation of twelve Hebrew tribes. (One of these twelve tribes, the tribe of Judah, winds its way through history to become today's Jews.) The entire twelve-tribe populace camped at the foot of Mount Sinai. This time Moses climbed the mountain and disappeared from view because of low-hanging clouds. On the mountain's top Moses again confronted the voice.

Here Sinai functions as an *axis mundi*, the cosmic pillar that connects heaven with earth. Sinai is a natural mountain, not a manufactured pyramid. Moses functions as the shaman, personally embodying the connection of heaven with earth, mediating the beyond of God with the intimate needs of the foragers and farmers who follow him. Not evoked at this time is a different sensibility, *autochthony*.[7] That will come later in the narrative, when Israel prepares to settle in the "Promised Land."

---

6. Norman K. Gottwald, *The Tribes of Yahweh* (Maryknoll, NY: Orbis, 1979), 685.

7. Autochthony pertains to that which is indigenous or originates in a particular region or culture.

When Moses descends from the mountain, he brings God's law. Later tradition organized and abbreviated the law into the Ten Commandments. The first three deal with humanity's relationship with God, and the final seven with human community.

1. You shall have no other gods; you shall not worship idols.
2. You shall not make wrongful use of God's name.
3. You shall remember the Sabbath Day to keep it holy.
4. You shall honor your father and mother.
5. You shall not murder.
6. You shall not commit adultery.
7. You shall not steal.
8. You shall not bear false witness about your neighbor.
9. You shall not covet your neighbor's house.
10. You shall not covet your neighbor's wife, slave, ox, or donkey, or anything else belonging to your neighbor.

For the people of ancient Israel to accept the Ten Commandments and commit to obeying them meant they were accepting a covenant with Yahweh to become God's "Chosen People." Yahweh was offering this covenant, including a divine promise. Yahweh promised that the Hebrew slaves would return to the land of their origin—the Promised Land—even if this meant making war against the Canaanites, who were unwelcome squatters in Israel's land. God would lead Israel's army to victory and pillage, while the people of Israel would keep God's covenant law.

Hear O Israel: The LORD is our God, the LORD alone. You shall love the LORD your God with all your heart, and with all your soul, and with all your might. . . . When the LORD your God has brought you into the land that he swore to your ancestors, to Abraham, to Isaac, and to Jacob, to give you—a land with fine, large cities that you did not build, houses filled with all sorts of goods that you did not fill, hewn cisterns that you did not hew, vineyards and olive groves that you did not plant—and when you have eaten your fill, take care that you do not forget the LORD, who brought you out of the land of Egypt, out of the house of slavery. (Deut. 6:4–5, 10–12)

The symbol of the Promised Land evokes the power of autochthony, a power that influences global affairs right down to the present day.

Once the Hebrews had taken up residence in the Promised Land about 1000 BCE and established a monarchy, it became the task of the kings to oversee the keeping of the covenant law. Some did better than others, but in nearly all cases the kings failed to live up to covenant expectations. Israel's first king, Saul, coveted the booty of battle and stole it. Israel's second king, David, coveted the wife of Uriah, Bathsheba, seduced her, and murdered her husband. Israel's third king, Solomon, brought idols into Jerusalem and sponsored their worship along with worship of Yahweh. No king could be trusted to keep the Ten Commandments. No king could be trusted to represent Israel's God on Earth. The king's immoral behavior disqualified him from playing the role of *axis mundi* or shaman. In contrast to the pharaoh in Egypt or the king in Babylon, Israel's kings were just human, all too human.

Prophets were anointed to criticize the king, to judge the king, to call the king and the people to repentance. Through the prophets, some of the children of Israel began to look forward to a future king sent directly from God, a messianic king who would write the law of God in people's hearts so that history could be fulfilled with peace on Earth. This meant that the future would be different from the present and the past. Through the mouth of the prophet Isaiah, the God of Israel promises a new future. "I am about to do a new thing" (Isa. 43:19). The mind of Israel became epigenetic, not archonic.

In sum, the Ten Commandments delivered on Mount Sinai appear within the larger story of Israel's liberation from Egyptian slavery and the taking possession of the Promised Land. The entire account, including the Ten Commandments, is found in the Hebrew Scriptures; the section that includes the Israelites' deliverance from Egypt and the establishing of the covenant at Mount Sinai is known as the Torah. Renowned Jewish scholar, Jon Levenson, asserts, "Sinai confronts anyone who would live as a Jew with an awesome choice, which, once encountered cannot be evaded—the choice of whether to obey God or to stray from him, of whether to observe the commandments or to let them lapse. . . . Sinai demands that the Torah be taken with radical seriousness."[8]

The God revealed to Moses evokes both beyond and intimate sensibilities in a profound way. Yahweh transcends the cosmos and establishes a trans-temporal standard of justice. The exacting of God's eternal justice within history would require upending current injustice by uplifting the downtrodden, feeding the hungry, and liberating the oppressed. "Happy are those whose help is the God of Jacob, whose hope is in the LORD their God, who made heaven and earth, the sea, and all that is in them; who keeps faith forever; who executes justice for the oppressed; who gives food to the hungry. The LORD sets the prisoners free" (Ps. 146:5–7).

8. Jon D. Levenson, *Creation and the Persistence of Evil: The Jewish Drama of Divine Omnipotence* (Princeton: Princeton University Press, 1988), 86.

Jesus in the New Testament

The Christian religious tradition begins with Moses and the prophetic expectation of a future kingdom of peace while adding a decisive historical moment wherein that future kingdom became present, becoming incarnate in a single person. In the New Testament, Jesus is hailed as the prophesied "Prince of Peace" (Isa. 9:6). In the eschatological New Jerusalem for which Jews and Christians are still waiting, there will be no more crying nor pain, for all suffering will have passed away (Rev. 21).

Jesus inherited belief in God in the axial mode from Moses, for Jesus was a Jew. Jesus' own teachings sought to interiorize faith and to universalize belief. Like his axial predecessors among the prophets, Jesus sought to cultivate the inner life of the soul. "You have heard that it was said, 'You shall love your neighbor and hate your enemy.' But I say to you, Love your enemies and pray for those who persecute you" (Matt. 5:43–44). The God of Israel is a loving and gracious God, taught Jesus; and Israel has been called by God to be a light to all the nations regarding this truth.

Paul Kurtz, mentioned above, disregards the teachings of Jesus as well as the entire Christian religion. He argues that the New Testament accounts are not historically reliable, that no unbiased historian was present to record events. He further argues that the people who listened to Jesus were "gullible."[9] As gullible, they were susceptible to affirming Jesus' appeal to a transcendent God. "Surely the transcendental temptation was as strong in the days of Jesus as it is today."[10] Kurtz's spurning of transcendence is curious. According to axial historians, transcendental consciousness was dawning in culture, and it had already begun in Israel with the tradition of Moses. Jesus could rely on transcendental awareness as he developed his teachings. But before his listeners could become susceptible to the so-called "temptation," they necessarily would have needed to be on the receiving end of an effective history that included transcendental consciousness. Kurtz cannot provide an adequate alternative account for this.

In Jesus' own day he confronted both those who believed in him and those who disbelieved so vehemently they put him to death on a cross. Jesus' teachings forced a decision upon his listeners then as now.

The Story of Jesus with Its Significance

One must distinguish between the teachings *of* Jesus and the teachings *about* Jesus, although the two belong together and certainly cohere with one another. The teaching about Jesus, which Christians call the *gospel*, is basically the story

---

9. Kurtz, *Transcendental Temptation*, 139.

10. Ibid., 144.

of Jesus told with its significance. It is a narrative. The gospel did not originate as a philosophy of life, a speculative metaphysical system, or a political program.

There is, however, one giant exception. Jesus is designated by the New Testament, written in the Greek language, as the *logos*.[11] By saying that, the New Testament is not claiming that Jesus' mind was critical like that of Socrates. Rather, the New Testament means that in this human being the divine *logos* by which all of creation is structured and through which each of us reasons is present in the flesh, incarnate in the biography of this one person, Jesus of Nazareth (John 1:1).

Logos becomes embedded in narrative, not mythical narrative but historical narrative. What happens within history now becomes decisive for eternity. With this the historical Jesus picked up titles of eternal consequence: Messiah, Christ, Lord, King, and Savior.

One can read the story of Jesus told with its significance in the four New Testament books that are also called *Gospels*: Matthew, Mark, Luke, or John. An abbreviated biography of Jesus can also be found in the sermons of the Apostles Peter and Paul in the book of Acts. Because Peter and Paul had to get the message out quickly before boredom would set into their audiences, they reduced the chronicle of events to a bare minimum, to only the essentials. Four essential elements appear whenever the story of Jesus is told: (1) the

A ceramic tile Crucifixion by Emilio Palacios adorns St. Cecilio Church, in Granada. For Christians, in Jesus' death on the cross God experiences injustice, suffering, and death. Jesus' resurrection promises forgiveness and cosmic transformation.

© Renata Sedmakova / Shutterstock.com

fulfillment of prior prophetic expectations, (2) the unwarranted death of the righteous one on the cross, (3) Jesus' Resurrection from the dead, and (4) the forgiveness of human sins. The apostles typically recited briefly the history of Israel understood as pointing forward toward fulfillment. This was followed by reporting the execution of Jesus on the cross on Good Friday and his vindication by

---

11. The ancient Greek word *logos* combines many important meanings, especially "word," "reason," and "study." It appears in many English terms such as *logic*, *anthropology* (the study of humanity), and *biology* (the study of life). The *logos* refers to the underlying rational structure of the cosmos, which can be perceived by the rational human mind. In the New Testament, the *logos* becomes incarnate in the person of Jesus.

God through the Resurrection on Easter Sunday. It was further explained that all this happened to effect the forgiveness of sins and the redemption of Israel (Acts 3:12–26; 5:24–32; 10:34–43; 13:16–41). In short, the gospel begins with the story of Jesus told with its significance.

The significance of the story of Jesus is that it announces cosmic salvation. The so-called *gospel in miniature*, John 3:16, includes the word *cosmos*. "For God so loved the world (*cosmos*) that he gave his only Son, so that everyone who believes in him may not perish but may have eternal life." When theologians reflect on this story, they draw out its significance in light of three covenantal promises: new creation, justification, and proclamation.

The Gospel as New Creation

The promise of a future new creation—sometimes symbolized as the "kingdom of God" brought by the Prince of Peace—is reiterated by God by raising Jesus from the dead on the first Easter. The axial dimension of God shines through when Saint Paul contends that the power of resurrection is tantamount to the power to create, and this power belongs only to God, "who gives life to the dead and calls into existence the things that do not exist" (Rom. 4:17). According to Paul, the Resurrection of Jesus confirms the long-standing Hebrew hope for the final triumph of God's justice. Jesus Christ is "the first fruits of those who have died," Paul tells the Corinthians (1 Cor. 15:20b; cf. Rom. 8:19; Col. 1:18). The gospel communicates that, on account of Christ, God's future is spiritually present now, imbuing believers with newness of life and inspiring hope while granting peace of mind. "So if anyone is in Christ, there is a new creation; everything old has passed away; see, everything has become new!" (2 Cor. 5:17).

The Resurrection victory of Christ is an advance incarnation of the yet-to-come new order of creation, the true *logos* that structures reality. Since New Testament times, however, the size of the cosmos has expanded in human imagination. No longer do people limit the scope of God's creation and redemption to planet Earth. The concept of creation now includes an immense universe with a past of 13.8 billion years and perhaps a future of a hundred billion years, with billions of galaxies and uncountable stars and planets. When today's theologian repeats the biblical promise of a coming new creation, it applies to all that exists both in the depth of the human soul and the breadth of a nearly immeasurable universe. Fordham University's Elizabeth Johnson points to the inclusive eschatological new creation: "The coming final transformation of history will be the salvation of everything, including the groaning community of life, brought into communion with the loving power of the God of life."[12]

---

12. Elizabeth A. Johnson, *Ask the Beasts: Darwin and the God of Love* (London: Bloomsbury, 2014), 209.

The Gospel as Justification

The second way Jesus' story is significant has to do with justification, a theological way of understanding the forgiveness of sins. Justification is the means by which God redeems each individual soul. The gospel "is the power of God for salvation," writes Saint Paul (Rom. 1:16). When comparing the New Testament concept of justification with inherited traditions, such as Sinai's Ten Commandments or other religious laws, Paul responds, "A person is justified not by the works of the law but through faith in Jesus Christ" (Gal. 2:16). Paul excludes works of the law from the content of the gospel. If this were not true, he says, "then Christ died for nothing" (Gal. 2:21). If Christ is the anticipatory embodiment—*prolepsis*—of the fullness of God's justice in the new creation, and if believers are united with Christ through faith and therefore with that righteousness, then conformity to the laws of the old creation simply has no influence on their salvation.

Recall how Socrates in Plato's *Gorgias* warned us that the soul deformed by injustice will be unable to find attunement with supra-cosmic order beyond death. It is imperative, therefore, that one achieve justification (*dikaiosynē*) within this life in order to find unity with what is eternal in the next life. The New Testament gospel speaks to this by contending that faith in Jesus Christ—the universal *logos*—is what justifies, and this justification is valid in and beyond death.

The social effect of this interpretation of the gospel is to establish equality at the foot of the cross. Paul trumpets, "There is no longer Jew or Greek, there is no longer slave or free, there is no longer male and female; for all of you are one in Christ Jesus" (Gal. 3:28). The gospel of Jesus cannot be used to support hierarchy in the social order.

As both sinful yet justified, today's Christian believers are called by God to work for justice in an unjust world. No matter how hard they work to increase justice, they themselves will not establish complete justice. Only the future kingdom of God will do that. Yet, curiously enough, that future justice becomes available now, ahead of time, proleptically. Believers in Christ are now both sinful and just in their personal relationship with God, awaiting the perfection of justice in the social order.

The Gospel as Proclamation

The good news of the gospel requires proclamation. In Christian understanding, the gospel is the report of divine grace that establishes justification and opens the door to experiencing new creation ahead of time. But the gospel is more than a mere report. The very telling of the gospel participates in the reality of God's grace itself. The gospel by definition is news, and as such presses to be told and retold. The gospel when preached is not merely information or even revelation about justice; rather, the preaching itself makes that divine justice a present reality.

The idea of the spoken word—the word of God—is key to understanding the living tradition of the Christian gospel. The whole life and destiny of Jesus are in their unique way God's word spoken to the world. Jesus Christ is the living Word, the *viva vox*. This makes telling the story of Jesus divine address. So for Christians to present the gospel through preaching or teaching is to participate in the very activity whereby God addresses the world. Christians believe that, through re-presenting the symbols of the gospel experience as reported in the New Testament, God actually calls people to live in the light of the revelatory action. Telling and listening to the story of Jesus with its significance are themselves part of the ongoing work of God.

By raising Jesus Christ from the grave, God broke the chains of death and blessed Jesus with the fulfillment awaiting the entire cosmos. As Jesus rose from the dead, so also will the entire creation be transformed.

Finally, Jesus is thought by Christians to be the incarnation of the ultimate mystery sensed by previous axial seers. Because of God's self-communication in the Incarnation, writes theologian Karl Rahner, human history becomes "a history which knows itself safe in God's love."[13] A few centuries after the New Testament writings were collected, theologians asserted that the Holy Spirit binds together the incarnate Son of God with the mysterious cosmic creator—symbolically termed the *Father*—in an intra-divine and ever-active loving. Cosmic History is safe within the eternal love of the Trinity of Father, Son, and Holy Spirit, say the early Christians.

Omnipotent Allah in Islam

"There is no God but Allah, and Muhammad is his prophet" is the profession of faith (*shahadah*) offered by the adherent to Islam. How does the God of Muhammad (571–632 CE) relate to history?

---

13. Karl Rahner, *Theological Investigations*, 22 vols. (London: Darton, Longman, and Todd, 1961–1976; New York: Seabury, 1974–1976; New York: Crossroad, 1976–1988), 5:14.

The word *Islam* literally means "surrender to God." An adherent to Islam is called a *Muslim*, one who surrenders. Everything Islamic flows from a single source, the Holy Qur'an, the divine recitation from God to his prophet, Muhammad, in the seventh century of the common era.[14] Whereas the eternal God became incarnate in Jesus Christ for the Christians, something akin to this applies to the Qur'an for the Muslims.

This divine recitation to Muhammad places him in the role of the shaman, the human *axis mundi*. A report by Christian monks at Saint Catherine's Monastery on Mount Sinai also places Muhammad in this role. According to tradition, the monastery is located on the very spot where Moses encountered the burning bush. One monk, upon watching Muhammad walking toward the monastery, reported seeing a lone cloud just above Muhammad's head. Symbolically, this signifies that Muhammad was recapitulating Moses' ascent to the cloud atop Mount Sinai, receiving divine revelation. The authority of Moses has now been transferred to Muhammad, Allah's superseding prophet.[15] Because this ascent was allegedly witnessed by a Christian, it symbolically suggests that Muhammad's authority includes while superseding both Jewish and Christian claims.

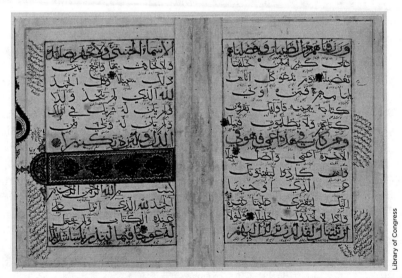

Bihari Qur'an. The Holy Qur'an, Muslims believe, is the definitive revelation given by Allah to the prophet Muhammad. The Qur'an was verbally inspired; the original Arabic text preserves the actual words of God.

---

14. "Muslims tend to read the Koran [Qur'an] literally. They consider it the earthly facsimile of an Uncreated Koran in almost exactly the same way that Christians consider Jesus to have been the human incarnation of God." Huston Smith, *The World's Religions* (New York: Harper, 1991), 232.

15. See John Andrew Morrow, *The Covenants of the Prophet Muhammad with the Christians of the World* (Kettering, OH: Angelico, 2013), 8–11.

Central to Islamic belief is the oneness and ineffability of God, Allah. To believe in one's heart that God is one is to assert *tawhid*. To associate or worship anything else with the one God is to commit the sin of *shirk*—much like disobeying the first of the Ten Commandments given to Moses. Muslims therefore avoid shirk at all costs.

From the Muslim point of view, Islam is aboriginal. Both Judaism and Christianity are deviations from Islam, not the reverse. Moses anticipated Muhammad, who supplants all the prophets, including Jesus. Muhammad is the final shaman, the human *axis mundi*, the one to whom God has spoken directly, word for word. Muhammad's recitation of these words would later be written down and compiled by his followers as the Qur'an. The proper way to read the Qur'an, therefore, is in its original Arabic and usually in a literal fashion. Reading the Qur'an literally makes it possible for the mind of the average Muslim to house the very utterances of God, especially God's law.

> The most fundamental religious attitude of Islam: to maintain wholeness and proper order, as the opposite of disintegration, by accepting God's law. It is in this sense that the entire universe and its content are declared by the Qur'an to be *muslim*, that is, endowed with order through obedience to God's law; but whereas nature obeys God's law automatically, humanity ought to obey it by choice."[16]

This divine law that pervades the cosmos is called *shari'ah*. The core of *shari'ah* can be found in the Qur'an, but over time provisions were added. Like the Ten Commandments, *shari'ah* is divided into two tables, the first for one's direct relationship to God and the second for community. One's relationship to God is supported by Five Pillars: (1) performing prayers five times per day (*salat*), (2) pilgrimage to the holy city of Mecca (*hajj*) once in a lifetime, (3) fasting every year during the month of Ramadan (*sawm*), (4) giving alms (*zakat*) and (5) professing faith (*shahadah*). These are the Five Pillars of *'ibidat*, the table of religious obligations. "The other main category of *shari'ah* rules is that of the *mu'amalat*, which regulate conduct of interpersonal relations," says Ann Elizabeth Mayer.[17]

Is *shari'ah* intra-cosmic or transcendent? For the Muslim, *shari'ah* derives from a transcendent origin, from the God of axial revelation. *Shari'ah* has its origins in the Qur'an, but is significantly derived also from the actions and words of Muhammad as recorded by his followers in the thousands of writings collected and commented upon—called *hadith*. *Shari'ah* is therefore a mix of

---

16. Fazlur Rahman, "Islam: An Overview [First Edition]," in *Encyclopedia of Religion*, ed. Lindsay Jones, 2nd ed., 15 vols. (New York: MacMillan, Gale, 2005), 7:4560–77, at 4560–61.

17. Ann Elizabeth Mayer, "Islamic Law: *Shari'ah*," in *Encyclopedia of Religion*, ed. Jones, 7:4691–4705, at 4693.

divine inspiration and human interpretation and commentary as well as shaped by multiple schools of law (both Sunni and Shia). On the one hand, *shari'ah* is a total system that unites religion, politics, culture, and the inner world of the individual psyche. On the other hand, today many Muslims find themselves living in pluralistic societies with secular governments. They have adapted. Modern Muslims have figured out how to carry out *shari'ah* in pluralistic and even communist settings.[18]

One God and One Social Order

The problem of the social order, as Muhammad perceived it in the seventh century, was tribal division, rivalry, and violence. Loyalty to local and ethnic tribal deities on the Arabian Peninsula only promoted inter-tribal competition and fighting. Could a theological belief create multi-tribal unity? Could the axial doctrine of a single divine reality that transcends history become a focal center that could, simultaneously, become a social center? This is how Karen Armstrong describes early Islamic logic. "Only by acknowledging him as *as-Samad*, the Uncaused Cause of all being, would Muslims address a dimension of reality beyond time and history and which would take them beyond the tribal divisions that were tearing their society apart. Muhammad knew that monotheism was inimical to tribalism: a single deity who was the focus of all worship would integrate society as well as the individual."[19]

Although Islam is unique and complex in many ways, the theology of Allah in Islamic thought belongs to the axial type, according to which the ultimate reality of God so transcends both cosmos and self that the divine remains ineffable even in revelation. Allah is supra-cosmic.

A Skeptic on Islam

If one rejects all belief in God, this will entail rejection of the entire axial history of Israel right through Judaism, Christianity, and Islam. Kurtz speaks for non-believers who call themselves *secular humanists*.

> Unfortunately, Islam has serious negative features. It has enshrined a set of moral values of which not all are any longer relevant to the postmodern world. The primary failure of the system, for the humanist at least, is its first promise: that we ought to submit obediently to God.

---

18. "American Muslims in the United States," Teaching Tolerance, *http://www.tolerance.org /publication/american-muslims-united-states*.

19. Karen Armstrong, *A History of God: The 4000 Year Quest of Judaism, Christianity, and Islam* (New York: Alfred A. Knopf, 1994), 149.

This is rooted in faith in the Koran and its message, but we have no reasonable evidence that God/Allah exists, that Mohammed received revelations from God, or that there is an afterlife. Why should we entrust our entire destiny to a false doctrine and submit to its authority?[20]

The modern and emerging postmodern culture in which we live makes belief in God or denial of God a matter of choice. No one can avoid this choice. Kurtz chose the secular humanist faith. Muslims, like Jews and Christians today, must make a choice either to believe or not believe. For those who believe, submitting completely to God's will evokes ineffable joy. The decision to believe can be just as intellectually honest and critical as the opposite decision. Being condemned to unavoidable choice is one implication of the differentiated consciousness to which post-axial civilization is heir.

Israel's History as World History

The Torah's account of Moses' experience with the burning bush is a history. It includes a revelatory experience, but the revelation is nestled within a story, a historical narrative. Reality for ancient Israel was essentially historical.

History for ancient Israel was not merely the chronicling of past contingent events. History was where God's reality was discerned. History is a drama. History has a plot. The plot of this history begins with God's promise to Abraham and continues through enslavement in Egypt, Moses' liberation, and the prophets. For Christians, it continues in the biography of Jesus and the promise of an eschatological fulfillment to history. For Muslims, it continues in Allah's revelation in the Qur'an and the attempt to establish divine justice in society through *shari'ah*.

The life-and-death threshold of the story is crossed with the Sinai covenant. Disobedience to the covenant means divine judgment and destruction. Obedience means divine blessing and prosperity. Even if this moral logic requires nuance and constant reinterpretation, the axial insight remains important down to the present era. As a child of axial parents, the modern standard for social justice is presumed to be grounded transcendentally in God and is not intra-cosmic. The dialectic between temporal subjects such as the people of Israel and the eternal God makes history what it is. History is the theater for the divine drama.

The transcendent social order by which the prophets of Israel judged their historical social order was future; it was *adventus*. The future reached back to judge the present. The God of Israel promised a future kingdom of peace in which all of society and even all of nature would be healed, transformed, redeemed.

---

20. Kurtz, *Transcendental Temptation*, 228.

Theologians today apply the term *eschatology* to this promised future kingdom of peace.

Conclusion

In axial Israel, the answer to the question of God was God. The God of Israel is personal, and this God constitutes ultimate reality. No supra-personal Dao or Brahman transcends Yahweh. And God's interaction with history makes history itself real, meaningful, and significant. What happens in history counts in God's eternity.

Of the three explanatory options for the axial insight—emergence, revelation, or a combination—revelation is the explanation that one would expect from devout Jews, Christians, and Muslims. Not only is ultimate truth revealed here, but the human soul becomes transformed through this revelation. God's revelation at Sinai elicited a differentiation within the human soul. According to Jerusalem theologian Martin Buber (1878–1965), "both the conduct of a [person's] life and his [or her] happiness in their nature transcend the realm of ethics as well as that of self-consciousness. Both are to be understood only from a [person's] intercourse with God."[21]

Many today in the Jewish tradition no longer revere this axial commitment to "intercourse with God." Judaism has come to mean people-hood, community over time, multi-national locations with a single ethnic identity. With people-hood as primary, many individuals today consider themselves Jewish even though they are not religious.

Regardless of how today's Jewish community thinks about the divine, the God of Israel long ago escaped the particular identity of the Chosen People. Yahweh is God of all the world, of all peoples, of the entire cosmos. Axial philosopher Voegelin remarks, "The prophetic experience moved toward the clarity of understanding that Yahweh was not only the one God beside whom Israel should have no other gods, but the one God for all [humanity] beside whom no other gods existed. . . . Yahweh tended to become a universal God of all mankind."[22]

For the larger world beyond the borders of Hebrew and subsequent Jewish culture, what happened in ancient Israel affects all subsequent global history.[23] At least, this is the biblical perspective. Rahner draws out the implication: "The world receives God, the Infinite and ineffable mystery, to such an extent that

---

21. Martin Buber, *Good and Evil* (New York: Charles Scribners' Sons, 1952), 54–55.

22. Eric Voegelin, *Order and History*, 5 vols. (Baton Rouge: Louisiana State University Press, 1956–1987), 1:357.

23. The early Israelites were known as Hebrews, and the language they spoke was Hebrew. The term *Jew* is an eponym derived from the tribe of Judah, one of Israel's original twelve tribes. After the reign of Solomon, the Kingdom of Israel split in two: Israel, in the north, and Judah, in the south. *Judaism* applies to the faith practices developed by the descendants of the ancient Kingdom of Judah. Robert M. Seltzer, "Jewish People," in *Encyclopedia of Religion*, ed. Jones, 7:4854–4865, at 4856.

[God] himself becomes its innermost life."[24] Finally Voegelin makes the axial point, "History is not merely human but a divine-human process."[25]

Even if history is a divine-human process, it is still agonizingly difficult to interpret Jewish history. From the time of ancient Israel to the present, the children of Israel have experienced untold victimization and tragedy. Perhaps the most devastating was the *Shoah*, the attempted Nazi genocide during World War II. No salvation within history seems possible, once this sequence of contingent events is chronicled and interpreted. The meaning of history is not immanent within history. It is so very difficult to perceive in the chronicle of events that God has maintained the covenant. The problem of evil—the problem of injustice and innocent suffering—has been so overwhelming that many victims found they could no longer believe they had been blessed by the God of the covenant. Some Jews have taken to secularism or even atheism. Yet a devout Jew today can still pray to the God of Abraham and Moses. "For this we pray: that we enjoy enough peace to allow the Jewish love of *this* world to flower. In such a time, we may enjoy Being's face, and give our trust to the conventional reasonings—religious law—that arise out of such enjoyment and wonder and observation."[26]

Review Questions

1. Why might Moses, Jesus, and Muhammad awaken shammanic and *axis mundi* sensibilities?
2. Why did the voice in the burning bush refuse to give a name to Moses?
3. According to Christians, what is the gospel?
4. What do *tawhid* and *shari'ah* refer to?

Discussion Questions

1. What role do resurrection and the promise of a new creation play in Christian thinking?
2. Compare justice in Greece with justice in Israel and justification in Christianity.
3. According to Islam, how does *shari'ah* connect the cosmos and the soul?

24. Rahner, *Theological Investigations*, 5:172.

25. Voegelin, *Order and History*, 4:304.

26. Peter Ochs, "The Renewal of Jewish Theology Today: Under the Sign of Three," in *The Blackwell Companion to Postmodern Theology*, ed. Graham Ward (Oxford: Blackwell, 2001), 324–48, at 336.

4. Do you believe that religion leads to violence? How do you understand occurrences of religiously-inspired violence in human history?

5. In your judgment, should non-Muslims fear Muslims?

Additional Resources

Print Sources

Iqbal, Muzaffar. *Islam and Science*. Aldershot, UK: Ashgate, 2002.

> Muzaffar Iqbal is editor of the journal *Islam and Science*. In this book, Iqbal puts classic Islamic theology and modern Western science in creative interaction.

Jenkins, Philip. *The Lost History of Christianity*. New York: Harper, 2008.

> Western culture in general, and Western Christians in particular, have ignored their brothers and sisters in the faith living in northern Africa, the Middle East, central Asia, and the Far East. Jenkins retrieves the history of Syriac and Byzantine Christianity, which for nearly a millennium enjoyed a golden age. The interweaving of Islam and Christianity is vividly traced: the two traditions overlapped, borrowed from one another, and fought one another. "The histories of Christianity and Islam remain quite inextricable, and repeatedly, even in dissolution, each faith has shaped the other" (p. 206).

Matt, Daniel C., *God and the Big Bang: Discovering Harmony between Science and Spirituality*. Woodstock, VT: Jewish Lights, 2016.

> Daniel Matt is perhaps the world's leading expert on Jewish mystical writings. In this clearly written book, Matt engages big bang cosmology in light of his belief that the cosmos as a whole—God—is present in every person's soul.

Moltmann, Jürgen. *The Source of Life: The Holy Spirit and the Theology of Life*. Minneapolis: Fortress, 1997.

> Moltmann is a Reformed theologian at Tübingen University in Germany and a fine writer. This book begins with the Christian doctrine of the Holy Spirit and then develops it into a way of life, a spirituality.

Pelikan, Jaroslav. "Christianity: An Overview." In *Encyclopedia of Religion*, edited by Lindsay Jones, 3:1660–72. 2nd ed. 15 vols. New York: MacMillan, Gale, 2005.

> The late Jaroslav Pelikan is perhaps the most erudite church historian of the twentieth century. He understands his subject matter from within, and he explains it plainly to the reader without. This brief overview of Christianity is excellent.

Smith, Huston. *The World's Religions*. New York: Harper, 1991.

Because Smith is such a clear and engaging writer, his chapters on Judaism, Christianity, and Islam provide lucid exposition of this grand religious tradition.

Winter, Tim, ed. *The Cambridge Companion to Classical Islamic Theology.* Cambridge, UK: Cambridge University Press, 2003.

This collection of scholarly essays is aimed at the advanced student interested in details of Islamic history and thought.

Web Sources

A Common Word. *http://www.acommonword.com/index.php?lang=en&page=option1.*

A carefully constructed manifesto by Muslim theologians demonstrating that much can be shared regarding belief in God and the pursuit of peace and justice in society.

Pope Francis. *Laudato si.* Crux. *http://www.cruxnow.com/church/2015/06/18/read -the-encyclical-for-yourself-laudato-si/.*

While the occasion for this papal letter is the crisis of the terrestrial environment, Pope Francis begins by presenting the essential elements of the Christian faith in order to enlist Christians and other people of good will in this planetary enterprise. This is a fine example of Christian theology.

$$17$$

CHAPTER

Models of God

You have made us for yourself,
And our heart is restless until it rests in you.
—Augustine (354–430), *Confessions* 1.1[1]

I n this book the question of God arises in two modes. First, taking history as the chronicle of past events, some of those events include developing ideas about the divine. The chronicle of cultural traditions includes reports on various times and places—including axial periods in different locations—where the question of God was posed and answered. In the second mode of asking the God question, we critically interrogate history so as to uncover its ground. Would Big History and World History be more coherent if a divine creator and redeemer belonged to the chronicle? This chapter addresses only the first mode: how have various people in the past answered the question of God? Later chapters will demonstrate that viewing the cosmos as God's theatre of creation makes the whole drama more coherent.

Many answers to the question of God that have appeared in history need to be catalogued. In this chapter, each category of answers will be called a conceptual *model*. The models explicated in this chapter are atheism, agnosticism, deism, pantheism, polytheism, henotheism, monotheism, and panentheism. Within critical consciousness, these various beliefs in the divine will be compared and contrasted, dissected and diagnosed, separated and integrated.

Atheism

The English word *theism* means belief in God. The term *atheism* puts the privative "a" in front of "theism" to mean belief that no god exists. It could refer mildly to a lack of belief in God, or refer more strongly to an assertive belief that there is no God. Although there are very few records of atheists in the ancient world, there were some allusions, as the Psalmist acknowledges: "Fools say in their hearts, 'There is no God'" (Ps. 14:1).

---

1. Saint Augustine, *Confessions*, trans. Henry Chadwick (Oxford: Oxford University Press, 1991), 3.

In post-Enlightenment culture, modern atheism is associated with a naturalism or secular humanism that is purportedly based on science. Marxists (communists who follow Karl Marx) and Maoists (communists who follow Mao Zedong) are the chief examples. Science is not itself atheistic, but naturalism and secular humanism are. The essential tenet of modern atheism is that physical nature is the only reality, and nature is self-explanatory. The only knowledge that counts as knowledge comes from science, and science makes no conceptual room for God to create the world or to act within the world. This belief system is also known as *scientism*. From the point of view of an atheist, what religious people believe is false knowledge or old-fashioned superstition.

Atheist philosopher Paul Kurtz denies transcendence to the object of religious devotion: "Prayers to an absent deity . . . merely express one's longings. They are private or communal soliloquies. There is no one hearing our prayers who can help us. Expressions of religious piety thus are catharses of the soul, confessing one's fears and symbolizing one's hopes. They are one-sided transactions. There is no one on the other side to hear our pleas and supplications."[2] To pray is to fool oneself, even if it might seem comforting. Should Kurtz rewrite Psalm 14, he would likely say, "Fools say in their hearts, 'There is a God.'"

The most aggressive form of atheism on the current scene is represented by Oxford evolutionary scientist, Richard Dawkins. Dawkins says he is not denying the existence of any specific divine figure such as Yahweh, Jesus, Allah, Baal, Zeus, or Wotan. Rather, he is denying all of them at once. All belief in such divinities can be swept up into a single "God hypothesis," which Dawkins attempts to falsify. "I shall define the God Hypothesis more defensibly: *there exists a super-human, supernatural intelligence who deliberately designed and created the universe and everything in it, including us.*"[3] If the materialist worldview is exhaustive, then no god—whether the intra-cosmic gods of myth or the sublime deity of axial belief—has room to exist.

Dawkins is a proponent of categorical atheism: the rejection of belief in every god, whether the intra-cosmic gods of mythology or the supra-cosmic deity of classical theism. Other atheists are much more specific about the divine they reject. Recall, for example, how Socrates was judged to be an atheist because he relativized the multiple gods of intra-cosmic polytheistic myth by affirming the existence of God in something like classical theism.[4] Similarly, in our own era, those calling themselves *post-theists* embrace a specified atheism

2. Paul Kurtz, *Transcendental Temptation: A Critique of Religion and the Paranormal* (Buffalo: Prometheus, 1986), 22.

3. Richard Dawkins, *The God Delusion* (Boston and New York: Houghton Mifflin, 2006), 31, italics in original.

4. Socrates's position was in fact rather more complex than this summary conveys; he appears not to have denied the existence of the gods and demigods of classical Greek mythology, as he makes clear in his *Apology*. Nevertheless, by affirming the existence of God in the theistic sense he effectively undermined the validity of the traditional pantheon.

that specifically rejects Socrates' theism. In addition to Socrates' God, these atheists also reject the God of Israel.

Is Buddhism atheistic? If so, certainly not in the materialistic form Dawkins advocates. Unlike materialist atheism, which declares material reality ultimate, Buddhism denies ultimacy to the material realm in favor of an underlying emptiness. Rigorous Buddhism admits to no god, either beyond or intimate. This makes Buddhism categorically atheistic. Denial of reliance upon a supra-human deity is part of the enlightenment a Buddhist adept seeks. Realization of this emptiness holds out profound spiritual promise. Buddhist David Loy writes, "When I look inside and see that I am nothing, that's wisdom. When I look outside and see that I am everything, that's love. Between these two my life turns."[5]

Agnosticism

This word, *agnosticism*, places the privative 'a' in front of the Greek word for knowledge, *gnōsis*. An agnostic is one who affirms that he or she does not know whether a god exists and, further, that it is in principle impossible to know for certain. Thomas Huxley, a friend of Charles Darwin, gave the modern world this term. He associated it with evolutionary science. Within the scientific mindset, one cannot know let alone prove whether or not any transcendent reality exists.

In this spirit, Michael Shermer, publisher of *Skeptic* magazine, finds no grounds for affirming or denying God. "We cannot prove or disprove God's existence through empirical evidence or deductive proof. Therefore, from a scientific or philosophical position, theism and atheism are *both* indefensible positions as statements about the universe."[6]

Agnosticism makes much of critical consciousness. One defining characteristic of modern critical thinking is the principle of doubt. When pursuing what counts

The word *agnostic* refers to "not knowing." Militant agnostics assert that God cannot be proven scientifically, therefore claims about God made by religious people are unjustifiable. But is scientific proof the only valid form of knowing?

---

5. David R. Loy, "A Buddhist God?" *Tikkun* (Summer 2014): 38–39, 68, at 39.

6. Michael Shermer, *How We Believe: The Search for God in an Age of Science* (New York: W. H. Freeman, 2000), 8, italics in original.

as genuine knowledge, the modern person begins by doubting inherited and accepted explanations. Doubt of established knowledge opens space for further inquiry, and often leads to new scientific or technological discoveries. It should come as no surprise that a component of agnosticism would accompany all modern and emerging postmodern belief in the divine.

This means, among other things, that one can both believe in God and intellectually entertain doubt at the same time. Faith and agnosticism can exist side by side in a single person with modern critical consciousness. "Faith embraces itself and the doubt about itself," comments theologian Paul Tillich.[7]

Deism

Deism is an English word based on the Latin for God, *Deus*. Methodologically, deism draws its belief from natural reason alone rather than supranatural (*supranatural* means "above nature") revelation. Doctrinally, deism affirms a single God who created the world at the beginning out of nothing. God created matter and energy. God also established the laws of nature, the same laws of nature that scientists discover. Once the world was established, the God of deism withdrew. God no longer intervenes in the world. The laws of nature take care of everything.

Deism and the mechanistic model of nature complement each other. According to the mechanistic model, the natural world works like a giant clock. It's gears mesh and grind and continue indefinitely to run the universe through the strict interaction of cause and effect. God designed the clock to work on its own. God for the deist is a clockmaker or a watchmaker. "According to this model," writes theologian Kurt Anders Richardson, "the divinely engineered, lawful world could run on its own as it were, because it did so according to the will of its Designer."[8] There is no need for a deity outside the cosmic machine to intervene in the mechanical process. An intervening deity would be superfluous.

Among the implications of deism are the elimination of miracles and petitionary prayer. Because God does not intervene in natural events, what appear to be miracles must in fact be natural events that humans only interpret as extraordinary. Because God does not intervene, no one should expect God to end a drought with rain, heal the sick, or save victims from adversity. Divine transcendence—the sensibility of the beyond—is affirmed, but the intimacy of God experienced by the faithful person in prayer is eliminated.

Deists were very influential in Great Britain, France, Germany, and colonial America in the seventeenth and eighteenth centuries. They were impatient with

---

7. Paul Tillich, *Biblical Religion and the Search for Ultimate Reality* (Chicago: University of Chicago Press, 1955), 61.

8. Kurt Anders Richardson, "Deistic Distance: The Shift in Early Modern Theology from Divine Immanence to Divine Design," in *Models of God and Alternative Ultimate Realities*, ed. Jeanine Diller and Asa Kasher (Heidelberg: Springer, 2013), 511–24, at 511.

the denominational wars in Europe. Deism became a religious position associated with reason and the Enlightenment. Freemasons openly embraced deism, as did Unitarians. The pyramid pictured on the obverse of the U.S. dollar bill depicts the all-seeing eye of the deistic God. Mozart's *Zauberflöte* (Magic Flute) is dedicated to deism.

Pantheism

The English word *pantheism* places *pan*, meaning "all," in front of the Greek word for belief in God, *theism*. Pantheism is the belief that all things are divine. The being of God and the being of the world are co-spatial and co-temporal. The underlying philosophical concept is monism, the ontological doctrine that all things are really only one thing. As a theological term, *pantheism* adds that this unity is a divine unity. Ultimate reality is divine, according to the panetheist.

Pantheists distinguish between plurality and unity. Human everyday experience seems to indicate that the world is plural, made up of a wide diversity of things. Each subjective person seems to be an individual, one person among others. Pantheism, however, says this is a delusion. Down deep, below the level of perception, all things are only one thing. That one thing is the divine reality.

Pantheism is operative in Brahmanism and Hinduism, even if the Buddhists took the path toward atheism. For today's Hindu, all is divine because all gives expression to the single supreme reality, Brahman. Traditional Hindus may be polytheistic as well as pantheistic, but their worship of gods such as Vishnu or Shiva or goddesses such as Laksmi or Shakti presume that such divine beings are conduits for the more sublime divinity, Brahman.

The American Transcendentalist movement of the 1830s, which included Ralph Waldo Emerson and Henry David Thoreau, mixed together deism as described above, pantheism borrowed from India, along with romanticism and idealism borrowed from Europe, to come up with the enticing doctrine of the *over-soul*. Like Brahman, the over-soul was said to be a single underlying spiritual reality, and each person possesses a piece of it. Each individual soul belongs inherently to the single over-soul. This ontology justified a fierce individualism called "self-reliance." Because one's soul is immediately grounded in the over-soul, the individual can step back from the social order and declare radical independence. "Ineffable is the union of man and God in every act of the soul. The simplest person, who in his integrity worships God, becomes God," wrote Emerson in "The Over-Soul," triggering both beyond and intimate sensibilities.[9]

In the late twentieth and early twenty-first centuries, pantheism has been on the rise in the West. People who embrace New Age and related spiritualities—including many who consider themselves spiritual but not religious—have

---

9. Ralph Waldo Emerson, "The Over-Soul," *http://www.emersoncentral.com/oversoul.htm.*

incorporated pantheism. Many new religious movements emphasize the sacredness of all things.[10] This often translates into enthusiasm for ecological ethics. By emphasizing that the planet Earth is divine and hence sacred in its depths, some ecologists argue that we should leave nature alone. We should withdraw our attempts to transform nature through technology, because this is a form of profaning what is sacred. We should acknowledge that the natural world is intrinsically valuable and protect the ecosphere from further deterioration.

This pantheistic tendency has fed into an increasingly popular form of spirituality, *religious naturalism*. A religious naturalist may view the natural realm as saturated with divine presence. Like materialistic naturalism, the new pantheism opposes traditional supranaturalism. No supranaturalism is required if nature is already divine. Accordingly, the central doctrine of religious naturalism is this: nature is divine. Divinity within nature manifests itself as creative energy, consciousness, and the power of transformation.

Feminist theologian Rosemary Radford Ruether offers her version of a religious naturalism: "God is not an old man outside the earth living in the sky, but rather a creative energy that is in and through the whole earth."[11] Similarly, Jewish progressive Michael Lerner believes the cosmos combines male and female energies as a divine "*Force* for transformation that makes possible a world based on love and generosity."[12] What people experience as consciousness is God at work, the same consciousness that governs the many universes of multiverse physics. "God is consciousness of all possible universes and more. All the actual and possible universes are in this consciousness in the same way that my thoughts are in my body but not reducible to any part of my body. My body swims in a field of consciousness."[13] According to the pantheistic version of religious naturalism, divinity provides the cosmos with consciousness.

The spiritual task of nearly every pantheist is to get beneath the surface illusion of daily plurality and discover the deeper unity, to realize that he or she as an apparently independent self is at one with the All, the divine whole of reality. A mystical realization of one's unity with the All is the goal of pantheistic spirituality. "That which is experienced in the loftiest flights of the spirit is a coming-to-oneself within Being, or as *unio mystica* as becoming one with the Godhead," comments philosopher Karl Jaspers.[14]

---

10. See Ted Peters, *The Cosmic Self: A Penetrating Look at Today's New Age Movements* (San Francisco: Harper, 1991).

11. Rosemary Radford Ruether, "The Empty Throne: Reimagining God as Creative Energy," *Tikkun* (Summer 2014): 28–29, at 28.

12. Michael Lerner, "God and Goddess Emerging," *Tikkun* (Summer 2014): 23–27, at 25, italics added.

13. Ibid., 26.

14. Karl Jaspers, *The Origin and Goal of History*, trans. Michael Bullock (London: Routledge, 1953, 2010), 3.

Polytheism

Polytheism is belief in many gods, as the prefix *poly* implies. In its most primitive or basic form—animism—polytheists believe spirits inhabit and direct the forces of nature. Amerindians before the arrival of the Europeans believed in the *manitoos*, spirits belonging to various species of animals they would hunt. The master of the animals was the king of the manitoos.

Enuma Elish belongs in the polytheistic category. A welter of deities populates the intracosmic stage of compact consciousness in pre-city-state cultures. Ancient foragers and farmers and citizens lived in an enchanted cosmos.

In the polytheism of ancient Greece and Rome, the gods are associated with natural forces. Zeus in Greece, Jupiter in Rome, is the sky god with the thunderbolt as his emblem. Poseidon in Greece, Neptune in Rome, controls the deep oceans and at will sends storm or calm to sailors. Aphrodite in Greece, Venus in Rome, is the goddess of love; her son, Eros or Cupid, is still seen on Valentine cards with an arrow aimed right at someone's heart.

In the polytheism of Chinese Daoism, the gods play quite a different role from that found in Greece and Rome. Especially in the Chinese tradition known as Highest Clarity Daoism, which flourished from the fourth to fourteenth centuries CE, the gods are "perfected persons," former earthly persons who have become transfigured into celestial deities. Daoists believe that it is possible for the average human person to metamorphose from earthly status to

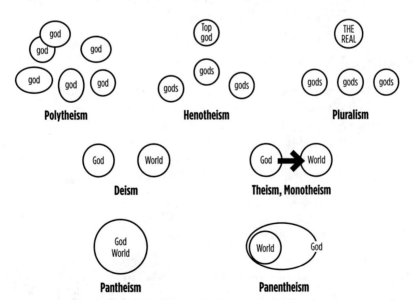

Not everyone uses the word "god" in exactly the same way. Here is an inventory of various conceptual models of the divine in ancient religious traditions and contemporary theology.

celestial status, and copying those who have already accomplished it becomes a method for self-transformation. The transformation may even include bodily ascension, not considered a miracle but rather a natural potential that is becoming actualized. "Both gods and humans are subject to the same universal law, the pattern of the Dao," writes James Miller; "gods are important not because they are loving or kind, but because, as instantiations of the Dao, they are compelled to follow inexorably the fundamental laws or patterns of the cosmos."[15]

Indian Hindus combine polytheism with pantheism, as previously noted. Personal gods such as Brahma, Vishnu, and Shiva constitute a so-called Hindu Trinity. Vishnu's wife is Laksmi, while Shiva's wife is Shakti. Tall temple towers connect heaven with the earth's goddess: Laksmi in the tradition of Vaishnavism, Shakti in Shaivism. The earth-mother goddess is responsible for the feminine energy that runs through creation, animating and transforming.[16] These and countless other gods and goddesses stimulate a kaleidoscope of symbols, artwork, architecture, rites, and worship.

It might seem that polytheism and pantheism are irreconcilable, yet, as already mentioned, Hindus find the two quite compatible. When the Brahman philosophers reflect on the matter, they resolve the tension easily by ranking reality. Brahman is dubbed the ultimate and all-inclusive reality, thereby adopting pantheism. The individual gods and goddesses become personalized emanations from the underlying Brahman. As we saw above, the personal gods and goddesses become avatars or incarnations who reveal to human perception the reality of transcendent Brahman. The avatars stand between true reality, Brahman, and human delusion, manifesting the former to the latter.

Henotheism

Henotheism is polytheism that emphasizes loyalty to only one of the gods, or the superiority of one god over other deities. Henotheism comes in two varieties, hierarchical and geographical. In its hierarchical form, a polytheistic pantheon will be organized so that one god is the top god, the god to all the other gods as well as humanity and creation. In its geographical form, henotheism respects the religions of foreigners and, on occasion, subordinates foreign gods without denying their existence.

---

15. James Miller, "Nature, Impersonality, and Absence in the Theology of Highest Clarity Daoism," in *Models of God*, ed. Diller and Kasher, 669–80, at 670–71.

16. One Western scholar of Asian religions, Rita Gross, takes a feminist stand against the alleged subordination of female goddesses to male gods in Western interpretations of India. "Laksmi is Vishnu's wife and is often portrayed as submissive to him. But she is also an important deity in her own right, often portrayed without her consort." Rita M. Gross, "Toward a New Model of the Hindu Pantheon: A Report on Twenty-Some Years of Feminist Reflection," in *Models of God*, ed. Diller and Kasher, 681–92, at 690.

Geographical henotheism can coincide with nationalities or ethnicities. For one nation to worship its favorite deity does not require denying the existence of the deities worshipped in other nations. Except, of course, during war. It often happened in the ancient world, when one nation would conquer another, that the statues of the native gods would be torn down and replaced with statues of the conquerors' gods. Change rulers, change gods.

According to geographical henotheism, in peace time the gods of every nation were simply assumed to be valid without objection. In the biblical story of Ruth, Ruth from Moab tells her Hebrew mother-in-law, Naomi, that she will follow Naomi back to Israel. "And Ruth said, 'Intreat me not to leave thee, or to return from following after thee: for whither thou goest, I will go; and where thou lodgest, I will lodge: thy people shall be my people, and thy God my God'" (Ruth 1:16, KJV). Note that when Ruth moves to Israel, she will worship the God of Israel. Change countries, change gods. This is geographical henotheism.

Hierarchical henotheism is making an appearance today in what many call *religious pluralism*. Philosopher of Religion John Hick provides an example of the renewal of henotheism. The "pluralistic hypothesis," he contends, holds that "the great world faiths embody different perceptions and conceptions of, and correspondingly different responses to, *the Real* from within the major variant ways of being human; and that within each of them the transformation of human existence from self-centeredness to Reality-centeredness is taking place."[17] Hick's term, "the Real," designates what others mean when speaking of Dao, Brahman, God, the Sacred, the transcendent, the ultimate reality, and such. When persons claim experiences of divine revelation, Hick refuses to call them "illusory." Rather, "they are empirically, that is experientially, real as authentic manifestations of the Real."[18]

This means that Daoism, Confucianism, Hinduism, Buddhism, Judaism, Christianity, and Islam each proffers its own non-illusory model of the divine. But each of these is historically conditioned, partial, and distorted. No historical religion enjoys an undistorted or accurate perception of the divine, according to Hick. Hick affirms each specific historical religion while, at the same time, subordinating each view of the divine to his own universal and all-encompassing concept of "the Real." One could imagine a three-way conversation such as the following.

Muslim, "Allah is ultimate."

Hindu, "Brahman is ultimate."

Religious Pluralist: "Only *the Real* is ultimate, and both Allah and Brahman are non-illusory yet partial manifestations of the one true ultimate, *the Real*."

---

17. John Hick, *An Interpretation of Religion: Human Responses to the Transcendent* (New Haven and London: Yale University Press, 1989), 240, italics added.

18. Ibid., 242.

Theism or Monotheism

Usually only the religions of the Abrahamic traditions—Judaism, Christianity, and Islam—are considered monotheistic. The terms *monotheism* and *theism* are used interchangeably, and both mean belief in one and only one God as the ultimate reality. The word *theism* simply indicates belief in God; and *monotheism* confirms belief in one divine reality, not many.

Modern theism comes in two brands: the personal God and the philosophical God. At the level of compact consciousness, the Bible in symbolic language depicts God as personal; God has a face, a backside, and an outstretched arm with a mighty hand. These anthropomorphic traits of God are both affirmed and denied by the Bible's symbolic language, because the God of Israel is not literally an overgrown human person. When the Bible's symbolic testimony is run through the critical filter of axial consciousness, the result is the second brand of modern theism: classical theism, a form of philosophical theism. The more personalistic language of the biblical Hebrews becomes augmented by the less personal philosophical language of the Greeks. "*Classical theism* is the name given to the model of God we find in Platonic, neo-Platonic, and Aristotelian philosophy and in Christian, Muslim, and Jewish thinkers who appropriate those traditions of classical Greek philosophy."[19] The God of classical theism overflows with instances of the prefix *omni*: God is omnipotent, omniscient, omnipresent, and omnibenevolent. Philosopher René Descartes (1596–1650) describes God in a way that makes all classical theists feel at home.

> By the name God I understand a substance that is infinite [eternal, immutable], independent, all-knowing, all-powerful, and by which I myself and everything else, if anything else does exist, have been created.[20]

Note the somewhat impersonal character of the attributes of God—for example, God is an "infinite substance." Such attributes are rational renderings of the more personal divinity depicted in the Bible.

What is distinctive to theism has to do with God's relationship with the world. According to theists, God is *a se*. That is, God is being unto itself; God has *aseity*. God is totally independent and totally free. Without the cosmos, God could exist. Without God, the cosmos could not exist. According to Eastern Orthodox theologian John Zizioulas, "Between God and the world there exists an otherness founded on the fact that the world's being is based on the will, not the substance, of God."[21] The world is not made out of the divine substance; rather, the world is brought into existence out of nothing as an act of the divine will.

---

19. Thomas Williams, "Introduction to Classical Theism," in *Models of God*, ed. Diller and Kasher, 95–100, at 95.

20. René Descartes, *Meditations on First Philosophy*, 3, *Descartes Selections*, ed. Ralph M. Eaton (New York: Scribners, 1927), 118.

21. John D. Zizioulas, *Being as Communion* (Crestwood, NY: St. Vladimir's Seminary Press, 1993), 86.

Most theists claim that God created the cosmos out of nothing. Without God, the big bang could not have banged. Even today, the world of nature is utterly dependent on the will of God to sustain it. Should God change the divine mind and withdraw support, all of reality would suddenly drop into nonbeing. In our sudden unconscious state we would not even be aware of the loss. Everything, including our consciousness, would blink out of existence. Conversely, the fact that we wake up in the morning and celebrate the singing of the birds is a gift of God's grace through creation.

Here is one significant implication of theism: the created world becomes disenchanted. If the cosmos is created from nothing and does not consist of an emanation from divine being, then the cosmos is not in itself divine. God may be present in spirit or mind or reason, to be sure, but the physical world itself can claim no sanctity or divinity. This disenchantment of the world makes room for its secularization and for scientific understanding.

Theism is like a tree trunk sprouting many branches. We will look at a few of these branches: perennialism, supranaturalist theism, naturalist theism, open theism, and Trinitarian theism. When the wind blows, the twigs and leaves so interweave that it's difficult to identify which branch is which.

Can a Perennialist Be a Monotheist?

"The three Abrahamic religions assert the fundamental truth of *creatio ex nihilo* as a means of negating all reality independent of God," asserts philosopher Seyyed Hossein Nasr.[22] Yet Nasr is both a Shiite Muslim and a follower of perennialist philosophy—which Nasr calls *esotericism*—who is sympathetic to pantheism. Pantheism is incompatible with theism, even if pantheism may be compatible with polytheism. Pantheism affirms that the everyday world emanates from the divine substance; whereas theism holds that the created order does not share the divine substance. The cosmos and God are ontologically distinct, say theists. Nasr is aware that he has blurred the line between pantheism and monotheism. Should Nasr be considered a theist or not?

To address this problem, Nasr describes the creation as an emanation from God yet different from God in substance.

> While rejecting the kind of emanationism that would deny Divine Transcendence, monotheistic esoterisms emphasize the basic truth that, although God transcends all limitations, the cosmos is, symbolically speaking, like "His garment," which at once veils and reveals His Reality. The order of nature is not only created by God through His Will, but derives from the Divine Substance. The root of the order of

---

22. Seyyed Hosssein Nasr, *Religion and the Order of Nature* (Oxford: Oxford University Press, 1996), 63.

nature is to be sought in the Divine Order, and the order of nature *is* none other than the Divine Order manifested upon the particular level of cosmic existence that we identify as nature.[23]

It appears that Nasr wants it both ways: the world is an emmanation from divine being, but it does not participate in the divine being. The former would belong to pantheism, while the latter to theism. Nasr wants to avoid being expelled from the theism club.

Nasr appeals to a simile: the natural world is like a garment worn by God. The sweater one wears is not made out of one's own skin. It is a separate substance. So also the cosmos is a separate substance. Whether Nasr solves the problem well enough to qualify as a monotheist is not entirely clear. In any case, his point is that the order of natural history is not an order that is independent of God. Natural history is grounded in the eternal order of its creator, the one God.

Must a Theist Believe in Prayer and Miracles?

There is more to theism. In contrast to deism, God for the theists is active. Rather than let the world just run itself, the God of theism monitors nature and history in such a way as to ensure that over the long run the divine will is done. God daily provides for the world; and theologians use the word *providence* to describe God's continued activity in the world.

Theists tend to believe in miracles and also in prayer. Miracles are rare, because God's main way of providing for the world is through matter, energy, and the laws of nature. Theists are close to deists here, because both theism and deism are consonant with the mechanistic model of nature. Yet there is a difference. Whereas for the deist nature's mechanical laws are exhaustive, for the theist, God may intervene from time to time in an act of special providence. Such a providential intervention is a *miracle*. Miracles are invisible to science, say theists, because they cannot be reduced to an incident within the laws of nature that appear to be in effect.

On the issue of the miraculous, we may divide theists into supranaturalist and naturalist camps. The supranturalists emphasize the interventionist quality to divine action: God's causal activity impacts the causal nexus of the natural order. Other theists attempt to avoid supranaturalism, however, contending that divine action is *compatible* with an exhaustive causal nexus. God acts, but divine actions are not discernible as separate efficient causes. Supranaturalists are inteventionists, whereas the more naturalistic theists are non-interventionist. The latter group seldom uses the word *miracle* even when affirming that God acts.

As a correlate, theists pray for rain and healing and comfort and world peace. When theists pray, they expect God to listen and to incorporate such prayers

---

23. Ibid., italics in original.

into the divine will for one's personal life as well as for the entire creation. The language of prayer as well as the language of worship is typically personal in character, treating God as a person. Trinitarian theists designate Father, Son, and Holy Spirit as personal, not the single Godhead.

Can an Open Theist Be a Monotheist?

Recently, some American evangelical Protestant theologians have been proposing *open theism*.[24] By *open* they mean God is open to an inter-dependent relationship with the cosmos. God begins with *aseity* and freedom, to be sure, but then God sacrifices this divine independence. God decides freely to limit the divine self. This act of divine self-limitation is called *kenosis*. So as to avoid overwhelming the world, God decides to limit the exercise of divine power. This divine self-limitation opens up freedom for the world to engage in self-organization and even to fall into sin and evil. By being open, God then voluntarily abides with the fallen world and works within the world for its redemption. God willingly agrees to suffer with the very world God loves. Open theism demonstrates the impulse within theistic models of God to emphasize divine involvement in the world of creatures.

Most classical theists would want to deny that open theists are theists, because classical theism, including that of Nasr, affirms divine immutability. According to the classical theist God is unchangeable, unable to suffer or die as creatures do. Open theists want God to respond to the world, whereas more traditional theists affirm that the eternal deity is beyond change.

Can a Trinitarian Theist Be a Monotheist?

Divine involvement in the world of creatures is a distinctive emphasis of Trinitarian theism as proffered by late twentieth-century Christian theologians. Because they affirm divine interaction with the world in a manner akin to open theists, the new Trinitarians reject divine immutability. Trinitarians affirm the existence of only one God; there is only one divine reality. But they also affirm that the three persons—Father, Son, and Holy Spirit—relate to one another *through* the world. This is the key: when the Son, Jesus, prays to the Father within time and space, the Second Person of the Trinity is relating to the First Person through the created world. The Holy Spirit, who binds together the

---

24. See Clark H. Pinnock, *Most Moved Mover: A Theology of God's Openness* (Grand Rapids: Baker Academic, 2001) and "Open Theism: An Answer to My Critics," *Dialog* 44, no. 3 (Fall 2005): 237–45. Philip Clayton tries to tie together open theism, process theology, and Trinitarian theology: "Kenotic Trinitarian panentheism is a view that open theists can, and should, accept. Yet, at the same time it also retains the most fundamental contributions of process theology. The being of God is not *identical* to the events in the world . . . almost no process theologian actually accepts a *full identity* between them. . . . There are a number of viable ways for process thinkers to be Trinitarian theologians." Philip Clayton, "Kenotic Trinitarian Panentheism," *Dialog* 44, no. 1 (Fall 2005): 254.

eternal Father with the historical Son, binds together eternity with time. Historicity is taken up into the eternal divine life. Only a God who is affected by interaction with the world could do this.

If inclusion in the classical theist camp requires divine immutability, then these Trinitarians may not qualify. A second sticking point has to do with divine oneness. If classical theism insists that divine oneness trumps the dynamic interaction of the three persons, so that Father, Son, and Holy Spirit become only superficial traits of an otherwise simple divine unity, then the Trinitarians may not qualify as strict monotheists. So decisive is this point that Reformed theologian Karl Barth holds that belief in the Trinity separates Christian belief from the other monotheisms.[25] Barth is quite happy being excluded from membership in the club of classical theists.

From the Muslim point of view, no Trinitarian Christians qualify as monotheists. Christians are only disguised polytheists, says the Qur'an. Here is the definitive passage: "The Messiah, Jesus son of Mary, was only the Messenger of God, and His Word that He committed to Mary, and a Spirit from Him. So have faith in God and His messengers, and do not say 'Three.' Refrain, better it is for you. God is only One God" (Qur'an 4:171).

Outgrowing the Theistic Model

Despite what has been said, open theists and interactive Trinitarians see themselves as theists. In contrast to deists, theists believe God acts in the world. In contrast to polytheists, theists believe there is only one divine reality. In contrast to pantheists, theists believe God as ultimate reality is personal and that God is qualitatively different from the world; God loves the world as one person would love another. What theists or monotheists achieve is an adequate conceptualization of divine transcendence; yet it is difficult to move coherently within this model of God toward divine immanence.

The classical theist model fits Muslims well. It also fits some Jews and many Christians. But some contemporary Christians want to emphasize divine immanence along with divine transcendence. The theistic model adequately presents God as beyond, as transcendent, as redeeming people from the vicissitudes of history. But when it comes to divine presence within history and within the human soul, classical theism fails to resonate sufficiently with the intimate sensibility of many people. Numerous Christian theologians at present are struggling to shed the constraints of the theistic model. They are considering other options, including open theism and interactive Trinitarianism. A third option some Christians are considering is panentheism.

---

25. Karl Barth, *Church Dogmatics*, trans. G. W. Bromily, 4 vols. (Edinburgh: T. & T. Clark, 1936–1962), 1:1.

Panentheism

In Acts 17:28, Saint Paul is reported to have said, "For 'In him [God] we live and move and have our being.'" Which model best interprets what is said here? The model of panentheism stands ready.

As the word *panentheism* (*pan* meaning all; *en* meaning in; and *theism* referring to belief in God) indicates, what is affirmed here is that all things exist within God's being.[26] The entire world of nature and history exist within God's being; but they do not exhaust God's being. There is a little bit of God left over, so to speak. Whereas pantheism holds that the divine and the world are co-extensive; panentheism holds that the world is located within the being of God while some aspects of God still transcend the world. Both contrast with theism, which holds that God completely transcends the world even though God freely enters and engages the world.

Panentheism, according to process theologian John Cobb, "differs from much traditional theism insofar as the latter stressed the mutual externality of God and the world, with God conceived as occupying another, supernatural, sphere. It differs from pantheism when pantheism is understood to be the identification of God and the world."[27]

Sometimes panentheists use a human analogy. They say that God relates to the world like our mind relates to our body. Our mind is totally dependent on our body to exist, yet our thinking seems to transcend our body at certain points. Our mind can look at our body and even guide our body. The world is God's body; and God is the mind of the world.

This means that God is totally dependent on the world to exist and that God did not create the world out of nothing. Panentheists reject *creatio ex nihilo*. They prefer the idea of continuing creation, *creatio continua*, to emphasize the shared temporal relationship between the world and God. Continuing creation for the panentheist is similar to providence for the theist.

This further implies that the world must have existed backwards in time just as long as God has. Similarly, the world will continue to exist into the future as long as there is a God. According to panentheism, God lacks *aseity*, independence. The world and God are mutually inter-dependent. Similar to pantheists, panentheists believe that everything in the world is connected to everything else, and everything is connected to God. God's being and the being of the world are inseparable.

The God of panentheism is finite, not infinite. The physical body of God is co-extensive with the physical make-up of the universe. Only the mind of God transcends the physical plenitude. Ontological transcendence is sacrificed.

---

26. The term *panentheism* goes back to K. F. Krause (1781–1832), an interpreter of Hegel and Fichte. See Charles Hartshorne, "Pantheism and Panentheism," in *Encyclopedia of Religion*, ed. Mircea Eliade, 16 vols., 1st ed. (New York: MacMillan, 1987), 10:6960–65. See also Philip Clayton, "Introduction to Panentheism," in *Models of God*, ed. Diller and Kasher, 371–80.

27. John B. Cobb Jr., *God and the World* (Louisville: Westminster John Knox, 1969), 80.

This also means that God cannot love the world as we would love another person. Rather, God must love the world as we would love our own body. God's love for the world is a form of self-love.

Process theologians and some contemporary feminist theologians find panentheism attractive. They object to the cultural connotations of theism, where God is pictured as an omnipotent king or lord or father. These symbols of dominance have tended to reinforce hierarchical thinking and patriarchy over the centuries. Feminists object as well to the idea of creation out of nothing, because it implies total power over the world. Panentheism provides an attractive alternative model for feminists, because it pictures God as connected, as more relational.[28] The love of God for the world according to the panentheist is an extension of God's love for God's own body; and feminists find this a good model for a woman. A woman should love others as an extension of her own self-esteem and self-care.

From the point of view of most theists, panentheism is an unacceptable model for explicating the biblical experience with the God of Israel and the God of Jesus Christ. The chief complaint against panentheism is that the image of interdependence between God and the world compromises God's freedom and omnipotence, eliminating divine *aseity*. Yet panentheism's emphasis on divine involvement in the world of creatures is attractive to Christian sensibilities.

Comparing Models of God Chart

CONCEPT OF GOD	CREATOR?	ACTIVE IN THE WORLD?	ASEITY?
Atheism	No	No	No
Agnosticism	No?	No?	No?
Deism	Yes	No	Yes
Pantheism	Yes	No	No
Polytheism	No	Yes	No
Henotheism	Yes	Yes	No
Theism	Yes	Yes	Yes
Panentheism	No	Yes	No
Trinitarian Theism	Yes	Yes	Yes

---

28. "Theology, as the way in which we interpret existence in a world where God is for us, will be expressed in relational language," writes Marjorie Hewitt Suchocki in *God, Christ, Church: A Practical Guide to Process Theology* (New York: Crossroad, 1982), 3. She adds, "It is not theology about feminist issues, but it *is* feminist theology" (Ibid., vi, italics in original).

Conclusion

A human who thinks critically about being human is like a paddler sitting in a kayak with "history" written on the bow. The kayak navigates white water. That white water is like the mystery within which cosmic history is being borne. To ask about the water is to ask about the mystery within which history is set. The question about this mystery is the question of God. According to Lutheran theologian Wolfhart Pannenberg, "The idea of God or—to put it impersonally—of a mysterious ground of all reality transcending one's own and all other finite existence, is so implied in the movement of human existence beyond everything finite that [human consciousness finds itself] referred to this transcendent mystery and can have a well-founded hope for the fulfillment of . . . existence only from it."[29] In *God in Cosmic History*, the first mode of answering the question of God shows that our ancestors provided a variety of answers. The text's second mode suggests that cosmic history itself requires that the question of an ultimate grounding be explored.

God in Cosmic History has been plumbing this mystery by asking, what is ultimate? Wherever the pursuit of ultimate reality is followed, the question of God arises. The very asking of this question suggests an implication for spirituality, namely, authentic human life is oriented around what is important, true, and of ultimate value. Jewish theologian Eliot Dorff provides inspiring advice on this matter.

> Confusing the unimportant with the important, the finite with the infinite, leads us mistakenly to devote our time and energy to what are at best only partial or instrumental goals. Only getting a grasp on what is ultimately important in life—in theological terms, learning to discern the difference between idols and God—can save us from such serious mistakes. In practice, we human beings are all too often tempted by the sirens of temporary and improper goals, and it is the ongoing function of religion to remind us of what is really important."[30]

Review Questions

1. Identify one culture that is polytheistic and another that is henotheistic.
2. Look at the obverse side of a U.S. dollar bill. Explain the symbolism.
3. Distinguish atheism from agnosticism. How can faith and agnosticism be compatible?
4. How can polytheism and pantheism be compatible?

---

29. Wolfhart Pannenberg, *Basic Questions in Theology*, trans. George H. Kehm, 2 vols. (Minneapolis: Fortress, 1970–1971), 2:102.

30. Eliot Dorff, "Jewish Images of God," in *Models of God*, ed. Diller and Kasher, 111–24, at 114.

5. Among your friends, can you identify individuals who hold one or another of the alternative models of God?

Discussion Questions

1. Compare the God of classical theism with *Brahman* in Hinduism.
2. Why do panentheists think they have a better view of God than monotheists do?
3. Why do Christians affirm the Trinity? Why do Muslims reject the Trinity?
4. What do open theists and panentheists share in common?
5. Modern people must choose whether or not to believe in the divine, because we live in a religiously plural culture. How should a modern person select what to believe?

Additional Resources

Print Sources

Cobb, John B., and Christopher Ives, eds. *The Emptying God: A Buddhist-Jewish-Christian Conversation.* Maryknoll, NY: Orbis, 1990.

This collection of essays by scholars from differing religious traditions will initiate the reader in the finer points of conceptualizing the divine in inter-religious dialogue.

Diller, Jeanine, and Asa Kasher, eds. *Models of God and Ultimate Realities.* Heidelberg: Springer, 2013.

This is the most comprehensive collection of scholarly chapters on the ideas of the divine across cultures and philosophies. This superb book is for the advanced student.

Peters, Ted. *God as Trinity: Relationality and Temporality in Divine Life.* Louisville: Westminster John Knox, 1993.

This book for advanced students traces the exciting and complex development of Trinitarian theism in the late twentieth century. While showing how Roman Catholics and Protestants debated the issues, the book compares and contrasts multiple understandings of the divine.

Web Sources

Peters, Ted. "Models of God: Comparing Concepts." Theological Briefs. *http://tedstimelytake.com/wp-content/uploads/2016/11/2013-ModelsGod-300dpi-Peters.pdf.*

Science and Scientism in Europe and China

The social orders we live in are not grounded cosmically.

—CHARLES TAYLOR[1]

The model of God belonging to theism disenchanted the world. Because the physical world is created from nothing and exists in discontinuity with a supra-cosmic God, the cosmos is no longer sacred, spiritual, or magical. This divorce of divinity provided Jews and Christians along with Muslims (especially in the early centuries of Islam) with a big hint: the physical world can be studied on its own. The world is contingent, and the only way to know the world is through observation.

In addition, this disenchanted world just might be organized mathematically, as the ancient Greeks had surmised. If one could discern the mathematical laws by which nature is ordered, one would then discern the mathematical mind of the God who created all things. Western science could study the world and the mind of God at the same time. With this effective history in place, knowledge exploded.

The knowledge explosion was followed by detonations that burst into nationalism, colonialism, industry, technology, democracy, freedom, dignity, secularization, and religious revival. Once the fallout was cleaned up from these cultural explosions, a new way of life was constructed. This new way of life is termed *modernity*.

The breadth of modernity includes nearly the entire globe. Where is the depth? What is thought to be ultimate? To find out, one must dig below the surface of the modern era. Without such digging, the question of God cannot be asked. Digging is the task of this book.

---

1. Charles Taylor, *A Secular Age* (Cambridge, MA: Harvard University Press, 2007), 540.

Science and Scientism in the Modern Era

The defining traits of the modern era—*modernity*—include science and its close cousin, scientism. Science is the pursuit of new knowledge; and in the modern world science is systematic and well-funded. Science shares its findings with its sibling, technology. Technology transforms our environment and even ourselves. Virtually every day we expect to see new things, thanks to science and technology.

To understand the modern mind, one needs to understand the role of effective history in modern consciousness. What happened in the past did not just go away. It remains present in today's language, idioms, and frameworks of thought. The role of reason in ancient Greece and the role of contingent history in ancient Israel continue to influence modern and emerging postmodern self-understanding. Greek reason provides the foundation for science, and the Hebrew expectation of newness provides the foundation for technology. But there is much more to the modern mind. Modernity invented scientism, something unknown in previous history.

Scientism is the belief that the kind of knowledge science produces is the *only* knowledge. Because science pursues knowledge of the physical domain and only the physical domain, scientism claims that the physical domain is the *only* reality. Nothing supra-physical or metaphysical exists. Nothing is supra-cosmic; rather, it is all intra-cosmic. The material world is devoid of enchantment, unconnected to anything spiritual. Nothing in poetry, art, religion, or culture can contribute to genuine knowledge, because science has an exclusive patent on what can be known. Paul Kurtz, a skeptic cited in previous chapters, commits himself to the proposition that "there are no ultimate questions, only penultimate ones."[2]

To repeat with emphasis: science does not require scientism. Most of our living scientists do not embrace the myth of scientism, yet those who do embrace scientism wield considerable influence in both Western and Chinese society.

Scientism's Tenets

"The Cosmos is all that there is or ever was or ever will be," said Carl Sagan, Cornell's famous cosmologist.[3] Sagan's wife, Ann Druyan, agrees: "Science is a way of looking at absolutely everything."[4] According to Harvard geneticist Richard Lewontin, the challenge of scientism is to get the public "to reject irrational and supernatural explanations of the world, the demons that exist only

2. Paul Kurtz, *Transcendental Temptation: A Critique of Religion and the Paranormal* (Buffalo: Prometheus, 1984), 56.

3. Carl Sagan, *Cosmos* (New York: Random House, 1980), 4.

4. Ann Druyan, "Ann Druyan Talks about Science, Religion, Wonder, and Awe, and Carl Sagan," in *Science under Siege*, ed. Kendrick Frazier (Buffalo: Prometheus, 2009), 38–47, at 44.

in their imaginations, and to accept a social and intellectual apparatus, *Science*, as the only begetter of truth. . . . Materialism is absolute, for we cannot allow a Divine Foot in the door."[5] Michael Shermer, prominent skeptic and agnostic, mentioned in an earlier chapter, admits that scientism "is a secular religion in the sense of generating loyal commitments (a type of faith) to a method, a body of knowledge, and a hope for a better tomorrow."[6] The religion of scientism has no churches, because it operates more at the level of presupposition than supposition.

Philosopher Huston Smith objects, asserting that science should remain science and not attempt to become an anti-religious religion or ideology. "The problem is not science, but scientism—namely, to assume that what science turns up and can turn up is the sum of all there is."[7] Job Kozhamathadam of Pune, India, founder of the journal *Omega*, similarly objects. "Scientism is basically an attitude that accords undue confidence to the power and importance of science. In its extreme form it believes that science can do everything, solve all problems. . . . Seen through the eyes of scientism, religious and related matters became meaningless non-issues."[8] Pope John Paul II similarly observes, "Scientism is the philosophical notion which refuses to admit the validity of forms of knowledge other than those of the positive sciences; and it relegates religious, theological, ethical, and aesthetic knowledge to the realm of mere fantasy."[9] Scientism is an anti-religious religion with a missionary zeal to convert traditional believers into non-believers.

Science effects a powerful impact on culture that extends way beyond the laboratory. The temptation to usurp and dominate other forms of cultural expression has been too hard to resist by many champions of science. Scientific explorers have become colonizers of the modern mind, exterminating traditional thoughts and obliterating inherited values. The thorough colonization of culture is the missionary goal of those who have turned science into scientism.

Smith, who taught world religions at MIT, revolts against the hegemony of scientism. "Science is great. Scientism, though, is bad. What's the difference? Science is the positive finding, through controlled experiment, of truths about the physical universe—and that's good. Scientism, by way of contrast, says two

---

5. Richard Lewontin, review of *The Demon Haunted World*, by Carl Sagan, *New York Review of Books* (January 9, 1997).

6. Michael Shermer, *How We Believe: The Search for God in an Age of Science* (New York: W. H. Freeman and Co., 2000), 61.

7. Huston Smith, *The Way Things Are: Conversations with Huston Smith on the Spiritual Life*, ed. Phil Cousineau (Berkeley: University of California Press, 2003), 118.

8. Job Kozhamathadam, "Science and Religion: Past Estrangement and Present Possible Engagement," in *Contemporary Science and Religion in Dialogue: Challenges and Opportunities*, ed. Job Kozhamthadam (Pune, India: ASSR Publications, Jnana-Deepa Vidyapeeth, 2002): 2–45, at 18.

9. Pope John Paul II, *Fides et Ratio*, http://w2.vatican.va/content/john-paul-ii/en/encyclicals /documents/hf_jp-ii_enc_14091998_fides-et-ratio.html.

things. The first is that science is the best if not the only probe of truth. The second fallacy of scientism is that it holds that the most fundamental substance in the universe is what scientists deal with, namely, matter. There is no scientific basis for those two corollaries."[10] Scientism is not itself scientific.

Next the modern cultural family will be considered, including science and scientism. Scientism is prominent not only throughout the West, but in China as well. Twentieth-century China adopted scientism explicitly as the state ideology. In the West, scientism operates at the level of presupposition while, in the East, at the level of supposition. Scientism in the West is quietly assumed, but in the East its ideology is stated explicitly. In both West and East, scientism has been trying to bury the question of God.

Modernity's Family

"The modern era, or modernity, got under way about 250 years ago," say world historians Dunn and Mitchell. "It represented the sharpest turn in the human venture since the invention of farming 12,000 years ago."[11] Modernity is home to dynamism, innovation, and growth. Its effects include the nation-state, Western Colonialism, industrial revolution, technology, democracy, freedom, dignity, secularization, religious revival, and the Anthropocene effect.

The Nation-State

A few city-states remain in the twenty-first century, such as Monaco and Singapore, but the days when city-states combined into empires is long gone. With the arrival of modernity, a new form of government has appeared, the nation-state. Because of revolutions in America, France, Great Britain, Germany and, later, Russia, kings lost their power. The modern state grants more rights and privileges to its people than did previous monarchies, making the new government stronger and more involved in the lives of its citizens. Despite the modern idea of freedom, however, historians aver that today's governments "have come to exercise both military power and command over the lives of their own citizens on a scale unknown in premodern times."[12]

Modern states do not overtly rely upon myths to legitimize their authority. Even so, the autochthony sensibility remains powerful. Modern governments create ceremonies with pageantry to celebrate their own history on their own

---

10. Huston Smith, "The News of Eternity" in *Healing our Planet: Healing Our Selves*, ed. Dawson Church and Geralyn Gendreau (Santa Rosa, CA: Elite, 2005), 43–58, at 46.

11. Ross E. Dunn and Laura J. Mitchell, *Panorama: A World History* (New York: McGraw Hill Education, 2015), 632. It might be more accurate to say that modernity began four or five hundred years ago. Curiously, Thomas Aquinas in the twelfth century spoke of his theology as "modern."

12. Dunn and Mitchell, *Panorama*, 575.

particular portion of global real estate. This elicits patriotism and the willingness to wage war for one's native land.

Western Colonialism, Science, and Technology

Italian explorer Cristóbal Colón (1451–1506), remembered as *Columbus*, was sent by Spain's royal family westward across the Atlantic Ocean to find a direct route to India. Instead of finding India, Columbus's three ships landed in the Bahaman archipelago in 1492. From the European perspective, this threshold event marked the discovery of a new world, the Americas. European explorers began voraciously gobbling up real estate around the globe through colonization. From the colonies Europe extracted agricultural produce and valuable minerals, developing the slave trade to supply the labor.

European explorers often took scientists on board their ships, with instructions to bring back new knowledge to Europe. "European imperialists set out to distant shores in the hope of obtaining new knowledge along with new territories. . . . The conquest of knowledge and the conquest of territory became ever more tightly intertwined. . . . Almost every important military expedition that left Europe for distant lands had on board scientists who set out not to fight but to make scientific discoveries," observes Harari.[13] In addition to cotton and gold, scientific knowledge produced in the colonies enriched the universities of the colonizers.

Because science feeds the growth of technology, and because technology leads to stronger armies, outnumbered European soldiers were able to conquer and establish colonies wherever they wished. Harari observes that "from 1850 onward European domination rested to a large extent on the military-industrial-scientific complex and technological wizardry."[14]

Progress in technology meant progress in culture, thought the Europeans. Europeans came to believe they were superior because, technologically, they were the most progressive people in the world. "They judged other people and cultures as inferior and took on the arrogance of believing themselves superior to all others. In many cases, this belief was added to their already existing belief in the superiority of their religion, Christianity."[15] The historical significance of the colonial period was that European ideas spread, and included in the inventory of ideas was admiration for what science and technology could accomplish. Because of the hegemony of science and technology, Europeans convinced themselves their culture was more progressive than those they colonized.

---

13. Yuval Noah Harari, *Sapiens: A Brief History of Humankind* (New York: Harper, 2015), 284.

14. Ibid., 280.

15. David Christian, Cynthia Stokes Brown, and Craig Benjamin, *Big History: Between Nothing and Everything* (New York: McGraw-Hill, 2014), 257.

Industrial Revolution

Between 1760 and 1840, in Europe and in many of its colonies, technology underwent a huge advance. This transition, now called the *Industrial Revolution*, included replacement of hand crafts with machine production in the factory system. Power was generated by flowing water, coal, and eventually petroleum. Capital investment fired the engines of economic growth, and the world became modern in the technological sense. Farmers left their rural homes to become factory workers in the cities, and urbanization followed.

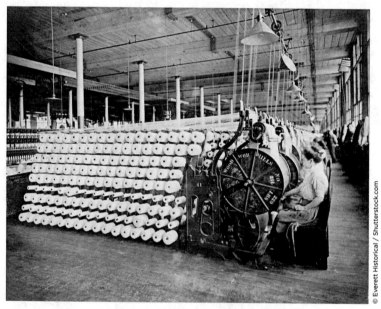

During the industrial revolution, artisans and craftsmen were replaced by machines and mass production. The mechanistic worldview, based on Newtonian physics, seemed vindicated by the growing capacity of machines to turn a profit.

The Industrial Revolution could accomplish so much so fast because of the four stage movement: (1) raw materials flow from the peripheral colonies to the center, to the colonizing nations, where (2) manufacturing takes place, then (3) the manufactured products flow back to the colonies, and (4) surplus value or profit flows back to the center. "The industrial revolution," observes Charles Mann, "depends on three raw materials: steel, fossil fuels, and rubber."[16] This accumulation of wealth seemed to confirm the sense of superiority developing in European self-understanding.

---

16. Charles C. Mann, *1491: New Revelations of the Americas before Columbus* (New York: Vintage Books, 2006), 354.

Democracy

The European Renaissance followed by the Enlightenment benefitted from the axial insights of ancient Greece and Israel. Specifically, the belief that the mind of God could be apprehended directly in the human mind through reason had a double revolutionary impact: it undercut the authority of the king to tell people what to do and the authority of the priest to tell people what to believe. Kings lost their heads and churches lost their public privileges. Democracy—one person, one vote—rose up like Fourth of July fireworks. Modernity "planted in the human imagination the novel idea that a community of people welded together by shared rights and responsibilities could form a sovereign state."[17] The implications of the axial insight—human equality based on transcendent justice—mushroomed in modernity, a gift of effective history.

Freedom

The kind of freedom on the minds of early moderns was political liberty. As already noted, the new mood in Europe was to deny kings the authority to tell people what to do and to deny priests the authority to tell people what to think. Democracy came to be thought of as the form of government free people would choose. In time, freedom came to take on many additional meanings, such as self-expression.

The modern mind is not entirely coherent. Politically, modern people celebrate freedom. Physically, modern people presume with Newton that the world is a closed causal nexus. Are these two compatible?

Modernity inherited from its Christian past the debate over human free will. The idea of democratic freedom depends upon a prior assumption, namely, individual persons possess free will and by law they should be permitted to exercise free will in society. However, this assumption is incompatible with the scientific worldview—specifically the Newtonian mechanical worldview—which grew to dominance during the Industrial Revolution. Newton's closed-causal worldview is deterministic. There is no room for contingency let alone human free will. Jumping forward to the twenty-first century, deterministic philosophers of neuroscience are asserting that the human mind is determined by the physical brain. Free will is a delusion. "There is a puzzle about everyday life: we all feel like unified conscious agents acting with self-purpose, and we are free to make choices of almost any kind," says neurophilosopher Michael Gazzaniga. "At the same time everyone realizes we are machines . . . [we are] completely determined."[18] The mechanistic model of Newton now applies to human

---

17. Dunn and Mitchell, *Panorama*, 603.

18. Michael S. Gazzaniga, *Who's in Charge? Free Will and the Science of the Brain*, 2009 Gifford Lectures (New York: Harper, 2011), 7.

persons, eliminating free will. By denying free will, determinists deny one of the foundations upon which the modern culture of democracy and personal freedom is built.

German theologian Markus Mühling prophesies a forthcoming culture conflict. "Whenever science becomes scientism, science not only ceases to be science and changes into religion, but becomes an intolerant danger for liberal societies."[19] The pseudo-religion of scientism seems to be built on the mechanistic model of nature, not the quantum model that implies contingency, free will, and unpredictable history. Because scientism functions as a pseudo-religion and is so pervasive in the Western mind, we will here dub it a *myth* in the third sense of the term: a conceptual set or worldview. It is a myth that precludes the most precious value of modern society, freedom.

Perhaps a caveat should be entertained. Currently, scientific researchers rely upon freedom of inquiry. Science thrives in democracies but suffers in totalitarian states such as the previous Soviet Union and today's fundamentalist theocracies. Science and freedom come together in a single package, sociologically speaking. Yet, at the theoretical level, the determinism of Newtonian physics risks undercutting the very cultural foundations on which freedom is constructed.

Dignity

According to the doctrine of human dignity, each human individual should be treated as a moral end, never merely as a means to a further end. Enlightenment philosopher Immanuel Kant (1724–1804) codified for all of modernity the concept of dignity and its moral corollary: "Act in such a way that you always treat humanity, whether in your own person or in the person of any other, never simply as a means, but always at the same time as an end."[20] Each person is inherently a locus of value, and never merely a means to some other higher value.

Prior to modernity, people believed that God alone should be treated as the moral end, the ultimate moral end. How did something belonging to God get transferred to humanity? Human dignity is an indirect gift of the Christian gospel wending its way through effective history. The gospel claims that God participated in a sacrifice on behalf of the human race (indeed, on behalf of all creation). Theologically, the human person is God's moral end. The modern world could not rob God of something God had already given.

---

19. Markus Mühling, *Resonances: Neurobiology, Evolution and Theology* (Göttingen: Vandenhoeck & Ruprecht, 2014), 27.

20. Immanuel Kant, *Groundwork of the Metaphysic of Morals*, trans. H. J. Paton (New York: Harper, 1948), 96. Arizona State University religious studies professor Gaymon Bennett offers a postmodern analysis, suggesting that dignity is a social construction. *Technicians of Human Dignity* (New York: Fordham University Press, 2016).

Historically speaking, the modern doctrine of human dignity emerged in the social order; it developed within a popular reaction against royal and ecclesial hierarchies. On the eve of the Enlightenment, the sixteenth-century Protestant Reformers had trumpeted that God graciously relates to each individual directly, bypassing the authority of the church or the state. This led eventually to the affirmation that all individual persons are equal. Equality pulled the rug out from under the privilege claimed by the priestly class and the royal class. The trend towards modern individualism also enhanced human dignity.

The doctrine of human dignity is the implicit if not explicit moral ground for what happens today in the courtroom, in legislatures passing laws, in protests against police profiling, in the civil rights movement, the women's liberation movement, LGBTQ (Lesbian, Gay, Bisexual, Transsexual, and Queer) claims for equal rights, and even in the worldwide call for compassion on behalf of refugees and migrants.

In the later Middle Ages and in earlier modernity, dignity was associated with rationality, with intellectual capacity. Humans were thought to be the *rational animal*, as Aristotle had taught. Rationality provided the justification for dignity. Recently this understanding has been challenged. Young children suffering from Down Syndrome and elderly persons suffering from Alzheimer's cannot be judged according to their abilities to reason: they possess inherent dignity. Regardless of one's capacity to reason, each person is a moral end and not merely a means to somebody else's end. Infanticide and euthanasia are ruled out.

Modern society is morally obligated to *confer* dignity on every person regardless of rational capacity, age, gender, ethnicity, religion, or political affiliation. This obligation relies on a presupposed belief in the existence of a transcendent standard of justice that applies to all persons, in all times, and in all places. Only by implicit appeal to the divine reality of the axial breakthrough could we guarantee such a transcendent standard of justice or dignity or freedom. These modern convictions spring from the answer to the God-question provided by the axial seers and have been mediated to us by effective history.

Modern culture does not represent a revolutionary rejection of its prehistory. Rather, the modern mind burst into cultural history by retrieving its biblical roots during the Protestant Reformation and its Greek roots in the Renaissance. By fertilizing these axial roots, the modern mind has blossomed in creative and even unpredictable ways.

Secularization

One unpredictable outgrowth of modernity is the spread of secular thinking. In common usage, the term *secular* indicates a domain of life that is ordered without recourse to religion. Philosopher Charles Taylor observes that the modern world represents a change "which takes us from a society in which it was virtually impossible not to believe in God, to one in which faith, even for the staunchest believer, is one human possibility among others."[21] Religious faith in a secular age must be chosen from among an array of alternatives, including unfaith. The secular dimension of modern culture has led to pluralism, to the inescapability of choice.

Secularity is a noun that *describes* the last several centuries; the noun *secularism*, on the other hand, *prescribes* an ideology that promotes what is secular. The first is descriptive; the second is prescriptive. Secularism is a popular ideology. Theologian Ingolf Dalferth identifies three ways the term comes into play: "(1) In a political sense, it [secularism] insists on the idea that religion should not interfere with or be integrated into the public affairs of society. (2) In institutional terms, it insists on a separation of church and state. . . . (3) In an ideological sense, it rejects religious belief as a key to understanding the world, asserts an unbridgeable gap between reason and religion, and consigns all religious views and orientations to an outdated pre-rational past."[22] When secularity becomes secularism, choice is removed in favor of an anti-religious ideology that claims that "the human good is in its very essence sensual, earthly; whoever identifies a transcendent goal departs from it, betrays it."[23] Or, as Tillich puts it, "The secular is the realm of preliminary concerns. It lacks ultimate concern; it lacks holiness."[24]

While Judaism and Christianity adapted to secular modernity, Islam has found it more problematic. Sunni Muslim leader Muhammad ibn Abd al-Wahhab (1703–1792), known for his emphasis on the principle of *tawhid* (relying solely on the oneness of God and one's unity with God), reacted negatively to what was happening in Western Europe. A secular interpretation of the world could not be reconciled with the idea of revering the one God in every aspect of daily life. Secularity right along with secularism must be rejected, vehemently denounced. A retrieval of premodern Islamic commitments must lead to an immediate and thorough reform, he contended. Al-Wahhab formed a pact with a local leader, Muhammad bin Saud, founder of today's House of Saud dynasty that rules petroleum-rich Saudi Arabia. Petrol dollars today fund the Wahhabi ideology that adamantly opposes the secular way of life pervading Western Europe and its former colonies, including the Unites States. Wahhabism seeks to purify Islam from contamination by both European secularism and Shiite Islam. This strand of spirituality is fighting back against modern secularity and secularism, sometimes with violence.

---

21. Taylor, *Secular Age*, 3.

22. Ingolf U. Dalferth, "Post-Secular Society: Christianity and the Dialectics of the Secular," *Journal of the American Academy of Religion* 78, no. 2 (June 2010): 317–45, at 329–30.

23. Taylor, *Secular Age*, 547.

24. Paul Tillich, *Systematic Theology*, 3 vols. (Chicago: University of Chicago Press, 1951–1963), 1:218.

The doctrines of secularism presuppose what some European and North Americans call the *secularization theory*. Accordingly, with every advance in science and democracy there is a corresponding decline in religious belief. As secularity grows, religion declines. In time, religion will simply wither away. Such a theory could be valid if, and only if, secularism would itself be thought of as an ideology occupying the space formerly belonging to religion. The secularization theory conflates science and secularity. More importantly, it conflates scientism with secularism.

The data tend to refute secularization theory. According to sociologist of religion Peter Berger, for example, the once dominant *secularization theory* held, very simply, that "modernity inevitably produces a decline in religion." However, Berger recently noted, "the data doesn't support this." Yes, some countries in northern Europe are heavily secular and there certainly exists an intellectual elite in the globe's metropolitan areas who affirm a secular worldview, but "the rest of the world is massively religious. In some areas of the world more religious than ever. The theory is wrong."[25] The key is to recognize that secularity in public life has led to pluralism in religious life. Religious faith is today a matter of free choice, and many individuals are making the choice for religion. The connection between religion and free choice has, in part, plowed the field where spiritual fervor could grow.

Religious Revival

While governments in many cases sought to become secular so as to show impartial justice to a variety of religions, the populace discovered a new interior energy to their personal faith. The intimate sensibility has been enlivened during modernity. The Protestant Reformation of the sixteenth century had already turned to personal faith over against ecclesiastical authoritarianism; this seed bore fruit again in the eighteenth and nineteenth centuries. Revival began in Prussia (Germany) among the Lutherans, who called for a renewal of individual faith. In North America, under the leadership of Jonathan Edwards, John and Charles Wesley, and other revivalists, a *Great Awakening* took place just prior to and subsequent to the American Revolution (1776). This was followed by the *Second Awakening*, 1805 to 1835.[26] Individuals were urged to take Jesus Christ as their "personal Lord and Savior." This form of spirituality promoted a relationship to God that was individual and immediate, not mediated by government or church, and it fittingly complemented the rise of democracy with its "one person, one vote." Freedom applied equally to both faith and citizenship.

25. Cited in Gregor Thuswaldner, "A Conversation with Peter L. Berger: 'How My Views Have Changed,'" *The Cresset* of Valparaiso University 77, no. 3 (Lent 2014): 16–21, at 16.

26. Bonnie G. Smith, Mark Van De Mieroop, Richard Von Glahn, and Kris Lane, *Crossroads and Cultures: A History of the World's Peoples* (Boston: Bedford/St. Martin's, 2012), 785.

What is distinctive about religious revival in a secular context is the axiomatic requirement, tolerance. Modern secular values will not tolerate intolerance between rival religions. Secularity, plurality, and tolerance come together in a single modern package. The insightful professor of missions at Yale Divinity School and expert on Muslim-Christian dialogue, Lamin Sanneh, explains that radical religion makes pluralism difficult.

> A version of secularization theory has survived to the effect that globalization has required the plural expression of religion, and pluralism means in that context the availability of choice in religious affiliation. One may be born into a religion, but that is not enough in an age of globalization. One has to choose to become consciously religious, with the stress on consciousness as an independent variable. . . . It is fair to add that the culture of relativism that has been the driving force of pluralism has nevertheless failed to cope with issues of religious and ideological radicalism. Radicals do not wish to play by the rules of a tolerant pluralism, and tolerant pluralism in turn cannot be intolerant of the radicals without being inconsistent with itself. Tolerance is thus exposed as either inadequate or evasive, or both. That situation creates the urgent need to match the rhetoric of an inclusive pluralism with commitment to some standard or idea of what is true and worthwhile.[27]

If *plurality* becomes *pluralism*, does it become another ideology? John Hick identifies the concept of pluralism with his own supra-denominational religious ideology: "Religious pluralism is the view that there is no one-and-only true and salvific faith. . . . Pluralism regards all the great world faiths as equally authentic and salvific."[28] In this perspective, pluralism implies that Hinduism, Christianity, and other traditional faiths, along with ISIS and suicide cults, should be tolerated because each is authentic and salvific. This is pluralism as ideology. Sanneh, in contrast, appears to presuppose a non-ideological meaning to *pluralism*. Regardless, Sanneh's point is this: modernity requires an inclusive pluralism if religious fervor is to be encouraged within the context of a non-ideological secularity. Intolerant religious radicals, however, risk destroying the peaceful cooperation that pluralism could preserve. Modern values such as religious tolerance make pluralistic social units possible.

The problem with scientism (not science!) is that it is intolerant. Because it functions as a myth at the level of presupposition, it flies under the radar and escapes being designated as one religious position among others. The Western

---

27. Lamin Sanneh, "Why Is Christianity, the Religion of the Colonizer, Growing So Fast in Africa?," (Santa Clara Lecture, Santa Clara University, Santa Clara, CA, May 11, 2005), 11. *https://www.scu.edu/media/ignatian-center/santa-clara-lecture/scl-0505-sanneh.pdf*.

28. John Hick, *The New Frontier of Religion and Science: Religious Experience, Neuroscience and the Transcendent* (New York: Macmillan, Palgrave, 2006, 2010), 153.

myth of scientism has provided the framework within which some big historians have chronicled natural and human history.

From Confucius to Science to Scientism in China

"The basic dynamics of the Axial Age and Modernity seem similar, from the social breakdown and political fragmentation through the intense social, political, and technological innovation, from the terror roused by periods of intense warfare through the evolution of new world stories," comments Ken Baskin.[29] This certainly applies to twentieth century China, where the Confucian story is replaced by the modern story.

Culturally, up until a century ago, Confucius and Chinese culture compatibly blended. Confucius provided the design for the social order for two millennia. The educated class was required to take and pass thorough examinations on Confucius's teachings. This blend remained intact until 1911.[30]

The change was slow at first, then sped up. It began with modern Christian missionaries. Nestorian Christians had established educational institutions in Xian, China, which lasted from the seventh to the ninth centuries. Then, for unknown reasons, these Christians disappeared without a trace. When modern Western missionaries arrived in China they had no knowledge of their Syriac predecessors.

Near the end of the Ming Dynasty (1368–1644) and the beginning of the Qing 1644–1911), Jesuit Roman Catholic missionaries from Europe showed up. Along with their faith, these Europeans brought unheard-of science and technology, including military technology. From the Chinese point of view, the Christian gospel and awesome science came together in a single package. Both Roman Catholic and Protestant missionaries set to establishing schools and universities. By 1939 the Protestants alone had built nineteen universities, most of which were later confiscated by the Maoist regime and are still operating today.

The fascinated Chinese leaders initially applied the new science to their own calendrical studies and related subjects such as astronomy, geometry, and mathematics. At first, the absorption of Western science had very little impact on the Confucian worldview. Chinese intellectuals added new Western knowledge to their cultural inventory, but Chinese scientists did not adopt the European scientific method of systematic discovery or technological progress. Not until young Chinese scholars traveled abroad and returned with Western educations

29. Ken Baskin, "The Dynamics of Evolution," in *Teaching and Researching Big History: Exploring a New Scholarly Field*, ed. Leonid Grinin, David Baker, Esther Quaedackers, and Audrey Korotayev (Volgograd, Russia: Uchitel, 2014), 220–42, at 242.

30. This section draws upon the research of Frank Budenholzer, Professor in the Department of Chemistry, Fu Jen Catholic University in Taipei, Taiwan, especially his unpublished lecture, "Religion and Science in Taiwan/China."

The Temple of Heaven in Beijing, China, is an example of an *axis mundi*, the tower that connects heaven and earth. The emperor would enter the temple to make court judgments, symbolically blessed by heaven. The emperor's authority derives from heaven's blessing.

did the full impact of a scientized worldview begin to register on the yet-to-be modern Chinese consciousness.

Things changed dramatically in 1911. During what is called the Xinhai (or Hsin-Hai) Revolution, the Republic of China deposed the Qing dynasty and replaced two thousand years of imperial rule with a secular government. The republican revolutionaries despaired at the weakness of traditional Chinese culture and its inability to resist the powerful impact of Western colonialism. The two Opium Wars of the nineteenth century, wherein Great Britain forced Chinese markets open to the sale of opium and to the pacification of the populace, had been humiliating. The once proud and dominant China had been reduced to a cowering servant within the British Empire.

The revolutionaries believed that the cause of China's weakness was Daoism, Confuciansim, and all forms of religion. The cure would be science. The process of either augmenting or even replacing traditional religion with science became known as *Chinese scientism*.

Sun Yat-sen and Chiang Kei-Shek in the era of the Republic of China typify a "middle path" between preservation of China's cultural treasures while absorbing Western science. The Marxists who followed the Republic of China dumped the middle path in favor of a brutal and exhaustive scientism. By 1945, Mao Zedong and his communist or "red" army had replaced the Republic of China with the People's Republic of China, which continues to rule the Chinese mainland today. The Republic of China still exists, but it is confined to Taiwan.

On the mainland, Mao Zedong ramped up the replacement of religion with science, albeit science tainted with Marxist ideology. The contemporary rise of China as a world power is attributed to its scientism, at least by the Chinese who sponsor it.

As might be predicted, a metaphysical debate broke out. The revised philosophy of one revered scholar, Wu Chih-hui, is described by a student, Hu Shi: the "old scholar unreservedly accepted the mechanistic conception of the universe, and built up a philosophy of life, which in his own words, 'ruled out the term God and banished the soul or spirit.'"[31] What was primarily a cultural movement in Europe and the Americas became an intentional political movement in Eastern Asia. In both cases scientism has taken the form of an anti-religious ideology with a missionary zeal to convert traditional believers into non-believers. By employing reeducation programs, backed by the threat of force, scientism triumphed among the Chinese.

On the whole, the Chinese variant of scientism has less to do with metaphysical materialism and much more to do with technological innovation. The Chinese turned out to be more practical, less philosophical. Chinese scientism emphasizes the pragmatic value of science, science as a tool for nation building and for declaring independence from the colonial West. This is the view that dominates both the People's Republic of China and Republic of China today. In the People's Republic of China, Confucianism has been declared a philosophy, so some citizens may now retrieve the middle path. In the Republic of China's Taiwan, religious fervor remains both abundant and pluralistic.

Conclusion

The question of God in a modern secular society has very little to do with statistics about worship attendance, the separation of church and state, or the religious affiliation of elected officials. Looking at religious institutions is not the same thing as asking the question of God.

When asking the question of God in a modern secular society, one must look for the dimension of ultimacy buried beneath the topsoil of secular culture. We must ask about the topsoil: what are the "isms" that provide the mythical framework through which the culture interprets itself? In modern Western and Chinese societies, the twin sisters of secularism and scientism dominate. Even if secularism and scientism cannot claim exclusive hegemony, their roles in defining modern and emerging postmodern understanding are significant. The problem, from a theologian's point of view, is that secularism and scientism prevent the human psyche from honestly asking about ultimate reality. Modern and postmodern cultures keep religious sensibilities buried.

---

31. Ibid.

Langdon Gilkey (1919–2004), an American Protestant theologian who was a prisoner in a Chinese labor camp during World War II, asks the question of God by exploring the dimension of ultimacy buried beneath modern culture. His theological method is called the *hermeneutic of secular experience*. With this method, Gilkey attempts "to see what religious dimensions there may be . . . in ordinary life . . . which will uncover what is normally hidden and forgotten."[32] What Gilkey "seeks to uncover . . . are those aspects of daily experience which the secular mood has overlooked. . . . There are levels latent in secular life of which our age is undoubtedly aware but about which it is unable to speak or to think intelligibly. These elements are the dimension of ultimacy presupposed in all our interaction with the relative world, and the presence of ambiguity within our freedom and creativity, of the demonic and the despairing in life as well as the joyful, with both of which secular experience is suffused."[33] In short, Gilkey asks the question of God by trying to unearth ultimacy buried below secularism and scientism.

To dig for ultimacy requires a spiritual shovel, an awareness of religious sensibilities, which may be hidden within or under secularism and scientism. Without such digging, the question of God cannot be asked. The goal of this book is to dig.

Review Questions

1. How should we use terms such as *secularity, secularism, science, scientism, plurality,* and *pluralism*?
2. What characteristics of the Axial Age have been mediated to modernity via effective history?
3. Why did the Republic of China attempt to convert people away from Confucianism and Daoism to scientism?
4. What are the economic and political motivations for becoming modern?

Discussion Questions

1. How is belief in human freedom foundational for modern democracy?
2. How is belief in human freedom threatened by belief in a closed causal nexus?
3. Why might a revival of religious commitment occur in modernity?
4. Why must one dig below the surface of secularism and scientism to ask the question of God?

---

32. Langdon Gilkey, *Naming the Whirlwind: The Renewal of God-Language* (Indianapolis and New York: Bobbs-Merrill, 1969), 234.

33. Ibid., 260.

Additional Resources

Print Sources

Christian, David, Cynthia Stokes Brown, and Craig Benjamin. *Big History: Between Nothing and Everything.* New York: McGraw Hill, 2014.

Chapter 10, "Toward the Modern Revolution," identifies three drivers that led to crossing the threshold to modernity: (1) increasing size and variety of exchange networks; (2) growing efficiency of systems of communication and transportation; and (3) expansion of commercial activity, competitive markets, and capitalism. In chapter 11, "Breakthrough to Modernity," the authors define *modernity* in terms of the Industrial Revolution as the Anthropocene Epoch; that is, modernity is characterized primarily as human control over natural resources.

Dunn, Ross E., and Laura J. Mitchell. *Panorama: A World History.* New York: McGraw Hill Education, 2015.

Chapter 20, "Waves of Revolution," and chapter 21, "Energy and Industrialization," provide a lucid narrative running from our premodern predecessors to our modern world through the story of political revolutions and cultural change. In both chapters, Dunn and Mitchell make their position clear: "In our view, the development on which all other transformations turned was the onset of what we call the *energy revolution*" (p. 574). Excellent reading.

Mann, Charles C. *1491: New Revelations of the Americas before Columbus.* New York: Vintage Books, 2005.

Mann, Charles C. *1493: Uncovering the New World Columbus Created.* New York: Vintage Books, 2011.

In these two thick books filled with data in delightful narrative form, Mann provides the reader with the best of what Big History has to offer. The role of nature in the years prior to Columbus's discovery and colonial expansion in the centuries following is informative and fascinating.

Robinson, Marilynne. "Sacred Inwardness: Why 'Secularism' Has No Meaning." *The Christian Century* 132, no. 14 (July 8, 2015): 24–25.

The word *secularism* "means the ground gained in society and culture by agnosticism or atheism as religion recedes," observes Robinson in this lucid article. In a tolerant and liberal society, each individual must choose his or her own belief system. Robinson pleads that one choose "universalism, toward extending the courtesy of nonjudgment very broadly indeed in deference to human mystery and divine grace."

Smith, Bonnie G., Mark Van De Mieroop, Richard Von Glahn, and Kris Lane. *Crossroads and Cultures: A History of the World's Peoples.* Boston: Bedford/St. Martin's, 2012.

Chapter 23, "Atlantic Revolutions and the World," provides a brief yet informative tracking of Enlightenment ideas and their effect on modernity.

Taylor, Charles. *A Secular Age*. Cambridge, MA: Harvard University Press, 2007. This extraordinary tome chronicles the rise of modernity along with in-depth interpretations of secularity. Although Taylor fails to see the difference between science and scientism, his other assessments are by and large both accurate and insightful.

The Evolution Controversy

From what flat wastes of cosmic slime,
And stung by what quick fire,
Sunward the restless races climb!
Men risen out of mire!

—Don Marquis (1878–1937),
"Unrest"

Cosmic History borrows a number of elements from Big History: (1) placing World History within the context of the story of the big bang and evolution, (2) taking note of the influence of nature on human history, and (3) respecting the contributions of science to our understanding of the past and present. In addition, Cosmic History gives attention to the differentiation in human consciousness that takes place over time and, in its own way, constitutes a special dimension of history. This concern over differentiation within human consciousness has led to the special attention given in this book to claims about a purported axial breakthrough two and a half millennia ago. This concern has also led to the special attention given to the modern mind, especially to the way in which the modern Western mind has constructed the concept of science.

This chapter will analyze the century and a half long controversy over Charles Darwin's theory of evolution. This study will try to get beneath the superficial descriptions of this controversy propagated by media as well as scientism's disciples. Scientism's disciples and the media lead us to believe falsely that this controversy pits religion and science against one another in a war. As will appear in the course of this discussion, the warfare idea is disastrously misleading. What has prompted this misconception? The discussion that follows will attempt to answer this question.

Who Is Fighting with Whom about What?

Are religion and science in conflict? According a 2014 PEW Research Center survey, nearly six of ten Americans say science and their own religious beliefs are often in conflict. Certainly some sort of cultural battle is taking place. But a more critical examination of the data demonstrates that only a tiny minority of religious believers actually repudiates science. Just what is going on?[1]

There is no doubt that a culture war is raging, even if the popular trope of a war between religion and science mislabels it. There are multiple armies fighting in this cultural struggle, not just two.

The following discussion will identify the various camps, their positions, and their opponents. The primary contenders include the following: (1) the *science alone* camp, made up of laboratory researchers who employ evolutionary theory in their research programs; (2) ideologists who rely upon *Darwinian scientism* to support their capitalistic ethics and anti-religious materialism; (3) *young Earth creationists*—including both *biblical creationists* and *scientific creationists*—who hold that Darwinian theory is both scientifically wrong and morally dangerous; (4) *intelligent design* theorists, who hold that Darwinian theory is scientifically wrong but that standard evolutionary theory could be improved by incorporating the principle of intelligent design; (5) *theistic* or *pantheistic evolutionists*, who synthesize Darwinian science with a Christian philosophy of history; and (6) *transhumanists*, who wish to take control of humanity's future evolution. The creationists and intelligent design school include conservative Protestant Christians and conservative Muslims. The theistic evolutionists include more mainstream Protestants and Roman Catholics, but virtually no Muslims. Most transhumanists are atheists, but some Christians and Buddhists are exploring an alliance with transhumanism.

The prize in this conflict is meaning. In light of the long natural history from the big bang through the evolution of life on Earth to the recent appearance of *Homo sapiens*, we must ask, is our life meaningful? The laboratory scientists must regretfully admit that they cannot answer this question, because evolutionary biologists do not ask the question of meaning when examining their data. The materialists and atheists answer this question by denying that nature provides any meaning to human life; contemporary civilization must take the responsibility for inventing its own meaning. Both creationists and intelligent design advocates hold that human life is already meaningful because all of physical reality is the creation of a loving and gracious God. Similarly, theistic evolutionists affirm that human life and the entire physical creation find meaning in God's creative love and gracious promise. In sum, the very concept

---

1. Pew Research Center, "Most Americans Say Science and Religion Conflict, But Fewer Say Their Own Beliefs Conflict with Science," *http://www.pewinternet.org/2015/10/22/science-and-religion /pi_2015-10-22_religion-and-science_0-01/*.

of Darwinian evolution raises the question of God, and since 1859 multiple answers have been proffered.

Science Alone: Darwin's Theory of Evolution in the Laboratory

The scientist in the laboratory or in the field must rely upon basic Darwinian principles if his or her research program is going to be fertile and lead to new knowledge. Of course Darwin's 1859 theory regarding variation in inheritance and natural selection has been refined and updated. The most significant update was merging Darwin's original theory with genetics to establish the neo-Darwinian synthesis, which is now almost a century old. Evolutionary theory continues to be refined. Yet Darwin's basic conceptual framework still inspires creative hypotheses and research agendas for anthropologists, paleontologists, biologists, astrobiologists, geneticists, virologists, medical researchers, and countless other scientists. Until a better theory comes along, evolutionary theory will be indispensable for everyone working in the life sciences. "No serious biologist today doubts the theory of evolution to explain the marvelous complexity and diversity of life," contends Francis Collins, a prominent evangelical Christian who at this writing directs the U.S. National Institutes of Health.[2]

If we ask the laboratory researcher to explain the meaning of life, he or she will demure. One reason why the research scientist will not report on the meaning of biological evolution has to do with the evidence. The evidence with which the scientist works does not demonstrate meaning. Francisco J. Ayala, former president of the American Association for the Advancement of Science and author of the statement on evolution for the U.S. National Academy of Sciences, makes this point: "The evidence of the fossil record is against any directing force, external or immanent, leading the evolutionary process toward specified goals. Teleology . . . is, then, appropriately rejected in biology as a category of explanation."[3]

Ayala adheres strictly to the rule of survival of the fittest. When the human race goes extinct, he surmises, the surviving cockroaches will declare themselves more fit. No in-built teleology guarantees the evolutionary success of *Homo sapiens*, regardless of how intelligent human beings think they are. The human being is not the apple of evolution's eye.

The second reason the scientist will not report on meaning is methodological. The research scientist tacitly adopts *methodological naturalism* as a conceptual

---

2. Francis S. Collins, *The Language of God* (New York: Free Press, 2006), 99.

3. Francisco J. Ayala, "Darwin and the Teleology of Nature," in *Science and Religion in Search of Cosmic Purpose*, ed. John F. Haught (Washington, DC: Georgetown University Press, 2000), 19.

framework through which to look at nature. According to methodological naturalism, only physical causes count as explanations for phenomena. The laboratory scientist does not look for divine interventions, miracles, or teleology (purpose). In principle, evolutionary biology like all sciences is neutral on questions dealing with meaning, purpose, and direction.

This applies to all scientific research, not merely evolution. Arno Penzias, winner of the 1978 Nobel Prize in Physics for discovering the first physical evidence to support big bang theory, asserts that science "cannot know the mind of God. Because the meaning of the world, if any, is an issue which can't be described, could not be handled by a self-consistent physical description of the world."[4] Or, more succinctly, "The meaning of life isn't in science."[5]

Religious sensibilities are not triggered by lab research. Lab findings do not draw the human imagination toward the beyond; nor are there any biological candidates nominated for the office of *axis mundi*. This implies that the laboratory scientist has no reason to engage in the evolution controversy. There is no controversy from his or her point of view, because in scientific research evolutionary theory stands or falls on the basis of scientific criteria—and thus far it has stood firm. The question of how the theory does or does not relate to ultimate meaning is simply not part of the equation.

Darwinian Scientism in Eugenics and Atheism

Sometimes Darwin's science comes packaged in scientism. In order to get at the science, one has to cut away the wrapping. Darwinian science frequently comes wrapped in either a eugenics ideology or an atheistic ideology. It's advantageous to avoid confusing the wrapper with the science.

The eugenics wrapper also goes by names such as *evolutionary ethics* and *social Darwinism*. This ideology constructs an ethical ideal based upon "nature." *Nature*, in this context, refers fundamentally to a struggle for existence in which only the fittest survive. Social Darwinists contend that the social order should mimic nature by benefitting the fit and eliminating the unfit: the weak, the sickly, the inferior. Social Darwinism supports *laissez faire* economics, in which clever businesses survive while non-competitive, less adaptive businesses go extinct. Social Darwinism advocates that governments withdraw all social welfare programs for the sick and the poor, because the human race progresses along its evolutionary course when the unfit are culled from the gene pool and only the fit survive. Investing public money to support the sick and the poor is counter-evolutionary.

4. Arno Penzias, "The Elegant Universe," in *Faith in Science: Scientists Search for Truth*, ed. W. Mark Richardson and Gody Slack (London and New York: Routledge, 2001), 18–34, at 28.

5. Ibid.

The eugenics movement within social Darwinism sought to speed up human evolution through planned breeding of healthy and intelligent babies. The word *eugenics* means good birth, and eugenics programs were set up in Great Britain, France, the United States, and Germany. The Nazis in Germany adopted eugenic principles in their program of *Rassenhygiene* (Racial Hygiene), which led to the systematic genocide of persons deemed unfit. Initially the Nazi regime sent children born with physical disabilities or mental retardation to the gas chamber to die before they could reproduce. Eventually Jews, gypsies, and homosexuals were defined as genetically inferior, and the gas chambers were used to eliminate their heritable traits from the human gene pool.

Social Darwinism is the ethical wrapper within which Charles Darwin's legacy was sold to many Western societies from the late nineteenth century up to the Second World War. One nineteenth-century philosopher, Charles Sanders Peirce, foresaw the degrading effect social Darwinism would have on civilization. "The *Origin of Species* of Darwin merely extends politico-economical views of progress to the entire realm of animal and vegetable life. . . . As Darwin puts it on his title-page, it is the struggle for existence; and he should have added for his motto: Every individual for himself, and the Devil take the hindmost! Jesus, in his Sermon on the Mount, expressed a different opinion."[6] In short, the social Darwinists' dog-eat-dog ethic is inconsistent with the Christian ethic of loving one's neighbor.

The second wrapper that often covers Darwin's science is scientism, even atheism. The key tenet of ideological scientism is that physical nature is the only reality, so it is foolish to search for a spiritual or divine reality beyond nature. One can proffer such an ideology without any reference to Darwin, but many of today's promoters of scientism try to invoke Darwin in support of their position.

Outspoken atheist Richard Dawkins provides an example: "Although atheism might have been logically tenable before Darwin, Darwin made it possible to be an intellectually fulfilled atheist."[7] Darwin, however, appears to disagree: "My views are not at all necessarily atheistical."[8]

Laboratory science presumes *methodological naturalism*. Dawkins's ideology goes further by tacitly embracing *metaphysical naturalism*, the view that nature and only nature constitutes reality. Whether identified as scientism, atheism, naturalism, or materialism, this ideological wrapping insists that

6. Charles Sanders Peirce, *Collected Papers of Charles Sanders Peirce*, ed. Charles Hartshorne and Paul Weiss, 8 vols. (Cambridge, MA: Harvard University Press, 1931–1958), 6:293. See also *The Essential Peirce: Selected Philosophical Writings*, ed. Nathan Houser, Christian Kloesel, and Peirce Edition Project, 2 vols. (Bloomington, IN: Indiana University Press, 1992, 1998), 1:358–60.

7. Richard Dawkins, *The Blind Watchmaker* (London: W. W. Norton, 1986), 6.

8. Charles Darwin, *The Life and Letters of Charles Darwin, Including an Autobiographical Chapter,* ed. Francis Darwin, 3 vols. (London: John Murray, 1888), 2:312.

natural history is without meaning. Dawkins writes, "The universe we observe has precisely the properties we should expect if there is, at bottom, no design, no purpose, no evil and no good, nothing but blind, pitiless indifference."[9] This near celebration of meaninglessness runs profoundly counter to the beliefs of Christians, Jews, or Muslims, for whom the world of nature is the creation of a gracious God.

The point we stress here is that one can appreciate the science of Charles Darwin without committing oneself to either evolutionary ethics or metaphysical naturalism. Ayala reminds us, "The message has always been twofold: (1) evolution is good science and (2) there need not be a contradiction between evolution and religious beliefs."[10] For Darwinian scientism, however, evolution and religion are incompatible; in fact, they are at war.

To be clear, this war is not between *science* and religion. Rather, it is a war between *scientism* and religion. If one understands scientism to be a form of anti-religious ideology, then, in effect, it is a battle between two religions.

Young Earth Creationism

Young Earth creationists assert that Charles Darwin's theory of evolution is mistaken. The human race is not the product of a long history of variation in inheritance acted on by natural selection. Rather, God created *Homo sapiens* just as they are today, and this creation took place somewhere between ten thousand and six thousand years ago.[11]

Young Earth creationists show their opposition to Darwinian science in two ways: the biblical creationists argue by appealing to the authority of the Bible while the scientific creationists argue by appealing to scientific evidence. Does this make creationists anti-science? Not as such. Creationists of both stripes strongly affirm mathematics, physics, geology, chemistry, and all the rest of the physical sciences. Young Earth creationists object to only one scientific theory, namely, Charles Darwin's theory of evolution. Many creationists hold doctorates in one or another science, even biology in some cases.[12]

---

9. Richard Dawkins, *River Out of Eden* (New York: HarperCollins, Basic Books, 1995), 133.

10. Francisco J. Ayala, *Darwin's Gift to Science and Religion* (Washington, DC: Joseph Henry, 2007), 5.

11. Actually, one can identify many types of creationism beyond the two explicated here. See Eugenie Scott, "The Creation/Evolution Continuum," National Center for Science Education, *http://ncse.com/creationism/general/creationevolution-continuum*.

12. One might argue that, despite what they say, young Earth creationists are anti-science: by insisting on earth's creation only six to ten thousand years ago, they must logically reject the findings of big bang cosmology, geology, paleontology, and such. However, if you ask these creationists, "Are you anti-science?" they will say, "No, of course not." Very few religious people, even creationists, think of science per se as the enemy.

One of the strongest voices raised to support *biblical* creationism is that of Ken Ham, whose Creation Museum in Petersburg, Kentucky, attempts to show that the fossil record supports a literal reading of the biblical creation account. He summarizes his ministry this way: "Answers in Genesis [Ham's website] seeks to give glory and honor to God as Creator, and to affirm the truth of the biblical record of the real origin and history of the world and mankind."[13] Ken Ham's goal is for all the peoples of the world to read the Bible, respect the Bible, and find salvation in the message of the Bible. In short, the Bible trumps Darwin.

But don't make the mistake of concluding this means that the Bible trumps science by dismissing science. At the Creation Museum, paleontological discoveries of dinosaur skeletons count as evidence to support Ham's biblical point of view. This amounts to a positive enlistment of science in support of a theological position. Biblical creationism sees itself as pro-science, not anti-science.

In addition to *biblical* creationism, there is *scientific* creationism. One of the strongest voices raised to support scientific creationism is the Institute for Creation Research, formerly located in San Diego, California, and now in Dallas, Texas. Like biblical creationists, the Institute for Creation Research critiques Darwinian theory, but on the basis of science, not scripture. "Creation is true, evolution is false, and real science confirms this," writes the institute's founder, Henry Morris.[14] It is important to note in this statement that Morris relies upon "science" to confirm his position.

Morris, who has a doctorate in hydraulic engineering, and his colleague Duane Gish, whose doctorate is in biochemistry, contend that Darwinian theory fails to account adequately for the fossil evidence. Even if Morris's and Gish's scientific arguments ultimately fall short, it is important to note that they believe themselves to be making a *scientific* argument against evolution. They are not anti-science, at least in their own self-understanding.

One of the chief scientific arguments raised by creationists against evolution's concept of speciation is the alleged absence of transitional forms, what are popularly called *missing links*. If one species gradually gave way to a subsequent species and then died out, one would expect its fossil remains to chronicle the transition. Yet, claim the creationists, no such fossil record of transitional species has been found. Establishment scientists counter that numerous transitional forms have in fact been found, such as fossils of reptiles with wings that demonstrate evolution from land reptiles to flying creatures. Note what is happening here: it is a battle between interpretations of fossil evidence, not a battle between biblical authority and science.

---

13. Answers in Genesis, *https://answersingenesis.org/about/good-news/*.

14. Henry Morris, *History of Modern Creationism*, 2nd ed. (Santee, CA: Institute for Creation Research, 1993), 308–9.

After reviewing the evidence, one might safely say that virtually every scientific argument raised by the creationists has been successfully refuted by scientists defending the Darwinian model of evolution. Even if creationists believe science supports their position, it is relatively poor science. The point remains, however, that the war here is over scientific evidence, not over the authority of the Bible. These creationists are not anti-science, even if they are anti-evolution.

Here is the key that unlocks the clarity of what is transpiring in the controversy over evolution: Darwin's opponents see themselves as supporting science. In his 2016 commencement address at Cal Tech, surgeon and public health researcher Atul Gawande turns the key the right direction. "People don't argue

© By Maija Karala (Own work), via Wikimedia Commons

In 1859 Darwin accurately predicted that scientists would find fossils of transitional forms, such as these that document the evolution of four-legged animals from fish. Such forms confirm Darwin's theory of speciation.

back by claiming divine authority anymore. They argue back by claiming to have the truer scientific authority. It can make matters incredibly confusing. You have to be able to recognize the difference between claims of science and those of pseudoscience."[15] The war is not between religion and science, because all sides respect science. The war is over what constitutes sound science. The creationists will lose this war because their science belongs on the pseudoscience side.

Creationists find the ethics of Darwinism even more problematic than the science of Darwinism. Social Darwinism, eugenics, *laissez faire* capitalism, gas chambers, and genocide are values incompatible with the Christian gospel's focus on love. Creationists argue that the science of Darwinism leads ineluctably to social Darwinism and to an ethic that disregards the unfit in favor of the fit. If Darwin-based ideology is so heinous, then the science that underlies it must be wrong, argue the creationists. Henry Morris of the Institute for Creation Research once said,

Evolution is inconsistent with God's nature of love. The supposed fact of evolution is best evidenced by the fossils, which eloquently speak

15. Atul Gawande, "The Mistrust of Science" (California Institute of Technology Commencement Address, June 10, 2016), *http://www.newyorker.com/news/news-desk/the-mistrust-of-science?mbid=social_facebook.*

of a harsh world, filled with storm and upheaval, disease and famine, struggle for existence and violent death. The accepted mechanism for inducing evolution is overpopulation and a natural selection through extermination of the weak and unfit. A loving God would surely have been more considerate of His creatures than this.[16]

Devout creationists find themselves experiencing incalculable tension between their faith commitment to a God of love, on the one hand, and the description of a violent dog-eat-dog and apparently meaningless creation, on the other hand. Their chosen avenue for relaxing the tension is to dismiss Darwin's account and substitute their own interpretation of the biblical account.

Conservative Muslims similarly oppose Darwinian science. Haran Yahya (the pen name of Adnan Oktar) in Turkey says Darwinism is nonsense: "To believe that all the living things we see on Earth, the flowers with their matchless beauty, fruits, flavors, butterflies, gazelles, rabbits, panthers, birds, and billions of human beings with their different appearances, the cities built by these human beings, the buildings they construct, and bridges all came about by chance from a collection of mud, means taking leave of one's senses."[17] Yahya goes so far as to claim that evolution is satanic; it is a deceptive device to woo people away from Allah. Yahya makes alliances with Christian creationists to help him in his battle against Darwinism as taught in the Turkish public schools.

For most of Judaism, evolution is not a problem. The Jewish understanding is that God's creation at the beginning was unfinished; so it is no surprise that a scientific theory such as evolution might arise that shows creation as continuing. In addition, the Hebrew concept of *tikkun olam*, according to which we in the human race are mandated by God to fix what is broken in creation, leads to the strong emphasis in Jewish culture on healing, including the scientific pursuit of medicine. A conflict with the Darwinian model of evolution is less likely to arise in Judaism than in other religions in the Moses tradition.

Intelligent Design

The intelligent design school wants to modify Darwin's exclusive reliance on natural selection. Intelligent design advocates look at advanced life forms, and they see complexity. Michael Behe, a professor of biochemistry at Lehigh University, for example, describes living organisms as *irreducibly complex.* "By *irreducibly complex* I mean a single system composed of several well-matched, interacting parts that contribute to the basic function, wherein the removal of

---

16. Henry M. Morris, *Scientific Creationism* (Green Forest, AK: Master Books, 1974, 1985), 219.

17. Harun Yahya, "The Theory of Evolution: A Unique Deception in the History of the World," *http://www.harunyahya.com/en/Articles/4314/the-theory-of-evolution-a*. See his book, *The Evolution Deceit* (Istanbul: Okur, 2000).

any one of the parts causes the system to effectively cease functioning."[18] If living creatures are in fact irreducibly complex, then two implications obtain. First, complex creatures could not have evolved in a long, slow, step-by-step process. Second, irreducibly complex creatures must be designed by an intelligent designer. This is the core of the intelligent design argument.

Today's advocates of intelligent design refrain from applying the word "God" to the intelligent designer, because they want to be scientific and not religious. So, within the framework of science, their position supports evolution understood as change over time. Yet intelligent design advocates deny that random variation and natural selection can provide an adequate explanation for the appearance of complexity in the natural world. Appeal to an intelligent designer provides a superior scientific explanation, they say.

Political activism in the form of lobbying school boards and legislators to disestablish Darwinian science in public education have been bankrolled by the Discovery Institute in Seattle, Washington. A motto of the Discovery Institute is "teach the controversy." The goal here is to present intelligent design as a scientific theory that provides an alternative to the Darwinian model. This alternative should be offered to children in the public school system, they say.

Defendants of the Darwinian model accuse intelligent design disciples of being mere creationists in disguise, trying to sneak sectarian religion into the public schools in violation of the first Amendment to the U.S. Constitution. Some opponents use the term *intelligent design creationism* in an attempt to equate intelligent design with creationism.

Theologically, the intelligent design position differs from that of young Earth creationism. The creationists, as their name indicates, are concerned about the beginning moment of creation—that is, they assert that God created all species in their respective "kinds" at the beginning. No evolution has taken place since. Intelligent design, in contrast, is less concerned about creation's beginning and more concerned about creation's evolution over time. Intelligent design finds it can accept something like evolution; but it adds that intelligent design rather than natural selection better explains nature's history. Both scientific creationists and intelligent design supporters claim to be making scientific arguments. Neither young Earth creationists nor intelligent design proponents see themselves as anti-science; rather, they see themselves as sponsoring a better science.

Theistic Evolution

The key concern of the theistic evolutionist is to celebrate the achievements of Darwinian science while affirming the providential love of the divine creator.

---

18. Michael Behe, *Darwin's Black Box: The Biochemical Challenge to Evolution* (New York: Touchstone/Simon Schuster, 1996), 5.

Theistic evolution is not a tightly organized school of thought akin to either young Earth creationism or intelligent design. Rather, the term *theistic evolution* refers to a collection of various views, including both theists and pantheists, including both scientists and theologians. Theistic evolutionists define their position first by granting full acceptance of Darwinian evolutionary theory along with more recent emendations, such as new discoveries in paleontology and genetics. Theistic evolutionists then describe God's ongoing creative work in a manner compatible with the history of nature as evolutionary biology describes it. Theistic evolutionists reject ideological overlays such as eugenics and scientism. On Sundays theistic evolutionists are most likely to be found worshipping in Roman Catholic and mainline Protestant churches.

The *de facto* founder of theistic evolution theory, renowned Jesuit paleontologist and theologian Pierre Teilhard de Chardin, followed a pantheistic path toward theistic evolutionism. "As St. Paul tells us, *God shall be all in all*. This is indeed a superior form of pantheism . . . the expectation of perfect unity, steeped in which each element will reach its consummation at the same time as the universe. . . . God, the Centre of centres."[19]

Most of today's proponents of theistic evolution are theists. Many are Trinitarian theists. According to theistic evolution, writes Robert John Russell at the Center for Theology and the Natural Sciences in Berkeley, California, "God creates the world *ex nihilo* with certain fundamental laws and natural constants, and God acts everywhere in time and space as continuous creator (*creatio continua*) in, with, and through the processes of nature. God's action is trustworthy and we describe the results through these laws of nature. The result is the evolution of life. In essence, evolution is how God is creating life."[20] The central tenet in the theistic evolution position is this: God works in, with, and through natural processes.

Transhumanism

Transhumanism extends Darwinian scientism by renewing the commitment of the effete social Darwinists to take control of humanity's future evolution. The transhumanist method, however, does not refurbish gas chambers. Rather, transhumanism plans to transform human nature through technology. *Homo sapiens* will be transformed into *Homo cyberniticus*, into post-human *technosapiens*.

"The human species can, if it wishes, transcend itself," evolutionary biologist Julian Huxley wrote in 1967, introducing the term *transhumanism*. "We need a

19. Pierre Teilhard De Chardin, *The Phenomenon of Man* (New York: Harper, 1959), 294.

20. Robert John Russell, *Cosmology, Evolution, and Resurrection Hope: Theology and Science in Creative Mutual Interaction*, ed. Carl S. Helrich, Fifth Annual Goshen Conference on Religion and Science (Kirchener, ON: Pandora; Adelaide, South Australia: ATF, 2006), 28.

name for this new belief. Perhaps *transhumanism* will serve: man remaining man, but transcending himself, by realizing new possibilities of and for his human nature."[21]Writing more than four decades later, Nick Bostrom, founding director of the Future of Humanity Institute and of the Programme on the Impacts of Future Technology at Oxford University, explains that the term *transhuman* "refers to an intermediary form between the human and the posthuman."[22] Today's transhumanist, then, is someone dedicated to "increasing the chance that we will have competent successors."[23] Transhumanists think of their task in terms of humanity plus, or "H+."

The transhumanist movement is progressive, optimistic, and promises a form of technological redemption. According to the "Transhumanist Declaration" of the World Transhumanist Association, "Humanity will be radically changed by technology in the future. We foresee the feasibility of redesigning the human condition, including such parameters as the inevitability of aging, limitations on human and artificial intellects, unchosen psychology, suffering, and our confinement to the planet earth."[24]

Customarily the term *singularity* refers to that ball-bearing-sized beginning of the big bang when all things were only one thing, but for the transhumanists the singularity lies in the future. Actually, the near future. The year 2045.

The singularity transhumanists look forward to is the creation of smarter-than-human intelligence. Leading up to the singularity, the pace of technological change will be so rapid and its impact so deep that human life will be irreversibly transformed.

The first phase of this transformation will be enhanced human intelligence, according to Ray Kurzweil of Singularity University, located at NASA's Ames Research Center in California.[25] The next phase will entail human intelligence leaping from human bodies to machines, making high tech machines more human than we are. This can happen because intelligence is not dependent upon our biological substrate; rather, as information in patterns, intelligence can be extricated from biological bodies. Human intelligence can live on in an enhanced form even when extricated from fleshly bodies and placed in a computer. "Uploading a human brain means scanning all of its salient details and then reinstantiating those details into a suitably powerful computational

21. Julian Huxley, *Religion without Revelation* (London: C. A. Watts, 1967), 195.

22. Nick Bostrom, "Introduction—The Transhumanist FAQ: A General Introduction," in *Transhumanism and the Body: The World Religions Speak*, ed. Calvin Mercer and Derek F. Mather (New York: Palgrave, 2014), 1–9, at 4.

23. Nick Bostrom, *Superintelligence: Paths, Dangers, Strategies* (Oxford: Oxford University Press, 2014), 256.

24. "Transhumanist Declaration," Humanity+, *http://transhumanism.org/index.php/wta/declaration*.

25. Ray Kurzweil, *The Singularity Is Near: When Humans Transcend Biology* (New York: Viking, 2005), 136. See also Ray Kurzweil, *How to Create a Mind: The Secret of Human Thought Revealed* (New York: Viking, 2012), 4.

substrate. This process would capture a person's entire personality, memory, skills, and history."[26] Rather than a biological substrate, posthumans will rely upon a machine substrate. Consciousness will be able to live as long as it wants. "By the end of this century, the nonbiological portion of our intelligence will be trillions of trillions of times more powerful than unaided human intelligence."[27]

Transhumanists see their movement as a scientific replacement for traditional religion. The former religious glue that held our culture together in a common spirit is coming undone. What we need at this moment is an inspiring philosophy that reveres scientific reason and will pull us toward a positive future, they say. To meet this need, transhumanism offers a "totalized philosophical system" with a three-level worldview: a metaphysical level, a psychological level, and an ethical level.[28]

First, at the metaphysical or cosmological level, the transhumanist sees a world in a "process of evolutionary complexification toward ever more complex structures, forms, and operations." Transhumanists see meaning in evolutionary history, a direction that leads via complexity to increased intelligence. Second, at the psychological level, the transhumanist believes we human beings are "imbued with the innate Will to Evolve—an instinctive drive to expand abilities in pursuit of ever-increasing survivability and well-being." These two lead to the third level, the ethical, where "we should seek to *foster* our innate Will to Evolve, by continually striving to expand our abilities throughout life. By acting in harmony with the essential nature of the evolutionary process—complexification leading to enhanced intelligence—we may discover a new sense of purpose, direction, and meaning to life, and come to feel ourselves *at home in the world* once more."[29] What Simon Young plans is to replace "Darwinian Evolution with Designer Evolution—from slavery to the selfish genes to conscious self-rule by the human mind."[30] In the past, evolution was what happened to us; in the future, human beings will bend evolution to their own will and design.

The transhumanist foresees an evolutionary future that includes a cosmic imbuing of matter with consciousness. "Liberated from biological slavery, an immortalized species, *Homo cyberniticus*, will set out for the stars. Conscious life will gradually spread throughout the galaxy . . . until finally, in the

---

26. Kurzweil, *Singularity*, 198–99.

27. Ibid., 9.

28. Simon Young, *Designer Evolution: A Transhumanist Manifesto* (Amherst, NY: Prometheus, 2006), 87.

29. Ibid., 19, italics in original; see also p. 202. Big historian Ken Gilbert holds a parallel view, metaphysically attributing an underlying *telos* to evolution understood as cosmic evolution. There is an *"evolutionary force"* in nature analogous to the force of gravity." Ken Gilbert, "The Universal Breakthroughs of Big History: Developing a Unified Theory," in *Teaching and Researching Big History: Exploring a New Scholarly Field*, ed. Leanid Grinin et al. (Volgograd, Russia: Uchitel, 2014), 122–46, at 135, italics in original.

30. Young, *Designer Evolution*, 207.

unimaginably distant future, the whole universe has come alive, awakened to its own nature—a cosmic mind become conscious of itself as a living entity—omniscient, omnipotent, omnipresent."[31] What traditionally were attributes belonging to God will become human attributes. Transhumanism is a form of technological messianism, a raising of the human into the sphere of the divine.

Some religious people have expressed enthusiasm about transhumanism. "Transhumanism is a Christian concept," contends Ronald Cole-Turner, a systematic theologian at Pittsburg Theological Seminary.[32] "I am a self-identified Buddhist transhumanist," confesses Michael Latorra; "Reducing suffering and increasing happiness are goals common to Buddhism and transhumanism."[33] According to Mormon theologian Lincoln Cannon, "Mormonism actually mandates transhumanism."[34]

Camps in the War over Evolution

APPROACH	METHOD	GOD'S ROLE	NATURE
Darwinian Science	Science	Law-Like Behavior	Physical Causes
Darwinian Scientism	Ideology	None	Physical Causes
Biblical Creationism	Bible	Creator	Divine Causes
Scientific Creationism	Science	Creator	Divine Causes
Intelligent Design	Science	Interventionist	Intelligent Causes
Theistic Evolution	Theology	In, With, Under	Natural Causes
Transhumanism	Scientism	None	Nature's Goal = Intelligence

Some transhumanists are not willing to trade away their heart just to gain more intelligence. The Brighter Brains Institute of Northern California, for instance, a transhumanist organization describing itself as "a think-and-do tank raising cognitive potential via conferences and charity projects," raises funds to build health clinics in the world's poorer regions, such as the Philippines and

---

31. Ibid., 44.

32. Ronald Cole-Turner, "Going beyond the Human: Christians and Other Transhumanists," *Theology and Science* 13, no. 2 (May 2015): 150–61, at 150.

33. Michael Latorra, "What Is Buddhist Transhumanism?" *Theology and Science* 13, no. 2 (May 2015): 219–29, at 220, 219.

34. Lincoln Cannon, "What Is Mormon Transhumanism?" *Theology and Science* 13, no. 2 (May 2015): 202–18, at 213.

Uganda. The clinic in Bwethe, Uganda is called H+ Clinic ("transhuman+" is often abbreviated H+ or h+).[35]

Conclusion

The evolutionary chapter in the cosmic story raises the question of God because it raises the question of ultimate meaning. Actually, the question of meaning arises whenever science is pursued within the constraints of methodological naturalism. Post-axial believers in God find it difficult to conceive of the natural world as meaningless, because the natural realm is God's creation; God's love and grace provide meaning for Cosmic History. The problem from a religious perspective is that the scientific method is blind to meaning.

The publication of Darwin's *Origin of Species* in 1859 set off a culture war of varying intensity. It is popular but misleading to describe this war as a battle between science and religion. Most of the religious combatants fully embrace science, and even those who reject evolution from a faith-based perspective do not see themselves as waging war against science. The dispute centers primarily upon one domain within science, Darwinian evolution, even if for young Earth creationists it does tend to spill over into related areas, such as the geological age of the earth and the cosmos.

This chapter has identified six camps in this war, some of which seem quite pacific at the moment. These camps are (1) Darwinian science alone, (2) Darwinian scientism, (3) young Earth creationism, (4) intelligent design, (5) theistic evolution, and (6) transhumanism. Both theistic evolutionists and transhumanists attach the future to their history. "The notion of an unfinished universe still coming into being . . . opens up the horizon of a new or unprecedented future. . . . In its depths, nature is promise" contends Georgetown theistic evolutionist John Haught.[36]

Does Cosmic History have meaning or not? Research scientists, regretfully, admit that they cannot answer this question, because evolutionary biologists do not perceive meaning when examining their data. The materialists and atheists, in contrast, answer this question negatively by denying that nature provides any meaning to human life. Both the creationist and intelligent design schools hold that human life is already meaningful because all of physical reality is the creation of a loving and gracious God. Similarly, theistic evolutionists affirm the meaningfulness of Cosmic History because it is the creation of God's love accompanied by a gracious promise of redemption. Transhumanists do not need to rely upon any traditional deity, because they plan to evolve themselves into

---

35. The author of this book serves on the board of the Brighter Brains Institute. *http://brighter brains.org/*.

36. John Haught, *Deeper than Darwin* (Boulder, CO: Westview, 2003), 170, italics in original.

omnipresent divinity. In short, the very concept of Darwinian evolution raises the question of God, and since 1859 multiple answers have been proffered. Cosmic History, which includes the evolutionary history of life on Earth, should not assume that the God-question has already been satisfactorily answered.

Review Questions

1. Compare and contrast Darwin's evolutionary package with its wrappers, eugenics and atheism.
2. Compare and contrast biblical creationism with scientific creationism.
3. What do theistic evolutionists believe?
4. What does the future look like according to transhumanists?
5. In what way are transhumanists and social Darwinists alike? Unlike?
6. How do theistic evolutionists handle the question of meaning or purpose?

Discussion Questions

1. Why is it a mistake to describe the evolution controversy as a war between science and religion?
2. What is the "transitional form" debate about?
3. Transhumanists believe that progress is built into evolutionary biology. Do you agree?
4. Do you think the arguments for a pantheistic variant of theistic evolution are strong?
5. Of the various armies fighting in the war over evolution, with which would you identify? Why?

Additional Resources

Print Sources

Cole-Turner, Ronald, ed. *Transhumanism and Transcendence.* Washington, DC: Georgetown University Press, 2011.

This is one of the best collections of essays by scholars analyzing, evaluating, and in some cases applauding transhumanism from a religious perspective. Those who register criticism doubt that transhumanism should rely upon the doctrine of progress or promise more redemption from the human condition than any historical agency can deliver.

Darwin, Charles. *Origin of Species by Means of Natural Selection.* 7th ed.
This edition is available from many sources. Consider reading it on disc, which is included in the paperbound edition of Ted Peters and Martinez Hewlett, *Theological and Scientific Commentary on Darwin's* Origin of Species (Nashville: Abingdon, 2009)." Note: this change will conform the entry here and the similar entry on p. 63.

Gould, Stephen J. *The Structure of Evolutionary Theory.* Cambridge, MA: Harvard University Press, 2002.
This comprehensive exposition of Darwinian theory and its successors is a giant of a book written by a giant of a scholar. A must read for the serious student of biology.

Ham, Ken, Carl Wiel, and Don Barten. *One Blood: The Biblical Answer to Racism.* Green Forest, AK: Master Books, 1996.
In their fight against social Darwinism and eugenics, biblical creationists struggle to defend the equality of persons in different races. By reaffirming that all human beings on Earth are descendents from a single Adam and Eve, they provide a biblical argument in support of the notion that we are all brothers and sisters and, hence, responsible for one another.

Johnson, Philip E. *Darwin on Trial.* Downer's Grove, IL: InterVarsity, 1991.
This exciting and readable diatribe against Darwinian science helped put intelligent design into the news in the 1990s. Johnson, a lawyer, put Darwin on trial and found him guilty of flawed science. This book is stronger on rhetoric than it is on the actual marshalling of scientific evidence.

Kurzweil, Ray. *The Singularity Is Near: When Humans Transcend Biology.* New York: Viking, 2005.
This is the Bible of the singularity, so to speak. Kurzweil invites glee in those readers enamored with the prospects of new technology.

Moritz, Joshua M. *Science and* Religion: *Beyond Warfare and Toward Understanding.* Winona, MN: Anselm Academic, 2015.
In chapter 6, "The Forming of Life from Cosmic Dust to Consciousness," Moritz provides a lucid description of the creationist positions within the larger evolution controversy. This may be the single best book for a student to read to get a clear grip on the controversy.

Morris, Henry M. *History of Modern Creationism.* 2nd ed. Santee, CA: Institute for Creation Research, 1993.
Morris is one of the patriarchs of modern scientific creationism. In this book he argues that his position is grounded in a traditional battle between authentic Christian belief and competition from humanism and atheism.

Numbers, Ronald L. *The Creationists.* Berkeley: University of California Press, 1992.
Numbers is the leading historian who analyzes creationism, both biblical and scientific. A serious student of the controversy must read one or more works by Numbers.

Peters, Ted, and Martinez Hewlett. *Can You Believe in God and Evolution?* Anniversary ed. Nashville: Abingdon, 2009.

Peters, Ted, and Martinez Hewlett. *Evolution from Creation to New Creation: Conflict, Conversation, and Convergence.* Nashville: Abingdon, 2003.

These two books co-authored by a theologian and biologist attempt to clarify the controversy. The earlier volume, *Evolution from Creation to New Creation*, is longer and more thorough in its exposition of the competing positions. Aimed at theologians and scientists. The later volume, *Can You Believe in God and Evolution*, summarizes the first book in a much more readable and accessible medium. It provides an excellent overview helpful for college students and high school science educators.

Teilhard de Chardin, Pierre. *The Phenomenon of Man.* New York: Harper, 1959.

This is the classic first example of theistic evolution, even though Teilhard's doctrine of God looks more like pantheism. Teilhard is a maximalist, that is, he thoroughly integrates all Christian doctrine with the understanding of Darwinism regnant in the 1920s.

Web Sources

Answers in Genesis. *https://answersingenesis.org/.*

This website promotes biblical creationism.

Bigliardi, Stefano. "Harun Yaha's Islamic Creationism: What It Is and What It Isn't." *Skeptical Inquirer* 38, no. 1 (January/Februrary 2014). *http://www.csicop.org/si/show/harun_yahyas_islamic_creationism_what_it_is_and_isnt.*

This article discusses Islamic creationism.

Clergy Letter Project. *http://www.theclergyletterproject.org/.*

This website promotes theistic evolution.

CTNS: The Center for Theology and the Natural Sciences. *http://www.ctns.org/.*

This website promotes theistic evolution.

Discovery Institute Center for Science and Culture. *http://www.discovery.org/id/.*

This website promotes intelligent design.

Harun Yaha. *http://www.harunyahya.com/.*

This website promotes creationism from an Islamic perspective.

Nick Bostrom's Home Page. *http://www.nickbostrom.com/.*

This website promotes transhumanism.

Richard Dawkins Foundation. *https://richarddawkins.net/.*

This website promotes atheism and evolution.

Ted Peters' Website. *http://tedstimelytake.com/.*

This website promotes theistic evolution.

Do We Share Our Galaxy with Extraterrestrial Neighbors?

Our universe is infinite,
spreading outward without end.
Don't you think it's possible
somewhere we'd find a friend?

What is the most amazing thing
in this world that you'll find
is that the entire universe
fits within your mind.

—SUSAN ELIZABETH HANFORD,
"THE UNIVERSE"[1]

Cosmic History traces the appearance of life on Earth and the evolution of life over the last 3.9 billion years. Might something like this have happened on other habitable planets as well? If life began on another planet, might it also have evolved? And if extraterrestrial life evolved, might it have produced intelligent creatures such as ourselves? If so, might we meet them some day? Will the concept of Cosmic History include an interstellar community?

This chapter introduces the field of astrobiology, which includes the search for extraterrestrial life. It will consider the possible significance for life on Earth should knowledge of space neighbors become confirmed. It will try to correct a number of popular misunderstandings regarding the rigidity of traditional religious beliefs about sharing the cosmos with extraterrestrials.

Cosmic History includes so much more than merely the history of life on planet Earth. It includes an immensity that lies beyond the heavens. The

---

1. Susan Elizabeth Hanford, *Seeking Emily*, 2nd ed. (Geneseo, IL: Rabbit Hole, 2015), 23. Used with permission.

immensity of outer space evokes within the human soul a sense of infinity, incomprehensibility, unending depth. Space evokes our beyond sensibility. Space is inherently religious. How might religious traditions established during the Axial Age when the cosmos was so small adapt to the scientific picture of the immense universe?

Astrobiology and the Search for Extraterrestrial Life

The term, *astrobiology*, combines *astro*, referring to the realm of the stars, with *bio*, the term for life. According to Chris Impey, the professor who directs astrobiology research at the University of Arizona, astrobiology is "the study of the origin, nature, and evolution of life on Earth and beyond."[2] Note in this definition how *evolution* is assumed to connect life both on Earth and elsewhere.

Beginning in the 1990s, NASA began using the term *astrobiology* to refer to its research into life elsewhere in the universe. NASA's "Astrobiology Roadmap" of 2003 orients the field around three fundamental questions: (1) How does life begin and evolve? (2) Does life exist elsewhere in the universe? (3) What is the future of life on Earth and beyond?[3] According to Christopher McKay at NASA's Ames Research Center, "Astrobiology has within it three broad questions that have deep philosophical as well as scientific import. These are the origin of life, the search for a second genesis of life, and the expansion of life beyond Earth."[4]

Within the encompassing field of astrobiology, one should distinguish between unintelligent and intelligent life. The sub-field of exobiology focuses on the search for microbial or biologically simple forms of life, non-intelligent life forms. Currently, the focus is on the planet Mars, where signs of water have been discovered. One might refer to this as extraterrestrial non-intelligent life. This distinguishes the search for extraterrestrial non-intelligent life from extra-terrestrial intelligent life or ETI. The search for extraterrestrial non-intelligent life focuses on our local solar system, while the search for extra-terrestrial intelligent life looks at star systems elsewhere in the Milky Way.

Astrobiology is clustered with cosmology, astronomy, astrophysics, spectroscopy, evolutionary biology, bioinformatics, and many other fields. "Astrobiology concerns itself with life in the universe—its origins, evolution, and future.

---

2. Chris Impey, *The Living Cosmos: Our Search for Life in the Universe* (New York: Random House, 2007), 4.

3. "Astrobiology Strategy," NASA, *https://nai.nasa.gov/media/roadmap/2003/*.

4. Christopher McKay, "Astrobiology: The Search for Life beyond the Earth," in *Many Worlds: The New Universe, Extraterrestrial Life and the Theological Implications*, ed. Steven Dick (Philadelphia and London: Templeton, 2000), 45.

Astrobiology is a highly inter- and multi-disciplinary endeavor, which incorporates both the physical and biological sciences," says Grace Wolf-Chase, a University of Chicago astronomer and director of the Adler Planetarium.[5] Lucas Mix, a former Harvard research scholar, emphasizes the multi-disciplinary nature of the field. "Astrobiology is the scientific study of life in space. It happens when you put together what astronomy, physics, planetary science, geology, chemistry, biology, and a host of other disciplines have to say about life and try to make a single narrative."[6]

In the search for extra-terrestrial intelligent life, one must give attention to radio astronomy and the research pursued at the SETI (Search for Extraterrestrial Intelligence) Institute. Optical SETI (OSETI) at Harvard uses an optical telescope, while in Mountain View, California, SETI scientists use radio telescopes. Radio SETI's goal is to detect intelligent life outside Earth's solar system. Among the SETI approaches is the use of radio telescopes to listen for narrow-bandwidth radio signals from space. Such signals are not known to occur naturally, so a detection would provide evidence of extraterrestrial technology.[7] An extension of SETI is METI (Messaging Extraterrestrial Intelligence) International, which actively sends radio wave messages; METI rings ET's telephone, so to speak, hoping some intelligent creature will pick up.[8] Will meeting extra-terrestrial intelligent life precipitate a new Copernican revolution? SETI's Seth Shostak thinks so: "Proof of thinking beings beyond Earth would be one of the most profound discoveries ever."[9]

Since the mid 1990s, excitement regarding meeting new space neighbors has been rising due to the discovery of exoplanets. Astronomers have confirmed thousands of extrasolar planets orbiting other stars within our Milky Way.[10] Of special interest are planets in the habitable zone—the Goldilocks zone where it's not too hot and not too cold; it's just right. As of this writing Proxima Centuri b has caused the greatest excitement, because it is only 4.24 light years away. It is roughly the mass of Earth (1.3 Earth masses) and in just the right location where, if it has an atmosphere, it would have liquid water.[11] The search has

---

5. Grace Wolf-Chase, "Astronomy: From Star Gazing to Astrobiology," in *The Routledge Companion to Religion and Science*, ed. James W. Haag, Gregory R. Peterson, and Michael L. Spezio (London: Routledge, 2012), 103.

6. Lucas John Mix, *Life in Space: Astrobiology for Everyone* (Cambridge, MA: Harvard University Press, 2009), 4.

7. See the SETI homepage: *http://setiathome.berkeley.edu/sah_about.php*.

8. See the METI homepage: *http://meti.org/*.

9. Seth Shostak, "Are We Alone? Estimating the Prevalence of Extraterrestrial Intelligence," in *Civilizations beyond Earth: Extraterrestrial Life and Society*, ed. Douglas A. Vakoch and Albert A. Harrison (New York and Oxford: Bergbahn, 2011), 31–42, at 41.

10. See "The Extrasolar Planets Encyclopaedia," *http://exoplanet.eu/*.

11. John Wenz, "The Exoplanet Next Door," *Astronomy* 44, no. 11 (November 2016): 26–29.

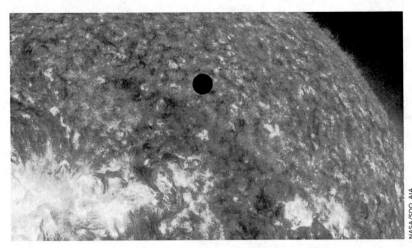

NASA/SDO, AIA

Passing between the Earth and the sun, Venus appears as a black dot, slightly reducing the amount of light reaching Earth. Astronomers searching for exoplanets watch stars for similar events.

begun in earnest to find Earth's twin somewhere in the Milky Way. Galaxies beyond the Milky Way are simply too distant for terrestrial scientific equipment to detect stars with planets.

Astronomers watch for two phenomena that can indicate the presence of an extrasolar planet orbiting a star within the Milky Way: wobbles and transits. Radial-velocity surveys analyze the motion of a star induced by its orbiting partner—that is, by measuring a star's wobble astrophysicists can speculate that it might be caused by the gravitational pull of an orbiting planet. The High Accuracy Radial Velocity Planet Searcher (HARPS) can detect wobbles of less than one meter per second.

Star watchers pursue visual searches for planets that transit in front of their primary star. Astronomers observe a black dot in front of a brightly lit star; this could be the shadow side of an orbiting planet. They then take a series of photos over a period of time to see if it moves in a regular pattern. If so, the black dot might be considered a transit—that is, a planet in orbit passing in front of its home star. Direct imaging is difficult, because each star is bright whereas each planet only reflects the star's light. High contrast techniques are being developed.

These two methods are best suited to locating large planets, nicknamed *Jupiters*. As the technology improves, astronomers may in the future find themselves able to detect more Earth-sized and biophilic objects as well. Once an exoplanet is located, its atmosphere must be analyzed spectrascopically to see whether it could support life. "The obvious biosignatures to look for are oxygen, ozone, and nitrous oxide, unique products of life on Earth which a distant civilization could detect in the spectrum of our atmosphere. Another candidate is dimethyl sulfide, which oceanic phytoplankton produce on Earth."[12]

In early December 2013 five exoplanets with water in the atmosphere were discovered. The U.S. House Science, Space, and Technology Committee held a hearing titled, "Astrobiology." Steven Dick, who held the Blumberg Chair in Astrobiology at the Library of Congress, told the congressmen that it's time to get ready.[13]

Infinity and Ultimacy

As observed in earlier chapters, the sheer scope of the material cosmos connotes infinity; and infinity connotes ultimacy. Physically speaking, the universe is not infinite. The universe is estimated to be ninety-three billion light years across. But, to the human imagination, its immensity arouses a sense of infinity allied with ultimacy. These are not developed concepts of infinity or ultimacy, to be sure. Rather, we are talking here about pre-conceptual sensibilities. With an awareness of ultimacy enkindled, the question of God arises. Outer space evokes the "beyond" sensibility.

Outer space evokes a sense of intimacy as well. Outer space stimulates the inner soul. At first the inner soul feels squashed, tiny, insignificant, lost. Then the very cognitive grasping of this immensity seems to enlarge the soul, embolden a sense of identification of one's self with the all, the totality, the whole. Many astronauts who traveled in space report having religious experiences, some even mystical experiences.

The impression outer space makes on the inner soul includes the question, are we alone? Might God have provided other sentient creatures on other planets to share this magnificent universe with us? Atheist Carl Sagan wrote, "Space exploration leads directly to religious and philosophical questions."[14] Scientist and Christian believer Francis Collins asked, "If God exists, . . . why would it be beyond His abilities to interact with similar creatures on a few other planets or, for that matter, a few million other planets?"[15] When outer space sings silently of ultimacy, our inner soul dances to its rhythms.

---

12. Yudhijit Bhattacharjee, "A Distant Glimpse of Alien Life?," *Science* 333, no. 6045 (August 19, 2011): 930–32, at 932.

13. U.S. House Committee on Science, Space, and Technology, "Full Committee Hearing— Astrobiology: Search for Biosignatures in Our Solar System and Beyond, December 4, 2013, *https:// science.house.gov/legislation/hearings/full-committee-hearing-astrobiology-search-biosignatures-our-solar -system-and*. See also Chris Spitzer, "Congress Ponders Life on Other Worlds," AAAS, *http://member central.aaas.org/blogs/capitol-connection/congress-ponders-life-other-worlds*.

14. Carl Sagan, *The Cosmic Connection* (New York: Dell, 1973), 63.

15. Francis S. Collins, *The Language of God: A Scientist Presents Evidence for Belief* (New York: Free Press, 2007), 71.

When outer space stimulates the inner soul, one steps beyond astrobiology to *astrotheology*, from science to religion. "The discussion of topics teetering between religion and science has broadened with the rise of astrobiology. Scientific questions about the origin, distribution, and future of life in the universe touch on basic issues of human existence,"[16] observes psychologist Albert Harrison. Natural observations, scientific definitions, and spiritual connotations warrant a theological analysis and perhaps even a theological construction.

Just how might theologians ponder what is happening in space exploration? What might they think about the prospect of sharing our creation with extraterrestrial neighbors? Perhaps a brief look at yesterday's theologians will provide a hint about tomorrow's theologians.

Are There Many Worlds in Outer Space?

In ancient Greece, the question of many worlds arose. Might there exist other worlds in space with inhabitants just like Earth? Aristotle said, no: a nicely ordered cosmos with the Earth in the center signifies perfection. Against Aristotle, Democritus led a group called the *atomists*, who asserted that many worlds exist, and on each planet in space we should expect to find intelligent beings living in civilizations.

The Latin Christian tradition inherited the Greek dispute. Thomas Aquinas (1225–1274), a professor of theology at the University of Paris, repeated Aristotle's argument supporting only one world. John Buridan (1295–1358), also a professor at Paris, argued that we should trust that God could make many worlds in space with many civilizations. Thomas Aquinas argued on the basis of philosophy, whereas John Buridan argued on the basis of biblical faith. Neither seemed to have any compunction about entertaining the possibility of many worlds. This debate on the theological meaning of extraterrestrial life took place centuries before Copernicus was born.

German theologian Nicholas of Cusa (1401–1464) argued that extraterrestrials were living on another world. "Life, as it exists here on earth in the form of [humans], animals and plants, is to be found, let us suppose, in a higher form in the solar and stellar regions." This theological speculator shied away from stating as fact what was not empirically known. "For since that whole region is unknown to us, its inhabitants remain wholly unknown." The title of Nicholas's work, after all, was *De docta ignorantia* or, in English, *Of Learned Ignorance*. Nevertheless, this ignorance did not restrict the theologian from conjecturing about the relative level of spiritual attainment of extra-terrestrial intelligent life. According to Nicholas, "In the area of the sun there exist solar beings, bright and enlightened intellectual denizens, and by nature more spiritual than such as may

---

16. Albert Harrison, "Russian and American Cosmism: Religion, National Psyche, and Space-Flight," *Astropolitics: The International Journal of Space Politics & Policy* (June 20, 2013): 11:1–2, 25–44, at 39, *http://www.tandfonline.com/doi/pdf/10.1080/14777622.2013.801719*.

inhabit the moon—who are possibly lunatics—while those on earth are more gross and material."[17] Nicholas's extraterrestrial speculations were not considered heretical in his day. He was elevated to Cardinal in 1448, eight years after writing about extra-terrestrial intelligent life.

In the centuries following Copernicus, this type of theological speculation continued with little or no obvious change due to the heliocentric cosmology. In 1714, Anglican clergyman and chaplain to the future King George II, William Derham (1657–1735), published a book, *Astro-Theology; or, A Demonstration of the Being and Attributes of God from a Survey of the Heavens*. In this book Derham broke the history of science into three epochs: the Ptolemaic, the Copernican, and the Derham system of the universe, his own third epoch. According to this less than modest proposal, Derham contends that each star is itself a sun like ours with a family of orbiting planets, also like ours. These planets orbiting fixed stars he declares "to be habitable worlds; places . . . accommodated for habitation, so stocked with proper inhabitants."[18] Among other legacies, Derham bequeathed to the twenty-first century the term *astrotheology*.

None of these premodern speculations contribute any scientific data to modern astrobiology. Yet history shows that the questions of today's science have been asked and re-asked many times before.

From Gods to Aliens

In 2010 the History Channel premiered a five-part series, "Ancient Aliens." According to this origin story, a series of visits by highly advanced ancient aliens explains why things are the way they are today. Modern life is the product of an ancient event: extraterrestrials came to Earth with their advanced science and engaged with our ancestors, either primates or early hominins. Extraterrestrial engineering augmented that of our primitive ancestors. And this augmentation accounts for the Egyptian pyramids, the architecture of the Incas and Aztecs, the placement of statues on Easter Island, Stonehenge, and numerous other ancient wonders. In addition, alien scientists genetically modified the terrestrials, thereby giving a jump start to the evolution of *Homo sapiens*. We modern humans benefit from alien DNA in our genome.

Purported evidence of this alleged dramatic visitation to Earth from space appears in the petroglyphs and scriptures of ancient peoples such as those in Mesopotamia, Egypt, and Israel. If, when reading the Bible, one replaces reference to God or angels with reference to aliens in spacecraft, it all fits together. Gods and extraterrestrial intelligences are the same. Alternatively, between the

---

17. Nicholas of Cusa, *Of Learned Ignorance*, cited by Michael J. Crowe, *Extraterrestrial Life Debate from Antiquity to 1915: A Source Book* (Notre Dame, IN: University of Notre Dame Press, 2008), 27–34.

18. Cited by Crowe, ibid., 125.

inexpressible deity of the beyond and us is a layer of extraterrestrials. So say the ancient astronaut theorists.

In general, the theorists do not reject what the Bible says. Rather, they reinterpret the Bible by removing God and substituting ancient aliens. Scott Alan Roberts, founder and publisher of *Intrepid Magazine*, reinterprets the Adam and Eve story in Genesis to show how the evolution of the human race was jumpstarted by an alien. Earth's evolution was moving too slowly, so a visiting geneticist from outer space inserted some extraterrestrial DNA.

According to Roberts, the serpent in the Garden of Eden was actually a reptilian alien. Eve engaged in sexual intercourse with both the serpent and with Adam, giving birth to two boys, Cain and Abel. Abel was Adam's progeny. Cain was the hybrid, carrying DNA from both Eve and the alien serpent. Cain killed Abel. This meant Cain's genes would survive and provide a DNA boost to the rest of humanity, expanding the genetic distance between primates and humans. "So let's engage in a little gap-filling exercise of our own; the so-called missing link may very well have been DNA provided by visitors from another world."[19]

Note how this reinterpretation treats the Adam and Eve story as historical, an event that occurred in a specific location at a specific time. As noted in an earlier chapter, the Adam and Eve myth took place *in illo tempore*,[20] not intra-historically. It is a timeless story, an enduring story. But the ancient astronaut theorists treat it as a literal event within human history.

Philip Coppens, frequently interviewed on TV, summarizes the secular theology presupposed by ancient astronaut theorists. "It is clear that civilization was indeed guided by gods, by a nonhuman extraterrestrial intelligence. Though today we would consider this to be the bailiwick of religion, it is not; it is about directly experiencing another reality and contacting this intelligence."[21] Note what motivates ancient astronaut theorists, namely, the goal of replacing religion with science. NASA and SETI scientists think this is rubbish, to be sure; but the ancient astronaut theorists think of themselves as defending materialism against spiritual claims. What is invisible to the protagonists is their own religiosity, their own turning of the scientific mindset into a religion of its own. While it may appear that science is replacing religion here, it is more accurate to say that science is becoming a re-expression of religion in secular form. Scientism has become the tacit religion of a culture where people can actually believe the claims of ancient astronaut theory.

---

19. Scott Alan Roberts, "Race Interrupted: Ancient Aliens and the Evolution of Humanity," in *Lost Civilizations and Secrets of the Past*, ed. Michael Pye and Kirsten Dalley (Pompton Plains, NJ: New Page, 2012), 156. For a more extensive analysis of the UFO phenomenon and ancient astronaut theorists, see Ted Peters, *UFOs: God's Chariots? Spirituality, Ancient Aliens, and Religious Yearnings in the Age of Extraterrestrials* (Pompton Plains, NJ: New Page, 2014).

20. Latin for "at that time." See chapter 7 for the use of this phrase in conjunction with creation myths.

21. Philip Coppens, *The Ancient Alien Question* (Pompton Plains, NJ: New Page, 2012), 288.

Here is what is important for our treatment of Cosmic History: so-called ancient astronaut theorists think of themselves as scientists. They think of themselves as providing scientific explanations for ancient phenomena just like big historians do. This is why both Big History programs and ancient astronaut programs appear together on the History Channel.

But, we might ask, is this the best science? Or, more precisely, do ancient astronaut theorists simply speculate based on the myth of scientism? By introducing the idea of ancient space visitors who are more advanced than earthlings in science and technology, they can reduce any ancient insights into transcendent reality to strictly physical causes. What our ancestors thought were religious realities turn out to be merely advanced technological gadgets, accordingly.

The question of the existence or non-existence of extraterrestrial intelligent neighbors is important for both scientists and theologians to ask. The answer offered by ancient astronaut theorists is strictly speculative and premature.

Conclusion

If Tillich is correct—that questions about the ultimate ground of reality are fundamentally religious questions—then many such questions remain even after the ancient astronaut theorists are done: If ancient astronauts created human intelligence on Earth, who originally gave intelligence to them? Where did the sky with all its stars and planets come from in the first place?

The transcendent divine reality pointed to by axial experiencers ought not to be confused with physical astronauts. A transcendent or supra-cosmic God, according to believers in the Bible, is the origin and destiny of the entire cosmos, including the Earth and any space neighbors that might exist. Even if extraterrestrial aliens like us do in fact exist, they are most likely saddled with the same basic religious concerns that we have. They will necessarily be finite creatures, perhaps battling evil for the sake of the good, perhaps struggling for meaning in life, perhaps looking toward our planet to make new friends.

This is where history helps us to gain perspective. It appears that both prior to and following Copernicus theologians could honestly ask the question of extraterrestrial life and dispassionately consider answers both pro and con. There is no reason to suppose that the theologians of today or tomorrow will shy away from confronting what might turn out to be amazing scientific discoveries on other planets or moons or asteroids.

This book is concerned with the existence or non-existence of God implied by the nature of our physical history. If there is a God to create, one must also consider the scope of God's creation. For those who feel comfortable living in a cosmos created by a supra-cosmic divine creator, this scope includes the entire universe and all its creatures, both terrestrial and extraterrestrial.

Review Questions

1. Define *astrobiology*. What does it include?
2. What are NASA's three "road map" goals?
3. What are the two methods for identifying exoplanets?
4. What is the ancient astronaut theory?

Discussion Questions

1. What role does evolution play in NASA's road map?
2. For religion, what is the significance of the prospect that we share our universe with extraterrestrial neighbors?
3. Have you encountered ancient alien theory before? If so, where did you encounter it?
4. Why do some scientists criticize ancient astronaut theorists? Do you agree or disagree with the ancient astronaut theory?

Additional Resources

Print Sources

Davies, Paul. *The Eerie Silence: Renewing the Search for Alien Intelligence.* New York: Houghton Mifflin, 2010.

Paul Davies may be the most widely read author in the field of science and religion. He is superb at demonstrating how religious questions rise up out of fields such as physics, cosmology, and biology. In this lucid book, Davies provides a description of astrobiology and assesses the likelihood that we on Earth may be alone in this vast universe.

Dick, Steven J. *Life on Other Worlds: The 20th-Century Extraterrestrial Life Debate.* Cambridge, UK: Cambridge University Press, 1998.

Steven Dick is one of the best historians of the long debate regarding the existence or non-existence of extraterrestrial life. Philosophers and theologians debated the matter long before Copernicus and Galileo. In this volume, Dick chronicles the recent controversies.

Herrick, James A. *Scientific Mythologies: How Science and Science Fiction Forge New Religious Beliefs.* Downers Grove, IL: IVP Academic, 2008.

In this insightful volume by an evangelical Christian, the convergence of science with science fiction produces cultural tropes that exhibit religious dimensions. Herrick demonstrates more clearly than most how scientism rivals traditional religion.

Impey, Chris. *The Living Cosmos: Our Search for Life in the Universe*. New York: Random House, 2007.

Chris Impey directs the astrobiological research program at the University of Arizona in Tucson, one of the nation's leading centers for astronomy. This book is clearly written and conveys some of the excitement scientists feel as the search for space neighbors progresses.

Peters, Ted. *UFOs: God's Chariots? Spirituality, Ancient Aliens, and Religious Yearnings in the Age of Extraterrestrials*. Pompton Plains, NJ: New Page, 2014.

This book provides a description and analysis of the contemporary UFO phenomenon along with the ancient astronaut theory. It applies the principles of Paul Tillich as well as other scholars in dissecting the cultural anatomy of extraterrestrial consciousness at work in society.

Wilkinson, David. *Science, Religion, and the Search for Extraterrestrial Intelligence*. Oxford: Oxford University Press, 2013.

David Wilkinson is both an astrophysicist and a Christian theologian at St. John's College, Durham University, in England. To date, this is the best book on astrotheology. Wilkinson traces recent scientific developments in space exploration and then maps out theological issues that require public attention.

Web Sources

"Ancient Alien Theory." History: Ancient Aliens. *http://www.history.com/shows/ancient-aliens/articles/ancient-alien-theory*.

This site provides information about ancient alien theory as well as access to the television series *Ancient Aliens*.

Astrobiology at NASA. *https://astrobiology.nasa.gov/research/astrobiology-at-nasa/astrobiology-strategy/*.

This provides information about NASA's astrobiology research strategy.

METI International. *http://meti.org/*.

METI actively sends messages to targeted locations in the Milky Way, seeking to evoke a response from extraterrestrial civilizations.

Peters, Ted. "Astrotheology." *http://tedstimelytake.com/theological-briefs/*.

Among these theological briefs are items dealing with the religious and ethical implications of space exploration.

SETI Institute. *http://www.seti.org/*.

For more than half a century, SETI radio astronomers have been listening for signals transmitted by advanced extraterrestrial civilizations.

CHAPTER

Toward a Just, Sustainable, Participatory, and Planetary Society

Climate change is much more than an issue of environmental preservation. Insofar as human-induced, it is a profoundly moral and spiritual problem. To persist in the current path of ecological destruction is not only folly. It is no less than suicidal, jeopardizing the diversity of the very earth that we inhabit, enjoy and share.

—His All Holiness, Ecumenical Patriarch Bartholomew[1]

Cosmic History has been winding its way from the big bang through galaxy formation to planet formation and the appearance of planet Earth within our solar system. Here on Earth life began mysteriously about 3.9 billion years ago. Since then, life has been evolving. *Homo sapiens* are one legacy of the multi-billion-year process. Acknowledging this inextricable connection between the human and the natural is one of the fundamental principles of Big History. Philosopher and ecologist Holmes Rolston III speaks like a big historian: "Nature remains the milieu of culture—so both science and religion have discovered . . . humans need to get themselves 'naturalized.'"[2]

Earth is home for humanity. The God question raises issues about the beyond, the more, the transcendent. Yet the God question never divorces the human species from its home in nature. Human beings resonate at the point of tension between soil and spirit, earth and heaven, historicity and eternity.

---

1. Ecumenical Patriarch Bartholomew, "Statement by His All Holiness Ecumenical Patriarch Bartholomew for the WCC Working Group on Climate Change, August 12, 2005," in *Climate Change* 67, World Council of Churches, *https://www.oikoumene.org/en/folder/documents-pdf/Climate_Change_Brochure_2005.pdf*.

2. Holmes Rolston III, "Environmental Ethics and Religion/Science," in *The Oxford Handbook of Religion and Science*, ed. Philip Clayton and Zachary Simpson (Oxford: Oxford University Press, 2006), 908–29, at 912.

We historical human beings have befouled our nest, polluting the home nature has given us. Axial experiencers report being saddened by the human condition, by the state of estrangement within which human beings find themselves. What people actually experience in history seems estranged from the transcendent vision of the ideal social order. The transcendent stands in judgment against historicity.

Yet the transcendent vision also provides hope, because the ideal social order, according to the axialists, is more real than the historical one in which we live. Might an axial-based faith offer something of value to *Homo sapiens* as humanity faces a crisis in its natural environment?

This chapter will consider what it means to live in the Anthropocene Epoch. The chapter will analyze the ecological crisis and then propose an ethical structure to move the present generation toward historical transformation. One of the gifts bequeathed to the modern age from the Axial Age is a criterion for prophetic judgment against the injustices within history. Among those

Earth may be small on a cosmic scale, but it is humanity's only home. There is but one planetary family living in this home. How shall we take care of it?

injustices is the human maltreatment of the Earth that sustains life. This problem requires ethical deliberation. One of the virtues of the Big History program is its commitment to ecological ethics. This book endorses and expands this important ethical commitment.

At the center of this chapter's ethical recommendations will be a positive vision of the future derived from axial awareness of a transcendent order of justice. This positive futuristic vision projects a just, sustainable, participatory, and planetary society for planet Earth. In contrast to today's marginalization of the poor, misdistribution of health benefits, institutional racism and sexism, and terrorist blood-letting, the future society envisioned here will be *just*. In contrast to today's wanton draining of our planet's life-giving energy and desecration of the natural beauty bequeathed to us by evolutionary history, the future society envisioned here will be ecologically *sustainable*. In contrast to today's oligarchical governments of both elected officials and behind-the-scenes billionaires rigging the laws, the future society envisioned here will be *participatory* for everyone regardless of economic class or political affiliation. In contrast to today's divisions into competing nation-states and competing trans-national businesses each demanding its own self-interest, the future society envisioned here will be *planetary* in scope; a single planetary society will become the community of moral deliberation.

The Anthropocene Epoch

The modern world—not just Europe but the entire planet—has entered a new stage in Earth's evolutionary history, the *Anthropocene Epoch*.[3] Without intending it, the human species has become a force in altering the ecology of our world. Natural selection must move over as *Homo sapiens* take the driver's seat to steer their own evolutionary future. As discussed in the exposition of transhumanism, many people consciously and deliberately want to take direct control of evolution; they want to manufacture a future of their own design. Before turning to the future, however, it is well to pause to understand with a bit more clarity just where modern humans stand within planetary history.

According to big historians, "Humans have begun, without fully understanding what they are doing, to transform the chemistry of the atmosphere; the range, variety, and distribution of plant and animal species; the nature of the water cycle; and fundamental processes of erosion and sedimentation. We have become the first single species in almost 4 billion years that is powerful enough to transform the biosphere single-handedly."[4] From an ecological point of view, modern *Homo sapiens* are no longer adapting to their environment; their environment is adapting to *Homo sapiens*. This portends disaster. Planet Earth will be unable to support modern human civilization for very long. The Club of Rome, made up of business and government futurists, dubbed the current environmental crisis *the world problematique*.[5]

Many secular and religious thinkers have dubbed the *world problematique* the most urgent ethical issue of our time. "Climate change involves a complex global set of both causal practices and felt impacts, and as such requires

---

3. The term *Anthropocene Epoch* was coined by Nobel Prize winning chemist Paul Crutzen in 2000.

4. David Christian, Cynthia Stokes Brown, and Craig Benjamin, *Big History: Between Nothing and Everything* (New York: McGraw-Hill, 2014), 285.

5. Donella H. Meadows et al., *The Limits to Growth* (New York: Universe Books, 1972). Fred Spier believes this Club of Rome study still obtains today. Fred Spier, *Big History and the Future of Humanity* (Oxford: Wiley Blackwell, 2015), 302.

coherent global action—or, at minimum, coordination across some critical mass of global players," say the editors of *The Oxford Handbook of Climate Change and Society*.[6] The community of moral deliberation to deal with the *world problematique* must be a single planetary society. As long as human civilization is hopelessly divided among competing businesses and warring nations, the human race lacks even the opportunity to make the moral decisions needed to confront the crisis.

According to Seyyed Hossein Nasr, the environmental crisis is at root a religious crisis brought on by scientism and secularism. "The environmental crisis is before everything else a spiritual crisis," he writes. Modern civilization has failed to appreciate the natural world. Instead, like the mythical Prometheus, modernity has attempted to rob nature of its enchantment, its holiness, its sacred dimension. Modern Prometheus, "cut off from his own center as well as the spiritual principles governing the cosmos, has no interest in nature other than its subjugation and dominion."[7]

Shiite Muslim Nasr and Pope Francis share a reverence for creation. The global challenge to care for the creation raises the question of God, according to Pope Francis.

> We know how much violence has resulted in recent times from the attempt to eliminate God and the divine from the horizon of humanity, and we are aware of the importance of witnessing in our societies to that primordial openness to transcendence which lies deep within the human heart. In this, we also sense our closeness to all those men and women who, although not identifying themselves as followers of any religious tradition, are nonetheless searching for truth, goodness and beauty, the truth, goodness and beauty of God. They are our valued allies in the commitment to defending human dignity, in building a peaceful coexistence between peoples and in safeguarding and caring for creation.[8]

With this the Club of Rome announced, the "Vatican has it right."[9]

---

6. John S. Dryzek, Richard B. Norgaard, and David Schlosberg, "Climate Change and Society: Approaches and Responses," in *The Oxford Handbook of Climate Change and Society*, ed. John S. Dryzek, Richard B. Norgaard, and David Schlosberg (Oxford: Oxford University Press, 2011), 12.

7. Seyyed Hosssein Nasr, *Religion and the Order of Nature* (Oxford: Oxford University Press, 1996), 285.

8. Pope Francis, Audience with Representatives of the Churches and Ecclesial Communities and of the Different Religions, March 20, 2013, *https://w2.vatican.va/content/francesco/en/speeches/2013 /march/documents/papa-francesco_20130320_delegati-fraterni.html*.

9. "On the Edge: The State and Fate of the World's Tropical Rain Forests," The Club of Rome, *http://www.clubofrome.org/report/on-the-edge/*.

The *World Problematique*

Founded in 1968, for nearly five decades now the Club of Rome, an independent organization of leading personalities in politics, economics, science, and other fields, has addressed the urgent concern for the future of humanity and the health of the planet. Along with other futurists in the 1960s and 1970s, the Club of Rome assumed the role of the modern prophet and trumpeted that the world needs to repent of its covetous and greedy exploitation of the planet's natural resources and its relentless discrimination against poor and marginalized peoples. The world did not listen to these prophetic voices, so now in the twenty-first century this over-populated world has allowed global warming to begin melting the polar ice caps, leading to flooding and storms of unprecedented ferocity. Despite the deafness of world leaders, the prophets continue to utter their dramatic warnings.

Among the modern eco-prophets is former vice president of the United States, Al Gore. According to Gore, the *world problematique* is at root a spiritual problem. The symptoms of the spiritual problem are expressed by a complex network of destructive forces including climate change. Climate change is a global phenomenon. Its effects are not limited to one's own neighborhood or one's own country. "The essence of the emergent crisis of global warming is that we are importing enormous amounts of energy from the crust of the Earth and exporting entropy (that is, progressive disorder) into the previously stable, though dynamic, ecological systems upon which the continued flourishing of civilization depends.[10] A finite planet cannot quench the infinite thirsts of its current inhabitants.

Axial theorist Robert Bellah has heard the prophetic warning. "The hour is late: it is imperative that humans wake up to what is happening and take the necessarily dramatic steps that are so clearly needed but also at present so clearly ignored by the powers of this earth."[11] Big historians have also listened to the eco-prophets, and include in their agenda support for ecological ethics.

Four items should appear on every eco-ethicist list of concerns.

1. *Human population growth.* At the current rate, the population of the planet doubles every fifty-eight years. Futurist estimates for the population in 2050 range between 7.4 to 10.6 billion. Soon the entire planet will be "standing room only."

2. *Depletion of non-renewable resources.* Despite flamboyant announcements of new oil discoveries, the supply of fossil fuels is finite. Civilization will run out. Soon the dead dinosaurs will be all burned up. Futurists are

---

10. Al Gore, *The Future: Six Drivers of Global Change* (New York: Random House, 2012), xvii.

11. Robert N. Bellah, *Religion in Human Evolution from the Paleolithic to the Axial Age* (Cambridge, MA: Harvard University Press, 2011), 602.

experimenting with renewable energy sources such as wind power and solar power. Civilization needs to recover from its addiction to carbon-based energy.

Notre Dame eco-ethicist Celia Deane-Drummond contends that *sustainable economics* challenges the market system as such "by making production decisions not on the basis of market or consumer demand, but on the basis of the rate at which resources could be replenished."[12] The peoples of the planet must gain a measure of control over the economic system in order to steer it away from depleting non-renewable natural resources and toward renewables.

3. *Destabilization of the Climate.* Pollution production not only befouls the human nest, the carbon emissions (CO_2) in the atmosphere have led to the *greenhouse effect*, constructing an atmospheric ceiling that keeps heat from escaping into outer space. The planet is warming up faster than it would without anthropogenic (human) influence.

Despite many nay-sayers, the threat of climate change is not pseudo-science. It is serious, says physicist and former U.S. Secretary of Energy, Steven Chu. "Overwhelming scientific evidence shows that CO_2 emissions from fossil fuels have caused the climate to change, and a dramatic reduction of these emissions is essential to reduce the risk of future devastating effects."[13] Much of this climate change is *anthropogenic*, the product of human consumption and pollution. "On the one hand, climate change is driven by activities that provide comfort, mobility, and a high material standard of living to members of the present generation," says Richard Howarth, writing on inter-generational justice. "On the other hand, greenhouse gas emissions pose a threat to the long-term sustainability of ecological systems and the services they provide to human societies."[14]

4. *Ecosystem damage.* Soil erosion, deforestation, depletion of groundwater, reduction of fish populations, rapid extinction of species, and countless other forms of ecosystem damage are the result of overpopulation and disregard for natural environments. Acidification, deforestation, and desertification are everywhere destroying the natural habitat our ancestors inherited. There is nowhere one can go to find nature in its natural state.

Regarding repair of damaged ecosystems, Wangari Maathai (1940–2011) has provided a voice of hope. She established the Green Belt Movement in 1977 with the modest goal of planting trees in denuded Kenya, her

---

12. Celia Deane-Drummond, *Eco-Theology* (London: Darton, Longman, and Todd, 2008), 21.

13. Steven Chu, "Carbon Capture and Sequestration," *Science* 325 (September 25, 2009): 1599.

14. Richard B. Howarth, "Intergenerational Justice," in *Oxford Handbook of Climate Change and Society*, ed. Dryzek et al., 338–52, at 338.

native land. She received the Nobel Prize in 2004, awarded for her impact on sustainable development, peace, and democracy.[15]

5. *Structural Injustice.* The global economic system is structured in such a way that natural resources flow from the marginal periphery toward the wealthy center; then manufactured products flow back out to the markets. Profits, in the form of surplus value, flow back toward the center, toward the investors, businesses, and banks located in selected geographical locations primarily in North America, Western Europe, China, and Singapore. The economic divide between the rich and poor in the world is exacerbated because the negative effects of the *world problematique* are borne initially by the poor. The poor breathe the exhaust-pipe gasses of the wealthy.

Lutheran eco-ethicist Cynthia Moe-Lobeda terms this *structural violence.* "*Structural violence* refers to the physical, psychological, and spiritual harm that certain groups of people experience as a result of unequal distribution of power and privilege."[16] Structural violence in the form of class separation, institutional racism, and economic injustice would exist with or without the ecological crisis. Inequality is one expression of human estrangement. Yet the *world problematique* exacerbates the divide between haves and have-nots. Even though the challenge of the global crisis faces the entire human race and mandates, among other things, removing the divide between haves and have-nots, the haves delude themselves into thinking they can continue to have more and more without end.

For Nasr, Pope Francis, and Gore, today's crisis is at root a spiritual crisis. It is spiritual because in humanity's haste to bulldoze its way through nature people have forgotten that *Homo sapiens* are embedded in nature. What is called *ecological consciousness* reminds the human race that we belong to the soil, that '*adam* (Hebrew for "human being") comes from '*adamah* (Hebrew for "earth"). "Underlying the ecological view of life is the ontological view that there is no isolated self. Ecology assumes that humankind evolves and transforms together with the environment," writes Confucianist Lai Pan-Chiu; "The relationship between the human being and his/her environment is internal rather than external."[17] This identification of Earth's soil with the human spirit is important to those who have active religious sensibilities.

---

15. Ross E. Dunn and Laura J. Mitchell, *Panorama: A World History* (New York: McGraw Hill Education, 2015), 849.

16. Cynthia D. Moe-Lobeda, *Healing a Broken World: Globalization and God* (Minneapolis: Fortress, 2002), 72.

17. Lai Pan-Chiu, "Christian-Confucian Dialogue on Humanity," *Studies in Interreligious Dialogue* 14, no. 2 (2004): 202–15, at 212.

> ## Listening to the Cry of the Earth
>
> "A Spiritual Declaration on Climate Change," by Faith Community Participants at the United Nations Climate Change Conference on December 4, 2005, declares the following:
>
> - We hear the call of the Earth.
> - We believe that caring for life on Earth is a spiritual commitment.
> - People and other species have the right to life unthreatened by human greed and destructiveness.
> - Pollution, particularly from the energy-intensive wealthy industrialized countries, is warming the atmosphere. A warmer atmosphere is leading to major climate changes. The poor and vulnerable in the world and future generations will suffer the most.
> - We commit ourselves to help reduce the threat of climate change through actions in our own lives, pressure on governments and industries and standing in solidarity with those most affected by climate change.
> - We pray for spiritual support in responding to the call of the Earth.[18]

From the prompting of the autochthony sensibility, the field of eco-theology has been born. "Eco-theology . . . is that reflection on different facets of theology in as much as they take their bearings from cultural concerns about the environment and humanity's relationship with the natural world," according to Deane-Drummond.[19]

Anticipatory Ethics for a Positive Vision of the Future

Big historians believe their work will contribute to the uniting of the peoples of the world into a single planetary society. Lowell Gustafson, for example, asks, "Can the study of Big History be formative enough to teach us how to combine families, ethnic groups, cities, nations, empires, humans, and our environment in ways that protect all of them?"[20] Big historians should be thanked for their

---

18. Faith Community Participants at the United Nations Climate Change Conference, "A Spiritual Declaration on Climate Change" (December 4, 2005), World Council of Churches, *https://www.oikoumene.org/en/resources/documents/commissions/international-affairs/climate-change/a-spiritual-declaration-on-climate-change*.

19. Deane-Drummond, *Eco-Theology*, x.

20. Lowell Gustafson, "From Particles to Politics," in *Teaching and Researching Big History: Exploring a New Scholarly Field*, ed. Leonid Grinin, David Baker, Esther Quaedackers, and Audrey Korotayev (Volgograd, Russia: Uchitel, 2014), 65–89, at 87.

earnest intention to contribute to a healthy future for Earth. More than history is needed, however. What is needed is an ethical vision of a just, sustainable, participatory, and planetary future accompanied by middle axioms that will connect that vision with an action plan. Middle axioms build a bridge between the comprehensive ethical vision and practical moral action.

Because human history is filled with contingent events, we are all too aware that today's human race can choose either a utopian future or oblivion. With this in mind, it would be wise to begin with a positive vision of the future, perhaps even a utopia. The positive is more effective than the negative. Prophetic warnings to repent from past ecological sins will not suffice as a motivation to change direction. Threats of planetary self-destruction seldom persuade people to do what is right. What might precipitate a transformation in global consciousness would be a positive vision of the future. Hope inspires.

Like a belated Christmas present, the archaic axial insight sends a gift to us in the modern world. That gift is the transcendent standard of justice and peace. This transcendent standard judges as fallen what actually happens in history. But judgment is not all. The transcendent vision also provides hope that the future can be better than the past. Should people lift up a vision of a better future, they would have a better chance of enlisting enthusiastic efforts to make that potential future an actuality. Genuine justice and peace are possible.

Proleptic ethics will be the term employed here to guide planetary resolve toward making a better future.[21] The term *prolepsis* refers to an active anticipation of the future, a present embodiment of one's vision of the future. What follows will entertain a vision of the future with moral drawing power. This vision derives in part from the New Testament promise of a new creation, buttressed by the vision of a transcendent social order shared by so many axial experiencers. The vision of a transcendent order could itself contribute to making the history for which the present generation is responsible. To this vision will be added some middle axioms to aid movement from the vision to an action plan.

1. **Project a vision of the coming society that is just, sustainable, participatory, and planetary.** Dutch sociologist and pioneer futurist Fred L. Polak proposed that positive images of the future are the primary causal factor in cultural change.[22] Such positive images pull a civilization together and unite its people in a single task. Nothing is more practical than a good idea, an idea that inspires and directs.

   The vision of a just, sustainable, participatory, and planetary society would not be merely the product of an active imagination. Rather, for axial

---

21. The seven-point structure of proleptic ethics is drawn from a number of previous iterations, most recently from Ted Peters, "Proleptic Ethics," chapter 14 in *God—The World's Future*, 3rd ed. (Minneapolis: Fortress, 2015), 740–72.

22. Fred L. Polak, *The Image of the Future*, trans. Elise Boulding (New York: Elsevier, 1973).

believers, it would find its ethical ground in the transcendent mystery, which demands a transformation of the social orders we know in history. Projecting this vision would take up the task of the prophet in ancient Israel or the task of the philosopher in ancient Greece.

2. **Promote a single planetary society.** Climate change is not local. Population overgrowth is not local. The economy is not local. Everything is interconnected, shared, and planetary in scope. The peoples of the world together should become the single community of moral deliberation.

The *world problematique* prompts with uncanny urgency the necessity for a single global community of moral deliberation. Al Gore says that to meet the climate change crisis we need to advance "to the Global Mind; from families to tribes to communities to nations" to the global mind.[23] Pope Francis puts it this way:

> There has been a growing conviction that our planet is a homeland and that humanity is one people living in a common home. An interdependent world not only makes us more conscious of the negative effects of certain lifestyles and models of production and consumption which affect us all; more importantly, it motivates us to ensure that solutions are proposed from a global perspective, and not simply to defend the interests of a few countries. Interdependence obliges us to think of *one world with a common plan*.[24]

The prospect of a single planetary society leads big historian Fred Spier to ask, will our future be utopia or oblivion? "The most fundamental question concerning our human future is whether the inhabitants of planet Earth will be able to cooperate in achieving the goal of reaching a more or less sustainable future in reasonable harmony, or whether the current large division between more and less wealthy people, as well as the unequal distribution of power within and among societies, will play havoc with such intentions."[25] Economic justice is a prerequisite to planetary sustainability.

3. **Provide for posterity.** Population ecologist Lester R. Brown uncovers the tacitly assumed we-they thinking of our generation this way: "We have not inherited the earth from our fathers, we are borrowing it from our children."[26]

The cure for the we-they mentality is to think in terms of a single planetary society that exists not only in space but also over time. Proleptic ethics

23. Gore, *The Future*, 361.

24. *Laudato si'*, http://w2.vatican.va/content/francesco/en/encyclicals/documents/papa-francesco_20150524_enciclica-laudato-si.html.

25. Spier, *Big History*, 313.

26. Lester R. Brown, *By Bread Alone* (New York: Praeger Publishers, 1974), cover.

are inter-generational ethics. Today's generation has a moral obligation to future generations. Today's families have an obligation to bequeath to all future children a planet that is fertile, life-giving, and sustainable. Harvard sociobiologist Edward O. Wilson admonishes, "If there is any moral precept shared by people of all beliefs, it is that we owe ourselves and future generations a beautiful, rich, and healthful environment."[27]

4. **Protect human dignity.** To understand dignity in the modern world, one should rely on Immanuel Kant's assertion that one should always treat another person as an end and not merely as a means. Because of dignity, the single planetary society must be participatory, that is, all persons of moral resolve should be encouraged to participate in ethical deliberation and planning.

5. **Proffer the distinction between needs and greeds.** Part of the *world problematique* is structural injustice. The wealthy consume too much, while the poor are struggling merely to stay alive. In the proleptic vision, the distinction between needs and greeds must be articulated. The current problem is that the overconsumption of the wealthy sectors of the global economy justify their excesses by describing them as *needs*. No one needs everything that unbridled covetousness can buy, especially when such buying skews the market away from meeting the genuine needs of the poor. Prophets need to deconstruct the concept of need, distinguishing it from greed.

6. **Propose alliances.** "We call on all groups to join us in collaboration, co-operation and friendly competition in this endeavour and we welcome the significant contributions taken by other faiths, as we can all be winners in this race," say the composers of the "Islamic Declaration on Climate Change."[28]

> We particularly call on the well-off nations and oil-producing states to—
>
> - Lead the way in phasing out their greenhouse gas emissions as early as possible and no later than the middle of the century;
> - Provide generous financial and technical support to the less well-off to achieve a phase-out of greenhouse gases as early as possible;
> - Recognize the moral obligation to reduce consumption so that the poor may benefit from what is left of the earth's non-renewable resources;
> - Stay within the '2 degree' limit, or, preferably, within the '1.5 degree' limit, bearing in mind that two-thirds of the earth's proven fossil fuel reserves remain in the ground;

---

27. Edward O. Wilson, *The Creation: An Appeal to Save Life on Earth* (New York: Norton, 2006), 5.

28. "Islamic Declaration on Global Climate Change," International Islamic Climate Change Symposium, *http://islamicclimatedeclaration.org/islamic-declaration-on-global-climate-change/*.

- Re-focus their concerns from unethical profit from the environment, to that of preserving it and elevating the condition of the world's poor.
- Invest in the creation of a green economy.[29]

Regardless of religious affiliation or even anti-religious belief, the call for a planetary society is the call for cooperation. Pope John XXIII wrote in *Pacem in terris* that Catholics could cooperate with "all [people] of good will" in working for world peace.[30] Religious leaders along with political leaders and scientific leaders should lead the peoples of the world together toward a society that is just, sustainable, participatory, and planetary. According to theological ethicist John Hart, "Religious thought can have a positive impact on ecological ethics in theory and in practice, and complement scientific thought, research, and development, as a corrective for ecologically harmful industrial, commercial, or military technological exuberance and arrogance."[31]

7. **Profess faith.** Christians, Muslims, and other axial experiencers have hope. They hope that the transcendent reality—the God of grace—will provide grounding and justification for a future transformative vision. This hope is built on faith. Hopeful faith takes the form of trust. Even though life within history does not look like the transformed life of the Christian vision of the new creation, it takes faith as trust to believe that this vision is attainable. Such trust translates into enthusiastic action aimed at social change. Professing this faith may itself help to bring the projected new order into being ahead of schedule proleptically—that is, fragmentarily yet authentically. It is the Christian's way of embodying the Lord's Prayer, "Thy will be done on earth as it is in heaven."

Conclusion

The 13.8 billion-year history of a cosmos that is now 93 billion light years across seems big when compared to the time and space occupied by our little Planet Earth.[32] Certainly a contaminated and life-extinguished Planet Earth would not be missed by the larger universe! If in fact Cosmic History is meaningless and directionless, then what happens on Earth will contribute nothing to the larger cosmic picture.

29. Ibid.

30. Pope John Paul XXIII, *Pacem in terris*, nos. 1, 166, *http://w2.vatican.va/content/john-xxiii/en/encyclicals/documents/hf_j-xxiii_enc_11041963_pacem.html*.

31. John Hart, *Cosmic Commons: Spirit, Science, and Space* (Eugene, OR: Cascade Books, 2013), 378.

32. See David J. Eicher, "How Immense Is the Universe?," *Astronomy* 43, no. 12 (December 2015): 20–23.

From whence, then, comes the grounding for an eco-ethic? Why should the human race of the present generation assume moral responsibility for the health of future generations? Why should we respect or even love our planet? Why bother? To ask about the warrant for caring for the Earth raises the question of God.

Review Questions

1. What is the *world problematique*?
2. What factors constitute the global eco-crisis?
3. What does it mean to be a secular prophet?
4. What is distinctive about the proleptic approach to ethics?

Discussion Questions

1. How does the *world problematique* exacerbate the split between haves and have-nots?
2. Which religious or spiritual sensibility is triggered by climate change?
3. When it comes to climate change, on what do Muslims and Christians agree?
4. Do you have hope? If so, why? If not, why not?

Additional Resources

Print Sources

Dryzek, John S., Richard B. Norgaard, and David Schlosberg, eds. *The Oxford Handbook of Climate Change and Society*. Oxford: Oxford University Press, 2011.

This book is authoritative in the scientific and political sense, because the authors derive their forty-seven chapters from the respected work of the Intergovernmental Panel on Climate Change (IPCC). "Climate change presents perhaps the most profound and complex challenge to have confronted human social, political, and economic systems. It also presents one of the most profound challenges to the way we understand human responses" (p. 17).

Gore, Al. *The Future: Six Drivers of Global Change* (New York: Random House, 2012).

The former U.S. vice president provides a clearly-written and inspiring analysis of the ecological challenges facing the present generation. The call for planetary transformation could not be more reasonable and forceful.

Moe-Lobeda, Cynthia D. *Resisting Structural Evil: Love as Ecological-Economic Vocation*. Minneapolis: Fortress, 2013.

To the world-wide discussion of the eco-crisis, Moe-Lobeda adds attention to the social structures that repress certain classes and races of people. She designates these structures as evil. Resistance to structures of evil takes the form of active loving, loving that pursues justice and transformation.

Peters, Ted. *GOD—The World's Future: Systematic Theology for a New Era*. 3rd ed. Minneapolis: Fortress, 2015.

Chapter 14, "Proleptic Ethics," presents a full explication of the eco-crisis combined with the structure of ethical deliberation within a proleptic framework.

Afterword

Asking the Question of God

Cleave ever to the sunnier side of doubt,
And cling to Faith beyond the forms of Faith!
　　—Alfred Lord Tennyson (1809–1892),
　　　　　"In Memoriam"

This book has been inquiring about God's existence and God's creation of the world. Our method has been to pose the question of ultimacy and then assess various historical attempts to answer this question. This method has also included critical interrogation of Big History and big bang cosmology in order to crack open the question of ultimacy, which then could lead to the question of God. Many different concepts of the ultimate and of the divine have been compared and contrasted; comparing and contrasting is itself a form of questioning. This final chapter will add another question: if God exists, is God gracious?

If God is gracious, the cosmos in which we live comes to us as a divine gift. One might ask, why is there a cosmos when there could be only nothing? A possible answer is that God created the cosmos out of divine love so that its creatures could experience divine love. To realize this would produce a daily life characterized by an attitude of gratitude.

To say that God is gracious adds something to the axial vision of an ideal social order. The ideal social order renders judgment against every historical social order, condemning us for inequality, injustice, violence, and genocide. If God is gracious, then one would look for a divine promise to establish that just social order by divine power despite historical resistance. God's graciousness would then entail forgiveness; it would entail not only compassion for the victims of injustice but also for the perpetrators of injustice. Justice would come as a divine gift even for those who had not earned it. Might such a gracious God make it into our catalog of divine models?

As the author of this book, which poses the question of God within the frame of cosmic history, I have sought with diligence to explicate the varied answers given in various human cultures and epochs. I have sought to avoid microcolonizing various systems of thought with my own answers. Rather, by demonstrating how the question of ultimacy has led repeatedly to sublime reflection by genius seers in different eras and different cultures, I have sought to demonstrate that we human beings have a built-in ontological thirst, a thirst that can be slaked only by ultimate reality. The biblical attempt to quench this thirst with the message of a personal and gracious God is an answer to which I would like to give special attention here in this afterword.

The Big Bang Asks the Question of God

In many theories about the origin and future of the cosmos, the idea of God as a cosmic engineer or designer seems to be required to make the theory coherent. When a theory preemptively excludes God from its description of reality, one may well ask, what presuppositions led to an answer that excludes appeal to God? They are not the presuppositions of solid science. Rather, they are the presuppositions invoked by scientism.

It is reasonable to ask if God exists. Tillich avers, "Within itself, the finite world points beyond itself. In other words, it is self-transcendent."[1] This becomes vivid in the case of big bang cosmogony. God's existence becomes plausible, because the anthropic principle includes God as one of the possible explanations for the initial conditions. To ask the question of God is coherent, given the big bang model of the cosmos.

But is this enough? For those whose religious sensibilities include the dialectic of the beyond and the intimate, the decisive question is this: is God gracious, loving, and transforming? If God exists, does God care for what happens within each human soul? If God exists, will God sponsor a historical transformation to replace war with peace, suffering with joy, meaninglessness with meaning? Will God redeem a creation bent on self-destruction? To date, neither Big History nor World History has addressed these questions. Even if the idea of a divine engineer is consonant with big bang cosmogony, affirming the existence of this creating divinity would leave the human thirst unquenched. The beyond without the intimate is unsatisfying.

Cosmic History does ask these questions, for the simple reason that we *Homo sapiens* are here. We did not put ourselves here. We are the beneficiaries of what happened at the big bang and what happened during the millions of years of evolutionary history. In a sense, our very presence on Earth within this magnificent cosmos comes as a gift. We did not ask for it. We did not demand it. We did not accomplish it. We simply woke up to discover that we are present, and this presence is a gift from a source well beyond our control. A theologian would call this giftedness *grace*.

---

1. Paul Tillich, *Systematic Theology*, 3 vols. (Chicago: University of Chicago Press, 1951–1963), 2:7.

Is our presence in time and space an accident? Or is it the product of a divine purpose establishing history and working within history?

Evolution Asks the Question of God

We saw how life "miraculously" began on Earth and then evolved over 3.9 billion years to produce *Homo sapiens*. The word *miracle* is used euphemistically by some simply to indicate that scientists have not yet discovered how abiotic chemistry first became biota, how non-life produced life. This is an enigma waiting for an explanation.

One might be tempted to say, "God did it!" But unless one is able to demonstrate just *how* God created life, and why only God could have been responsible, this would not count as a scientific explanation.

Should one wish to say, "God did it," it would be important also to claim that God did it without an obvious miracle. Most evolutionary theists contend that God works in, with, under, and through natural processes. God does not intervene in nature like a cheater rigs a Las Vegas roulette wheel. God is the author of nature's laws and is quite happy to join in nature's history without miraculous intervention. Robert John Russell, for example, recognizes that God works "in, with, under, and through" natural processes.

> Evolution, in short, is God's way of creating life. God is both the absolute, transcendent Creator of the universe and the continuing immanent Creator of biological complexity. God gives the universe its existence at every moment *ex nihilo* and is the ultimate source of nature's causal efficacy, faithfully maintaining its regularities which we describe as the laws of nature. God provides the world with rich potentialities built into nature from the beginning, including the combination of law and chance which characterize physical and biological processes. God also acts in, with, under, and through these processes as immanent Creator, bringing about the order, beauty, complexity, and wonder of life.[2]

One need not deny the presence of occasional miracles in order to see the important point Russell is making: God's providential care is exercised in, with, under, and through normal natural processes. God's action is not added to nature's action. God's action is conflated with natural events. Therefore, once a scientific explanation for life's origin is found, it may look like other natural processes even if God is at work.

With regard to the creatures' relationship to their Creator, Tillich says, "God is neither alongside things nor even above them; he is nearer to them than

---

2. Robert John Russell, *Cosmology from Alpha to Omega* (Minneapolis: Fortress, 2008), 212.

they are to themselves. [God] is their creative ground, here and now, always and everywhere."[3] If Russell and Tillich are correct, then each moment of our existence is blessed by a gracious God acting at the quantum level to include us in a divinely guided purpose. Divine action at the quantum level insures contingency in history and makes newness possible. If genuine newness—*adventus*—is possible, then the divine promise for transformation becomes plausible. The New Testament has promised an eschatological transformation, a new creation, the advent of the kingdom of God. In, with, under, and through present history, God is working to bring this promise to fulfillment, according to theistic evolutionist Russell.

The Axial Insight and a New Form of History

One might think of history as merely one darned event after another. In this view, once the historian has chronicled a string of events, his or her job is done. It appears that this is what big historians and world historians have been assuming. But in each case they salt their chronicles. Big historians salt their chronicles with reminders that natural processes influenced the course of human events. World historians salt their chronicles by eliciting awareness of historical relativity, awareness that many different cultures in different eras experienced their own respective histories. History as a discipline cannot be anything other than the chronicle of events accompanied by a salting of those events.

The cosmic historian salts history as well. Unfortunately, neither Big History nor World History have liked the taste of Cosmic History's salt. This suggests that Cosmic History becomes something quite different once the course of events is salted by axial insight. Because the axial insight frequently includes belief in a transcendent order of justice, what lies beyond history comes to judge history. The failings of the historical social order are measured against the standard of the ideal social order, at least in China, Greece, and Israel. Awareness of human historicity, recall, is awareness that we are mortal, deficient, judged. But to be historical is also to be gifted by grace, because the power of the ideal social order draws people toward it. In revelation, the biblical God promises that the ideal will become actual. The kingdom of God is imminent.

In this perspective, history is the stage on which the drama between God and creation is played, a drama still awaiting its final act. "World history is the basis of the history of revelation, and in the history of revelation world history reveals mystery," says Tillich.[4] Voegelin weighs in enigmatically, "History, thus, reveals itself as the horizon of divine mystery when the process of differentiation is discovered to be the process of transfiguration."[5] Morrissey restates this

---

3. Tillich, *Systematic Theology*, 2:7.

4. Ibid., 1:157.

5. Eric Voegelin, *Order and History*, 5 vols. (Baton Rouge: Louisiana State University Press, 1956–1987), 4:314.

message with a little more clarity: Voegelin "views history as the revelatory process that discloses divine mystery in a diversity of revelations, all of which point to the transfiguration of all things within the cosmos. This transfiguration is not the result of human will but of the grace of God."[6] Future redemption will come as a gift of divine grace, not as the achievement of the next political revolution.

The claim here is that the social order—kings, hierarchies, ideologies, injustices, violence, and ecosphere destruction—which we experience within history is judged by a divine promise that a transcendent social order will eschatologically transfigure history, redeem history. At present, those who have effective axial consciousness have become aware that what they experience within history misses the mark of the transcendent order of justice. This eternal order of justice renders judgment against what happens within history. Yet it also announces hope. It announces a future transfiguration. Beyond the judgment, God promises salvation. The ideal order judges the historical order as deficient, yet the God of grace promises a new order replete with justice, peace, and freedom.

The axial revelation effects a differentiation in human consciousness, and this process of differentiation itself constitutes a historical process worth chronicling. "What happens in history is the very process of differentiating consciousness that constitutes history."[7] Once a transcendent judge has been revealed, "*history* could mean either the dimension of objective time in which civilizations run their course or the inner form which constitutes a society."[8] The inner form of a given society—the society's orientation toward justice—is what stands under divine judgment and hope. It also stands under the divine promise of grace.

The Vision of Universal Human Equality

A prime example of differentiated consciousness is belief in a counterfactual reality, namely, human equality. Factually speaking, human equality does not exist within history. Yet modern people still believe in human equality. Moderns believe in something they cannot see. Modern civilization believes in human equality as an ideal, as the measure to which society must aspire, as the judge when society falls short.

The world in which people actually live day to day is replete with discrimination, class pride, racial superiority, degrading ideology, and even genocide. Yet axial consciousness prompts awareness that, despite this historical experience, there is but one, single, universal, planetary human race. "Universal mankind is not a society existing in the world, but a symbol which indicates [human]

---

6. Michael P. Morrissey, *Consciousness and Transcendence* (Notre Dame: University of Notre Dame Press, 1994), 252.

7. Voegelin, *Order and History*, 4:332.

8. Ibid., 1:126.

consciousness of participating, in this earthly existence, in the mystery of a reality that moves toward its transfiguration. Universal mankind is an eschatological index."[9] People strive for human freedom, dignity, and equality based solely on this transcendental vision and the hope for transfiguration. The God of grace has promised such transfiguration for the future, for *adventus*.

In sum, once the axial insight has dawned, neither natural history nor human history can be thought of exclusively as the chronicle of events according to somebody's private or professional perspective. Rather, history becomes nested within eternity. The social order within history becomes measured by the ideal and judged to be deficient. For believers, the God of grace has promised that the future will be more than what historicity itself can achieve. The future will include transformation, redemption, and salvation. This will be eternity's gift to history.

"Things do not happen in the astro-physical universe; the universe, together with all things founded in it, happens in God."[10] The awareness that the entire cosmos is nested within something still grander, God's grace, becomes itself something the historian should pay heed to. If a big historian or a world historian would pay heed to divine grace, the gifted character of history might become more visible right along with a vision of history's future transformation.

Axial Theory under Criticism

It would be too much to ask of axial theory to bear the entire burden of posing the question of God plus the question of whether or not God is gracious. This book has relied in large part on axial theory to help chronicle the course of differentiating human consciousness. However, some problems with this approach must be confessed and addressed.

One critique of axial theory notes that the concept of axial ultimacy privileges certain religions over others. This critique is raised by historical relativists and postmodernist deconstructionists. The so-called *higher religions* with their sublime and universal doctrines should not receive privilege over more indigenous traditions among today's foragers and farmers, they argue. It is admittedly the case, of course, that these indigenous religious worldviews are strictly intra-cosmic and retain the type of myth of origin analyzed in earlier chapters. Yet, in principle, the modern world should not look upon non-axial religious traditions as less highly evolved or inferior. It is unjust, say critics, to rank religions with the post-axial traditions on top.

However, there is an internal inconsistency to this complaint. The very appeal to justice that would equalize higher religions with indigenous religions derives

---

9. Ibid., 4:305.

10. Ibid., 4:334.

from the axial insight. It is the effective history of the axial insight (in the form of belief in universal justice) that makes it possible for modern people to appeal to a cross-cultural standard of justice. In short, one must rely upon axial justice in order to protect the right of indigenous peoples to preserve their traditions. Protecting indigenous cultures is seen as a moral responsibility of the dominant society specifically because of modernity's belief in the ideal of human equality.

A second objection to axial theory takes the form of a complaint that it is nothing but Christianity without Christ. Theologian Wolfhart Pannenberg, for example, complains that Jaspers overemphasizes the role of the transcendental insight in forming human subjectivity. This "does not justify systematizing this epoch into the axis of world history. This step was already problematic insofar as Jaspers admits that he wants to replace the axis which the Christian understanding of history has provided up until now by a construction accessible to non-Christians as well."[11] To say it in other words, the influence of God on the human soul taking place within Christian faith has been illegitimately broadened by Jaspers and then used to describe non-Christian experience. That is, Pannenberg objects to the axialists' method.

Voegelin similarly criticizes Jasper's method. Jaspers, he says, "forms an oddly doctrinal conception of Christian faith that will permit him to remove Christ from his epochal status together with a religion in which the majority of mankind does not believe anyway."[12] In short, axial theory is, at bottom, Christian theology stripped of Christ and then imposed upon non-Christian cultural settings. "I conclude that the concept of an epoch or axis-time marked by the great spiritual outbursts alone is no longer tenable."[13]

Jaspers took a step out of the Christian faith and into the world of religious traditions to identify something many such traditions hold in common, namely, the axial insight into ultimate reality. The historical report of the axial experience in each individual tradition looks different from the others, as one would expect. After all, each axial experience took place in a different historical context. Yet this does not diminish the value of observing what they all share: they all share an experience with supra-cosmic mystery combined with a supra-historical standard for a just social order.

This book has used axial theory as a hypothesis—the revelatory version of the hypothesis—for examining certain chapters in human history. This hypothesis has been illuminating. By asking the question of God as an axial theorist would ask it, much has been learned about the differentiation of consciousness taking place during the rise of the so-called higher religions twenty-five hundred years ago. What seems undeniable is that a level of awareness of transcendence

---

11. Wolfhart Pannenberg, *Basic Questions in Theology*, trans. George H. Kehm, 2 vols. (Minneapolis: Fortress, 1970–1971), 2:92, n. 39.

12. Voegelin, *Order and History*, 4:310.

13. Ibid., 4:312.

and even universality dawned on the minds of seers, sages, prophets, and philosophers. Our historical past is different because of this dawning experience. So also is the effective history operative within modern and postmodern consciousness. Analyzing the axial leap to transcendental consciousness—whether this leap was emergent, the product of divine revelation, or a combination—makes reasonable our posing the question of God to all historical knowledge.

It would be a mistake to dogmatize the axial insight and turn it into a religious stance. Rather, as a working hypothesis, the idea of the axial breakthrough functions for the cosmic historian as a pair of glasses, so to speak, to help see more clearly the course of historical events.

Is God Gracious?

"In the name of Allah, Most Gracious, Most Merciful," is included in everyday Islamic greetings. Allah is the merciful one (*Al Rahman*). Can the Creator God be relied upon to have mercy? Is the God beyond all other gods loving, compassionate, forgiving, and redeeming? This may be of greater value to the human soul than merely affirming the existence of an engineer who designed the big bang.

What does a human person want, really want? According to Huston Smith, each person wants three things. First, "we want being. Everyone wants to be rather than not be; normally, no one wants to die. . . . Second, we want to know. . . . The third thing people seek is joy, a feeling tone that is the opposite of frustration, futility, and boredom. These are what people really want."[14] What people really want is being, knowledge, and joy. If God as the ultimate reality is gracious, would this fulfill all three wants?

It is one thing to want a gracious God and quite another to get one, of course. "Grace is the favor, mercy, and gratuitous goodwill of God toward us," says Reformation theologian Philip Melanchthon (1497–1560).[15] There are some who proclaim the gospel of such a gracious God. But such a claim must be based on special revelation, not as the conclusion of a scientific quest.

Swedish hymn composer Carl Boberg (1859–1940) offers an answer to the God question with his song, "How Great Thou Art."

> O Lord my God, when I in awesome wonder
>   consider all the works thy hand hath made,
> I see the stars, I hear the mighty thunder,
>   thy pow'r throughout the universe displayed.

---

14. Huston Smith, *The World's Religions* (New York: Harper, 1991), 20–21.

15. Philip Melanchthon, *Loci Communes*, in *Library of Christian Classics* 19 (Louisville: Westminster John Knox, 1969), 88.

> Then sings my soul, my Savior God, to thee,
>> how great thou art! How great thou art!

In this first stanza, note how the beyond sensibilities are enlivened by reference to stars and thunder. In the refrain, note how the intimate sensibility is enlivened by eliciting a response from the inner soul. God is both beyond and intimate. Still we must ask, is God gracious?

> But when I think that God, his Son not sparing,
>> sent him to die, I scarce can take it in,
> that on the cross my burden gladly bearing
>> he bled and died to take away my sin;
> Then sings my soul, my Savior God to thee,
>> how great thou art! How great thou art![16]

The divine sacrifice takes away one's sin. This song interprets the gospel in miniature: "For God so loved the world (*cosmos*) that he gave his only Son, so that everyone who believes in him may not perish but may have eternal life" (John 3:16). The gift of eternal life is a gift of divine grace.

This is one of the answers to the God question reported in axial history. It is the author's preferred answer.

Conclusion

What has been said and what has not been said in this book? Contingent existence has been shown to be distinct from necessary existence. Thereby, necessary existence could aptly apply to a divine creator who gave the cosmos a future at the big bang. Plausibility arguments have been provided so as to demonstrate that affirming God's necessary existence would be consonant with big bang cosmogony and with the anthropic principle.

The Vatican gets is right. "Since the Big Bang theory does not in fact exclude the possibility of an antecedent stage of matter, it can be noted that the theory appears to provide merely *indirect* support for the doctrine of *creatio ex nihilo* which as such can only be known by faith."[17] What also can be known only by faith is that the God who caused the big bang also gave to *Homo sapiens* their existence in this magnificent universe as a gift.

---

16. Text by Carl G. Boberg (1859–1940). Translation by Stuart K. Hine (1899–1989). Music from a Swedish folk tune, adapted by Stuart K. Hine. © S.K. Hine 1953. Manna Music Inc., *http://mannamusicinc.com/*.

17. International Theological Commission, *Communion and Stewardship: Human Persons Created in the Image of God* (2004), no. 67, *http://www.vatican.va/roman_curia/congregations/cfaith/cti_documents/rc_con_cfaith_doc_20040723_communion-stewardship_en.html*.

The human thirst for transcendent being becomes nuanced when a person wishes that ultimate reality be gracious, when a person asks for love, compassion, forgiveness, renewal, transformation. Any logical argument for God's existence or conventional spiritual practice will not be good enough unless it is grounded in ultimate reality. The best we can do is pray, asking the God of grace to hear our prayers.

Index

Note: An italicized *f, n, s* or *t,* following a page number indicates a figure, footnote, sidebar or table, respectively.